Praise for Howard Swindle's
Deliberate Indifference

"Powerfully rendered . . . Virtuoso, enthrallingly authentic, Swindle demonstrates consummate art in bringing each player vividly alive in order to drive a gripping drama."
—*Kirkus Reviews*

"Swindle has an eye and an ear for the particulars of place. . . . It's a powerful story, and Swindle does it justice."
—Joe Holley, *Dallas Morning News*

"Swindle has done some spectacular reporting on the criminal justice system. . . . His work is a brilliant flesh-and-blood civics lesson on the courts."   —Bob Elder, *The Texas Observer*

"Those who enjoy the details of intricate investigations and the unfolding of real-life courtroom drama will find Swindle's *Deliberate Indifference* a gripping, disturbing and provocative reading."
—Judyth Rigler, *San Antonio Express News*

"In a powerful and poignant manner, Swindle has given us a fascinating history lesson that deserves to be read for years to come. Disturbing and thought-provoking, *Deliberate Indifference* is factual storytelling at its absolute finest."
—Carlton Stowers, author of *Careless Whispers*

"Inspiring . . . Swindle provides a careful account of the [Loyal Garner, Jr.] incident, painting a disturbing portrait of an insular community in which racism and police brutality were everyday realities. . . . *Deliberate Indifference* is recommended for all collections."
—Ben Harrison, *Library Journal*

"*Deliberate Indifference* should be read by anyone who thinks that violent backwoods racism is a thing of the past."
—Red Connelly, *Houston Public News*

PENGUIN BOOKS

DELIBERATE INDIFFERENCE

In the course of more than twenty years in journalism, Howard Swindle has won a George Polk Award for investigative reporting and edited and supervised three Pulitzer Prize-winning series. He is assistant managing editor of *The Dallas Morning News* and the author of *Once a Hero*.

Deliberate
INDIFFERENCE

*A STORY OF RACIAL INJUSTICE
AND MURDER*

HOWARD SWINDLE

PENGUIN BOOKS

PENGUIN BOOKS
Published by the Penguin Group
Penguin Books USA Inc., 375 Hudson Street,
New York, New York 10014, U.S.A.
Penguin Books Ltd, 27 Wrights Lane,
London W8 5TZ, England
Penguin Books Australia Ltd, Ringwood,
Victoria, Australia
Penguin Books Canada Ltd. 10 Alcorn Avenue,
Toronto, Ontario, Canada M4V 3B2
Penguin Books (N.Z.) Ltd, 182–190 Wairau Road,
Auckland 10, New Zealand

Penguin Books Ltd, Registered Offices:
Harmondsworth, Middlesex, England

First published in the United States of America by Viking Penguin,
a division of Penguin Books USA Inc., 1993
Published in Penguin Books 1994

1 3 5 7 9 10 8 6 4 2

THE LIBRARY OF CONGRESS HAS CATALOGUED THE HARDCOVER AS FOLLOWS:
Swindle, Howard.
Deliberate indifference/Howard Swindle.
p.   cm.
ISBN 0-670-83946-9 (hc.)
ISBN 0 14 02.3370 9 (pbk.)
1. Ladner, Thomas—Trials, litigation, etc.   2. Trials
(Murder)—Texas—Sabine County.
3. Police—Texas—Sabine County—Complaints
against.   4. Race discrimination—Texas—Sabine County.
5. Sabine County (Tex.)—Race relations.   I. Title.
KF224.L3S95   1993
364.1′523′09764177—dc20   92–50386

Printed in the United States of America
Set in Primer
Designed by Wilma Jane Weichselbaum

*For my children, Ashley and Stryker,
so they'll understand there's more gray
in the world than black and white.
And for my wife, Kathy,
who brightens the gray.*

ACKNOWLEDGMENTS

DELIBERATE INDIFFERENCE could not be told were it not for the trust and cooperation of many. A few jeopardized their standing in the community, even their safety, to tell a stranger a story they believe had to be told at any cost.

Among them are Vollie Grace, Ura Daniels, Janie Latham, Barbara Richard, Pearlie Henderson, Corrine Garner, Loyal Garner, Sr., Sarah Garner, Andrew and Nora Helms, W. B. "Bill" Beaird, Mary Pritchard, and Doris Sorter. Others cooperated in the research but asked to remain unidentified for reasons I understand and appreciate.

Others also were helpful in their perspectives, support, and cooperation, including Carlton Stowers; John Manasco; Sheriff James Brumley of Sabine Parish, Louisiana; Gayle Ladner; Stephanie Corley; Dr. and Mrs. Grover Winslow; Marnie Foster; Barbara Seale; Katie Morgan; United States Magistrate Judith Guthrie; United States Attorney Bob Wortham; David Baugh; Glenda Shelton; John and Velma Hannah; and Phil Latham.

Likewise, this endeavor was blessed with support from friends: Lorraine Adams, Dan Malone, Mary Ann Palmer, F. R. "Buck" Files, Jr., Lloyd Harrell, Judy Stratton, and Bob Mong.

I am particularly indebted to former Hemphill police chief Thomas Ladner, who, while he undoubtedly will take issue with much of this book, nonetheless extended me the courtesy of an interview. Diligent attempts were made to interview other key characters in this book, particularly Sheriff Blan Greer and former deputies Bill Horton and James "Bo" Hyden of Sabine County, Texas. For their own reasons, they declined to be interviewed, leaving me to rely on their voluminous statements in the public record and on interviews with those who know them.

The lawyers in the legal battle over Loyal Garner, Jr.'s death lent their considerable expertise to causes in which, I am convinced, they personally believed. It was a case that made no one rich. Quite the contrary, defense attorneys John Seale and Paul Buchanan financed the bulk of their cases from their own pockets. John Hannah, Jr., easily could have earned more from his private practice. Prosecutor Jack Skeen would have been paid whether or not he took the Garner case, but he had the courage to roll the dice, knowing he easily could bankrupt himself politically. Richard Cohen of the Southern Poverty Law Center received not a nickel beyond his regular salary for the effort he put into Garner's case. I am indebted to them all for their cooperation, and honored to call them friends.

Mindy Werner, my editor at Viking Penguin, believed in *Deliberate Indifference* from its inception; her confidence, suggestions, and frequent phone calls were an inspiration.

No expression of gratitude would be complete without including Janet Wilkens Manus: my agent, my confidante, my architect, and my friend.

CONTENTS

PREFACE

THE SUMMER OF 1963 was uncommonly hot and dry even by Texas standards, and it was on one of those searing days that I discovered race, class, and indignity.

I had gone to Trucktown to see my girlfriend, whose family owned the combination service station and restaurant. It was easily the busiest establishment in Hamilton. The truck stop catered to the heavy truck traffic along Texas 36, the main north-south artery for moving West Texas cotton down to the seaport in Houston. I came in the back entrance, through the kitchen, and when I opened the door the temperature hit me like a blast from a ruptured radiator.

Six pairs of eyes—those of black truck drivers whose rigs were being serviced outside—stared at me simultaneously from above their plates as they heard the door open. Their reaction, I remember, was like that of squirrels straining toward an alien sound to see if it posed danger. The black drivers were eating at two tables shoved together; grease from a nearby deep-fryer glazed the table like dirty shellac.

For reasons a seventeen-year-old didn't immediately understand, I was ashamed and embarrassed—and stunned that men were forced to eat in backrooms where greasy fans never beat the heat below 115 degrees. I walked fast, avoiding the men with my eyes, through the swinging door and into the air-conditioned restaurant, where white drivers were eating comfortably in booths.

I suspected then that the civil rights battles I'd seen on television in Montgomery and Selma had little to do with restaurants serving blacks. They had everything to do with human decency and respect.

Blacks had good reason to be cautious in Hamilton County. It was in the heart of predominantly white North Central Texas ranching country, and it was the whitest of the white. The fact that Hamilton County didn't have a single black was as worthy of bragging rights among some of its residents as the quality of their well water or the prices their steers had brought at auction.

Actually, what I and others in Hamilton knew about blacks was what we saw on the five o'clock news. Selma and Montgomery seemed halfway around the world from Hamilton. The only nonwhites we knew were a few wetbacks who lived out on the ranches, working eighteen-hour days for fifty cents an hour. And we barely ever saw them. The ranchers who worked them illegally bought groceries in town for them so that people wouldn't notice them.

Not that the civil rights movement in the Deep South didn't provide heated grist for small-town Texas gossip. As a sack boy, I listened to veiled threats as I toted groceries on Saturdays to dusty pickup trucks angle-parked around the town square. One man in khakis and cowboy boots referred to the civil rights demonstrations in Selma as "that crap in Alabama." "Them niggers know better than to come around here," he told a neighbor. "They know we wouldn't sit still for a bunch of that nonsense." The man was a strong churchgoer and a member of the American Legion post. I went to school with his son. They were a good family, and I had admired them.

Loitering near the coffee counter at City Drug one day, I overheard several men I knew and respected grumbling about the Postal Service transferring a black man to Hamilton. They were talking about putting up roadblocks before he could get to the city limits. "We've got to stop it before it gets started," one vowed. "Give 'em an inch, they'll take a mile." The talk scared me; but months later, when no black man had appeared at the post office, I forgot about the potential crisis.

Not long before I left home for college, a district judge with a perverted sense of justice moved a murder trial to Hamilton. The defendant was a black man accused of killing a white trooper on the outskirts of Waco, about sixty miles east. The black man's attorney said he couldn't get a fair trial in Waco. On the opening day of the trial, my stepdad, whom I admired more than any other man I've ever known, loaded his gun and carried it to his jewelry store, which was across the street from the courthouse. "You just never know what could happen," he told me vaguely.

Not surprisingly even to a teenager, the trial was over almost before it began. An all-white Hamilton jury took less than an hour to convict the black man of murder. There was no violence and no escape attempt. And except for the preoccupied merchants staring through their windows toward the courthouse, it was just another day in a dusty Texas town so small that even many Texans have never heard of it.

What I still can't figure—not after a trip to college, a trip to Vietnam, and more than twenty years as a journalist—is how otherwise decent people could be so blindsided and fanatical about an issue I saw so simply as one of human decency: how a family could take dinner to neighbors who had suffered a death in the family and still maintain they'd never live next door to a *nigger,* or how a white man could take a black man's money and still expect him to eat like an animal in the kitchen of a cafe.

Events that unfolded on Christmas Day, 1987, only added to my long-time quandary about racism. Loyal Garner, Jr., a black man from Louisiana, the father of six and never before arrested, was jailed for a minor offense in Hemphill, a tiny town in East Texas. Two days later, he was dead, the victim of massive brain damage. The last people to see him conscious were three white police officers.

As the case unfolded piecemeal in the media, and after the officers were indicted in Garner's death, residents of Hemphill and the rest of Sabine County rallied in defense of the officers. One of the town's best-educated and most prominent citizens posted bond for two of the officers. A volunteer fire department sponsored a cookout to raise funds for their defense. The town's mayor compared the beating death of Garner to an "industrial accident." Another noted that Garner should have been at home with his family on Christmas Day. "Far as I'm concerned," he said, "the nigger got what was coming to him."

The news accounts flashed me back nearly twenty-five years to that hot summer day in small-town Texas. Maybe, I thought, I had become as oblivious to my surroundings as I had been at seventeen. While insensitivity born of teenage naivete might be defensible, there was precious little mitigation for a forty-one-year-old journalist paid, ostensibly, for his objective observations of society. Again, I was daunted by the hypocrisy of my roots.

Hemphill, I imagined, was much like Hamilton, full of people who were God-fearing and hard-working and cared about their families and their neighbors. So what was it about the death of a black stranger in

Hemphill that had so permeated a whole town of otherwise decent folks with denial, defensiveness, and rationalization?

I saw the Garner case as an opportunity for a moral and social post-mortem of sorts, a chance to resolve questions that had gone unanswered since I was a teenager in rural Texas.

Before embarking on *Deliberate Indifference*, I discussed the Garner case with a friend and colleague, Peter Applebome of *The New York Times*. Peter, a native New Yorker, had been in Hemphill to cover the Garner story. He had been threatened as he interviewed townspeople. "It's a scary place, Howard," he had said. "I won't go back." With what I took as good-natured kidding and an obvious reference to my Texas drawl, Wranglers, and cowboy boots, Peter said, "You talk that talk. It'll be easier for you."

Peter, I discovered, had been overly optimistic: *anyone* who wasn't from Hemphill or Sabine County was suspect, regardless of race, dress, or drawl. The county was beleaguered by out-of-town lawyers and media. Forced unwillingly almost overnight into the national spotlight, its residents were distrustful of everyone. I felt a curious empathy and kinship with them. "We're no different from anyone else, I'll tell you that," one man told me on the town square. "But that's all I'll tell you, 'cause I got to live here."

While I was researching and writing this book, the saga of Rodney King, a black man beaten mercilessly by four white police officers in Los Angeles, was videotaped and replayed on TV screens throughout the nation. I watched the horror of the beatings and wondered how many other times in cities as big as Los Angeles officers had beaten people and gotten away with it. Had the victims' injuries, even deaths, been explained away with bogus police reports of resisting arrest and attempted escape?

Though both may be lethal, a gaping laceration is easier to identify than a tumor buried in a vital organ. And in tiny Hemphill, Texas, Garner's death was as obvious as a bloody wound to the forehead; it couldn't be concealed. That Garner's death and its fallout were rooted in racial distrust, maybe even racial hatred in a few cases, was equally obvious. Far more difficult to isolate were the other, more subtle forces that surfaced in the aftermath in Sabine County: abuse of authority, shortage of decent jobs, false community pride, a vacuum of courageous leadership, and fierce defense of the status quo.

But hadn't the King beating and the subsequent reaction in South

Central Los Angeles following the officers' acquittals been rooted in the same racial distrust and hatred?

I suspect the old man in Hemphill was right, at least to some degree, when he defiantly told me that people in Hemphill were "no different" from people anywhere else. The size of the body, he seemed to be saying, may make the illness harder to find; it doesn't make the illness any less devastating.

Many of the major events that led to the death of Loyal Garner, Jr., remain in dispute more than four years after his death. For purposes of narration, and to avoid a ponderous point-counterpoint presentation, I have attempted to use the most plausible of those disputed accounts, relying at times on decisions made by jurors who heard the same evidence. But I also have attempted to give equal weight to all the versions of the truth and, during the trial sequences of this book, to both prosecution's and defense's accounts. Such is the character of our justice system, and indeed of human beings, that sworn testimony concerning the same tragic event can vary so dramatically.

I have relied heavily on the voluminous court records spawned by Garner's death. To the extent that bureaucrats complied with open-records laws, I have supplemented court records with investigative reports and affidavits that weren't introduced in court. Some conversations I have reconstructed, based on interviews with people who claim to have had them.

> *Howard Swindle*
> *July 1992*

Deliberate
INDIFFERENCE

PROLOGUE

TROY LEE STARLING was the first, killed on a tarpaper night beside a deserted East Texas highway. A blue steel muzzle was pointed close to the back of his neck. One clean shot, with enough velocity to pierce the engine block of a car, tore through Starling's neck, blowing a gaping exit hole in his Adam's apple. The .357 magnum was issued by the Texas Department of Public Safety; the man who pulled the trigger was a state trooper.

Four months later, on Christmas night, 1987, Loyal Garner, Jr., was bludgeoned with a blackjack, then dragged out of the sight of witnesses into an isolated room. When his friends next saw him, his eyes were locked open in an eerie, sightless freeze frame. Propped against a cement wall, he slid like cold syrup along the wall and onto the floor. A pathologist later would characterize the injuries to Garner's head as similar to those of a person who had gone through a car windshield at one hundred miles an hour. Garner was last seen conscious in the company of three police officers.

Spring hadn't fully settled in East Texas when Kenneth "Hambone" Simpson died. There had been no more dignity in the man's death than in that of a road-killed armadillo left beside the highway. Ambulance attendants found Simpson's body hog-tied on the cement floor of a jail cell, his hands cuffed behind his back and his ankles bound together with disposable plastic cuffs. He wore no shirt; his pants had been pulled below his buttocks. A pool of blood beside his left shoulder had dried onto the cement floor. Rigor mortis had set in, posing no small problem for the attendants, whose job it was to remove Simpson's contorted body from the cell onto a gurney. Eleven officers admitted being in the eight-foot-square cell during five frenzied minutes of violence. All of them swore that Simpson had been alive when they left.

In eight months that straddled 1987 and 1988, Starling, Garner, and Simpson died within one hundred miles of each other in a triangular slice of wondrous pine thickets known as Deep East Texas. Nothing suggests that any of them ever had occasion to meet. Starling operated a forklift, Garner drove a truck, and Simpson was a sidewalk scammer, a nickel-and-dimer whose enterprises included gambling, drugs, and other people's property.

Indeed, the three men shared more in death than in life. Each met death under the color of law. Each fell into police custody for misdemeanor offenses that shouldn't have overly challenged the peace and dignity of local society—speeding, drunk driving, stealing a ballpoint pen. None of the victims was armed—no gun, no knife, not even the ubiquitous "shiny object" that officers inevitably claim to have mistaken for a weapon before electing to exercise lethal force.

Starling and Garner were black. The last faces they saw in life were those of white police officers. Simpson also was black. Eight of his eleven assailants were white officers, troopers, and deputies.

The similarities in death didn't end there. Among some members of the tiny communities in which the black men died, reaction was frighteningly similar: "Just another dead nigger."

For decades, long before the nation was outraged by the videotaped brutality of white Los Angeles police officers beating an unarmed and helpless black man, black life had been cheap in rural Texas—particularly if a black had the audacity, or ignorance, to step out of his "place."

By 1964, it was inevitable that Washington would mandate that blacks and whites would sit beside each other in public schools and in restaurants. But today, more than twenty-five years after the Civil Rights Act of 1964, a black's place in most of Deep East Texas doesn't yet mean a badge, an elected office, or an integrated church. As if the seventy-foot-tall pines were an inpenetrable social barrier, Deep East Texas lies stagnant in a civil rights time warp, more forties and fifties than eighties and nineties.

Texas, not Alabama or Mississippi, leads the nation in the number of federal civil rights investigations annually. And within Texas, the majority of those officers investigated for beating, torturing, and shooting defendants practice their professions in small towns east of Interstate 35, the major artery that splits the state in half. Ironically, it is within this same piece of geography, broadly known as East Texas, that history and culture also has situated the bulk of the state's black population. Not surprising, black residents of these farming and sawmill towns become victims in disproportionately high numbers of some of the toughest, most abusive cops in the nation.

In the deepest enclave of East Texas, the criminal-justice system is dominated by white cops, white grand juries, white jurors, and white judges. At best, the system tolerates black defendants. At worst, black defendants don't make it past the white cops even to be heard by the white grand juries: justice is administered swiftly and surely by a good ol' boy beside the road or in a booking room or jail cell.

Vollie Grace, a black contractor, deacon of his church and father of four, was born and reared on a family farm just outside Hemphill, Texas. He didn't set out to be a civil rights activist. He didn't *want* to be an activist. But when Loyal Garner, Jr., was beaten unconscious in the Sabine County Jail in Hemphill, just a rock's throw from the Louisiana state line, Vollie Grace felt like he would suffocate on his silence. Garner died two days later without regaining consciousness. Not only was there no official explanation from law enforcement about the cause of his death, there was not even an acknowledgment of his death.

Grace forced an explanation from law enforcement, a group that for two hundred years in Sabine County has been exclusively white and which, its current sheriff vows, will continue to be exclusively white as long as he's alive and wearing a badge. When the acknowledgment of Garner's death did come, it was passive. Loyal Garner, Jr., a valued, hardworking family man, had walked without threat or coercion into the one-story stucco jail, under his own power. The next morning he was rolled out on a gurney, his eyes locked in a half-open, surrealistic daze. Somehow, he "just got dead." A passive act, like "Well, he just took ill."

Troy Starling's and Kenneth Simpson's deaths never made it past grand juries. The white trooper who killed Starling was cleared without charges even before forensic lab tests were available. The tests proved that the officer's story of self-defense was scientifically implausible—about as likely, a forensic pathologist said, as "lightning striking the room while we're speaking." When the final vote came around, the grand jury's two black members abstained in disgust.

The eleven officers who last saw Simpson alive before he was found hog-tied and suffocated in his cell were neither disciplined nor indicted by the grand jury. A year later, one of the officers sauntered up to a writer and asked why he hadn't been interviewed about the circumstances of Simpson's death. "I know what happened," he sneered, moving his face close to the writer's. "The nigger killed hisself."

The death of Loyal Garner, Jr., perhaps no more heinous in circumstance than Starling's or Simpson's, was the only one of the three to be prosecuted in the criminal justice system responsible for law and order in Deep East Texas.

Justice for Garner wouldn't come easily. That it came at all, considering the legacy of human abuse in East Texas, was stunning enough to command two minutes of network news time and front-page headlines in *The New York Times*. Moreover, justice came reluctantly, and only when the good-ol'-boy system was dissected, magnified, and exposed. Garner's day in court came only after another jurisdiction fought to wrest responsibility from the tiny town that had tried so desperately to bury the evidence along with its sordid history of civil rights abuses. When the town realized it no longer could shield its officers from the glare of outside scrutiny, its residents rallied even more stubbornly behind the lawmen, pulling in ranks tightly and refusing to talk to outsiders. The people who lived in Hemphill called it community pride; outsiders called it paranoia. Whatever its genesis, the result was an impenetrable silence.

Beyond all else, Hemphill seemed to determine, its deliberate indifference should remain concealed within the familiar thickets of longleaf pines.

1

THE ARREST

TEXAS HIGHWAY 87 is a scenic and incongruous stretch of two-lane blacktop, conceived as much for tourism as for commerce. From its origin near Galveston, it runs flat and straight for sixty picturesque miles along the lip of the Gulf of Mexico. Only a few thousand yards short of Louisiana, the highway veers hard left, ducks beneath the steady congestion of Interstate 10, and heads quietly due north for country that makes the Texas Department of Tourism proud. Texas 87 assumes a new personality with each northward mile, heading first up subtle inclines, then rolling gently and, by the time it skirts the pine-laden Big Thicket, bogging down logging trucks with its deceptively steep grades.

Fifty miles north of the Gulf Coast, Texas 87 already is well into Deep East Texas, the state's easternmost colony of counties, clustered along the Sabine River, the natural boundary that keeps Texas from running into Louisiana. On either side of the highway, seventy-foot longleaf pines grow so densely that they choke sunshine in midday. Even on nights with full moons, Deep East Texas is darker than coal tar in a cellar.

About an hour after dusk on Christmas Day, 1987, a chilly, sporadic drizzle was threatening to turn into genuine rain along Texas 87. Loyal Garner, Jr., was less than two miles north of Hemphill, the county seat of Sabine County, when he saw the flashing red and blue lights in his rearview mirror. "Damn!" Garner muttered to the two friends beside him in the cab of the pickup truck. "I wonder if I didn't hook up those taillights?"

Moments later, as he stood beside the deserted highway, rain trickling from his brows into his eyes, Garner was looking up at one of the biggest cops he had ever seen.

It was part Good Samaritanism, part pride, and part his usual inability to say no that had prompted Loyal Garner, Jr., to pry himself from the controlled Christmas chaos that he knew as head of a household that included three daughters and three sons—six loud, stair-stepped kids from three to thirteen, each separated by exactly two years.

The holiday frenzy actually had begun in earnest on Christmas Eve at the Garner home, a modest but livable three-bedroom frame house set on concrete blocks. It sat in a half-acre clearing surrounded by pines just outside the city limits of Florien, Louisiana. The pines, and the Boise-Cascade plant that cut, pressed, and pasted them into plywood, were Florien's only reasons for being. No more than a fly speck on the map, Florien (pronounced "FLO-REEN" by locals) was barely even in Louisiana; it snuggled close to the Sabine River and the Toledo Bend Reservoir, which formed the state line between Sabine County, Texas, and Sabine Parish, Louisiana.

On Christmas Eve, by family custom, Corrine Garner took the three girls, Carmica, Kimberly, and Valerie, with her to Many, Louisiana, ten miles north, to buy groceries and to stop off at the Laundromat. Christmas, particularly *this* Christmas, was no time to discuss it, Corrine knew, but a washer and a dryer were necessities for a family with six kids who seemed to create dirty clothes the way rain created mud. Buying a washer and a dryer always had been a priority, even with Loyal; but food and clothing always seemed to move them down the list. The phone had been a priority, too, but it sat idle in the living room. Loyal and Corrine had been forced to choose between paying the phone bill and sandbagging a little extra for the kids' Christmas, and the phone bill hadn't made the cut. The phone had been disconnected.

Garner kept the boys, Loyal Lynndell, Marlon, and Corey, at home, enlisting—or more accurately, *tolerating*—their help in applying the final touches to his black Ford Explorer pickup truck, a spotless nine-year-old relic he had rejuvenated with a wholesale overhaul. Only days earlier, Corrine, in mock seriousness, had drawn the line when rain had forced her husband to retreat to the kitchen, dragging with him his greasy carburetor and intake manifold, which he had plopped down on newspapers spread on the table. He grinned under the threat, the way he always did. "It ain't no use worrying, Corrine. No grease going to get on your table. I already cleaned them in gasoline."

When Corrine and the girls returned from Many in the afternoon, she set Carmica, Kimberly, and Valerie to folding clothes and straightening up the house while she got an early start on Christmas dinner. Christmas morning was for the kids, she always said, and she didn't want to be trapped in the kitchen cooking while they were playing with their booty from Santa. Christmas Eve she reserved for baking the pies and getting the vegetables ready. She also made the cornbread dressing and readied the turkey, needing only to pop them into the oven in the morning.

After dusk, Garner cajoled Corrine into a test ride in the Ford Explorer. He was like a kid at Christmas, Corrine mused, busily explaining mechanical intricacies that he knew she'd never understand. His ability to work with his hands, to fix or build just about anything, was one of the traits she most admired in him in the fourteen years they'd been married. His reputation as a "shade-tree mechanic," in fact, had meant a little extra money from fixing cars for friends. So, dutifully, Corrine nodded and smiled as her husband rambled on about timing chains, valves, and whatchamacallits.

Before heading home, the couple stopped off at Mr. Albert's. Florien was "dry," and while you could buy everything from a pump-action shotgun to french fries at John's Country Store, you couldn't buy Budweiser or Jim Beam. Alcohol meant a ten-mile trip up U.S. 177 to Many. Mr. Albert, an elderly black man, operated under the entrepreneurial philosophy of supply and demand, or, more specifically, find a void and fill it. Mr. Albert was a bootlegger. Garner emerged from Mr. Albert's tiny lean-to house with a single can of Budweiser, which he swigged before they pulled up in their own muddy red driveway.

Thoughts of new toys had a grip on the two youngest Garners, five-year-old Marlon and three-year-old Corey, who successfully fought off sleep until midnight. Stern warnings from their father meant little on Christmas Eve, and the boys knew they were safe in pushing the limits. "We'll just have to get up a little earlier in the morning and get that bike put together before they wake up," Garner told Corrine, yawning and heading for the bedroom.

The bicycle, assembled and ready near the tree early Christmas morning, was a hit with the oldest boy, seven-year-old Loyal Lynndell—but no more than Corey's dump truck, which, his father explained, was just like the one he drove every day working for the Sabine Parish road crew. They were on the floor together, Garner and Corey, pushing the truck around the coffee table and behind the space heater, dodging the torn Christmas wrapping that littered the floor.

After Christmas dinner, around eleven-thirty, Gerome Garner, one of Loyal's ten brothers, showed up on the front porch. Corrine, busy directing kitchen cleaning, saw Gerome offer her husband a beer, but her duties took her away from the window, and she never saw whether he drank it. And she only casually noticed that Johnnie Maxie also had appeared from down the road—to borrow a wrench to fix his down-and-out Ford Granada, Loyal told her after Maxie had gone.

Corrine didn't own a watch, but she later would estimate that Johnnie Maxie returned sometime between one and two in the afternoon, carrying the wrench and wearing a forlorn look on his ample face. Johnnie's younger brother, Alton, was with him in their mother's car. The wrench hadn't provided the solution to the Granada's woes; Johnnie Maxie needed a timing chain for the engine.

"Corrine, I'm going to follow Johnnie and Alton on to their mother's and drop off her car," Loyal said. "Then I'm taking them over to Newton to pick up Johnnie's other car. He wants me to redo his engine. Shouldn't be gone more than two or three hours, I 'magine."

Newton was maybe fifty miles southwest of Florien, across the Sabine River on the Texas side. Garner walked out the front door wearing black boots, a freshly pressed striped shirt his wife had washed only the night before, and the new pair of jeans she had given him for Christmas.

The innocuous, over-the-shoulder conversation would be the last Corrine Garner ever had with her husband. When she next saw him, she would barely recognize him.

"Junior" Garner had known Johnnie and Alton Maxie all their lives, had gone to school with them and had socialized with their family. Like all the blacks and most of the whites around Florien, the Maxies were players in hardscrabble economics, always searching the system of too few good jobs for ways to make ends meet. Recently, the Maxies had signed on as roughnecks for a small oil drilling company in western Louisiana. The money was better than average, but the drilling rig was miles out in the pines. Alton, shorter and leaner, rode to work with his big brother. They had to have transportation to have a job.

Once he had collected them at their mother's house in his pickup truck, Garner suggested a change of plan.

"Corrine's brother up in Many does some mechanic work. He might know somebody who has a timing chain today. There's a bunch of ol' wrecking yards up in Zwolle. It's worth a try." Besides, Garner figured, the trip would be a good break-in for the Explorer's tight, reworked engine.

The three friends meandered leisurely up U.S. 171, first to Many, where they just missed Corrine's brother, then on to Zwolle, where they tried a series of junkyards without finding one open. Garner was disappointed; he would have bet good money that one of the proprietors would have come out on Christmas to make a cash deal.

Jerry Lane Cartinez was open. He had owned the liquor store south of Zwolle only since Thanksgiving, and since the state of Louisiana didn't have any objections about selling booze on Christmas, he figured he needed the business.

At some point between five and seven that afternoon, three black men walked into his store. Cartinez recognized Alton Maxie, the smallest of the three. The proprietor and his customers chitchatted, first about the drizzly weather, then about the men's trip to Texas to pick up a car. Cartinez rang up their purchases—a six-pack of Budweiser, a half-pint of Bacardi rum, and a half-pint of Crown Royal bourbon.

"I got this," Johnnie said, pulling his belt up over his belly with his left hand and dipping his right hand into his pocket for a small wad of bills. "You been running me around all day on this car. I owe you."

As an afterthought, the third man, the solidly built, muscular one who was driving the black pickup, put a dollar on the counter for a raffle ticket. Holder of the winning ticket, Cartinez explained, won a fifth of bourbon. The fact that the man generally drank only beer didn't dissuade him from entering the raffle. On the back of the card, he wrote his name: "Loyal Garner Jr., Florien, La."

Within thirty minutes, the black Ford pickup had passed from Louisiana over the Pendleton Bridge, a two-and-a-half-mile concrete span over the Sabine River, and into Sabine County, Texas, en route to Newton.

Cartinez would see Garner's name in the newspaper and hear it on television in the next few days. The name struck a vaguely familiar chord. The liquor store owner shuffled through his raffle tickets until he found Garner's. That Garner had been in his store on Christmas making idle talk chilled him. He'd remember to tell his wife when he got home. He'd never known anybody who'd ended up in the news—not like that.

"Well, Junior, just *try* a swig of this Crown Royal. It's smooth stuff."

Johnnie knew Garner drank only beer, but he extended the half-pint of whiskey over Alton's chest anyway and motioned the small bottle toward the driver.

Garner looked dubiously at his friend, then took only enough from the bottle to confirm what he already suspected. "Damn, that stuff makes me sick. Don't like it. Just gimme one of them Buds."

Johnnie leaned into the floorboard and came up with a red, white, and blue can almost hidden by his huge fist. Alton took it and handed it to Garner. Both brothers say the driver nursed the single Budweiser until shortly before they were stopped beside Texas 87 outside Hemphill.

"It's got to be a taillight," Garner said again as the officer approached his door. The police officer who approached Garner's window was a bear of a man, six-foot-one, 270 pounds, with a belly that plunged heavily over his belt, concealing its buckle. From Johnnie Maxie's vantage point on the passenger side of the pickup, the full frame of the driver's window was filled with the officer's chest, forcing Garner to lean back in the driver's seat, cock his head toward the window, and peer up at his accuser. As Garner was told to step out of the truck and walk to the back, a second officer—smaller, wiry, and angular—appeared at the right rear of the Ford pickup, eyeing the Maxie brothers in the cab.

"Go on and get in the backseat of the patrol unit," he said to them, as he opened the passenger door, his eyes fixed on Johnnie.

The big one continued to talk to Garner. Then Garner joined his passengers in the backseat of the patrol car. The officers removed Garner's hunting rifle from the cab of the pickup and locked its doors.

As the big one pulled the Ford patrol car into gear and steered around the pickup truck on the shoulder of the road, Garner asked apparently his only question: "What about my pickup?"

"It'll be all right for a little while," came the answer from the front seat.

Garner was thirty-four years old and had never been arrested in his life. He was clearly perplexed, and looked toward the Maxies for explanation. Alton, sitting cramped in the middle, sensed Garner's silent question, shrugged and rolled his eyes. Alton and Johnnie had been arrested before, but never for anything except for drunk driving. This arrest, the Maxies sensed, was strange, and nothing at all like the other times. Neither of the cops had told them what law they supposedly violated. They hadn't read them the Miranda warning. And even though the cops had to have noticed the beer and liquor on the floorboard of the pickup —Johnnie had made no effort to push it under the seat—the big one hadn't asked Garner to perform any field sobriety tests: no walking heel-to-toe, reciting the alphabet, or standing on one foot with his eyes closed. There was no mention of Breathalyzer or blood tests. There wasn't even mention of a faulty taillight.

Even more curious, Alton Maxie thought, the officers ordered them into the backseat of a patrol car that had no protective mesh screen without frisking them for weapons or even handcuffing them. Alton's mind was beginning to reel with paranoia; something, he sensed, was horribly wrong. What the hell's going on here?

The little one shattered Alton's thoughts. "Any of you boys got a gun or a knife back there?" It was a casual question, as if he were merely making small talk. Quickly, Johnnie Maxie dug into his left front pocket and surrendered a small fold-out pocket knife.

The ten-minute drive to the Sabine County Jail in Hemphill was ominously quiet. The three blacks huddled in the backseat asked no questions; the two white cops in front volunteered nothing.

After the men had been escorted through the sally port and down the cell block hallway, Alton could stand the uncertainty no longer. "Uh . . . so what are you charging us with?" he asked timidly. The officers didn't acknowledge his question, and continued transposing information from the men's driver's licenses onto five-by-seven-inch jail cards.

Hell, they wouldn't be filling out those cards if they weren't going to put us in jail, Alton thought, and repeated his question, this time louder.

"You boys just sit down there and be quiet," one of the cops said. Periodically, one or the other of the officers would ask a perfunctory question. The three black men exchanged puzzled glances.

The third time Alton asked, his voice carried a definite edge, more of fear than of anger. "Look, if y'all are going to lock us up, don't you have to at least tell us what we're supposed to have done? I mean, this ain't right, you know?"

The little one looked up at Alton from his paperwork. "You come on and go with me." The instruction froze the room. The officer opened a metal cell door and led the smallest of the three black men out of sight and into the bowels of the jail.

As if Alton's departure were a cue, Garner obligingly stood up. Balancing himself on one foot, he sought to clarify an obvious misunderstanding. "Look at this," he said, balancing himself like a little boy on a train rail. "If you think I'm drunk, well, just look. . . ."

"Sit down."

"Well, okay—but I'd take one of them breath tests if you want to give me one."

After Garner and Johnnie Maxie had been booked, the two officers escorted them down the hall to the detox cell, where Alton already had been deposited. As the two new charges entered the cell, the cops motioned to Alton, who followed them back down the hall to the book-in room.

Moments later, Alton, escorted by both officers, was returned to the detox cell. As the metal door echoed shut, the three men looked silently around the tomblike room. Except for a toilet and a raised cement slab with no mattress, the cell was simply floor, walls, and ceiling. Opening onto the hallway was a heavy metal door with a glass-and-mesh screen at about eye level and a rectangular "bean hole" through which food could be passed.

The prisoners' conversation was tentative at first. "Ain't we supposed to be able to call somebody and tell them where we're at?" Garner asked of no one in particular. "Man, I know Corrine's gonna be wondering. I mean, it's Christmas and all. . . ."

Rapidly, the grousing became more vocal, the tone angrier. "Man, this is bullshit!" Alton screamed, making no attempt to conceal his mood. "God damn it, this ain't right. Gimme the damn phone. I want to make a call. *Any*body hear me?"

Their screams echoed and fell on silence. In frustration, Alton and Garner hit and kicked the metal door, over and over again. They kicked and slammed at the door until they were exhausted; they screamed until they were hoarse; then they kicked again.

Next door in B cell, Angus Bozeman had been incarcerated with Keith Miller and Trent Taylor for a month by the time the three black strangers were brought in. Between theft and criminal mischief, in fact, the red-haired and wiry nineteen-year-old had been in some jail or other for most of the last two years. B cell was his most recent home. Sitting on the edge of his bunk, Bozeman was tired of the commotion next door. He resented the intrusion. "You bastards next door better shut up," he yelled. "Some of us got to live here. We ain't getting out tomorrow. So shut the fuck up."

"Look, man, this ain't your deal. We ain't drunk and we got a right to a phone call. Mind your own goddamn business."

The argument through the concrete wall between captive neighbors quieted down when Bozeman heard the familiar footsteps of Lawton Crain, the jailer, in the passageway. In his month in the Sabine County Jail, Bozeman had learned to identify his captors not only by their voices, but by their footsteps. He knew he was right when he heard Crain's same old toothless threat directed next door at detox:

"If you boys don't shut up and get away from that door, I'm gonna come in there and stomp your ass."

"What you gonna do? Bring four or five with you?"

Within minutes, Bozeman heard the locks unlatch on the metal security door at the end of the hall. He leaned forward on his bunk, straining to hear, like a startled deer. He heard Thomas Ladner and Bo Hyden, the same pair he'd seen earlier through the bean hole escorting the three black prisoners down the hallway.

"Shit," Bozeman whispered to Taylor across the cell, "is about to hit the fan."

The voice was unmistakable and clear. It belonged to Ladner. "Who in hell is raising hell back there?"

The answer came from Crain: "Them niggers you brung in a while ago."

There were two sets of footsteps, and the voices were closer. Bozeman suspected they stopped outside the door to detox. He heard the voice he knew as Ladner's yelling down the hall to the jailer with the automatic controls. "Open detox!"

Metal clanged on metal. A door creaked on its hinges.

The swinging door startled Alton Maxie and Loyal Garner, both of whom were sitting on the concrete ledge just inside the cell. Across the cell, his back leaning against the wall, Johnnie Maxie straightened.

The little officer, his right hand on the butt of his holstered pistol, stood half in, half out of the doorway. The big one, a black, leather-covered, lead-weighted slapjack in his right hand, was staring down on Alton and

Garner. It was Ladner, the huge one, who spoke. "Which one of you's beating on the motherfucking door?"

Garner was speaking even as he rose from the ledge. "I was. I just want to call my wife—"

The sound echoed next door in B cell, dropping Bozeman's eyes to the floor. Three times, staccato—*blap, blap, blap*—the sound of metal on skin and bone, like a bird hit by a car grille.

Immediately after the blows, Angus Bozeman heard a metal object—it sounded to him like a metal Zippo lighter—hit the floor and career like a hockey puck down the long hallway outside detox. Locked in B cell, he had no way of seeing that the metal object wasn't a lighter but the lead insert from Ladner's blackjack. The last of the three blows to Garner's head had split the stitching that held the lead inside its leather sheath.

Barely inside detox, Alton Maxie looked up helplessly from the concrete ledge as Ladner, his beefy arm still grasping Garner's neck from behind, pushed, shoved, and carried the dazed prisoner to the open cell door. Even before the blows had rained down on Garner, Alton instinctively had tried to stand. "Sit down," commanded Bo Hyden, his hand still on the grip of his holstered pistol, and Alton knew better than to try again.

After Ladner had wrestled Garner into the hallway, and as Hyden began closing the metal door, the smaller deputy made ominous eye contact with Alton. "See, boy," he said, "it didn't take no four or five of us."

Bozeman heard the sound of scuffling as the door to detox slammed shut. Before the footsteps faded with distance down the hallway, Bozeman recognized two distinctive sets. A third set of footsteps, he thought, sounded different, like a combination of walking and dragging.

"They got one of 'em out," Bozeman whispered. "Aw, shit."

Alton and Johnnie Maxie were pacing nervously at the rear of the detox cell ten minutes later when Ladner and Hyden returned with their prisoner. Garner, his chin dangling on his chest and his feet only half touching the floor, was suspended between the two officers like wet pants on a clothesline. The front and side of his shirt were bloody.

Together, the two uniformed men backed Garner toward the wall, then swung and pitched their load like a bag of oats onto the concrete ledge. Garner's back slid a few inches down the wall until the weight of his tilted head pulled his torso onto the ledge.

Relieved of their load, the officers motioned to Alton. "Come on, let's go."

The trip lasted only twenty-five feet or so, but it was the longest in Alton's life. His heart pounded and his mind raced. When the officers opened the door to the processing room, Alton's eyes fell first on the metal armchair on rollers standing conspicuously in the middle of the room, then to the floor. Splotches of blood the size of a kitten's paws were littered around the chair. His mind flashed back to the cell and the sight of his bloodied friend.

Alton didn't know how he got in the chair, but Police Chief Thomas Ladner had assumed a position over his right shoulder by the file cabinets. The chief's eyes never left Alton. In his right hand, the burly officer held a black nightstick about eighteen inches long, which he tapped methodically into the opened palm of his left hand. Deputy Sheriff Bo Hyden was in the prisoner's face.

"Do you want some?"

"No sir."

"I want to know. Do you want some?"

"No sir, I don't. *No sir*."

"Well, why are you back there raising so much hell?"

Alton braced himself in the chair, anticipating the worst. He heard his words come out apologetically. "Well, we just wanted to call somebody, you know, and let 'em know where we were."

"Let me tell you what's gonna happen. You're gonna go back there in that cell and keep your damn mouth shut. You understand that?"

"Yes sir, I do. *I do*."

As the door to detox clanged shut behind him, a relieved Alton still was shaking so badly he wasn't certain he could stand. When he looked down on Garner slumped half-prone on the bloodstained concrete, Alton knew he was about to be sick.

The blood covering Garner's shirt, Alton saw, had seeped from a deep gash in his head. The man's forehead and hairline were littered with random, marble-sized knots, as if he had dozed off in a hailstorm. In one place well into Garner's hairline, a circular swatch of hair bigger than a half-dollar was missing, as if it had been ripped out by its roots. But even more unnerving were Garner's eyes. They were locked open in an eerie stare at the beige cement wall across the cell. The only indication of life from Garner's body—and it periodically would jolt the Maxie brothers with renewed horror—was an unpredictable wheeze for air.

It was Garner's stuporous stare that sent Johnnie, by far the biggest man in the cell, retreating to the back of the concrete cage, as far away from his best friend as he could get.

At some point in the waning hours of Christmas, Chief Thomas Ladner appeared at the door to detox with Trent Taylor, Angus Bozeman's cell-mate in B cell and a trusty in the Sabine County Jail. At twenty-one, the clean-cut, docile Taylor looked like a fraternity boy, maybe pre-med or computers. Only a look at his rap sheet lent justification to Taylor's current plight: he was an overachiever at breaking into other people's businesses and had been hauled off the street six times for burglary and theft. In the month he had been imprisoned in Hemphill, the soft-spoken, obliging Taylor had inherited the job of trusty, sweeping and mopping the cell blocks and washing clothes. In return, he enjoyed more freedom than the other prisoners within the confines of the bars. Occasionally, as it had happened this night, Taylor was rewarded with a cup of coffee in the kitchen.

"Grab a set of those clothes for one of those guys in detox," Ladner had told him in the jail's utility room, "and clean up anything you see needs cleaning."

When Ladner opened detox, Taylor saw the results of the sounds he had heard earlier from his cell. An unconscious black man was lying on the concrete ledge. The man's shirt hadn't absorbed all the blood from his head wounds; a twelve-inch-wide reservoir of blood had collected beside him.

The chief directed his instructions to the two other black men standing nervously at the rear of the cell. "Get him up and change his clothes."

The Maxie brothers fidgeted under the order before the smaller one finally answered. "Uh, maybe we just ought to leave him be. He's not doing too good. He hasn't moved a bit and he hasn't said nothing. You know, I think he needs to see a doctor."

Ladner eyed the two men, then redirected the order to Taylor. "Go ahead. Get those clean clothes on him."

"I just can't do it. I mean . . . well, I just can't touch him, you know?"

The chief apparently underwent a change of mind. Before he shut the door, the bigger black man asked the trusty if he had a pinch of Skoal. The smaller one asked him for a cigarette. The trusty had neither.

Outside in the runaround adjacent to the cell block, Taylor busied himself cleaning. Retrieving a mop, he cleaned up blood outside detox. He found more blood at the other end of the hall, outside the inmate processing room, and mopped that up too.

Taylor stowed the mop and bucket and headed for the dispatcher-jailer's office, directly across from the processing room. Crain was sitting at the desk. A blackjack was lying nearby. Taylor picked it up, looking at it curiously. It was medieval, black leather, about a foot long and skinny, maybe an inch wide, with a looped handhold on one end. The opposite end, the "business end," spread into a two-inch circle. Taylor noticed that the stitching around the circular part of the leather was unraveled. When he elevated the skinny end, a deceptively heavy and rounded chunk of lead fell out into the palm of his other hand.

Crain noticed the young trusty's preoccupation with the blackjack, and grinned. "They don't make 'em like they used to."

Alton Maxie was on his knees peering through the bean hole, the rectangular hole about waist-high in the cell door, when he saw Chief Deputy Billy Ray Horton walk past detox. Horton, considerably older than the other two officers, wasn't a face Alton had seen before. Alton was losing his battle with panic. For what seemed an eternity, he and his brother had paced aimlessly at the rear of the cell, watching helplessly as their friend lay comatose and bleeding on the hard ledge. Now as he saw the new face in the uniform, Alton gambled.

"Uh . . . sir . . . could I come out and talk with you a minute?"

Soon the door rattled open and the older officer escorted him to the processing room in front of the jail. The prisoner searched the area with his eyes: Ladner and Hyden were gone; the rolling armchair had been returned to its position against the desk; there was no blood on the floor.

Playing out his gamble, the young black man studied his captor's face as he began talking, starting his tale innocuously with the uneventful arrest. Chief Deputy Horton, his face impassive, listened without saying anything. Gradually, the inmate related how the other officers had beaten Garner. Strategically, Alton structured his monologue to end with his two most important points: Garner, he emphasized, was in bad shape and needed a doctor; and could he *please* use the phone to tell someone their whereabouts?

Horton reached across the desk to the black phone and pulled it close. But before Alton was allowed to call his mother in Florien, the graying deputy established what Alton clearly understood to be guidelines. "It would be best," he intoned, "if you just tell her where you are and that she can't do anything about it until morning."

After Alton dialed his mother's number, Horton pulled the base of the phone away from him, leaving him with only the receiver. The inmate knew he had to follow the script; the deputy poised his index finger on the carriage of the phone just above the disconnect button, and listened intently.

2

COMA

THE SOUND of a jailer delivering breakfast outside the detox cell jolted Alton Maxie upright from the concrete floor. Alton was surprised that he had dozed off. Immediately, he looked to Junior Garner, still slumped on his side with his legs in front of him, his eyes still locked in the same blank stare, but now dried with a thin, scablike film over the pupils. The early-morning sounds of the jail routine had awakened Johnnie, too, and together the Maxies looked feebly at their collapsed friend.

Garner now was naked from the waist up; his shirt lay in the middle of the cell. Alton Maxie picked it up. It was damp, Alton thought, as if it had been washed but not dried. The blood that had stained it only a few hours earlier was gone. The two brothers looked at each other curiously.

Through the bean hole in the cell door, day jailer Clyde "Preacher" Kirk yelled into the cell at the two men. "How long's he been like that?"

"Ever since he was beat last night."

Kirk came through the door, bent over the concrete ledge, and searched Loyal Garner's wrist for a pulse. "I can't find nothing," he said, and left the cell. He returned within minutes, bearing a paper towel and water, which he handed to Alton Maxie. "Wash his face off and see if that helps. I'm gonna get an ambulance."

Another uniformed officer appeared moments after the jailer, and Johnnie Maxie left with them to retrieve a phone number for Garner's parents from his confiscated wallet. He was back in detox by the time the two ambulance attendants arrived.

Bill Barcheers, a heavyset emergency medical technician and owner of Hemphill's only ambulance, bent over the unconscious black man on the concrete ledge. The prisoner clearly was in rough shape. His eyes, Barcheers noted, were dried and dilated, and they didn't flinch when the paramedic shined the tiny ray of light from his flashlight, indicating a lack of blood circulation to the eyes. Demanding more immediate attention, though, were Garner's labored and faint attempts at breathing. Barcheers retrieved a plastic oral laryngeal airway from his medical kit and inserted it into Garner's throat, raising his tongue from the back of his throat and allowing him to breathe more easily.

As he moved the unconscious prisoner, Barcheers noticed smeared blood beneath the man's head, and clotted blood or mucus, or both, in his right nostril. The prisoner's pulse was a dangerously low eighty-four beats a minute.

When Barcheers had readied Garner, Preacher Kirk ordered the Maxie brothers to help load their friend onto the small jump cot. Barcheers's assistant walked with a cane, and Alton obligingly fell in behind the cot, pushing it down the hallway, through the sally port, and into the ambulance just outside the door. Silently, Johnnie followed the procession, carrying Barcheers's medical kit.

As the ambulance rolled away, the two brothers turned to the jail door. Something was wrong. They looked around. There were no jailers or deputies. The door was locked. They were alone.

Alton's mind contemplated escape. At eight-thirty on the Saturday morning after Christmas, not a soul was moving around the tiny town square diagonally across from the jail. In the other direction, across a vacant lot the size of a football field, was a darkened thicket of towering pines. He looked to his big brother for a sign, and saw uncertainty etched in his face. Without a word they began beating on the locked metal door. The irony was not lost on Alton. The only two eyewitnesses to Garner's beating were locked outside, and now they were begging to return to the scene of the crime.

You bastards ain't gonna set me up and shoot me!

"Hey in there!" Alton screamed. "Open the door! You got us locked out!"

The two brothers were panic-stricken by the time they finally heard the hinges move on the heavy metal door.

———

Corrine Garner first thought she had the wrong room. She had abandoned her in-laws near the nursing station at the Sabine County Hospital and ran as fast as she could. Now, from the doorway of the small hospital room, she knew the man in the bed couldn't be her husband. An orderly stood over him, and most of the patient's head was hidden with bandages tinged with fresh blood from his left ear and from a wound higher on the left side of his head. Gauze patches covered the man's eyes, and his mouth was forced open by a thick, clear tube that ran into his throat. She approached the bed reluctantly. The man's bandaged face was twice that of her husband's, as if it belonged to a three-hundred-pound man. It was unrecognizable. Slowly, she forced herself to pull back the sheet covering his legs. Junior, she remembered, still bore scars on his knees from a motorcycle wreck. The jagged, angry scars were unmistakable. Corrine had collapsed in sobs by the time her elderly in-laws, Sarah and Loyal Garner, Sr., appeared in the doorway.

The first message from Hemphill had jolted Corrine. Shortly before midnight on Christmas, with her husband long overdue from his trip to Texas, Corrine had heard a knock on her door. Sarah Garner had dispatched one of her sons next door to Corrine's with the message. "Rosie Maxie called Mother," he had said, "and Loyal and Alton and Johnnie are in jail over at Hemphill. But they said there wasn't anything we could do till in the morning."

That wasn't like Loyal. As long as they'd been married, he'd never seen the inside of a jail, and the mention of Hemphill made the arrest even more ominous. The town's white police officers were notorious in black communities on both sides of the state line for their brutal treatment of blacks. The few times the Garners had had to drive through Hemphill, Corrine recalled, Loyal had been adamant about not stopping for food or gas. He hadn't wanted to tempt fate.

It being Christmas and with the Maxie brothers as passengers, Corrine speculated, her husband must have been bolstered by a false sense of security. And while Corrine wasn't aware they had been coming from Zwolle, Texas 87 through Hemphill was clearly the shortest route to Newton.

The second message Corrine received, on Saturday morning, had been even more alarming. She had awakened at six A.M., dressed quickly, and was waiting for her in-laws to get ready for the trip to Hemphill. Shortly after eight A.M., Loyal's brother returned. "They called again, Corrine, and said you needed to come over to the Hemphill hospital quick. Said Loyal's taken ill."

Corrine's heart dropped as she ran next door to Junior's parents' house. Loyal had never been sick a day in his life. Hemphill? The coincidence defied reality. "My lord, Mother," Corrine told her mother-in-law, "they've beaten him bad. We *got* to go. Now!"

Dr. Grover Winslow had practiced medicine for thirty-six years, and for the last thirty-five of those years he had been a legend, if not a monopoly, in Sabine County. Accidents, cancer, births, heart attacks, and shootings had left him unflappable and direct. More times than he could remember, he had been Sabine County's only human buffer between life and death.

Moments before Corrine Garner was notified of her husband's "illness," Dr. Winslow was examining him in the emergency room. The patient's pulse was increased; his blood pressure was precariously high—262 over 130 at one point—and, Dr. Winslow suspected, he suffered either a blood clot or hemorrhage in his head. Sabine County Hospital was too small to own a CAT scan, and the doctor had a nurse phone forty miles away to Jasper for a mobile unit. But the veteran country doctor didn't need sophisticated computer imagery to render a bottom line. Despite his best efforts, Dr. Winslow wouldn't give two hoots and a holler for Garner's chances.

"Your husband is in critical condition, Mrs. Garner," the doctor told her just after she arrived. "We're going to get a CAT scan when the unit arrives from Jasper, and then I imagine we'll be transferring him some-place where there's a neurosurgeon. He needs some help we can't give him here."

Even before the heavy truck with the CAT scan pulled up beside the tiny hospital, Garner had stopped breathing, requiring a respiratory ther-apist to "bag" him, mechanically forcing air into his lungs. The techni-cians told the anxious woman the quarters in the mobile unit were too cramped for her to be inside while they tested her husband, and for forty-five minutes Corrine fidgeted outside the door to the truck.

The results of the scan came as no surprise to Dr. Winslow. Garner's brain literally had been rearranged. The pictures showed a mass on the right side of the head, apparently hemorrhaging, that had shoved the brain and the ventricles to the left. The only hope, however remote, was to relieve the pressure inside the skull. For all practical purposes, Dr.

Winslow figured, Garner had been a "flat line," or brain dead, when he arrived from the Sabine County Jail.

It was Christmas weekend, and phone calls to hospitals in Nacogdoches and Beaumont, both about eighty miles away, failed to produce an on-duty neurosurgeon. Medical Center Hospital in Tyler, more than one hundred miles to the northwest, agreed to accept the emergency transfer.

Garner hadn't breathed on his own for an hour and thirty-five minutes. As the staff readied him for the ambulance trip to Tyler, Ronnie Felts, a local timber-mill owner who doubled as Hemphill's mayor, had been notified of Garner's injuries in the jail and headed to the hospital to see for himself what had happened. Medical attendants had declined to allow Corrine to ride with her husband in the ambulance, again emphasizing the limited space, particularly considering the emergency procedures they'd have to use en route. Mayor Felts asked Corrine if she had enough money to pay for the gas and incidentals for her and her in-laws to get to Tyler. When he heard her reply, he reached into his back pocket for his wallet.

Paramedic Bill Barcheers once again was entrusted with what remained of Garner's life. As Barcheers loaded Garner into the ambulance, Dr. Winslow had serious doubts that the patient would survive the trip.

3

PINE THICKETS AND GOOD OL' BOYS

ANDREW HELMS had made the trip up Texas 87 many times before he surrendered to the siren song of Deep East Texas. As he drove late in the afternoons through the sprawling Sabine National Forest, occasional bursts of sun shot unpredictably through the pine thickets across the highway, striking the side window like lasers. After one of the frequent heavy rains, known locally as "frog stranglers," even a small crack in the side glass fills the car with the cleansing scent of pine.

This, Helms had told his wife, Nora, is God's country. *This*, he said in late 1973, is where we're going to live.

Sabine County, before it became one of Texas's original counties, was a breathtaking but tranquil transit point, first for the Indians, then the Spaniards and French headed west in the early 1600s to settle Texas. The main road, called the King's Highway in deference to the King of Spain, was blazed in 1691. The road ran from east to west through the northern part of Sabine County. Settlers—and some would say just as many outlaws and fugitives—made their way through Louisiana to the wide river the Spaniards called "Sabine," or cypress, crossing it north of Hemphill.

Nearly four hundred years later, Sabine County, Texas, still was statuesque pines rooted in rolling, rust-red dirt. But a conflux of industry, ecology, and recreation had sliced, diced, and flooded the county, changing its face so dramatically that the old wayfarers wouldn't recognize it. Eighty percent of the land still is covered in timber, however, 114,498 acres of that lies in the sprawling Sabine National Forest.

In 1968, even as Andy Helms was completing his second tour in Vietnam, the Army Corps of Engineers was flooding 54,717 acres in Sabine County to create Toledo Bend Reservior. Its 1,200 miles of shoreline straddling the Texas-Louisiana state line make it the largest man-made lake in the South. And even as game wardens were stocking the mammoth lake with bass, Sabine County, Texas, was billing itself as the "Fishing Capital of the World."

The tourism should have been a financial godsend for a cash-starved county. But even twenty years after Toledo Bend's opening, Sabine residents still earned an average of less than $10,000 a year. In the late 1980s, personal income in Sabine County ranked 225th of Texas' 254 counties, and more than 27 percent of its residents fell off the chart into poverty.

Lumber was still king, as it had been since the late 1880s, when T.L.L. Temple formed what would become the giant conglomerate of Temple-Inland. Today, in a county whose strongest assets are pine trees and whose towns are called Pineland, Yellowpine, and Pine Park, Temple-Inland's two-by-fours and plywood still pay the bills.

Sabine was nonetheless a sportsman's paradise—the lake, the bass, the deer—and it was more than Helms could resist. In 1974, he gave up his construction job near Houston, and Nora chucked her job as a hair stylist. They might not get rich, but they were moving themselves and their four girls to Sabine County.

Helms's daddy, a longtime justice of the peace and a keen observer of small-town Texas, had offered a word of caution to his son before he loaded up his family for the Piney Woods.

"You may go to church there, maybe you'll even join the Lions Club, and you can live there until you're eighty years old," the senior Helms had told his son. "But one day, you'll be sitting in the rocking chair and somebody'll drive by. They'll point to you and tell their friend, 'See that ol' boy over yonder? He moved in here not long ago. He ain't *from* here.' And that'll be 'nuff said."

The clannishness in Deep East Texas has been well documented, and by some authoritative people, who claim the explanation is rooted in history. That the region's distrust of outsiders has survived, some would say, is a matter of genealogy.

When the Louisiana Purchase failed to clearly designate the new western boundary of the United States in 1803, the governments of both the United States and Spain agreed that the swath of land along the Sabine River—the current Texas-Louisiana state line—would be neutral ground. Until the official boundary could be agreed upon, neither country would enforce its laws in the area. Virtually overnight, the area became a no-man's land, a safe haven for murderers, rapists, thieves, and fugitives from authority in both the United States and Spain. Not until 1819 was the western boundary of the United States fixed at the Sabine River, and it was another three years before an ambitious young lieutenant colonel named Zachary Taylor was dispatched to establish law and order in what had become known as the Free State. By the time Lieutenant Colonel Taylor's Seventh U.S. Infantry arrived at Fort Jessup, just north of Many, Louisiana, the outlaws had imported women, sired children, and established settlements all along the Sabine River.

Deep East Texas in the 1880s, according to Professor Robert S. Maxwell, a historian and former president of the East Texas Historical Association, still "was strangely isolated, and existing railroads merely skirted the Piney Woods. . . . The people were insular, largely uneducated, and suspicious."

The area still was sparsely settled, and old-time residents say it wasn't uncommon for the outlaws' descendants to marry their cousins and other close relatives. The unfortunate result was a family tree that didn't have many branches. The suspicion and paranoia of the outlaw patriarchs, so the story goes, became hereditary.

Even one hundred years and a new man-made lake, with the weekend hordes of fishermen and campers from Houston and Beaumont and the retirees with permanent houses, didn't change the clannish, suspicious attitudes of the *real* Sabine Countians. Some of the people who'd lived there all their lives, watching from the town square as four-wheel-drive trucks pulled trailers with Bass Trackers through Hemphill, referred to the drivers as "lake people," synonymous, in the same contemptuous tone, with "riffraff."

Old-time merchants would take your money, no doubt about that, Helms learned, and they'd be proud to get it. But don't expect them to offer you a cup of coffee from the percolator behind the counter, not like they did the "regular" people who lived in the county.

Anybody who met Andrew W. Price Helms figured pretty quickly that he wasn't one to shy away from a challenge. In 1968 Helms had emerged unscathed from two tours in Vietnam, and for the next six years, as a civilian, he had remained lean and tough working construction jobs. He was too young to appreciate his daddy's wisdom, and there's no indication that he ever read Professor Maxwell's piece in the *East Texas Historical Journal*.

Nora, herself not easily daunted, opened a hair salon in her house, a mobile home surrounded by idyllic pines about three miles out of Hemphill toward the lake. Jobs always were at a premium in East Texas, and Helms considered himself lucky when he fell into a job as Hemphill's city marshal.

That, however, was before he learned firsthand about law and order in Sabine County. He was too proud to admit his daddy had been right.

Hemphill City Marshal Andy Helms knew he was an outsider from his first night on patrol. He was parked at the intersection down by the First State Bank. He heard the roar of a pickup truck well before he saw it, and when he did, the truck was careening at a right angle off Texas 87 onto Highway 83, steering widely to avoid the parked patrol car. The novice marshal knew a highway patrolman and a deputy were parked only a few blocks up on 87. How come they hadn't stopped this fool when he passed them?

Twice more, the pickup truck came hurtling around the corner. Helms suspected someone was playing games. The next time, Helms turned on his siren and flashing lights and pulled the pickup over three blocks past the feed store. He had its driver bent over the hood and handcuffed when a trooper and a deputy pulled up in a highway patrol car. They were grinning.

Sabine County Deputy Lamar Williams emerged from the passenger side of the patrol car and headed for the newest member of Sabine County law enforcement. Putting his arm around Helms, the deputy was deliberately condescending. "You can go ahead and let him go. This here's my cousin. He was just fooling with you a little—you know, testing the new *po*-lice."

Helms shrugged off the deputy's arm but made no attempt to remove the handcuffs from his prisoner.

"I'm not interested in who he is. The man's going to jail for reckless driving. He could have killed somebody going round that corner."

Deputy Williams, the biggest man beside the road, forced himself between Helms's prisoner and Helms's patrol car. "You don't take those cuffs off him, there's going to be an ass whipping right here and now. I told you he's my cousin. Now cut him loose."

Helms stood his ground. "You ain't whipping nobody's ass, and damn sure not mine. This sonofabitch is going to jail one way or the other. Move your fat ass."

Blows were imminent when the gray-suited trooper finally interceded. Helms exploited the distraction and put his prisoner in the car.

At the jail, Helms phoned Sheriff Blan Greer, the county's senior lawman, at home. Helms knew it'd be better for the sheriff to hear the story from him than from one of his own deputies.

"I'll talk to him tomorrow," Greer said tersely. "Go ahead and let him go."

Within the same week, the infamous "Dr Pepper Affair" gave Helms new insight into the workings of Sabine justice. Two deputies insisted he accompany them to Pineland, southwest of Hemphill, for a rendezvous with Pineland's police chief. Notwithstanding the fact he was ten miles out of his jurisdiction, Helms nonetheless participated in the most curious law enforcement procedure he had yet witnessed. Setting up beside U.S. 96, the four lawmen systematically stopped every car with out-of-county plates as it headed south toward Beaumont.

It was into this unfortunate net that a seventeen-year-old drove his van at about ten P.M. He would have been stopped anyway—not only because of the out-of-county tags but because he was driving a van and had hair so obviously long that the officers noticed it as he drove by. Worse, the teenager chose that exact moment to toss an empty Dr Pepper can onto the highway. A deputy bolted to gather the evidence and barely managed to get most of his body back into the patrol car before the chief sped off in hot pursuit.

The scene down the road unreeled under flashing splotches of red and blue lights, like slow-motion action in a cheap disco. Pineland's chief yanked the startled teenager from the driver's seat of the van and onto the shoulder. "Where's the dope, asshole?"

"Dope? Man, you got to be kidding me. Why you stopping me? I don't have any dope."

The officer pulled him by his hair to the rear of the van and forced him spread-eagled, shoving his forehead against the back doors.

" 'Member where the dope is now?"

When the kid turned to answer, the chief slammed his .9 mm automatic into the back of his head. Handcuffing his prisoner and turning him over to a deputy, the chief appeared hell-bent on finding the stash of dope.

"There's dope in here, I guaran-damn-tee you," the chief told his colleagues. "That's why the hippie sonofabitch's driving a van."

The chief assaulted the vehicle. He pulled the front passenger seat out and tossed it onto the shoulder. The driver's seat wouldn't budge, so he used his pocket knife to slash the backrest and seat, groping his hand beneath the upholstery.

When they drove off—the teenager handcuffed in the backseat between Helms and a deputy—the van was beside the road. The seats and the boy's personal belongings were scattered on the gravel shoulder.

The boy would spend the night in Sabine County Jail and pay a hefty fine in the morning for a traffic violation. Helms was ashamed and embarrassed: no dope, only one empty Dr Pepper can.

Embarrassment was one thing; sheer anger was another. A few months later, Helms saw an unusual sight in the book-in room of the jail. Two elderly, well-dressed women, each loudly protesting their innocence, were being printed and mugged by two sheriff's deputies. After the deputies led them into the cell block, Helms casually asked the jailer the charges against the women.

"Drunk driving."

"Really? Which one was driving?"

The jailer shrugged. "Both of 'em are charged with drunk driving."

The older of the two sisters, who lived near Houston, refused to pay the fine as a matter of principle; the younger pleaded, saying she couldn't face spending the night behind bars.

July had pushed the temperature into triple digits when Helms came across the women's Cadillac parked beside the road on the outskirts of Hemphill. The windows were badly smudged from inside, and the upholstery was torn and ripped. Feces littered the interior. Peering into the backseat, Helms saw a lifeless German shepherd, dead, he surmised, of heat exhaustion.

After two days behind bars, the steadfast sister, tired of bologna sandwiches and her sister's sobs, acquiesced. She wrote out a check for her and her sister's fines, emphasizing that Sabine County hadn't heard the last from her. For weeks, Helms recalled, officers were cautious, dead certain they were going to be sued, particularly after the woman told them she was a diabetic.

Helms was surprised when the lawsuit never came. Apparently the women counted themselves fortunate just to be out of the county.

As bizarre as his brief law-enforcement career had been, Andy Helms had never feared for his life—not since Vietnam—until he met Thomas Ladner on his own turf.

In 1974, four years before he was appointed police chief in Hemphill, Ladner's turf was Yellowpine, a crossroads community where trees outnumbered people. Ladner at the time was a constable, who, like the hundreds of other constables in Texas, generally was entrusted with helping the sheriff serve civil papers—notices of divorces, damage suits, subpoenas, and delinquent tax statements. Though empowered by state law, only occasionally did constables involve themselves in criminal law enforcement.

But such apparently was the case on a chilly night in 1974 when a suspicious driver bolted from Marshal Helms and sped through Hemphill's city limits on Texas 87 south toward Yellowpine. It was only after the chase progressed into the city limits of Yellowpine that the driver swerved to a stop beside the road, partially blocking the driveway to a liquor store, one of Yellowpine's four businesses.

When Helms first saw a hulking officer walking from the county patrol unit, he silently welcomed the backup. But the conversation turned immediately hostile. Why, Constable Ladner wanted to know, had a city cop from Hemphill pulled over a driver in Yellowpine?

Helms explained that he *had* tried to stop the driver in his own jurisdiction, but the driver had done a rabbit when the red and blue lights went on, and he'd been in hot pursuit since. "I followed him five or six miles," Helms explained, "and he's drunk. He's been all over the road, and he's dangerous."

"You're not taking this man anywhere. You just get your ass back in your car and head on back to Hemphill."

As the grinning suspect watched unsteadily, Helms reiterated his story about the driver being too dangerous to be on the highway, but he could tell it wasn't swaying the other lawman.

Helms was stunned when Ladner's right arm went to his side and emerged with a pistol, which he leveled at the marshal from Hemphill. The constable motioned with the pistol toward Helms's Ford. "This man ain't going nowhere," Ladner said. "The only thing for you to do is get in your goddamn car and get the hell out of here."

For ten minutes, Helms tried to talk reason into the big constable, stressing that cops had to rely on each other, that law enforcement was dangerous enough even when cops cooperated. Grudgingly, Ladner allowed Helms to leave with his prisoner handcuffed in the backseat of the patrol car. En route back to Hemphill, Helms used his car radio to phone for a wrecker to impound the drunk's car.

Checking back at the jail later that night, Helms discovered that the man had been released in fifteen minutes.

Over coffee the next morning, Nora Helms was incredulous, as was Andy Helms's father, who was visiting, when the young lawman related the episode in Yellowpine.

"I don't understand these people," the younger Helms told them. "They don't trust anybody from outside the county. They want to run this county and they don't care who they step on. Everybody in law enforcement is so damn emotional about their job that they don't care about nobody. Nobody's got rights if they ain't from here. They just get upside their heads. Hell, it don't make no difference to them."

Coffee was interrupted when Sheriff Blan Greer and Hemphill Mayor Charlie Rice appeared at the Helmses'. Helms, they maintained, had made a "mistake" in impounding the car the night before. He should have let the driver, a retired serviceman, follow him back to the jail.

"I'm telling you," Helms said defensively, "the man was too drunk to follow anybody anywhere. He wasn't safe. That's why I impounded his car."

When Helms told the sheriff that one of his constables had pulled a gun on him while he was trying to take charge of the prisoner, the sheriff was disbelieving. "I've known ol' Thomas since he was just a boy," the sheriff said, "and that don't sound like nothing Thomas'd do."

The two visitors hadn't even gotten to the sheriff's car before Andy Helms's daddy issued his son some more unsolicited advice. "Best thing you can do, Andy, is give 'em back their damn badge."

This time Helms heeded his father's advice. In barely a year, he had witnessed innocent people arrested, and some of them had been beaten. A fellow officer had even pulled a gun on him. Eventually, he knew, he'd witness something that he'd either have to report or else become one of them. Neither option was acceptable.

In late 1974, after less than a year as marshal, Andy Helms arrived at another means of supporting his family. He had spent his off-duty hours in a bass boat on Toledo Bend with amazing enough results that marina operators were giving his name out to weekend fishermen as someone who knew where to fish. He made up his mind to become a full-time fishing guide, charging accountants and businessmen from Houston by the day to lead them to the big bass catches. With Nora's hair salon, they'd just have to make ends meet if they were going to stay in God's country.

His resignation was welcomed by the sheriff and the mayor, who determined the decision was in everyone's best interest. But it certainly wouldn't be the last that the local establishment would hear from Andy and Nora Helms.

4

SABINE LAW

SITTING AROUND the huge wooden table that dominates John's Country Store in Florien, Louisiana, Loyal Garner, Jr.'s hometown, a former Louisiana deputy sheriff was delivering a discourse on law and order as practiced by his colleagues across the state line in Sabine County, Texas.

"Tell you one thing," the former lawman said, "you sure as hell don't have the number of burglaries over there that you do here. Those officers over there, well, they put the word out. 'There won't be no burglaries in Sabine County.' Those ol' boys over there, they just won't tolerate it. And by God, the burglars know it, and they know better than to mess around over there. So if you live out there in the country, I 'magine you're pretty pleased with your law enforcement."

The erstwhile lawman paused long enough for a sip of free coffee, then grinned. "Course, now, if you're from out of town and driving through, then I 'spect you'd tell a different story."

That story—one long on badge-heavy law enforcement and short on probable cause—extended well beyond the picturesque limits of Sabine County, Texas. It was repeated as gospel, particularly among out-of-county motorists, fishermen, campers, so-called "lake people," poor whites, and, especially, blacks.

Indeed, one of Garner's brothers and his wife had been escorted out of Hemphill by officers eight years earlier. Two white officers approached their pickup truck as they pulled into Twitty's Restaurant, named for and once owned by country music star Conway Twitty. One officer, apparently suspecting that a cooler in back of the pickup concealed beer, sauntered up and lifted the lid—only to find soft drinks. His partner still found the Louisiana plates suspicious. "Y'all go ahead and eat," he told the couple. "Then you leave." When they left the restaurant, the patrol car fell in behind them and followed them to the city limits before pulling off beside the road and making a U-turn back toward Hemphill.

Strict enforcement of the law and maintaining the peace in Sabine County was more than getting drunk drivers off the highway and quelling domestic disturbances. It was a major business. In 1987 alone, by the time Loyal Garner, Jr., was pulled beside the road, ostensibly for drunk driving, Sabine County had collected $91,653.78 in criminal fines—about nine times the amount it had collected in state sales taxes. In the 1970s, shortly after Toledo Bend opened as a mecca for fishermen, criminal fines in the county had soared to $150,000 a year. The drop over the years was understandable to the fishermen who drove to Toledo Bend from their homes in Beaumont and Houston. It had taken a while for word to spread among fishermen and campers at the marinas that they would be contributing mightily, if not voluntarily or even justly, to Sabine County's coffers if they were stopped by law enforcement. And, word had it among sportsmen, being stopped by Sabine County cops was merely a matter of time. Gradually, some of the marinas at Toledo Bend were closed and boarded up, while marinas fifty miles away at Lake Sam Rayburn were turning fishermen away. The difference, fishermen knew, was that they didn't have to drive through Sabine County or Hemphill to get there.

Texas is notorious for speed traps, those jerkwater little hamlets that incorporate as townships, invest in a one-man police department, buy a Ford Mustang interceptor and a radar gun, then reap so much in fines from out-of-town motorists that its own residents live virtually tax free. Sabine County, word had it, was worse than any speed trap. If you were stopped in Sabine County, it was for a stiffer offense (frequently drunk driving) that would cost you appreciably more than speeding. And if you thought the probable cause for your arrest was bogus and had the audacity to complain, you ran the added risk of getting a good East Texas ass whipping which almost always was accompanied by the additional charge and fine of resisting arrest.

Norman Crory, who owned a small weekend fishing camp with his father, and Richard Abshire, a fishing buddy, had heard talk about the officers at the Cove, one of the slew of marinas that once thrived on

Toledo Bend. "I just heard, you know, you'd better be careful when you go through Hemphill," Abshire said.

Unfortunately, legend was to become fact for the two fishermen from Groves, near Beaumont. Chief Deputy Billy Ray Horton stopped them in Hemphill in 1984 as they were headed to the lake for a bass tournament. Crory was arrested for drunk driving and Abshire for public intoxication.

In the book-in room, Crory asked Horton if he could make a phone call, a request the chief deputy summarily refused. When Crory told the officer he believed he had a *right* to use the phone, Horton slammed a fist into his face. Abshire was stunned. "I was standing about two feet away and he hit Norman about two more times, and at that time one of the cops grabbed me by the shirt and threw me outside the door on the street. I stayed out there approximately twenty minutes. One of the officers came out and got me, brought me back in. Norman's eye was swollen and his lips were bleeding."

The fishermen spent the night in jail and paid fines the next morning.

If the reputation of Sabine County cops was common currency along the fishing marinas of Toledo Bend, neither had it missed the cramped bullpen of desks shoved together at FBI headquarters in Houston, 125 miles to the south. In late 1984, a member of one of the most notorious bank robbery gangs in Southwest history elected to turn himself in to Police Chief Thomas Ladner in Hemphill. Charles Ray Holden was one of a team of heavily armed airborne bandits, a group that used helicopter assaults to terrorize and loot small, isolated banks in Louisiana, Texas, and Nevada. Aware that the FBI had "made" his identity and had added him to its fugitive list, Holden gave himself up to Ladner, an old and trusted hunting buddy.

When Ladner phoned federal authorities to notify them he had a fugitive bank robber in his custody, the young FBI agent on the other end of the line dutifully took the information. But he was evasive about when agents would pick up the federal prisoner. When Ladner hung up, the young agent quickly phoned San Antonio, where his veteran partner was on emergency leave attending an aunt's funeral. The partner, Special Agent Denny Ploeger, was a native Texan and a good ol' boy who, uncharacteristically for a federal agent, was partial to cowboy boots, a hat, and a chewed-up cigar. He'd know how to handle the situation. But no way was the younger agent going to Sabine County alone to pick up a prisoner.

"I'll wait till you get back, Denny," the younger agent said.

In the county clerk's office, across the square at the newspaper office, or over coffee in the drugstore, people referred to Blan Greer with deference reminiscent of the antebellum South. They called him simply "Mr. Blan." Many extended the courtesy out of genuine respect; others offered it only because they believed his authority demanded it. Sheriff Greer was more than the titular head of law enforcement in Sabine County. Indeed, even his detractors, who were careful to confine their criticism and speculation to tight, trusted circles, acknowledged him as the most powerful and influential politician in all of the county.

Mr. Blan's law-enforcement career began as a deputy sheriff in 1951. And since 1965 when he became sheriff, the voters of Sabine had determined in overwhelming numbers that the aging Sabine native should wear the tiny gold badge that designated him as the county's top lawman. So great was their consensus that some election years found Greer, a Democrat, alone on the ballot. He was such a fixture in the sheriff's office that most knowledgeable political observers had written off the post to him for as long as he lived or wanted the job.

Despite having celebrated his seventy-first birthday in 1987, the ruddy-faced, erect lawman showed no signs of slowing down and, in fact, appeared a good ten years younger than his actual age. Health apparently wouldn't be a factor in determining his political future. A more likely scenario for the sheriff abandoning his post, some observers held, involved the rumors that he was independently wealthy and didn't need to piddle with a regular job, especially one that didn't pay any more than twenty thousand dollars a year.

The speculation about the career lawman's wealth was more than idle coffee-shop gossip; it was borne out in the tax appraiser's records. He lived on a ranch in Milam, six miles north of Hemphill, and counted 650 acres of land scattered throughout the county among his holdings, an expansive spread by modest East Texas standards. He also owned two houses, and a lake lot on Toledo Bend. The appraised value of his holdings, according to the records, totaled more than $500,000, making him one of the most substantial landowners in the area and easily one of the wealthiest sheriffs in Texas.

The sheriff's knack for making money, particularly in one of the poorer sections of Texas, was the source of good-natured kidding among friends. "We used to tease him about his cattle," recalled District Attorney Bill Martin. "We'd say he never fed 'em. All he had to do to fatten 'em up was take 'em home and let 'em wallow in his pasture."

Speculation about Sheriff Greer's political future came and went; but come time to announce for re-election, the best rumors of retirement due to health or wealth didn't hold up. Greer was there, just as sure as God made pine sap sticky. The reason, his most severe detractors held, was power. Power, of course, is what constituents want from their sheriff, a hard-fisted, no-nonsense officer who protects property and residents from society's bottom-feeders. But Sheriff Greer's more than three decades wearing a badge had polarized people on his use of that power.

Sabine Parish Sheriff James Brumley, Greer's counterpart across the Sabine River in Many, Louisiana, recalls tracking a runaway juvenile through Greer's county in the middle of the night. "It was about one A.M., and I was driving through Milam," Brumley recalled. "There's really nothing in Milam to speak of except a little convenience store there at the crossroads. And here it was well after midnight, and I see Sheriff Greer out checking the doors at the store, rattlin' them to make sure they were locked. I thought, Here's a guy who could buy and sell just about everybody in the county, been sheriff forever, and he's still out rattlin' doors. That tells me something about a lawman."

As there is with all politicians, there is an alternative assessment of Sheriff Blan Greer, one widely embraced, but seldom expressed publicly, by roughly a quarter of Sabine County's population, the black community.

"He still calls black men 'boys,' and all of us are 'niggers,' " said one lifelong resident. "A lot of folks have heard him say that as long as he's sheriff, there'd never be a black deputy in his department."

Technically, Sheriff Greer presided over one of the smallest sheriff's departments in Texas, embracing only three or four combination jailer-dispatchers, and three deputies commissioned by the state of Texas— Chief Deputy Billy Ray Horton and deputies Billy Don Sparks and James "Bo" Hyden. Not particularly surprisingly for small-town law enforcement in Texas, none of the deputies started their careers as officers.

Sparks, graying, tall and angular, had spent twenty-five years working for the United States Forest Service in Hemphill, where he had worked with Bo Hyden's dad. The $1,100-a-month deputy's job, which Sparks assumed in 1980, supplemented his government retirement. His wife, Ollie Fay, was the elected treasurer and maintained offices in the Sabine County Courthouse, a block from the jail.

At thirty-four, Hyden was the youngest and newest member of the Sabine County Sheriff's Department. Born in Center, just north of Sabine County, the father of four had worked as a logger before briefly joining the neighboring San Augustine County Sheriff's Department. He joined the Sabine County Sheriff's Department in 1984.

Mr. Blan's second-in-command, fifty-seven-year-old Chief Deputy Billy Ray Horton, had worn the deputy's badge more than ten years. Leather-faced, home-ground, and generally quiet, Horton lived miles out in the county, where he raised cattle. He was an Army veteran who had done everything from driving trucks to breaking horses. He was the father of grown children and had been a widower for about a year.

While the county's roster of deputies was indeed small, Sheriff Greer was also the leader of everyone who wore a badge in Sabine County, if not jurisdictionally, then certainly in practice. And that included the two officers who were assigned to Sabine County by the state of Texas, Department of Public Safety Trooper Bill Bradberry and Game Warden Robert Rawls of the Parks and Wildlife Department. The pair of state officers shared an office in Sheriff Greer's jail complex. Hemphill Police Chief Thomas Ladner, employed by the city, didn't have an office in the jail, but he was there daily, coffeeing down and swapping hunting stories with the county and state officers. In an agreement not unusual in rural Texas, Sabine County allowed the city of Hemphill to use its jail in return for the city's volunteer fire department answering calls out in the isolated areas of the county.

By custom and design, law enforcement in Hemphill and Sabine County was laissez-faire. Jurisdiction was a formality that bowed to expedience and preference. It was regular practice for officers to help each other, even when it didn't fit neatly into their prescribed areas of geography. It was not unusual for Chief Ladner to accompany Trooper Bradberry as he made a speeding arrest ten miles from Hemphill. (Indeed, on the night Garner and the Maxie brothers were arrested, the chief and Deputy Bo Hyden were returning in the chief's city patrol car from near Milam, where they had opened a car door for a man who had locked his keys inside.) More than two hundred miles from the state capital in Austin, and one hundred miles from their regional supervisors, the highway patrol trooper and the game warden, both of whom had been stationed in Sabine County for years, in actuality were more a part of Sabine County law enforcement than of their distant bureaucracies. Their most constant companions were deputies—in the patrol car, around the jail coffee pot, at dinner. Bradberry, the trooper, conducted the Breathalyzer tests for the county and city. If Rawls, the game warden, needed help finding hunters illegally luring deer with spotlights, the deputies and the chief were at his side. All the officers shared the same radio frequency and knew the others' families. Whatever badge they wore, Mr. Blan was either the man who hired and fired them or their benevolent mentor and landlord. The sheriff's post was one of concentrated power.

Even in major cities with major crime rates, officers sometimes retire after thirty years without ever having drawn their guns. They sometimes can even count on both hands the number of times in three decades they've had to use physical force to subdue suspects. The empire over which Sheriff Greer presided in remote Sabine County bore little similarity to big cities with urban violence. Yet only Deputies Sparks and Hyden, the two newest law enforcement officers in the county, hadn't been reported to higher authorities for alleged civil rights violations. Sheriff Greer himself, Chief Deputy Horton, Trooper Bradberry, Game Warden Rawls, and Chief Ladner all had been reported to the FBI at least once before Christmas 1987. The civil rights complaints bore two striking similarities. More often than not, the officers were accused of beating suspects. And in every case, the FBI file reflected the same final notation: "Case Closed." Almost never were there witnesses to police brutality, leaving FBI agents to weigh the citizen's account against the officer's version. Absent independent corroboration, the credibility of the badge tilted the scales in the officer's favor.

Not that the FBI files contained every instance in which citizens claimed they were beaten by officers. Some, like Earl Hall, a black logger who said he was handcuffed and beaten when he was arrested on a trumped-up drunk driving arrest, figured it was in their best interests to keep their mouths shut. "You don't want to tell off on them, because everybody lives around here," he said. "You're scared they might catch you on the highway and do something worse than they done did."

The old black man had lived his entire life around Hemphill, watching the comings and goings and generally keeping his recollections to himself. He hesitated, even with the guarantee of anonymity, in his description of Hemphill's chief of police, Thomas Elzie Ladner. "Best I could tell you," he told the stranger, "Thomas is like an ol' hound dog laying under a shade tree on a hot day. He's fat and lazy laying there—you know, napping off and on. He looks like he wouldn't have the energy to do nothing much. But you just *know* he's treed a lot of squirrels, and could be mean when he's mad. So you kinda walk around him—you know, stay out of his way."

The black man had no way of knowing that Chief Ladner's name appeared at least three times in confidential FBI civil rights files. One of those complaints was an allegation that he arrested and harassed a white woman for "her association with blacks in the Hemphill, Texas area."

Even in Hemphill, so small that news traveled quick as a heartbeat, Ladner was an enigma. All of the town's thirteen hundred residents knew him on sight, the burly police chief looming over a curbed motorist's window or coming out of a coffee shop or backed in a driveway watching the school zone. It was next to impossible to overlook a six-foot-one, 270-pound man in cowboy boots and hat. But few of even the old-timers knew him well. He certainly wasn't a fixture at social activities; apparently he elected to spend his spare time with his family at their place in a picturesque clearing south of town, or hunting, which was a passion. He was more a loner than a mixer, appearing at least to some as distant, uncommunicative, and surly.

It had been that way even when Ladner was a kid growing up in the tiny community of Fairmont, south of Hemphill near the Sabine River. Fairmont was so small the federal government recognized it with neither an official census count nor a post office. Some put the population at "about fifty," and eight of that number were members of the Ladner clan. Thomas was the only boy in a family that included five girls, all older. A former classmate at Hemphill High recalled that Ladner had taken off a year from school to help out on the farm.

"He lived so damn far out in the sticks that it took forty-five minutes to get to town," recalled Bill Barcheers, Hemphill's paramedic and a classmate of Ladner's in the class of '67. "That meant sports were out." Hemphill's football coach had to have been distraught. Even as an underclassman, Ladner had the bulk of a college lineman, and years of farm chores had left him strong enough to lift a mule. But the only time his classmates saw him out of the classroom was on weekends, when he'd occasionally borrow the family pickup and drive into Hemphill.

It was either cruel luck of the draw or perhaps a tribute to the thoroughness of the Selective Service System that it could even find a pencildot like Fairmont, but less than five months after he graduated from high school, Ladner was drafted. One old-time resident later quipped that Ladner's term in the Army was probably the only time he'd ever been out of East Texas.

Sabine is a small county, and several remembered Ladner's being drafted, but few remembered him ever talking about his time in the Army, even when the topic would surface years later in early-morning coffee klatches at the Three Sisters Cafe. "I left all that behind me," he would say. Some who thought they knew Ladner well didn't know, for example, that the town's police chief actually was a bona fide hero during the year he spent in Vietnam. On October 14, 1968, Ladner, then a twenty-one-year-old cannoneer with D Battery, Third Battalion, Thirteenth Artillery of the Twenty-fifth Infantry Division, came under heavy enemy attack along with his unit during the Tet Counteroffensive. "Ladner immediately left the safety of his position and ran to his howitzer section," the citation read. "When his howitzer was rendered inoperable by enemy fire, Specialist Ladner, with complete disregard for his own safety, exposed himself to intense enemy fire as he moved his section's ammunition to another section. His valorous actions contributed immeasurably to the success of the mission and the defeat of the enemy force."

Ladner returned from Vietnam to Sabine County, working in the timber business and operating heavy equipment for local construction companies. He'd been home only a short time when he accepted the constable's job in nearby Yellowpine.

On December 1, 1972, Ladner married a local girl from Sabine County, and two years later, he and Carolyn Ladner became the parents of a little girl, Rachael. In 1979, shortly after Ladner traded his constable's badge for the chief's, they divorced. Ladner remarried, had another child, a boy named Wes, and moved his new family into a mobile home on two acres south of Hemphill.

Ladner spent little time in town during his off-duty hours. He enjoyed guns and was an avid hunter, spending his leisure hours prowling the thickets for deer. Ironically, though, the chief was the only lawman in the county who never carried a pistol on his hip—a habit in which he seemed to take pride. While he kept a shotgun and a pistol within easy reach in his car, no one had ever seen him actually carry a sidearm. Maybe it was his reliance on his enormous size, but he apparently also depended on the ever-present blackjack in his back pocket to get him out of any bind he might encounter.

When word inevitably leaked into the *Beaumont Enterprise* about a black Louisiana motorist suffering head injuries in the Sabine County Jail, Hemphill Mayor Ronnie Felts would publicly portray Ladner as the endearing and amiable Sheriff Andy Taylor of Mayberry on "The Andy Griffith Show." "I thought this was Mayberry," Felts said. "I didn't think things like that happened here."

Privately, though, Mayor Felts had ample reason to wonder. He had cautioned Ladner about verbal abusiveness, a trait the mayor attributed to the chief's service in Vietnam. "The only thing Thomas had done, Thomas was a real bad mouth, foul mouth—cussed," the mayor would say later. "Of course, he's a Vietnam vet, and, you know, it becomes a habit sometimes. But I've heard instances where he would use abusive language, and I talked to him about that a couple of times."

And the mayor knew personally that Chief Ladner's words had led to violence on at least one occasion. The chief had come to him, explaining the mayor might get a complaint about his having hit a young man in the head with a nightstick or slapjack. The boy's father worked for Felts at the mayor's timber mill on the outskirts of Hemphill. "But I never heard a word about it," the mayor recalled. "I asked Thomas about it later, and he said he saw the boy later and the boy said, 'Hey, that was all my fault—you did what you should have done.' "

Unchecked, a practice, no matter how legally suspect or potentially lethal, becomes custom. And in Hemphill, the mayor apparently had grown accustomed to officers using slapjacks on people's heads. "He whopped him on the head," Felts recalled. "I didn't know you couldn't hit anybody on the head, I'll be honest with you. But it didn't bust any skin or didn't hurt him or anything like that."

5

OUTSIDE SCRUTINY

As THE CROW FLIES, Tyler is about one hundred miles northwest of Hemphill, but by the time highway engineers zigged and zagged to accommodate pine thickets, hills, and a few lakes, it had become a two-and-a-half-hour trip by ground. Medical Center Hospital lies in a medical complex southeast of Tyler's downtown district, easily distinguished from a distance by two skyscrapers that appear as bookends on an otherwise empty shelf.

Dr. Ron Donaldson first examined Loyal Garner, Jr., at 6:50 P.M. on December 26, 1987. The neurosurgeon's notes of the examination were abbreviated by necessity:

> This is a 34 y.o. black male transferred here from the hosp in Hemphill, Texas. He apparently was found in jail in a comatose condition and brought to the ER there. He was seen by the ER physician, Dr. Winslow, and a CT scan revealed an acute subdural. He was transferred here by ambulance. I have no other history available due to the fact that there is no family and this was taken essentially from the nurse there who called me.

Dr. Donaldson noted also that the unconscious patient showed "no response to very deep pain." Then he added a grim prognosis: "The outlook is extremely grave. I do not expect him to live, however, a craniotomy will be accomplished in an emergency situation due to the fact that there is no one here to give permission for the subdural."

The doctor saw the transferred patient in the emergency room before Corrine and her in-laws arrived. None of the Garners had ever been to Tyler before, and finding the hospital hadn't been easy.

The craniotomy—an emergency procedure to relieve the intense pressure on Garner's brain—began at 7:21 P.M. and lasted only thirty-four minutes. When Dr. Donaldson bored through the skull and made his incision, the pressure inside Garner's brain was so intense that a blood clot literally shot from the incision onto his latex gloves. And things were going from bad to worse. When the neurosurgeon removed the remnants of the major clot, the cortical surface itself filled up the subdural space.

The cortex—the gray matter that covers most of the surface of the brain—was beginning to show blood. It was pulsating, but by the end of the procedure, Dr. Donaldson saw that the brain surface itself was about to rupture through the incision, forcing him to close rapidly.

At 7:55 P.M., the neurosurgeon noted in his operative report: "Patient was unstable during the entire procedure. Outlook is extremely grave. Will be returned to ICU."

At 12:25 P.M. on December 27, about seventeen hours after Garner was delivered to Medical Center Hospital in Tyler, Dr. Donaldson filled out his final report in the Garner file. The doctor recorded the emergency procedures he had performed, then wrote: "At any rate, he never regained consciousness and was pronounced dead at 12:25 after EEG was flat. . . . Patient is discharged by death."

A local minister in Tyler had told Pearlie Henderson that a black man had been beaten so badly in Deep East Texas that he'd been transferred to Medical Center Hospital in critical condition. "It's one of *those* situations," the minister had told Henderson, "that you'd want to know about, might want to take an interest in."

Henderson first met Corrine Garner in the waiting room outside ICU. She was slumped in a chair with her eyes shut, but she wasn't asleep. They spoke a few minutes; then she led her new acquaintance past the nurse's station into a room.

"Loyal Garner was wrapped like a mummy," Henderson said later. "Nobody had told her yet, but her husband was already dead—or maybe they had, and she just couldn't acknowledge it. It was a sight I'll never forget."

Pearlie Henderson, built firm like a fire hydrant, speaks with an economy of words and delivers them with unflinching eye contact. Fifty years of being black in white-dominated East Texas had taught him calculated patience. Henderson was a strong believer in the Serenity Prayer and repeated it to himself often: "God grant me the serenity to accept the things I cannot change, courage to change the things I can, and wisdom to know the difference."

The black man waited and watched, and when he thought he had something documentable, something so irrefutably obvious that it couldn't be twisted and warped by the influential whites who would interpret it, he moved quickly.

Henderson wasn't smug, but neither was he oblivious to the reaction he created when he walked into courtrooms in Tyler. Prosecutors and defense attorneys, even judges, paid homage with their eyes, sometimes with an occasional nod of the head, when he slid into one of the courtroom benches. And many around the Smith County Courthouse knew that Henderson's presence—equaled perhaps only by that of black county commissioner Andrew Mellontree—frequently played an unspoken role in the outcome of jury verdicts and plea bargains that involved black defendants.

Henderson reluctantly had agreed to head the Tyler chapter of the National Association for the Advancement of Colored People. He was an insurance salesman, father of children he was trying to get through college, and active in his church. He had gotten a college education, at Texas College, a beleaguered, perpetually strapped all-black school in North Tyler; but he knew he'd still be working in a sawmill near Lufkin if an older brother hadn't quit school to help support the family. His brother had sacrificed to benefit the family. Pearlie Henderson regarded his commitment to the NAACP the same way: he was repaying a debt. "Too many people are afraid to say anything," he said, "and not one damn thing will change if they don't. So somebody's got to."

Henderson knew he had something in his lifetime that Garner hadn't, at least when Garner was arrested in Hemphill: rights. "The only blacks in East Texas who have rights," he told a stranger, "are guys like me, because I'm going to demand mine. I'm going to expect it. There's no giving here of equal rights. There's just toleration. Some whites just feel like you're not deserving of equal treatment."

As a teenager, Henderson and his black friends were relegated to the balconies of theaters, leaving fifteen minutes before the movies were over so they could get a head start on the white boys. "They catch you after a movie, they'd gang up on you and kick your ass. I was a grown man before I ever saw the end of a movie." As a young sales representative for a Fortune 500 company, he was turned away at an East Texas country club where the company had scheduled its annual sales meeting and golf tournament. "Here I was twenty-five years later, looking at Loyal Garner dead in the hospital, and I thought, 'Damn, nothing's changed. Not one damn thing.'"

When Henderson accepted the reins of the NAACP, he knew that if he was going to have an impact, he would have to focus his energy instead of scattershooting. He singled out the criminal-justice system. "If we can't get equal treatment in a courtroom," he had told his group, "we won't ever get it in jobs or housing."

Henderson had heard of Sabine County long before he met Corrine Garner in a hospital waiting room. Sabine and those surrounding it were legendary among East Texas blacks and what cops called "poor white trash" for racism and police brutality. From what he heard and saw of the Garner incident, Henderson figured he had a blatant, documentable case.

"Time's overdue, Mrs. Garner," he had told Corrine. "I'm real sorry that it was your husband that had to lead the change, but we're going to make sure this never, ever happens to another black man in Sabine County. God rest you, and may He bless Mr. Garner."

There was no serenity in Pearlie Henderson when he appeared early on December 28 in the Tyler offices of the Federal Bureau of Investigation. "This man is dead simply because he had the audacity to demand his right to a phone call, so he could call his wife on Christmas," Henderson told a young FBI agent. "Those cops been beating people forever."

Across Tyler, in a red brick Georgian two-story, John Henry Hannah, Jr., was alone in his first-floor law offices. He couldn't tell if he was actually getting an early start on 1988, which had been his mission during the holidays, or if he was merely shuffling the loose ends he'd left dangling from 1987. Paperwork and organization obviously were necessities in lawyering, but he damn sure didn't have to enjoy them. For most of the evening, he had had the television on just for background noise. Over time he had become oblivious to the screen, his attention absorbed by the legal files scattered across his desk.

But something on the television locked into a clear channel in Hannah's consciousness, drawing his eyes to the screen. Now he cursed silently, wishing he'd heard the first part of the anchorwoman's report: something about a black man—Hannah had missed his name—dying in a Tyler hospital from head injuries he'd suffered in a jail somewhere. He hurried from his desk to the television, turning up the volume quickly, in time to hear the words "Sabine County."

The forty-eight-year-old lawyer's brow furrowed in thought, but the news didn't shock him. Hannah's background guaranteed he wouldn't be shocked. Rather, he regarded the sketchy report the way a retired fireman reacted to the smell of smoke; it jump-started his adrenaline. It made him feel all dressed up with no place to go.

Until he was replaced by a Republican administration six years earlier, Hannah had been the United States attorney for the Eastern District of Texas, the top federal prosecutor in roughly one-quarter of the state. He had been a college professor, a state representative, the head of a public-integrity watchdog group, a state district attorney, and, most recently, a defense lawyer. But no other of his callings had he enjoyed nearly as much as being the United States Justice Department's chief prosecutor in East Texas.

Republican detractors and Democratic supporters agreed on at least one point about Hannah's tour as federal prosecutor: it wasn't an appointment; it was a crusade. When President Reagan replaced him in 1981 with a Republican appointee, Hannah and his staff had accumulated a 90 percent conviction rate, one of the highest in the nation.

Ironically, Hannah, a native son of Deep East Texas, earned his reputation by targeting the most unlikely of all suspects—good ol' boys, particularly the ones who were elected to office and who carried badges. He had grown up in timber country, and rather than being inured to the good-ol'-boy system, he'd been angered by its historically incestuous grip on the region he called home.

Not that anyone ever doubted his mission, but Hannah reinforced the message to good ol' boys throughout East Texas during closing arguments in a 1979 case. On trial were some of the most powerful public officials from neighboring Gregg County—its sheriff, two deputies, a justice of the peace, and a county commissioner. Hannah had accused them of a wide array of offenses against society, ranging from gambling to accepting kickbacks for "protection" and promoting prostitution. Worse, the sheriff,

Hannah alleged, had assembled a so-called shotgun squad of deputies in a thwarted attempt to murder three enemies.

"They took an oath," Hannah told jurors, "that they would uphold and defend the laws and constitutions of the United States and Texas. They sullied and spoiled that oath just as surely as though they had spat upon the flag. There is nothing more deadly to a society than a totally corrupt law-enforcement group." The five Gregg County officials were among many that Hannah sent to federal penitentiaries.

Now, as he pondered the TV report on the black man's death, Sabine County struck a vague chord in his memory. He long ago had lost access to his federal files, and there had been file cabinets full of cases since his days as federal prosecutor. Reluctantly, Hannah resigned himself to simply following the case on the news and picking up whatever morsels he could glean from courthouse sources.

Hannah lost interest in the manila folders littering his desk. He flicked off the television and turned off the lights. He headed upstairs to his living quarters, feeling peculiarly frustrated and dejected.

It would have improved his mood no end had he known that within three months he would be thrust into the maelstrom of Loyal Garner, Jr.'s death.

6

UNDER COLOR OF LAW

BEFORE WORD SPREAD through Hemphill that a man had been beaten unconscious in the Sabine County Jail, no one could have convinced Lloyd Armstrong that he was a lucky man.

In August 1987, four months before Loyal Garner, Jr., was arrested, Armstrong had adjourned to the front porch of his modest frame house in Hemphill. As was his habit, he'd had more than a few beers, and now he was mad as hell. What he had considered merely "words with the wife" had been construed by a neighbor as a "disturbance," and she had called the police. Within minutes, Police Chief Thomas Ladner arrived, threatened to haul his ass off to jail again for disorderly conduct, and removed from a dresser the pistol Armstrong's wife had pointed out.

When the chief left, so did Mrs. Armstrong, heading across the street to sanctuary at another neighbor's. Beer in hand, Armstrong defiantly postured himself in a rocking chair on the porch and, apparently, drank and seethed. The more he thought about the incident, the madder he got. One by one, he knocked his wife's flower pots off the railing of the porch and onto the front yard.

Minutes later, Armstrong saw Chief Ladner stop in front of his house again, look up and down the street, then head for the porch. Immediately, the lawman cut to the chase. "Lloyd, you're coming with me."

"Why?"

Ladner grabbed Armstrong by his left arm and twisted it up behind his back. Unsteadily, Armstrong wrapped his right arm around the porch post to keep from falling. The way Armstrong remembers it, the chief pushed his left arm up higher on his back, then reached around him with his left arm in a choke hold. It might have been the beer or his high blood pressure, maybe both, but Armstrong immediately went down under the weight of the huge officer. Prone on the porch, Armstrong looked up at his attacker. "What in hell's going on?"

"Something black," which he later surmised was a blackjack, hit Armstrong square in the face, obliterating his consciousness. When he came to, the forty-three-year-old Armstrong was in the emergency room at Sabine County Hospital. One tooth was missing and three were loose. Blood covered the front of his shirt, and his blood pressure had soared to beyond 300. Dr. Winslow sutured his tongue, his chin, and the insides of his mouth.

Unsuccessfully, Armstrong argued to spend the night in the hospital. Well, then, could he at least have his wife bring his blood pressure medicine to the jail? Again, his request was denied. A phone call? Not until tomorrow.

After Ladner escorted Armstrong to the Sabine County Jail, the chief, apparently aware that Armstrong could neither read nor write, read him the charges. Disorderly conduct, which Armstrong had anticipated, carried a fine of $73. But then Ladner read another: resisting arrest, $288.

"Resisting arrest? I didn't resist no arrest." But Armstrong was a drinking man and had been in jail before, though never for anything more serious than public intoxication or drunk and disorderly. He knew the process: pay or stay. And he knew that complaining about brutality would be like pissing into a heavy wind: it'd blow back on you and make things worse.

Before Armstrong paid out the next morning, he pleaded with the chief for the city's help in paying his dental bill. Three teeth were dangling by roots, and he couldn't eat. A few days later, the chief sent word that the city council couldn't do anything. Upon receiving the news, Armstrong went into the garage and emerged with a pair of pliers. He sat down on the steps of his porch and pulled the three teeth, wiping the gush of blood with the back of his hand.

Armstrong's beating was but one bloody chapter in the saga of unchecked police brutality in Sabine County. He'd heard talk about other incidents, but talk was cheap and never changed anything. That's the way the cops were. Poor, white, and uneducated, and with a long track record for drinking and raising cain, Armstrong never even tried to report the beating to authorities. "I have enough trouble trying to live here in Hemphill," he said later though the gaping hole in his mouth. "Wouldn'ta done no good at the time."

Leonard Green lived down past the First Baptist Church, where the pavement played out and the gravel began. The road ended in a heavily wooded cul-de-sac of sorts, its adjacent property littered with the skeletons of rusted pulpwood trucks long since abandoned. As if some scavenger had preyed on them, the hoods of the trucks had been ripped off and the engine compartments had been picked clean. Their usable parts had been recycled into other ailing trucks, jury-rigged to get them to the woods for another load of pulpwood.

Green, a forty-nine-year-old black man whose legs had been amputated, lived with his mother in one of the handful of long, narrow "shotgun" houses—so named, apparently, because you could fire a shotgun through the front door and the buckshot would go through every room in the house and out the back door.

When Lloyd Armstrong confronted Thomas Ladner in 1987, he was dealing with a notorious law-enforcement legend. Green met him in 1979, when Ladner had worn the police chief's badge only a year. But if at first he didn't know what to expect, he learned quickly.

Green caught the chief's attention when he was trying to negotiate his way onto the highway from the parking lot of the Dairy Queen. The back tires of his mother's car—which was equipped with a device that allowed Green to drive it—had trouble getting traction on the loose gravel. When he gunned the engine, he spattered the air with gravel, and when the tires finally took hold and lurched him onto the pavement, Green didn't make it more than a few blocks before Ladner and a highway patrolman pulled him over.

"Nigger, I think you been drinking," the chief told him. Green denied the allegation. Then Ladner told him to get out of the car. Green couldn't even have gotten *into* the car if a neighbor hadn't helped him, and he didn't have his wheelchair with him. Green later would swear that Ladner and Trooper Bill Bradberry jerked him out of the car by his armpits, handcuffed him, and threw him on his side into the backseat of the patrol car.

At the Sabine County Jail, Ladner propped Green in a chair while he filled out the paperwork for a charge of driving while intoxicated. The ailing suspect protested his innocence. "Mr. Thomas, I done told you I ain't drunk. They's putting new gravel on the highway, that's what it was. Maybe I was having trouble—"

"Shut up, nigger, or I'll kill you. Just keep your goddamn mouth shut."

It was advice Green should have heeded. When he next opened his mouth, Ladner turned and slammed him in the face, blurring his vision. With no legs to steady himself, he was only inches from hitting the floor when Bradberry grabbed him and returned him to the chair. Green believed the object in Ladner's hand had been a blackjack.

The two officers carried their suspect into the cell block and deposited him on the cement floor. There were bunks in the cell, but Green couldn't pull himself into one. Indeed, he couldn't use the bathroom without someone to steady him on the toilet. He spent the night on the floor in his own urine.

Shortly after his mother had paid $300 in fines for drunk driving and disorderly conduct, she took Green to Dr. Winslow's office to have the wound on his face examined. Green never received a bill from the doctor, and didn't know who paid the medical costs.

Green and his mother contacted the FBI, and an agent appeared at their home. The agent took a report, but Green never heard anything else.

Mark Hanlon, his lip swollen and his mouth bleeding, thought Deputies Bill Horton and Bo Hyden were taking him to Hemphill so he could file charges against the two bastards who had blindsided him with a beer bottle at a nightclub on Toledo Bend.

Hanlon remembered thinking Horton was driving uncommonly fast, and when the patrol car ran up behind a pickup truck, Hanlon ducked in anticipation of a certain collision. Instead, the pickup swerved to the shoulder to avoid the oncoming patrol car. When the patrol car finally came to rest, it was sideways in the highway, blocking both lanes.

"The guy's so drunk he can't keep that thing on the highway," Horton muttered, and headed for the pickup. He returned with the driver minutes later, the man's hands cuffed behind him. As Horton was putting his new prisoner into the backseat, another pickup pulled up beside the road. Inside were the two guys who had hit Hanlon at the marina club only minutes earlier.

Hanlon, a thirty-seven-year-old "lake person" who had migrated from

Chicago to operate a boat propeller shop near the Pendleton Marina, was stunned at what he saw through the windshield: Deputy Hyden was mixing drinks with his assailants on the tailgate of their pickup.

When they finally arrived at the jail, Horton told Hanlon that *he* was under arrest.

"Is it normal for the *victim* to be arrested?"

"You trying to get smart?"

"Look, could I at least see a doctor? I'm bleeding pretty bad here."

Deputy Hyden grabbed Hanlon and led him to an open cell door.

"Well," Hanlon said, "could you at least tell me what I'm charged with? I've got some money for the bond."

Hyden eyed Hanlon as he beat a nightstick into the palm of his hand. "Get your ass in there."

Complaining about the officers, Hanlon had heard countless times at the marina, only made things worse. He did nothing.

About a year after his arrest, Hanlon had occasion to meet Chief Deputy Horton on friendlier terms. They were exchanging chitchat when Horton began bragging about how to "get a confession out of a nigger."

"What you do," Horton explained, "is sit them in a chair and put their feet in another chair. Then you sit on their knees and light up a cigarette. I've never seen one yet that can make it through a whole cigarette."

Friday nights during football and basketball seasons are guaranteed to attract every kid from Hemphill and points nearby. They're there in droves at the football stadium or the gym, rooting themselves hoarse for their Friday-night heroes, the Hornets. The Hemphill Hornets compete in Class 2A, near the bottom rung of Texas athletic classifications, which go up to Class 5A, depending on the number of students in the school. It is not singularly school pride—though plenty of that exists—that fills the bleachers in Hemphill. As in maybe a thousand other widespots alongside Texas highways, there's nothing else for teenagers to do. Home games are not merely athletic events but social gatherings as well. Dates are built around The Game. Tack on a ten-dollar mum with a green and white ribbon before the game, a burger and fries afterward at the Dairy Queen, and if a guy gets lucky, a stop beside a pine-shrouded dirt road, and it's a night on the town.

Social successes on Saturday nights are dicier, depending on the re-sourcefulness of those who engage in the game. Hemphill has no theater, necessitating a sixty-mile drive to Lufkin, or the forty miles south to Jasper, for a movie date. Occasionally there's a dance on Saturdays, or somebody's folks might rent three or four videos and voluntarily turn their VCRs and dens over to a few of their teenager's favorite friends.

Generally, though, Saturday nights out of necessity evolve into cruising, a sometimes monotonous yet inexpensive means for teenagers to see and be seen. Punctuated by the occasional honking of horns and the flicking of dim lights to bright, the rambling conversations inside the cars and pickup trucks center on rumor, speculation, hearsay, and, occasionally, fact. And it was adopted as hard-and-fast fact by some teenage girls in Hemphill, passed down as gospel from their older sisters and friends, that it wasn't wise to be caught by law enforcement—*any* officer—if you were alone.

Teresa Cassidy, now a mother of two who lives in another city under her married name, had heard the stories. Always, she remembers, the stories were passed on with the inference that if the girls resisted the suggestive advances of officers, they would go to jail under trumped-up charges.

Teresa was nineteen years old in 1975, having graduated two years earlier from Hemphill High School. She was driving alone, she recalls, heading into Hemphill, when Police Chief Thomas Ladner and Bob Rawls, the commissioned game warden for the Texas Parks and Wildlife Department, pulled her car over beside the highway.

"They stopped me and told me to get into the car. I said, 'What'd I do?' They said, 'We'll think of something by the time we get to the jail.' "

Teresa was terrified, recalling all the stories she'd heard.

"They didn't handcuff me. When they stopped at a stop sign, I saw a bunch of kids at a service station. There were woods nearby, but I knew not to run into the dark. I threw open the door and ran toward the kids, yelling, 'Call my mother! Call my mother!' "

After chasing her down, the officers returned her to the patrol car and took her to the Sabine County Jail, where her mother was waiting for them. After charging Teresa with a routine traffic violation—one that she says was concocted, and for which normally a ticket would have sufficed—they released her on bond to her mother.

"I had heard the stories about the law. I was scared to death. I didn't know what they might do."

Outside maybe a telephone operator on a party line, there is no more active tap into the grapevine of a small town than a beauty shop. One story ends when a woman, her hair coiffed and sprayed, leaves the chair; another story begins when the next woman sits down. In and out they come, six days a week, the wives of bankers, law-enforcement officers, lawyers, and businessmen; each uses the respite from small-town boredom to pass on her observations and opinions. The beneficiary of all this intelligence, of course, is the stylist standing behind the chair, a woman who generally knows more about the town than the local newspaper editor.

The stories Nora Helms had been hearing with increasing regularity in her beauty shop were not what she had been reading in the *Sabine County Reporter*. She'd first heard about law-enforcement officers harassing teenage girls in the mid-1970s after moving to Hemphill, and she queried her daughter Kathy, at nineteen the oldest girl still at home.

Yes, Kathy informed her—a girlfriend, Nina, had been stopped near Milam in northern Sabine County by a state trooper who, according to Nina, had sexually harassed her. "She liked to never got him out of the car," Kathy said, "and he said the next time, he wouldn't be surprised if he didn't find dope in her car."

Nina's parents had been so outraged they went to the prosecutor and attempted to press charges against the trooper. The prosecutor, Nina's parents said, took their statement but declined to file charges unless he received more evidence.

"It's common knowledge among the kids, Mother," Kathy had said.

In the ensuing months, Kathy was stopped several times as she was driving home alone on Texas 83. She never was given a ticket, but during each stop, officers badgered her for dates. One, upon being rebuffed, told her he was aware she had black friends. Indeed, Kathy did have black friends, some of whom she had accompanied to school functions and some of whom she had given rides home. But clearly, she knew, that wasn't the kind of relationship the officer was implying. "What would everybody think if I put out the word you're running with niggers? Maybe even more than running with them?"

Andy Helms, Kathy's father, had seen officers harass young girls during the year he had been city marshal. He wasn't about to tolerate them messing with his daughter. "Tell you what," Helms told Kathy. "If you're out on the highway by yourself and they try to stop you, you just keep going and come straight on home. But don't stop for anything."

It was hot and humid in August 1979. If there was a breeze, the pine thickets smothered it before it reached any of the residents in the mobile homes clustered on the red dirt road near the intersection of Texas 83 and Farm Road 3121. It was after midnight, and the Helmses were in bed when they were jolted awake by a car careening onto the circular drive that ran from the dirt road around the rear of their mobile home. The sound of tires crunching, then sliding on gravel had just subsided when the back door flew open with a bang. Kathy was screaming.

"Mother, Dad! Help me! They're *shooting* at me!"

The teenager was hysterical, sobbing bits and pieces that didn't make any sense to her parents as they stood dazed in their bedclothes. Outside, a car screeched to a stop, and Chief Deputy Horton and Chief Ladner ran toward the door of the mobile home. Nora Helms opened the door for them. Horton was screaming as he stormed in. "God damn it, I finally got something I can lock her up for! That girl's going to jail. Right now, by God!"

Nora and Andy Helms were equally adamant. "She's not going anywhere with you," Nora said. "You're too crazy, too mad. Andy and I will drive her to the jail and you can follow us."

"By God, I'll get a warrant."

"You can get all the warrants you want, but she's not riding anywhere with you. No, she ain't riding with you so that you can beat the hell out of her like the rest of the kids. Not so you can say she got smart with you or tried to attack you."

Horton and Ladner bolted off to get an arrest warrant, but not before all the commotion had awakened the Helmses' neighbor C. G. Lewis. Nicknamed "Tiny" by someone with a perverse sense of humor, Lewis was a 250-pound former Dallas police officer who had carried a badge more than twenty years before he retired. The havoc past midnight had piqued Lewis's curiosity, and he'd hurriedly dressed and headed for the Helmses.

Lewis listened intently as Kathy explained to her parents the scenario that had created the chaos. She had been out with friends in Hemphill, dropped them off at their homes, and stopped by Eve's Grocery about midnight to pick up a Dr Pepper to drink on her way home. Less than a mile from home, Horton and Ladner turned on their flashing lights behind her. Remembering her father's advice, she continued to drive, her eyes glued to the speedometer to make sure she wasn't speeding. Chief Deputy Horton, Kathy swore, fired his gun out the window of the patrol car. The gunshot unnerved the teenager, and she stopped in the highway, so rattled she didn't kill the engine. Horton, she told her parents and Tiny Lewis, came running and screaming toward the passenger side of the car and flung the door open. Cursing, the lawman began yanking at her to get her out of the car. She panicked and slammed her foot on the accelerator.

"Mama, I swear to God I didn't know what he was going to do. He was a madman, yanking on me and all. I didn't know what he was going to do."

Just as the Helmses had gotten dressed and calmed their daughter, Ladner and Horton returned. As they emerged from the patrol car, another cruiser drove through the front lawn and stopped at a right angle to the mobile home. The deputy flashed on his brights, ran the beam of his spotlight over the front of the house, then crouched behind the opened car door with his pistol drawn and aimed at the house.

Tiny Lewis could tell the situation was turning evil, and he insisted on accompanying the Helmses as they followed the sheriff's car to the Sabine County Jail.

In the jail book-in room, as Horton and Ladner filled out the forms necessary to incarcerate Kathy Helms, Andy Helms tried once more to reason with the officers. "This girl's getting ready to start nursing school next month. Can you tell me what she did that's so bad she's got to go to jail?"

Ladner's face flushed with anger as he moved menacingly toward Helms.

"I'll tell you one goddamn thing," the chief said. "You say another word and your ass will be in here, too."

When deputies finally forced the Helmses from the jail lobby two hours later, Nora Helms sat all night on a brick fence outside the jail, yelling to carry on a conversation with her daughter locked behind a barred window. "Don't worry, Kathy," she shouted more than once during the night. "I won't leave you alone in that jail. I'll stay here long as it takes."

At 6 A.M., a deputy allowed Nora into the jail and even let her take her daughter a Dr Pepper. Then she deposited herself into a plastic chair to await the arrival of Sheriff Blan Greer so she could post bond for Kathy.

The deputy took advantage of the slack time to engage Mrs. Helms in conversation. "I hear you're allowing blacks in your beauty shop," he said.

"If they walk in and I've got an appointment open, yes, I am. The law says I have to, for one thing. Another thing, I don't have a problem with it."

"Well, I'll tell you one thing right now. This county won't sit still for that."

"That may be. But I'll tell *you* something, too. You fool with me about it and I'll have the NAACP on you."

The lobby was full when Sheriff Greer showed up about noon. "I'm sorry, Mrs. Helms," he said, "but the judge isn't going to be in today to set bonds, so your girl's just gonna have to stay another night."

In the corner of the lobby, Nora spotted the state trooper who had harassed Kathy's friend, Nina. Speaking loud enough to ensure that everyone in the room could hear her, Nora Helms responded. "What about that man over there in the uniform, the one who crawled into the car with Nina? You remember that night, Blan?"

The low roar in the lobby fell quiet, and people turned their attention to the petite woman standing toe to toe with the aging sheriff. The fair skin beneath the sheriff's hat flushed red, and his voice dropped so that only Nora could hear him. "Well," he said, "I 'magine a two-hundred-dollar cash bond would get her out."

Before Nora Helms left with her daughter, the sheriff confronted her in the hallway. "When that young lady finishes talking to that judge tomorrow, I want her back over here in my office. Me and that young lady is going to have a good little talk."

"Blan, she doesn't have any reason to come back and talk to you. We've made bond and we're going before the judge—she won't be back to talk to you. Oh, there'll be some talking, but it won't be with *you*."

Kathy Helms's infraction, the family discovered the next day in justice-of-the-peace court, was failing to stop for a stop sign at the bank well before she pulled into the convenience store for a soft drink. But Ladner and Horton hadn't tried to stop her at the store. They waited until she had driven nearly three miles on a deserted highway beyond the city limits of Hemphill. The justice of the peace assessed a fine of eighteen dollars. His secretary had to record the fine on the official docket. It was common knowledge around town—and sometimes a derisive joke among those who appeared in the court—that Hemphill had entrusted its misdemeanors to an aging justice of the peace who could neither read nor write.

Nora Helms paid her daughter's fine, but she managed to extract some peace of mind before leaving the courtroom. "Judge," she said, "you haven't heard the last of this. I'm sick to death of the law in this county. We're not taking it anymore."

The next day, Nora and three other residents of Sabine County, embittered by their own horror stories of law enforcement, drove ninety miles to Beaumont, headquarters for the federal Eastern District of Texas. After they were interviewed by an FBI agent, just as Leonard Green had been earlier, they were asked to give written statements.

It would take eight years, but a single sentence in Nora Helms's statement would appear tragically prophetic: "If something isn't done about these cops, they're going to kill somebody."

7

FIGHTING OVER THE BODY

EVERYTHING ABOUT Loyal Garner, Jr.'s final hours was alien to the simple and modest life he'd lived among family and friends in remote Louisiana. He was arrested in another state, in a town whose notorious reputation he feared. He died in a town he'd never visited. And the responsibility for investigating the tragic chain of events that led to his death was left to strangers in places he couldn't have imagined.

Except for its most prized product—the tearless Noonday Onion, guaranteed to be sweet instead of strong—Noonday, Texas, is a wholly forgettable town. There's no stop light, not even a flashing light, just two signs on either end of a few houses, a service station, and a wholesale nursery that warn motorists to drop their speed by ten miles an hour. Tucked back from the farm-to-market road and almost hidden amidst a clump of trees is a mobile home that houses the office and courtroom of Justice of the Peace W. B. Beaird.

Precinct Two runs ten miles northeast into metropolitan Tyler, a burgeoning city of about seventy-five thousand. But Judge Bill Beaird's courtroom is located in the country, giving Smith County government a presence among its rural constituents. Strangers who didn't heed the speed warning considered the prefabricated trailer a peculiar place for the administration of justice. But if they were surprised to plead their cases in a converted mobile home, they were no less surprised at the man behind the bench. At forty-two, Bill Beaird was probably a good twenty years younger than most of his colleagues on justice-of-the-peace benches in Texas. And even a fleeting glance at the judge undoubtedly convinced accused traffic offenders to reconsider the vigor and veracity of their defenses. Beaird, who for thirteen years before his election made tires at the nearby Kelly-Springfield Tire and Rubber Company, was an imposing, if not unorthodox, jurist. His head was as smooth as the town's namesake onion, an apparent irreversible reaction to anesthesia he'd undergone after a helicopter crash in Vietnam. He was built solid, like the corner post in a quarter-mile stretch of fence, and he was partial to scuffed cowboy boots and faded Levi's. No offense intended to the decorum of the court, but Judge Beaird looked more calf roper than jurist.

His eyes were direct, telegraphing the basic premise upon which he operated his court: "It'll be *my* way or the highway." He was Smith County's first elected Republican judge since the Civil War, and in the six years he had been on the bench, he had earned the reputation as a no-nonsense, unabashed advocate of law and order. In those rare occasions when people weren't astute enough to get his unspoken message and dared suggest he bend the rules or look the other way, Judge Beaird always delivered the same bare-knuckled response: "I don't go outside the law for *no*body." Not that Judge Beaird didn't have strong opinions of his own. It was more that he didn't allow his personal views to conflict with the law, which, whether he agreed or not with its legislative intent, he enforced to the letter.

On December 27, 1987, during what should have been a postholiday doldrum, Judge Beaird received a succession of phone calls at his austere office. The first was from a registered nurse at Medical Center Hospital in Tyler. "I've got a man here who died about an hour ago from major head injuries," she said. "And there's an ambulance already here from Hemphill to pick up his body."

Death notifications are not unfamiliar to Texas justices of the peace, who, in addition to hearing traffic and small claims cases, also act as coroners in smaller counties. In cases in which the cause of death is unknown or suspicious—and in all cases involving the death of a prisoner—the state of Texas empowers its justices of the peace to order autopsies and conduct inquests to determine which of the options will be checked on the death certificate: natural, accidental, suicide, homicide, or undetermined. The justices' decisions often mean the difference in whether insurance companies honor hundreds of thousands of dollars in life insurance policies, and in the case of homicide rulings, whether suspects will be apprehended and tried for murder. The decisions on cause of death traditionally have led to the strongest criticism of justices of the peace, whom state law does not require to have either a college degree or any medical training.

The significance of an unnatural death certainly didn't escape Judge Beaird, particularly when further questioning of the nurse revealed that Loyal Garner, Jr., the deceased, had been in jail when he suffered the head injuries. And Beaird thought it strange that Garner had been dead only an hour when the ambulance from Hemphill showed up to pick up the corpse.

"Well, I don't know who ordered an ambulance, but tell them to go on back to Hemphill. There's got to be an autopsy and an inquest. Tell them I'll release the body after we're through."

Within minutes, the nurse was back on the phone. The ambulance attendants from Hemphill, she said, were insistent about taking the body back to Sabine County.

"No way," said Beaird. "There's going to be an autopsy. Put the body on ice, and I'll schedule the autopsy as quick as I can. But that body isn't to leave the hospital under any circumstances until I say so."

The third phone call, less than ten minutes later, was long distance, from Sabine County's chief executive, County Judge Royce Smith. There were no pleasantries, and the elderly judge appeared agitated. "What seems to be the problem getting this body back down here to Hemphill?" he demanded, wheezing between words.

Three phone calls in rapid succession, aggravated by Judge Smith's condescending demeanor, arched the younger judge's back. Bill Beaird wasn't about to give ground. "Well, this man died in *Smith* County, and the law says that his inquest will be conducted in the county in which he died. And I'm going to do one. Now, I've got an autopsy scheduled, and as soon as it's over, you're welcome to the body. Is this some particular concern to you, or what?"

"Oh, no—it was just an accident that we had down here in the jail."

"Well, in the first place, it's not up to you to determine if an *accident* occurred in jail or not. That's my job. That's what I do. I'll make the decision whether it was an accident or not."

Judge Beaird had no more than finished his sentence when the line abruptly went dead. He had precious few minutes to steam about being hung up on when the phone rang a fourth time. Beaird wasn't surprised when he heard Judge Smith wheezing on the other end of the line. What he didn't know was that Smith was not alone in his office. Nearby were two of Hemphill's most prominent leaders, Sabine County Sheriff Blan Greer and Dr. Grover Winslow, the doctor who first had treated Garner. Also in Smith's office was Texas Ranger Roscoe Davis, the lawman entrusted with the independent investigation of Garner's death. (Dr. Winslow later would explain he wanted Garner's body back to ensure that, in fact, it would be autopsied; Davis recalled being in Judge Smith's office, but didn't remember a fight over the body.)

"Judge Beaird, I just wanted to call back and let you know it's all right to go ahead and send that body," Judge Smith tried again. "I've talked with everybody down here who's connected with it and we've determined it was an accident. So just go ahead and send the body."

The justice of the peace had to restrain himself from laying into the elderly judge, who, Beaird thought, either was oblivious to their earlier conversation or, more probably, was trying to twist his arm and bend the law. "Well, Judge, maybe you didn't hear me the first time. I'm not turning that body over to anybody until I have an autopsy. And I may schedule a formal inquest, depending on what the autopsy shows, to find out what happened to this man. I'm thinking I may just impanel an inquest jury of six good Smith County citizens and let them decide what happened down there."

"Well, the sheriff's standing right here. You want to talk to him about it? He'll tell you it was an accident."

"Hell, no. I don't want to talk to anybody about it. I don't really give a damn what the sheriff has to say about it, because it's not any of his business. It's *my* business, and you're not getting the body until I finish with it. That should be pretty damn clear."

Again the phone went dead.

That night over supper, Beaird discussed the series of strange phone calls from Sabine County with his wife, Darla. By most standards, the dinner conversations at the Beaird household would be considered ghoulish. But Darla and the children, Tara and Buddy, had become accustomed to hearing about the head of the family's unusual days at the office. Beaird had conducted eight hundred inquests, the most bizarre and puzzling of which inevitably became standard fare at the dinner table.

"Those ol' boys from Hemphill are sure in a hurry to get that body back, and I don't think it's just to give him a good funeral. There's something wrong with this one, and I'm going to make sure I find out what it is. I think somebody's trying to cover their asses."

That a black man from Louisiana had died after being incarcerated in the Sabine County Jail was common knowledge at Twitty's Restaurant and the Brookshire Supermarket in Hemphill well before the weekly *Sabine County Reporter* announced the death at the top of its front page on December 30, 1987. On the same page that noted that 10.3 percent of Sabine County's workers were jobless—higher than the rate in any adjoining county, and twice the average of the nation at large—the top story told readers:

> Texas Rangers and the FBI are investigating the death of a 34-year-old Louisiana man who died Sunday after being jailed at Hemphill for drunken driving.
> Sabine County Sheriff Blan Greer said Loyal Garner of Florien was found "in bad shape in his cell Saturday morning" and was hospitalized. The sheriff said he immediately notified the Texas Rangers and turned the investigation over to them. . . .

Actually, phone records later would show that Sheriff Greer didn't immediately notify the Texas Rangers. Though Greer had walked into the jail at about eight-fifteen A.M. on December 26, just as the unconscious Garner was being loaded into the ambulance, Texas Ranger Roscoe Davis's phone in Jasper didn't ring until 3:24 P.M., more than seven hours later. And by the time the Ranger changed clothes and drove the forty miles to Hemphill, it would be around five P.M.

Indeed, on this Saturday, the day after Christmas, there had been unaccustomed activity in the one-story stucco Sabine County Jail. The floors, even the cinder-block walls in the book-in room, had been scrubbed. The Ranger found what he thought was blood in one of the crevices in the wall, but there wasn't enough to submit for a good lab analysis.

Sheriff Greer explained that he hadn't cordoned off the detox cell or the book-in room to protect the evidence of a potential crime scene because his deputies "all pretty well knew what they had to do." And during the morning hours, all three potential witnesses to Garner's death, Chief

Ladner and deputies Horton and Hyden, had been in and out of the offices, talking with each other and to Sheriff Greer in his office.

The Maxie brothers, the only two eyewitnesses to the cell-block assault on Garner, had been locked outside the jail Saturday morning after being ordered to load their dying friend into the ambulance. When they beat on the door long enough to finally be readmitted to the jail, they were isolated in separate cells.

Jailer Clyde "Preacher" Kirk was following orders. For the first time in the more than two years he had been a jailer, Kirk had gotten an early-morning phone call from Bill Horton, the chief deputy, inquiring about the welfare of prisoners. Horton wanted to know if everyone in the detox cell was up. When the jailer checked and told him one of the inmates was still asleep on the ledge, Horton said he would stay on the line while Kirk went back to wake the prisoner.

Minutes later, the jailer returned to the phone and said he was unable to rouse the prisoner. He was going to have to call an ambulance.

Horton delivered a curious order before hanging up. "Get statements from the two Maxies, and be sure and try to get the drugs out of them, what they have to say about drugs."

By the time Ranger Roscoe Davis arrived from Jasper, the Maxie brothers were back in Louisiana, having paid fines of $22.50 each for public intoxication. The veteran Ranger, however, was given signed statements taken from the Maxies by Preacher Kirk—the only statements the jailer had ever been told to elicit during his career with the Sabine County Sheriff's Department, and undoubtedly the first affidavits ever taken from suspects who had pleaded guilty to merely being drunk. At Chief Ladner's request, the Maxies' statements had been typed by Trooper Bill Bradberry of the Texas Department of Public Safety, the parent organization of the Texas Rangers. Bradberry shared an office with the game warden in the Sabine County Jail complex.

The affidavits bore little resemblance to the events the Maxies would later describe. In fact, the Maxies would swear that Deputy Preacher Kirk actually wrote the accounts, had them typed, and told them to sign the papers, all within an hour of their loading Garner into the ambulance. After spending the night watching their friend die, they said, they would have signed anything put in front of them.

Both statements given to Ranger Davis had been witnessed and signed by Trooper Bradberry, who had spent the last fourteen of his twenty years with the Highway Patrol stationed in Sabine County. Both of the Maxie brothers later would swear they never saw a uniformed trooper or anyone who was introduced to them by the name of Bradberry.

That Trooper Bradberry would bear witness to the controversial affidavits, which later would be discredited by the men who purportedly gave them, was ironic. The only disciplinary action in the trooper's file, for which he was suspended in 1979 for five days without pay, stemmed from, among other things, falsifying an official government document. Trooper Bradberry had apparently heeded the Cop's Code of Silence: Never say anything incriminating about another police officer. In the 1979 incident, Bradberry's partner was having an extramarital affair with a divorcee who lived in a rural part of Sabine County. "You regularly assisted him by covering for him, as he absented himself from duty without authorization, on numerous occasions in connection with the above mentioned affair," the disciplinary committee found in Trooper Bradberry's case. "You have falsified official reports in an effort to keep the affair from being detected."

8

LEGACY OF SHAME

The frightening part is that I know this is going to happen again.
. . . There are certain counties in East Texas where blacks know they
have to be careful. My own county, Nacogdoches, is all right. There
are two blacks on the sheriff's force. But here in Sabine County and
up in Cherokee County, be careful. That's always been the word.

—Lawrence Jones, Nacogdoches, Texas, during a town meeting
in Hemphill to discuss race relations after Garner's death

"LORD, LORD, it just don't seem possible, now does it? But you know, darlin', some things, they're just real slow 'bout changin'. Makes a person wonder if they ever will change. Don't guess I'll see it. Maybe you will, though, son."

Always, the old black woman had held out hope, first to her children, then later to her grandchildren, that they would see change in Sabine County.

Ura Daniels's oldest son, Vollie Grace, brought her the news about the black stranger in the jail dying. She could see her son was upset, and she tried to comfort him, just as she had when he was a little boy, years before Vollie had children of his own. For more than seven decades, Mrs. Ura, as people called her, had lived peacefully in a white-dominated county that wasn't known for its benevolence to blacks. Sabine County was where she was born, and life had never been easy for blacks, or the "coloreds," as she still calls her folks. They were, for the most part, hardscrabble people, hauling pulpwood in worn-out trucks, working for wages in the woods and grabbing up temporary jobs when they could scratch them out. Much of their meals they grew in their yards, canning what they couldn't eat to get them through the winter.

Ura Daniels had heard all about the Civil Rights Act, but in the nearly quarter-century since it had been passed, she hadn't seen any more blacks working in government jobs for the city of Hemphill or Sabine County or working in "public" jobs in the stores around the square. The elected officials who determined what roads got paved were still white, and the roads in black East Mayfield were still rutted and unpaved. The men who carried the badges and guns and enforced the laws were still exclusively white, and young and old blacks alike still knew better than to test them.

No, Mrs. Ura knew there was a Civil Rights Act just like she knew there was a cool breeze, but the Piney Woods stifled one as easily as the other. The law certainly hadn't made the word "nigger" go away, or the demeaning impact the slur left on its victims.

Consciously, Mrs. Ura had fought to insulate herself and her family from the scorn and ridicule she'd observed and filed away with amazing clarity in her seventy-plus years. From outward appearances, it seemed that nothing Mrs. Ura had endured had disturbed her serenity.

The conversation about Loyal Garner reminded Vollie Grace of another example of white justice, one not recorded in official histories of Sabine County but passed down by blacks, generation to generation. It was one of his mother's stories that left an indelible mark on a young black kid growing up in Hemphill. It also was one of the most brutal racist acts he could imagine.

Shortly after the turn of the century, blacks in Sabine County held church socials on Saturday nights, their alternative to being barred by whites from activities in town. When the women had tidied up after the covered-dish dinners, the men moved the tables from the center of the floor to make room for dancing. A few musicians with guitars and fiddles provided the music, and the socials provided dancing well into the night.

The Rockwall Church in Geneva, in northern Sabine County, had a social planned one night in the summer of 1903, as Mrs. Ura recalled the legend. Hugh Dean, a young white man born into one of the county's most prominent families, planned to attend the social, as he had many others. Dean would appear, so the oral history goes, and select the prettiest black girl, with whom he would dance and ultimately force to leave with him. Blacks despised the exploitation of their women in general and hated Hugh Dean in particular. White men randomly choosing young black women smacked of the plantation days four decades earlier, when white men had their choice of slave women.

Leland Roberts, whose sister was known around Geneva as one of the most beautiful young women in the county, had been warned by other blacks that if he allowed his sister to attend the social, she almost certainly would fall victim to Hugh Dean's advances. "Not my sister," Roberts had vowed. "He's not going to mess with my sister."

Indeed, Hugh Dean's mother apparently was aware of her son's habit, imploring him on this particular Saturday night to accompany the family the twenty or so miles to Hemphill, where they were spending the night with relatives. "Hugh, those coloreds are going to get tired of you courting their girls," she supposedly told her son.

Young Hugh was undaunted. "Mama, I'll put a lightning bug on a corn stalk and make those niggers so scared they'll jump right into the Sabine River."

Hugh Dean showed up at the Geneva social and, true to habit, reportedly forced himself on Leland Roberts's sister. Roberts came prepared. The young black man pulled a pistol and shot Dean in the stomach, killing him almost instantly.

"Give me two hours to get across the river into Louisiana, and then tell the white folks," Roberts yelled. "But make sure you report it, 'cause there'll be hell to pay if you don't. Don't go all night without telling somebody."

Leland Roberts made good his escape. But none of the frightened gathering could force himself to tell a white man that a colored had killed another white man. The black men fled into the woods. Shortly after daybreak, a black woman who worked for whites confided to her mistress that Mr. Hugh had been killed at the church social.

White men, armed and on horseback, poured from all of Sabine County into the woods around Geneva. Within hours, they had tied six black men together by their necks and, as they rode behind them on horseback, forced them to walk the twenty miles into Hemphill. Word spread throughout the county: on Saturday, all six of the blacks were to be hanged. Their capital crime apparently was being present when a black man killed a white.

On Saturday, so the story goes, Hemphill was swept by a carnival atmosphere, with whites riding into town from farms throughout the county. Amid much fanfare, the black men were bound together by their necks, three rows of two men each, and marched toward a huge oak at the base of the hill leading out of Hemphill. One managed to escape into a pine thicket; the other five were hanged from the tree.

Legend among the blacks has it that a white woman heavy with child actually examined and touched the black men's bodies as they dangled from the tree. When the child was born a few weeks later, he could neither speak nor hear, and he spent his tortured life unable to even raise himself from bed. The implied moral among blacks was that God had punished the mother for her cruelty to blacks.

Years later, one of Grace's white friends, whose father worked in the courthouse, offered to show Grace some old photographs that his father had found of the dead black men. Grace had grown up fearing the story; he declined his friend's offer.

The legacy of racial violence was as certain in East Texas as the pine needles that fell and turned red. Just as its lush thickets and rust-red dirt distinguished East Texas from the rest of the state, so did its prevailing philosophy about blacks, which was more aligned with that of the Deep South. Racial violence flourished in East Texas. But except for hushed and scared word of mouth, the violence went unreported and uninvestigated by white law enforcement, some of whom today still refer to murders of blacks as "misdemeanor killin's," or, in cop shorthand, as "TNDs"—"typical nigger deals."

One of the more frightening throwbacks to the antebellum South occurred in the tiny, all-black Mayflower Community fifty years after the Hemphill hangings, and sixty miles to the north. In 1953, the justification and rationalization for segregated schools was called the "separate but equal" doctrine. In truth, only half the phrase—"separate"—was accurate; there was nothing equal about white and black schools in East Texas. The frame schoolhouse for blacks in Mayflower literally was falling down around its students. When the community's black residents fought for tax money to build a new school, it triggered anger among whites in Panola County.

Just as they had fifty years earlier, blacks socialized together, barred from movies and restaurants in town, which were reserved exclusively for whites. On October 22, sixteen-year-old John Earl Reese had joined several other black teenagers at a small cafe in Mayflower, listening to radio and drinking sodas. He was dancing with his cousin, Joyce Faye Nelson, shortly before midnight when a barrage of gunfire rained through the walls and windows of the ramshackle little cafe. One of the slugs slammed into John, knocking him off balance. Instinctively, he grabbed for Joyce, then fell dead to the floor. Joyce was wounded in the arm, and her sister, sitting in a nearby booth, also fell under the gunfire.

Outside, a car gunned its engine and tore off toward the black school-house. From the car's window, a rifle fired randomly into the school and at a school bus parked outside.

The sheriff refused to investigate, and the district attorney refused to prosecute. Not until Ronnie Dugger, the white editor of the liberal *Texas Observer* in Austin, made a public crusade of John Earl Reese's murder did law enforcement even make a halfhearted effort to investigate the slaying.

Ultimately, a twenty-two-year-old white man gave detailed descriptions of the shooting and was convicted of murder. But as if to underscore the worthlessness of a black life in East Texas, Reese's murderer was given a suspended sentence. Charges against his accomplice, another local white man, were dismissed. The wanton and senseless death of a black teenager was sordid enough, but the reluctance of the white criminal justice system to prosecute the murder underscored the pervasiveness of unequal treatment in East Texas.

The Reverend Guston H. Browning, a white Methodist minister who followed the saga of Reese's murder, conceded that there was "a general lack of regard for Negroes in East Texas." "A Negro is considered by many as something just a little less than human," he said. "Whether or not a direct connection between this murder and the conflict over the Negro school can be positively established, I do not know. But that a shameful, non-Christian feeling of racial superiority is at the base of it all, I would bet my life."

When he was a youngster growing up in Sabine County, the stories of black murders at the hands of whites sent shivers through Vollie Grace. He wondered when he saw white men if there was some silent, dark side that could be triggered almost instantaneously against blacks. And if there was this dark side of violence, he wondered about its catalyst, considering it imperative to understand so that he could avoid the provocation at all costs.

Now, as a forty-six-year-old man, Vollie Grace could give a good ac-counting of himself. He had served honorably in the United States Army during the Cuban missile crisis; he had worked hard to start his own successful concrete contracting business; he worked hard in his church; and he was devoted to his wife and four children. But after Garner's death, Grace found himself wondering how those racist stories he heard as a kid had *really* affected him—if they had influenced his decisions or even subconsciously changed the way he raised his children. Had he inadvertently bred fear into his children at the expense of their pride and self-respect? Maybe, he thought, that's why Hemphill blacks even today knew to stay in their "place." And maybe that was why the Civil Rights Act had meant virtually nothing in Hemphill—because black men were afraid to demand they be protected under its provisions. Maybe, he thought, it was the threat of violence from almost a century ago that stymied blacks from even trying to run for office.

Vollie Grace never met Loyal Garner, Jr. It was the legacy of oppression that gnawed at Grace, the realization that after nearly eighty-five years a black man not even convicted of a crime still could be killed without good reason by white lawmen. "Nothing's changed, Mama, not one damn thing. And it's not ever going to change unless we *make* it change."

Perhaps for the first time since Leland Roberts had defended his sister against a white man's advances more than eighty years earlier, a black man was about to stand up and be counted in Sabine County—in public, in broad daylight, and in the presence of whites. As her son left, Mrs. Ura knew there was nothing she could do to insulate him from the course he was charting.

9

RELYING ON OLD ADVERSARIES

IN A MOMENTARY RAGE nine years earlier, Thomas Ladner would have done foul things to John Seale if the chief had thought he could get away with it. Seale, who represented Ladner's estranged wife in a divorce case, had a surgeon's precision and a pit bull's tenacity. The veteran lawyer drew on both to make the court appearance one of the most abysmal days in Ladner's life. Afterward, Ladner told friends that Seale had "put the britches on me bad, hurt me real bad." The burly chief wasn't bashful in admitting he ought to kill John Seale.

Now, in the aftermath of Loyal Garner's death in the Sabine County Jail, Ladner was more than willing to put his fate in the hands of a man he once despised. "Believe me, I learned the hard way what John Seale could do in a courtroom," Ladner explained. "I wanted to have the best."

Ladner had been Hemphill's police chief less than a year when he filed for divorce in April 1979. The papers were personally served on Carolyn Ladner a week later by Sheriff Blan Greer. When she read them, she discovered that her husband of more than six years, and the father of their five-year-old daughter, believed their marriage was "insupportable because of discord and conflict of personalities." That discord and conflict, the legal boilerplate indicated, left "no reasonable expectation of reconciliation." According to the petition, Ladner's solution to the terminally ailing relationship was legal euthanasia—divorce. Carolyn Ladner scheduled an immediate appointment with Seale, the portly senior partner of Seale, Stover, Coffield, Gatlin & Bisbey in Jasper, forty miles south of Hemphill.

John Seale moved predictably in the divorce, much like a supremely confident running back who, before the ball is snapped, looks at the defensive linemen and says, "I'm running off-tackle—stop me if you can." Unlike some successful civil lawyers who rely on their ability to coerce and finesse settlements without ever entering a courtroom, Seale built his substantial reputation by arguing to judges and juries. As a young personal-injury specialist, he had learned that insurance companies, his most frequent adversaries, kept score cards on which lawyers avoid courtrooms and are willing to settle beforehand. And if insurance companies knew a lawyer was predisposed to settle out of court, that lawyer's clients were offered substantially lower settlements.

Not that John Seale wouldn't play the game, at least to some extent. He dutifully submitted to opposing lawyers a figure that he considered fair reimbursement for his clients' pain, grief, suffering, mental anguish, or other unwarranted invasion of their wholeness. The lawyers either paid the amount or Seale took them to court—no hemming or hawing, no protracted offers and counteroffers. The generally quiet-spoken and unassuming lawyer wasn't known for his willingness to compromise.

Seale knew his way to the courthouse, and he was intimidated by neither judges nor juries. Indeed, he had discovered in thirty-odd years of practice that he accomplished two goals when he argued his cases in courtrooms: generally, judges and juries blessed his clients with heftier sums than settlements concocted in smoke-filled rooms; and, equally important to Seale, he enjoyed the contest immensely. More accurately, he enjoyed *winning* immensely.

Rapidly, Seale filed a cross-action against Thomas Ladner on behalf of his new client and scheduled a hearing, in which Mrs. Ladner was named temporary managing conservator of the couple's daughter and recipient of $150 a month in temporary alimony and child support. But if Ladner and his lawyer thought $150 unduly stretched the modest salary of Hemphill's chief municipal law-enforcement officer, they would suffer a major setback in the nonjury trial before Judge O'Neal Bacon in August. Since the couple had no major assets, the most contested issue was child support. When the trial ended, Carolyn Ladner walked out of the courtroom with a decree that gave her custody of the couple's daughter, the house, a nearly new pickup truck, all the furniture, $500 in cash, and $280 a month in child-support payments. The child-support award was the highest in the history of modest Sabine County.

Eight months later, when Ladner had fallen behind on two support payments, Seale hauled the chief back into court on a contempt motion. Ladner made the back payments and determined it was in his best interest not to run afoul of the court again. When a fellow lawman suggested he simply refuse to pay, Ladner looked at him like he was crazy and said, "Bullshit!"

But Ladner was still bitter more than a year later, and he hired a lawyer from Beaumont to argue his motion for a reduction in child support. Seale didn't even argue the issue of reducing the payments. Ever the southern gentleman with impeccable, old-fashioned courtroom demeanor, Seale asked the judge for a ten percent *increase*—and, Ladner believed, almost convinced His Honor to raise the payments. The chief felt lucky to escape with his life, and the $280 payments suddenly appeared almost a bargain. "I just don't have the right damn lawyer, apparently," he muttered.

Ladner v. Ladner certainly wasn't a major case, but it paid ongoing dividends to Seale over the next few years. Periodically, new clients from Sabine County were showing up at Seale's rambling complex of offices, telling him they had been recommended by Thomas Ladner. "The chief says you're the best lawyer in East Texas," they'd say. The chief's be-grudging recommendation brought a smile to John Seale's face.

Thomas Ladner, embattled and under siege, was in need of a good lawyer when he showed up in Seale's office the week after Christmas, 1987. Seale saw the pressure etched in Ladner's face, and the chief, customarily stingy with words, was even quieter than usual. Already the lawman had endured the unpleasantries of being on the "other side," the humiliation of being questioned as a suspect in a potential criminal offense. He had talked briefly with Texas Ranger Roscoe Davis, and at Davis's direction he had submitted his written statement of the arrest of Loyal Garner, Jr., and the Maxie brothers on Christmas night. Two FBI agents appeared in Hemphill on Davis's heels, and they, too, were asking questions, not only of Ladner but also of Horton and Hyden.

FBI Special Agents Roger Humphrey and Gerard Savnik noted in their initial report that the chief advised them that he was retaining a lawyer and "did not want to discuss any facts of the case at that time." Ladner did, however, volunteer to supply the FBI with the same three-page report he had written at Davis's request. In their report the FBI agents wrote: "Ladner did state he had been involved in one previous civil rights complaint approximately four to five years ago. To the best of his recollection, it involved Leonard Green, and Ladner added that nothing ever came of the complaint."

The chief already had been told that Garner's death would be submitted to the Sabine County Grand Jury, probably before the week was out. He had anticipated the grand jury, a routine action in Texas any time a prisoner dies in custody or an officer uses lethal force. He'd also heard that the justice of the peace in Smith County was being a hardass about his inquest into Garner's death. The inquest hadn't yet been convened, but depending on Judge Bill Beaird's findings, there could even be a second grand jury investigation in Tyler.

Worse, though, the small-town rumor mill was churning with threats of race riots and an uprising among even some whites who, rumor had it, were fed up enough with brutal law enforcement to talk to the press. And everyone around the square had seen the reporters, big-city strangers with notepads and ballpoints, grabbing anybody they could and asking the same questions ad nauseam: "What do you think about the officers accused of killing the man in jail?" "Is there a race problem in Hemphill?" Word traveled fast in a town of thirteen hundred that reporters had arrived from the *Houston Chronicle* and *The Houston Post, The Dallas Morning News, The Beaumont Enterprise*, the *Shreveport Journal*, and the *Austin American-Statesman*. Before the week's end, *The Christian Science Monitor* and even *The New York Times* were in town, too.

Standing in the jail lobby, Ladner himself had seen the TV crews arrive with their mobile satellite uplink antennas, which he came to regard as a cruel and unusual form of high-tech torture. Camera crews aimed minicams at him as he walked silently from his car to the office; then, sometimes minutes later, he'd see his face on television with a baritone voice telling viewers the chief "had no comment." CNN appeared. The media was turning the square into a circus. Officers even had to scatter a covey of reporters from the jail parking lot to allow the sheriff to park his car.

With so many reporters concentrated in such a small space, it was inevitable that they would stumble onto the spit-and-whittle club that met daily under the cedar tree on the courthouse lawn. The crusty old men presented the epitome of "color" opportunity for the big-city reporters, validating the stereotype that ignorance and racism were indeed still alive and well in Deep East Texas. A few of the codgers wore bib overalls, others khakis. Spitting tobacco juice, they sat around a picnic table, pissing and moaning about taxes, the federal government, and the weather, occasionally slapping a domino onto the table with enough force to sound like a twenty-two shot. One crusty, toothless old bastard, who perhaps had grown tired of the intrusions into his ritual domino game, bristled under one of the reporter's questions and blurted a quote that became news the next day. "Far as I can tell," he said, "that nigger got exactly what he deserved."

Even before he was retained to represent Ladner, Seale had seen the stories in the papers and on TV. Intense media exposure in high-profile cases, the veteran lawyer well knew, was a dice roll; sometimes the exposure could work for the defense. This wasn't one of those cases. In the public's perception, the veteran lawyer feared, the Garner death had warts and wrinkles all over it: unarmed black man, father of six, no criminal background. Three white officers, one too big to fit in a phone booth. Jailed on Christmas Day. Black vs. white. Civil rights. Even in the preliminary "breaking" stories, Seale believed, the media already was convicting Ladner, a view the chief damn well shared.

John Seale was an accomplished litigator, no question, but he also was too savvy to ever rely solely on emotional appeals to the strangers who sat in jury boxes. Less obvious, but infinitely more important, he knew, was encyclopedic knowledge of the facts. Favorable facts were to be used aggressively, like weapons; unfavorable facts were to be dodged like incoming mortar rounds. With the Sabine County Grand Jury meeting any day now, the fifty-six-year-old lawyer sat his new client down and beat him with questions. The ordeal was worse, Ladner thought, than what he had experienced with the Ranger and the FBI agents combined.

Not surprisingly, Ladner's account of Christmas night conflicted dramatically with that of Johnnie and Alton Maxie, who had been located by reporters and whose version was common currency among readers and listeners throughout Texas and western Louisiana. Seale listened intently and made notes as Ladner led him through the scenario of a few nights earlier.

Ladner and Bo Hyden were driving into Hemphill on Texas 87 when they saw a pickup truck "driving very erratic." They followed it, and shortly after it crossed into the city limits, they turned on their flashing lights. As if the lights had startled its driver, the pickup crossed the center stripe into the left lane, headed almost off the road, then veered back across the center stripe and stopped on the shoulder of the right lane.

Ladner told his lawyer, and noted in his report to Ranger Roscoe Davis, that when Garner got out of the pickup he "was holding onto the bed of the pickup, very unstable and I could smell the odor of alcohol beverage strongly." Inside the cab, the chief said, he found two half-pints of liquor and a six-pack of Budweiser, along with "several" empty cans. The suspects declined an offer for a phone call, the chief said, "because they wanted to talk to the judge the next morning . . . to see how much cash they would need to get out of jail." After booking all three men, Ladner said he and Hyden returned to Garner's pickup and Hyden drove it back to the jail.

When the two officers returned, Ladner said, dispatcher Mary Russell told them the men in the detox cell were cussing and beating on the door so violently that it was activating the red warning light on her console, indicating a security breach. "Chief Deputy Bill Horton went back and told them to calm down and when they did, they could make a phone call," Ladner said. The cussing and pounding only worsened, he said, so he and Hyden went back to tell them to calm down.

"When the door was open, we went in and asked which one was doing all the cussing and kicking the door," Ladner said. The chief continued his account:

> Garner jumped up and said, "I am the motherfucker," and ran at me. I pushed him to the side and he came back and hit me. I grabbed him around the neck and held him. He got away from me. Deputy Hyden grabbed him and Garner slung him against the door. When Garner got loose from Hyden, he tried to hit me again. I hit Garner with a slapjack, the slapjack slipped from my hand and landed in the hall. He got quiet and said he wanted to make a phone call.

> We brought him to the booking room and he started cussing again, calling us "three white motherfuckers. . . ." He refused to make a phone call. We told him if he was not going to make a phone call, to come on and we would put him back in his cell. He said, "You three motherfuckers are not putting me anywhere." We started to get Mr. Garner and put him in the cell. He hit me again with his fist. He grabbed a flashlight off of the desk. Mr. Hyden grabbed him from behind, Bill Horton grabbed the flashlight and Mr. Garner slung

Mr. Hyden back against the file cabinets. We tried to get him again and he slung loose and fell, hitting his head against the wall. He got back up and started calling us "three white motherfuckers" again. We all grabbed him again and took him to his cell.

Ladner's recollection of the scenario didn't explain the prisoners' apparent change of mind about the phone call, from supposedly electing to wait until the next morning when they could see the judge to beating on the door to demand an immediate phone call.

In the hours he spent with his lawyer, Seale would recall, the police chief was adamant that he had merely subdued an unruly prisoner. "He jumped us and hit me and I tried to defend myself," Ladner told his lawyer. "And yes, I hit him with a blackjack, but I didn't even get a good lick on him, and the blackjack flew out of my hand. The next thing I know, they say he's in a coma, and the next thing I know, they say he's dead. I just can't believe it."

Seale knew he had to act fast. With the media exposure, the case already was a locomotive headed downhill. It had to be sidetracked at the grand jury level, before the wheels of justice produced a criminal trial, and before the media could incite the public any more than it already had.

"Don't worry, Thomas," Seale told his client. "We'll head it off in the grand jury. I don't think there'll be any indictments."

As a reassured Ladner left Seale's office for home, the lawyer truly believed his representation of the troubled chief would be short-lived. Seale had handled his share of criminal cases, but he was by no means a criminal-defense specialist. No matter, he thought; Garner's death wouldn't make it past the grand jury.

Ladner's fate, and that of colleagues Horton and Hyden, the lawyer knew, would be determined by neighbors with whom they had grown up. And if past experience held true, there was more than a fair chance that all the faces on the Sabine County Grand Jury would be white.

Never in their history had Sabine County and Hemphill, its tiny administrative center, been laid so naked as in the waning hours of 1987 and the first week of 1988. The county's residents were startled, like range cattle who weren't accustomed to human beings, when an influx of out-of-towners converged on them.

Sabine County is a dogleg out of the mainstream. Strangers don't come by accident; they have to know where they're going to even find it. Motorists simply don't "pass through" Hemphill going to or coming from any major city. A United States highway runs north-south, almost missing the western edge of the county, but the only roads into or out of Hemphill are narrow state roads, some of which dead-end into Toledo Bend Reservoir. Only one highway, Texas 21, even crosses the Sabine River into Louisiana, and it leads to Many, hardly a metropolis. Almost equidistant between Beaumont to the south and Shreveport, Louisiana, to the north, Hemphill clearly is off the beaten path.

Far from apologizing for their isolation, most Sabine Countians regard it, along with the pine thickets and the lake, as one of the county's biggest assets. They know their neighbors and often their neighbors' families for two generations back. They know the "little girl" the next-door neighbor's son is dating and the "ol' gal" who used to be married to the neighbor across the street—and behind their closed doors, they have opinions on both.

Neighborhood crime watches, considered so innovative in big cities, have thrived for decades in the country, bred not of staggering crime rates but of familiarity—and more than a little busybodiness. People know that if Mrs. So-and-So's car is gone from the driveway for an hour right after lunch on Saturday, she's doing her grocery shopping. And set your watch by it, every other Friday at 9:00 A.M., Mr. So-and-So is in the barber's chair "getting his ears lowered." While the "lake traffic" caused some in Sabine County to reconsider, many still leave their doors unlocked, and even leave the keys in the ignitions of their cars and pickups. Life is slow-paced and, outwardly at least, amiable.

The pace changed dramatically after Christmas, 1987, and many Sabine Countians were suspicious, resentful, and even paranoid.

Sharon Atkins, the veteran East Texas bureau chief for *The Beaumont Enterprise*, based in Jasper, was the catalyst for the change in pace. Her phone began ringing even before Garner died two days after Christmas. Was it true, callers asked Atkins, that a black man had been beaten to death in the Sabine County Jail? Working the phones from her tiny office in Jasper, Atkins confirmed that a black inmate from the Sabine County Jail had indeed been taken to Sabine County Hospital with injuries he apparently suffered in the jail. His condition was so critical, he was transferred to Medical Center Hospital in Tyler, where, according to hospital spokespersons, he died of "massive head injuries." After contacting Garner's parents in Florien and interviewing the Maxie brothers, Atkins wrote her story for the *Enterprise*. It was picked up by the Houston Bureau of the Associated Press and moved nationally on the wires, triggering an avalanche of generally unwelcome visitors to Hemphill.

Sabine Countians couldn't go to the square, and certainly not to the courthouse, without stumbling into the strangers. Some of the out-of-towners were easy to figure. A few of the faces residents even recognized from the ten o'clock newscasts from Beaumont and Shreveport. Except for an occasional mention on the weather forecast, when Hemphill was wetter or drier or hotter or colder than any other place in Deep East Texas, even old-timers couldn't remember the town ever being mentioned on TV. Now, with "this deal at the jail," many believed, the TV people couldn't wait to drag the town through a mudhole. The other strangers, though, residents were certain, were FBI agents dispatched from Beaumont and Houston to investigate Chief Ladner and Deputies Horton and Hyden.

Sociologists call it ethnocentrism, but residents of Hemphill and Sabine County called it community pride. Whoever the strangers were, most residents were reluctant to be seen talking to them. If they were reporters, the locals didn't want to appear on the nightly news talking about their neighbors. And if the strangers were FBI, well, they just didn't know anything anyhow, except that they'd known all three officers a long time and didn't think they'd intentionally do anything bad. Some people didn't stay around long enough to even find out who wanted to ask the questions. Before the strangers could introduce themselves, the locals would walk wide around them. "I don't have anything to say to you," they'd say.

The magnet for the strangers was the Sabine County Grand Jury, impaneled almost immediately after Garner died in Tyler on December 27. The grand jury was convened in the Sabine County Courthouse, a tired tier of aging bricks that rose from the epicenter of the tiny town. In a square that encompassed the courthouse, merchants from decades earlier had built storefronts that Norman Rockwell would have coveted for a *Saturday Evening Post* cover. The county's former jail, abandoned for the new law-enforcement complex a block away, still stood on the southeast corner of the courthouse lawn. A group of local ladies intent on preserving the county's heritage had commandeered the old jail and turned it into a combination museum-library, but they had been careful to restore the top floor of the old jail to its original state, even down to resurrecting the hangman's noose in its gallows. In 1922, Sabine was among the last counties in Texas to use its gallows. Two years later the state built "Old Sparky," its first and only electric chair, and transferred responsibility for executions from individual counties to the Texas Department of Corrections in Huntsville.

While the Texas Commission on Jail Standards had forced Sabine County taxpayers to build the new jail in the early 1980s, there were no state agencies to force improvements to courthouses. By intent or neglect, the Sabine County Courthouse still was locked in the 1930s; it appeared to have resisted any major attempts at a facelift. As ancient as the old building looked, there actually had been two courthouses before it. The first, built of wood in 1875, burned to the ground, destroying all the county's records and documents. A wooden building was used for a time until, finally, in 1906, county commissioners paid a local attorney and architect $30,000 to build the current brick structure. Fire struck again in 1909, gutting the building's fourth floor. The top floor never was rebuilt, and in 1938, the Works Progress Administration remodeled the remaining three stories.

When District Attorney Bill Martin convened the grand jury in the third-floor courtroom of the First Judicial District in the final hours of 1987, the courthouse, with one major exception, couldn't have appeared much different than from fifty years earlier. The stairs creaked, and the high ceilings were stained yellow by years of unchecked leaks. The men's restroom on the first floor bore a yellowed, handwritten warning over the urinal: "Don't spit tobacco in the urinal. It stops up the drain."

The only manifestation that the courthouse had been tampered with in modern times was the third-floor corridor outside the courtroom. After trekking up two flights of stairs virtually unaltered by time, visitors walked onto a top floor painted in garish electric blue—an effect as incongruous in the old building as a cummerbund on bib overalls.

It was in this aging courtroom that John Seale hoped that the investigation into the death of Loyal Garner, Jr., would end, like investigations in many similar courthouses for so many other police officers accused of crimes against suspects in their custody. The grand jury had massive discretion in Garner's death, from taking no action against the officers to indicting them on charges ranging from murder and civil rights violations to misdemeanor charges of official neglect.

With any luck, though, Seale thought, the Sabine County Grand Jury would determine that Chief Thomas Ladner and Deputies Bill Horton and Bo Hyden were merely victims of police officers' second-worst occupational hazard—that they used "only that force necessary" to subdue an unruly prisoner who "made them fear for their lives or their personal safety," and in the process, the prisoner unfortunately suffered injuries that killed him. Had the officers not exerted that force, traditional police defense strategy had it, the officers could have suffered their *worst* occupational hazard: killed in the line of duty. It was a time-honored—and uncommonly successful—defense for Texas lawmen.

10

PRECEDENT

THE GRAND JURY, at least in theory, is perhaps the most purely democratic step in the entire criminal-justice system. Average citizens exercise their common sense and community values in determining whether to turn a case over to the system's professional players, the lawyers and judges.

Ostensibly, grand juries are a major part of the checks and balances of criminal justice, the filtering system for the justice pipeline. Grand juries are designed to screen out those cases in which there is insufficient evidence to suggest that a person committed a crime, and to pass on for trial, or indict, those suspects whose cases show enough "probable cause" to indicate they indeed could have committed a crime. The grand jurors' role is to determine not guilt or innocence but merely probable cause that a crime was committed. In Texas, grand jurors are sworn to secrecy, and they arrive at their decisions—to indict or to no-bill—behind closed doors. Grand jurors are guided in their decisions by the district attorney, who determines the evidence that will be presented. The grand jury typically hears evidence and testimony from police officers, forensics experts (such as pathologists and fingerprint analysts), and witnesses to the crime, if there are any. Because of the Fifth Amendment guarantee against self-incrimination, suspects are not compelled to testify before the grand jury, though they may voluntarily request to address the group.

John Seale had been correct in his prediction about the makeup of the Sabine County Grand Jury. The jury that filed up the creaky stairs into the courtroom was all white. Still, and more importantly, Seale knew, the grand jurors, the three police officers—indeed, all of Sabine County—

were trapped in a fishbowl, photographed, taped, and quoted by reporters for the nation to see. He worried that the scrutiny would have an effect. The tension in the aging courthouse was heavy, like humidity in July.

His deep concern about media scrutiny notwithstanding, Seale had reason to feel optimistic about the grand jury no-billing Ladner and Horton and Hyden, even as the two deputies were negotiating for lawyers of their own. Throughout the nation, and maybe particularly in Texas, grand juries are legendary for granting police officers benefits of doubt that common citizens don't receive. Even in Dallas, a primarily white-collar city that appeared on the cover of *Time* magazine in the mid-1980s as "the City That Works," grand juries in the last three decades have returned only one indictment against a police officer for using lethal force. And in that case, in 1973, it took the death of a child to persuade grand jurors to indict.

A veteran Dallas police officer, trying to coerce a burglary confession in the backseat of his patrol car from twelve-year-old Santos Rodriguez, played Russian roulette with the youth. Officer Darrell L. Cain pointed the gun at the boy's head, asked a question, then spun the chamber on his pistol before asking again. Apparently not hearing the answer he wanted, the officer clicked the firing pin onto a live shell, blowing a .357-caliber slug into young Santos's head, killing him. Cain, who claimed he believed the pistol was unloaded, was sentenced to five years in prison.

In the 1980s, Dallas County grand juries refused to indict officers who shot seventy-year-old Etta Collins, an unarmed black woman, through the front screen door of her house; Larry Brice, an unarmed twenty-year-old white, who was shot nine times; David Horton, an eighty-one-year-old black man who, as a crime watch coordinator for his neighborhood, had phoned in a burglary report; and Sammy Stone, a black burglar who was shot to death after he had been handcuffed.

The expansive benefit of doubt accorded by grand juries to police officers nationwide, according to an essay in the American Bar Association *Journal* by Philadelphia lawyer David Rudovsky, is rooted in the public's fear of crime. The result, Rudovsky maintains, is a blank check for officers to "control the streets and enforce the status quo," which leads, he says, to "institutional toleration of police abuse."

The bottom line, says James Fyfe, a professor of justice at American University and formerly a New York City police officer for sixteen years, is that society gives cops de facto sanction to cut corners. "We have this notion of the cop as a soldier in the war against crime—so the cop is entitled to do what needs to be done," Fyfe said.

And perhaps nowhere was the grand jury's benefit of doubt toward officers more apparent than in East Texas. Except for recent aberrations in federal court, primarily those cases pushed by former U.S. attorney John Hannah, Jr., Texas lawmen were virtually bulletproof in state courts when it came to indictments on civil rights charges. Factor in that Garner was a black from out of state, and the odds of the white lawmen being indicted by an all-white grand jury were somewhere in the neighborhood of their chances of being struck on the head by a plummeting meteorite.

Proof of the officers' invincibility in East Texas had been offered in the case of another black man only four months before Garner's death. A grand jury in Rusk County, less than one hundred miles north of Hemphill, determined that there wasn't adequate evidence to file charges against a white Department of Public Safety trooper in the shooting death of Troy Lee Starling, an unarmed black motorist in Mount Enterprise in August 1987.

The five hundred or so residents of tiny Mount Enterprise knew twenty-four-year-old Starling as a working man who got up before dawn every morning to drive to his job at a fertilizer plant in nearby Nacogdoches. He was married, the father of a four-year-old son, and so quiet that many regarded him as "timid." The son of a timber hauler and a rest home worker, Starling had one passion in life, and it accounted for his only problems with law enforcement: he tinkered with cars, fine-tuned them for speed, and on occasion, apparently, was too heavy on the accelerator. Except for minor traffic offenses, mostly for speeding, the young black man never before had been in trouble with the law.

On the night of August 21, 1987, Trooper Jim Reese was patrolling near Mount Enterprise on U.S. 259. As he crested a hill, the trooper would later testify, he met an oncoming red 1981 Monte Carlo traveling north. The car was going 71 miles an hour in a 55-mile-an-hour speed zone. The trooper said he turned around and chased the speeding Chevrolet before it finally slowed and pulled onto the shoulder of the deserted highway.

Trooper Reese said he twice yelled "Highway Patrol—step out!" but the driver remained in the car, staring ahead through the windshield. With his .357 magnum pistol in his right hand, Trooper Reese said, he opened the car door with his left hand, again identifying himself as a highway patrolman, and nudged his left knee against the door to keep it from being slammed into him.

"The driver then made a quarter-turn or less in the seat," the trooper said later in a sworn statement. "I then reached into the car with my left hand to get hold of the driver. At this time, with me leaning in the car, I felt a sharp tug on my gun arm. Then I felt the pistol discharge."

Troy Lee Starling lay dead beside the red Monte Carlo, a bullet wound 1.37 inches to the left of the middle of the back of his neck. A search of his car failed to turn up a weapon of any kind.

Trooper Reese, in his debriefing with investigating Texas Rangers, said he approached Starling with caution, in part, he said, because Starling was black. Earlier in the night, the trooper said, he had monitored a radio alert from nearby Nacogdoches County that two black men were being sought for armed robbery. They had been seen traveling north on U.S. 259 toward Mount Enterprise. The same radio report also had said the two men were in "an older green Dodge pickup."

Legally at least, the shooting was cleared quietly within Rusk County even before word of the killing spread outside the county. The grand jury in Henderson, the county seat, refused to indict Trooper Reese—and determined the lawman's lack of culpability even before all of the forensic reports had been completed. The Department of Public Safety investigation, conducted by the Texas Rangers, had determined the killing was accidental, a view the grand jury endorsed when it no-billed Trooper Reese.

Had grand jurors read the lab and ballistics reports, as investigative reporter Lorraine Adams of *The Dallas Morning News* did later, they would have discovered that the trooper's account of the shooting was scientifically implausible. Had Starling "tugged" at the gun as Reese claimed, Starling's hand would have contained gunshot residues of "levels in the thousands," said renowned forensics pathologist Vincent DiMaio, the county medical examiner in San Antonio. Yet the Department of Public Safety's lab report reflected no gunshot residue on either of Starling's hands. And while the DPS ballistics report showed that Reese's department-issued Smith & Wesson .357 magnum was not defective, expert Wayland Pilcher—a criminal-justice professor at Sam Houston State University in Huntsville and a former police officer and police administrator in Corpus Christi—said he never had been aware of reports of a .357 magnum discharging accidentally with a "sharp tug" of the arm. "I cannot see how that wound, where it occurred, could have come about by Mr. Reese's statement of the events," Pilcher told Adams, who with her partner, Dan Malone, was researching a project on abuse by Texas law officers. Finally, the pathologist who conducted the autopsy on Starling discovered that the victim was "shot in the back of his neck at close range." An autopsy photograph shows an oval wound, "a few tears radiating from its margin." In his analysis of the autopsy, lab reports, and autopsy photographs for Adams and Malone, Dr. DiMaio concluded that Starling could not have been turned *toward* the officer, as Trooper Reese claimed; indeed, he determined, Starling's head was turned *away* from the officer when he was shot to death.

Curtis Stuckey, a mild-mannered transplanted Indianan who practices law in Nacogdoches, has made a living taking cases that most East Texas lawyers dodge. The Starling shooting was one in a long list of civil cases Stuckey filed in federal court against police, alleging civil rights violations. Starling's death had left the normally low-key and unassuming Stuckey indignant and vocal. "Mr. Starling's killing is an absolutely devastating and senseless tragedy," the lawyer told Adams and Malone. "I was taught when I was a little boy what's good enough for the goose is good for the gander. How many unarmed people do you know who have been 'accidentally' shot in the back of the neck at point-blank range? What would have happened to Troy Lee Starling if he had shot Reese in the back of the neck and claimed it was an accident?"

His years in East Texas had convinced Stuckey that a civil rights lawsuit in federal court—not a criminal trial in state court—would be the only chance Starling's survivors would ever have at justice. Cops who killed people almost never made it past the state grand jury.

In January 1991, more than three years after Starling was shot to death, the Texas Department of Public Safety, without acknowledging guilt or negligence for Trooper Jim Reese's actions in August 1987, paid Starling's family $180,000 in an out-of-court settlement. Trooper Reese, the subject of thirteen complaints of misconduct and two United States Justice Department civil rights investigations, all of which were determined to be unfounded, quietly was moved from the Highway Patrol to DPS's License and Weight Division in a "nondisciplinary transfer."

11

"AGAINST THE PEACE AND DIGNITY OF THE STATE"

WHEN THEY WERE SUBPOENAED to testify before the Sabine County Grand Jury in Hemphill, Alton and Johnnie Maxie were more than a little reluctant about returning to the scene of the crime. Being forced to witness the onset of Garner's anguishingly slow death in the small cell had had a profound impact on the brothers. Junior's death had plunged Johnnie Maxie into a dark cocoon. Even in crowds, the larger of the two brothers remained impervious to the conversation around him. And in the six days following Garner's death, his brother, Alton, was wracked by intrusive, distorted nightmares that usually involved jails and white cops. A decent night's sleep had been impossible, and being awake wasn't much better: the mere sight of a Texas license plate—not uncommon just across the state line in Florien—or *any* police officer or patrol car involuntarily seized Alton's mind and delivered him back to the Sabine County Jail on Christmas night.

When Johnnie and Alton Maxie did appear in Hemphill on December 31 to testify before the grand jury, it was in the company of Sheriff James Brumley of Many, Louisiana. The sheriff was widely respected and trusted by both blacks and whites in Sabine Parish, and the Maxies believed his presence was the only way to guarantee their safe passage. Despite the potential for putting him in a politically uncomfortable situation with his counterparts in Texas, Brumley had agreed to escort the Maxies to Texas. With only the three-mile span of bridge over the Sabine River separating their jurisdictions, Sheriff Brumley and Sabine County Sheriff Blan Greer had worked closely for years, and the Louisiana sheriff didn't want to jeopardize that relationship. But the Maxies refused to honor the out-of-state subpoenas unless Sheriff Brumley accompanied them.

New Year's Eve was easily one of the busiest days in all of 1987 at the Sabine County Courthouse. A procession of witnesses, some wearing badges and uniforms, others with their hands cuffed behind their backs, headed silently into the antiquated courthouse to the grand jury. And into the secrecy of the courtroom, they took major surprises.

Even before they laid eyes on Alton and Johnnie Maxie, grand jurors knew each of the Louisianians had given two dramatically different versions of Garner's death. Texas Ranger Roscoe Davis, the first witness to testify, read aloud the statements the Maxies had signed in the Sabine County Jail on December 26.

A portion of Johnnie Maxie's first statement clearly captured the grand jurors' interest when Davis read it: "Loyal Garner was going around Newton County to pick up and deliver some drugs, part or all to Sabine County." Johnnie Maxie's statement also described his friend as "hitting, kicking and yelling" at Chief Ladner and Deputy Hyden. Likewise, Johnnie described the two officers as "acting like gentlemen and [behaving] kindly."

The law-enforcement officers had remained silent in the aftermath of the affair at the jail, refusing to comment in the media. But reporters had been successful in getting the Maxies and Garner's widow, Corrine, to comment. And the media had portrayed Garner and the Maxies as nothing more than three friends who were arrested without cause. There had been nothing in the press about aborted drug deals and certainly nothing about Chief Ladner and Deputy Hyden "acting like gentlemen."

Except for the single sentence that Alton Maxie claimed he had demanded be added before signing his original statement, there was no explanation in either of the brothers' statements of how Garner could have suffered fatal head injuries in the jail. That sentence—"He [Garner] was bleeding because when the two officers opened the door, one of the officers hit him with a slapjack"—was the final sentence in Alton's original statement.

Ranger Davis told grand jurors that he and Sheriff Blan Greer drove to the Sheriff's Department in Many on December 27, the day Garner died, and asked Louisiana authorities to bring in the Maxies so they could be interviewed again.

Privately, the Ranger doubted the original, jail-house statements as soon as he saw them. From a police point of view, they were blatantly self-serving. "We told them [the Maxies] that we felt like we needed to take another statement from them," Davis told the grand jury. "And they agreed."

The second set of statements, given in Sheriff Brumley's office, told a starkly different account from those taken in Hemphill by jailer Preacher Kirk. Ranger Davis also read the Maxies' second affidavits aloud to the grand jury.

"The big officer hit Junior with a slapjack two or three times, and put a choke hold on him with one arm," Alton Maxie's more recent statement read, "and was hitting him and dragging him at the same time. They took him to a room down the hall, and I could hear him howling and pleading with them." Describing Garner after he was returned to the jail cell, Alton said in his second statement: "I looked at Junior and his eyes were open, but it was like he was asleep. There was blood all over his shirt and on the side of his face."

Johnnie, whose original statement mentioned nothing about Garner being beaten, wrote in his Louisiana statement that after they beat Garner with a slapjack in the cell, the officers carried him "to another place up front. . . . You could hear them beating him, and you could hear him, Loyal, moaning and hollering. They brought him back to the cell and he was real bloody and they left him there. He did not moan anymore after that."

The 250 or so pounds that burdened Johnnie's five-foot-ten frame necessitated that he move slowly and deliberately. Yet he walked into the grand jury room erect, with his shoulders tucked back, accentuating the ample belly in front of him. As he turned sideways to wedge himself into the witness chair, his self-consciousness filled the room and his eyes fell immediately to his lap. He testified he could read and write, but clearly the heavyset twenty-eight-year-old black man labored under the questions. Often his responses were jumbled and disjointed. He used pronouns instead of identifying people by names, leaving the grand jury to surmise whom he was talking about. And there was a gravelly softness to his voice that belied his size. Grand jurors found themselves craning forward, studying his lips to understand him.

District Attorney Bill Martin set out to resolve the conflicts in Johnnie's two statements, particularly the damning portion in the first statement that implicated Garner in drug trafficking.

"I'll show you this," Martin said, placing Johnnie's original statement in front of him. "Is that your signature here?"

"Yes," Johnnie replied. "Do you want me to tell you how that got there?"

"Yes."

"I was working with a guy down in Newton County on some drugs," Johnnie testified, referring to a constable to whom he had provided occasional information on illegal activities. "And I called him. I was supposed to tell him that night, you know, and find out whether they was gonna come by my house. And I called him from . . . the jail over there, that night when they let me make a phone call, and explained to him that I wasn't gonna be there. So they took it from that. After that incident happened, Mr. Bill Horton called . . . and he told the jailer what to write," Johnnie said, referring to his first statement. "And after that had happened, you know, I signed it. Because I went along with whatever they did after that happened, with no reason."

In fact, Johnnie in the past had had a quid pro quo arrangement with Constable Holton "Bubba" Johnson of Newton County, occasionally tipping the small-town lawman when he ran across information about burglaries or drugs. Having been arrested before in Newton County for drunk driving, and visiting the county frequently to see his estranged wife and children, Johnnie figured a friend in law enforcement couldn't hurt.

Near midnight on Christmas, after Garner was returned to the cell unconscious, and after Alton had been allowed to call their mother in Louisiana, Johnnie had asked to talk confidentially to Chief Deputy Bill Horton outside the cell. He had promised to call Constable Johnson about a drug suspect, Johnnie told Horton. Could he call Johnson to tell him he was in jail and wouldn't be able to provide the information?

The late-night phone call to Johnson from the jail and Johnnie's ambiguous rambling left the grand jurors obviously confused. "Did you say that you were calling this person in Newton to let them know why you couldn't deliver the drugs?" one juror asked.

"Not *deliver* them. I was *helping* him. He was supposed to be catching a person with some drugs. Now they took and wrote that in there, whatever it says, and told me to sign it."

Johnnie swore to the prosecutor and the grand jurors that he never said Garner was involved in drugs.

"No sir," Johnnie said. "They put that in there."

"Yeah," a grand juror said, "but you signed it, didn't you?"

"Yes sir."

"Was it already typed before you signed it?"

"Yes sir. It was already—"

"But, to your knowledge, he [Garner] was driving all right? He wasn't weaving or something when y'all were coming in?"

"No sir. He didn't weave."

A woman on the grand jury came to Johnnie's rescue. "Were you afraid not to sign that paper?"

"Yes ma'am. Because you can imagine laying there hearing a man dying all night. . . . My brother and Garner, they didn't know I was even working with the Newton Police Department. See, they wasn't even supposed to put that in no report or nothing. But that morning when I signed this, there was another police officer behind me. And they had already called from the Sabine County Hospital and told them what kind of shape he [Garner] was in.

"Then they went to writing out statements. They messed up two or three papers. They balled 'em up and threw 'em away and started all over again. When I talked to Mr. Bill Horton that morning . . . he told me that whatever he put down and stuff, says, 'you go ahead and sign it.' "

Alton Maxie fielded the grand jury's questions with all the confidence his older brother hadn't been able to muster. Chronologically, he led them through the arrest, confirming his brother's testimony about seeing Ladner hit Garner with the blackjack and later hearing Garner's screams from another part of the jail. He also told the grand jury that Ladner tried to cover up the bloody evidence of the beating.

"Later on that night, the big officer came back, and he had some clothes in his hands," Alton testified. "And he asked me to take Loyal's clothes off so he could wash 'em. And I told him I was not gonna take his clothes off. I told him it looked like he needed to go somewhere to get help. And he said, 'Oh, he'll be all right. . . .' Later on that night, I went to sleep, and I guess that's when they came in and washed his clothes. But that next morning, he was still laying there, eyes still open, and his mouth was just dry, and his eyes, all the water that be in your eyes had dried, and they was just wide open."

The younger Maxie told grand jurors that officials told them on the morning of December 26 that their fines would be "from sixty to seventy dollars" each. "Later on that day, they came in and told us that if we had forty-five dollars between us, we could get out," he testified. "And we got out about three-thirty or four o'clock [P.M.]."

"The judge said that?" a grand juror asked.

"Yeah."

"But they already knew how much y'all had?"

"I suppose. I figure they did."

Another grand juror sought clarification about why Alton had signed the first statement in the jail if he knew it was incorrect. "Were you scared not to?"

"Yes."

"Why were you afraid to not sign it?"

"Just from the way they had acted that night before," Alton said. "And just looking at the way he [Garner] was that night when they brought him back. I felt all over him and everything, and he had gashes, and cuts, and knots, and bruises."

"Would you have signed anything?"

"I probably would have."

None of the three officers appeared before the grand jury. Ranger Davis read to grand jurors the typed statements that Ladner, Hyden, and Horton had submitted at his request.

The lawmen's stories meshed generally with what Thomas Ladner had told his lawyer, John Seale. The incident began, the officers said, when Garner attacked Ladner after the chief and Hyden had gone to quiet the three black men in the detox cell. Notwithstanding the attack on the police chief, all three officers said in their statements, Ladner and Horton removed Garner from detox and took him to the processing room at the front of the jail to allow him to make a phone call.

In reading the officers' statements to grand jurors, Davis was careful to spare the grand jury from any cursing. When he reached a point in the statements that contained curse words—all of which were purportedly used by Garner—he merely inserted the word "profanity" in the verbal account.

"Thomas Ladner and James 'Bo' Hyden brought Mr. Garner to the booking room to make a call," Ranger Davis read from Chief Deputy Horton's account. "But he refused. They told him that he was going to have to go back to the cell. Mr. Garner said, 'You (profanity) is not going to take me anywhere.' They—Thomas Ladner and James 'Bo' Hyden—started to get ahold of Mr. Garner and he started fighting. Mr. Garner grabbed Mr. Hyden's [flash]light. Mr. Hyden got him from behind around the arms, and I, Bill Horton, got the flashlight. Then he slung Bo Hyden against the filing cabinets. They grabbed him again, and he whirled around and fell against the door. We got him up and carried him back to his cell."

At the end of Davis's testimony, a member of the grand jury asked if the panel could hear from Horton.

"Yes, if Mr. Horton wants to talk to us, he can," said District Attorney Martin. "You understand you can't just talk to a defendant?"

"Well," the juror replied, "I just didn't realize that there was any criminal implication toward him at this time."

"It doesn't appear to me to be any," the prosecutor said, exercising his prerogative. "But you have heard the testimony, in writing at least, that he was present in the ready room. . . ."

As New Year's Eve progressed, the grand jury heard from a succession of witnesses, including five inmates, all white, who verified a loud exchange between at least one black prisoner in detox and officers. All testified they heard what sounded to them like blows being delivered.

But no witness was more outspoken or cooperative than Angus Bozeman, the spunky, red-haired nineteen-year-old burglar who had been incarcerated in the cell next to detox on Christmas night. A concrete block wall separated the cells, but Bozeman testified he recognized the voices of Ladner and Hyden next door. The person administering the blows, Bozeman swore to the grand jury, had been Ladner.

"And when he opened detox, all I heard was *boom, boom, boom!* And he said, 'Get up off the floor, boy.' He hollered real loud. He said, 'Get up off the floor, boy!' And he reached down there and grabbed him, I guess. You know, I just heard it. I can't say for sure that's what he did.

"I heard two hits, and it wasn't with his fist. He got him out in the hall, and then I heard a light or a key chain or something fall. And they was rustling around in the hall. And so I heard a couple of more hits, and then Bo Hyden said, 'See there, boy. It don't take four or five of us.' And then they drug him down the hall, and he didn't never say another word, and you never heard another rustling out of him, you know."

Bozeman had refused on December 26 to give a statement to Ranger Davis. A grand juror wanted to know why.

"Because," Bozeman said, "I hadn't seen 'em, but I've heard people over there since I been over there get done the same way. Every weekend when somebody gets picked up for drinking—a person naturally, when he's drinking, he's going to start talking and running his head. And a police officer is supposed to be able to take care of it without trying to hit him or something like that. But they don't. They'd be slapping them around and stuff.

"So, I figured, well, I don't know if the Texas Ranger is in with them. Because, you know, all along I don't know if all the officers are in it, but I know a few that's in together."

"Has anyone ever hit you or hurt you over there?" Martin asked.

"Yeah, when I was a juvenile. I didn't say nothing about it because I figured, you know, they said that once I got an adult, my juvenile record didn't matter. So I figured, you know, he didn't *hit* me. Bill Horton slapped me, and pulled my hair, and called me a punk and all this. But I didn't say nothing."

A grand juror interrupted the prosecutor's questioning. "Every weekend there's slapping around in the jail?"

"Oh, yeah. If they pick up somebody drinking, they're gonna beat 'em up. I mean, not beat 'im up literally, but they gonna slap 'em or knock 'em around, and then that's just gonna make matters worse. Then when they get back there shaking that door, which they're gonna do if you get slapped around, they go back in there and slap 'em around some more."

Bozeman told grand jurors that he was moved to a one-man cell in another part of the jail after he refused to give a statement to Ranger Davis on December 26.

"What do you think is gonna happen to you when you get back [to the jail]?" a juror asked.

"I don't know," Bozeman said. "I been wondering that since the night they moved me out because I didn't write no statement on it. They moved me out and put me in a cell. And then when I went to raising cain on the door, [Deputy] Billy Don [Sparks] come back there. . . . I said that if they didn't something get done about this—if they don't start investigating this—I'm gonna call, I'm gonna get my mom to call some paper or something, and get them up here where I can talk to them.

"And when I said that, he said, 'Well, you fight us and you see who wins.' So I didn't say nothing else."

Testifying against Ladner, Horton, and Hyden was a calculated gamble for Bozeman and the other inmate-witnesses. The scrutiny of the lawmen by the grand jury, the Ranger, and FBI agents, they hoped, would provide an insurance policy against retaliation. Surely the cops knew they were being watched.

Ostensibly, Mary Russell, the sixty-year-old dispatcher on duty in the Sabine County Jail, was uniquely positioned to have observed whatever happened to Garner in the waning hours of Christmas. It was Russell who reportedly noticed on her console the red warning light that indicated the door to detox was being hit hard enough to pose a security violation, a fact she dutifully had reported to Chief Deputy Horton. She was stationed in an office equipped with an intercom that linked her to the detox cell, and her glass door faced the booking room where three officers claimed Garner attacked them.

But Russell saw no evil, heard no evil, and, at least in her testimony to the grand jury, spoke no evil. In her brief appearance before the grand jury, the dispatcher swore sixteen times that she didn't see or hear crucial events. She had turned off her intercom, she testified, and shut her door, and because she was seated in a chair, she couldn't see over the metal part of the door through the glass pane into the booking room across the hall. Furthermore, Russell swore, she hadn't discussed the incident with any of the officers in the six days since Garner had been killed.

"Could you see anything from where you were?" Martin asked.

"No sir."

"Could you hear anything?"

"No sir."

"Did they have any trouble there in that office?"

"I didn't see no trouble, no sir."

"Could you see from where you were?"

"No sir."

"Could you hear anything going on?"

"No sir."

"Did you, when you examined the cells, did you observe blood or anything on the deceased, this fellow Garner?"

"No sir."

On and on, until a grand juror asked if the officers had offered Garner or the Maxies Breathalyzer tests.

"They refused it anyway," Russell replied.

"Do they sign something when they refuse it?"

"Yes sir, I believe they do."

"How do you know they refused it?"

"Well . . ."

"You said you weren't in the booking room."

"I wasn't," the dispatcher responded. "But the door wasn't closed then, when they first brought them in. I closed the door after."

Sheriff Blan Greer had barely settled into the witness chair when a member of the grand jury chided him about Mary Russell, his dispatcher.

"She can't hear, Sheriff," the grand juror said in mock seriousness. "You need to carry her to a doctor."

"I understood she heard enough to get in and lock the door," the sheriff said. Having made his point, he acknowledged the good-natured jab, adding, "Do you think I better get some hearing aids?"

"Absolutely."

The collegial give-and-take established a tenor for the aging sheriff's testimony, which he personalized by calling prosecutors and grand jurors by their first names. Indeed, Sheriff Greer almost immediately voluntarily interjected a statement that solidified his status as an investigator trying to get at the truth rather than an elected official called in to account for the actions of his officers in his jail. "As a matter of fact, Bill, let me say this," said the sheriff, calling the prosecutor by his first name. "It might help a little bit.

"When I came in and found this on Saturday morning—this is the first thing of this nature that has ever happened since I've been here. We all have our first experience. And naturally there was nothing for me to do but begin the investigation. And I started to work on it a little. Then I thought to myself, 'This is not the proper way for me to do it. I need to call the Ranger in here so everybody can, you know, understand and not feel like I'm trying to sit on some evidence or something like that.' I wanted it to be open, and I wanted everybody to know exactly what the investigation was."

From that point, questions from prosecutor and grand jurors alike were directed with deference to Sheriff Greer as an expert of sorts on proper police procedure. At times, the sheriff's answers reflected an almost third-person detachment from the fatal events that occurred in his jail. While he was careful not to say anything blatantly perjorative about his deputies or the city's police chief, the sheriff at times was obliquely critical, particularly of Billy Ray Horton, his chief deputy.

"Let me ask you this," said Martin. "Do you think there was excessive force used, or can you give that kind of an opinion on what little you know about it?"

"Well, it appears that it was, Bill. I don't know. I haven't talked to the doctors."

Implying that the officers shouldn't have removed a belligerent Garner from the cell to offer him a telephone call, Sheriff Greer said: "He would have to stay right there until he gets to where you can take him to a phone. If he's in a fighting condition, he's not going to do much phone calling when you carry him out."

"Mr. Blan," asked a grand juror, "is this the first time this has ever occurred, to your knowledge, with Thomas?"

"This is the first time that this has occurred here with *anybody* that I know of."

"I mean, not just specifically in the jail?"

"Well, I'd just have to check back. I know that nobody has worked over a period of years and not had some kind of a round or scuffle, whether it'd be Thomas or be me or whoever. You're gonna run into some problems. It's not gonna all go smooth. If you're doing your job, that's going to happen."

A grand juror steered the questioning back to the officers on duty Christmas night. "Sheriff, in your opinion, in the past has Thomas made a good law officer for the city?"

"Yes, Thomas has done lots of work for the city."

"Is Mr. Hyden making you a good hand?"

"Yes, Mr. Hyden was doing a good job. He sure was. He was a young officer and hadn't been here all that long."

"Mr. Greer, exactly what was Mr. Horton's implication in this, other than his presence?"

"Well, to look at it from a different angle there, I don't know what to say. Other than, if you're talking for me, for my part, one of the things that I felt like that Mr. Horton, being chief deputy, he should have checked this patient a little closer. Or seen that I was called or something. You know, I just felt like he shouldn't have gone home and not called me. I felt like I was entitled to know."

"Are you saying now that Bill probably knew that the guy was hurt pretty bad?"

"I'm not saying he knew it," the sheriff quickly corrected. "I'm not saying that either of them realized how bad he was. But, you know, I just felt like he should have been checked a little bit closer."

The answer didn't satisfy the grand juror, who refused to abandon his questioning of Horton's involvement. "Evidently he felt something," the grand juror said, "because he called the jailer early the next morning and told him to check on him. So Bill was concerned about him. He wouldn't normally do that, would he?"

"No, not enough to call me, you see."

The grand juror never got the sheriff to acknowledge the obvious: that Horton had to have feared *something* was wrong with Garner to have called the jail the next morning. He tried a new line of questions on the sheriff. "Did you see blood back there in the cell?"

"A little," the sheriff said. "But very little. Not much blood. There was a little blood there, if I remember correctly."

Increasingly, Chief Deputy Horton's culpability was beginning to unfold in the grand jury room, particularly after a series of questions about the purported battle over the flashlight in the booking room. "Don't you think," asked a juror, "that Bill, being chief deputy, he could have stopped all that?"

"Well, that's the part I was disappointed in," the sheriff replied. "I felt like he should."

"He was taking your job," said the juror of Horton's being in charge in the sheriff's absence. "I believe if you were there you could have stopped it."

Modestly, the sheriff didn't acknowledge the vote of confidence.

At least one grand juror appeared skeptical after hearing the voluntary statements from Chief Ladner, Chief Deputy Horton, and Deputy Hyden. "Sheriff, do you think that these three fellows coordinated their testimony and statements prior to them being taken? They all seem close in every detail—what is included and what is not included. It kind of struck me as, you know, this is either all truth, or they all saw everything just alike, or—"

Sheriff Greer's answer cut off the question before the grand juror could add the other, more ominous alternative. "I personally think they all told it as near they could, you know. You can get in a fight out here with somebody, in a big fight and goings-on, you cannot tell exactly what happened. You can do your best. But you cannot tell just exactly."

Again, the sheriff seized the opportunity to state his opinion for the record. "Of course, you know, naturally I hate it. I work with all three of the boys here. It put me in a bind. But there again, I'm just like you people. I was sworn and put under oath that I would uphold the law to the best of my ability."

John Seale would have shuddered had he heard the final minutes of the secret grand jury's questioning of Sheriff Greer. The lawyer's instinctive fears about the "fishbowl effect" of media scrutiny on the grand jury were becoming reality. The grand jury was talking about public perceptions of a cover-up. "Well," said one member, "they [the public] would have said it was a cover-up job if you didn't get outside help."

"Yes, that's exactly why I called the Ranger on in," the sheriff said.

"I think you did exactly the right thing," the grand juror said. "It's a very unfortunate thing. I don't think you'll find anybody anywhere that wouldn't agree to that. But I appreciate the job that all your department, as well as the city department, has done in past years."

When Dr. Grover Winslow appeared before the grand jury, he brought with him more than his medical expertise. He had treated virtually every member of the jury and their families, and he had answered medical emergencies at the jail for longer than some of the grand jury members had been alive. But he also occupied a special niche that doctors in small towns enjoy. Not only was he perhaps the best-educated resident of Hemphill, he also was among the most socially prominent. His opinion was trusted and valued.

Just as he was with his patients, Dr. Winslow was direct and unpretentious in his appearance before the grand jury. He spared the grand jury the twenty-five-cent medical terminology, crediting on four occasions "the good Lord" with designing various attributes of the human body. "And the good Lord has protected it very well," Dr. Winslow said of the brain, "but we can get some very freakish accidents that will end it."

Dr. Winslow was folksy as he described how seemingly innocuous, freakish accidents had led to brain injuries that killed people they all knew, like the doctor's wife in nearby Kirbyville, the man who fell from a porch swing, and the youngster who had fallen from a pickup truck. The Kirbyville doctor's wife, he said, had merely bumped her head on the dash of the car.

"Two weeks later she was dead of a subdural [hemorrhage]," Dr. Winslow said. "That was the only injury she had, and it didn't knock her out or didn't give her any problem whatsoever.

"Ordinarily you think that one has to have a lick," the doctor said, "but, it doesn't require much lick at times."

"Licks to the head" occupied much of the grand jury's time with the doctor, who on occasion corrected himself in his usage of "lick" and its implication of force, substituting "laceration," a neutral noun that denoted consequence rather than means. Winslow said he found only one laceration, on the back of Garner's head, about an inch or an inch and a half long, with jagged edges. His assessment of the wound was compatible with the officers' account of Garner falling into the wall. "This would come from falling, blunt butting. In other words, one of you back off and run into this wall with your head, or one of you sit there and go to sleep today and fall off on here," Dr. Winslow said, pointing to the floor, "you're gonna have a jagged area. Kind of like you dropped a watermelon."

"Would that have killed this man?" a grand juror wanted to know. "Could that lick have done that?"

"I really didn't attribute it too much to that, because I've seen so many licks—I mean, not licks but lacerations—to the head that were so minor. If you had looked at this thing, you would have called it a minor injury." The major damage, the doctor pointed out, was a blood clot on the left side of the brain.

"I'm gonna say this," Dr. Winslow said. "I have seen a lot of licks to the head, and this—I mean, a lot of places on the head that I have sutured—and this required only about four or five or six stitches. And really this, on the surface, had an appearance of a minor wound to the head."

Garner's condition, of course, was far different from the doctor's examples of patients who initially showed no serious symptoms. The prisoner was in a state of unconsciousness when he was admitted to the emergency room at Sabine County Hospital. Dr. Winslow's account was a chronology of a frenzied few hours that only postponed the inevitable.

"I think from all practical purposes, the guy was as good as dead, probably brain dead practically, when we had him in the emergency room upon admission," Dr. Winslow said.

"If this patient had been brought to you immediately after the incident happened," a grand juror asked, "say, eight or ten hours earlier, what would his chances of survival have been?"

"Any subdural, if it is detected and diagnosed, you've got a much better chance of survival."

A grand juror asked if Garner's bloody clothes shouldn't have been a "warning signal" to the officers.

"In the past," Dr. Winslow said, "I can never recall the patient that I thought needed attention that I wasn't called. This time, I do question it. I'll be honest with you. I do question it."

But the doctor quickly tempered his remarks. "On the other hand, you've got to look at it in another way. If you had walked into the emergency room, either one of you, and saw this patient laying there on the stretcher . . . you would have said he was asleep. And that's all you would have said. You wouldn't have called the nurses or anything else. Because that's the way he looked. But we found when we began to check him, we found the things I have described. We didn't find those things from just casually staring as I'm looking at you.

"So I can see where, if I wanted to be critical, it'd be very easy to be critical of the care or something. But also I've got to realize that our findings came from people that are trained to look for these things, and not people that are not trained."

Dr. Winslow also volunteered two pieces of information that in a vacuum, without the perspective and comparison afforded by other testimony and evidence, had to have appeared highly credible and enlightening to the townspeople who sat on the grand jury. Early in his testimony, as he recounted Garner's vital signs and condition when he first was brought into the emergency room, Dr. Winslow noted that a drug screen from Garner's blood had failed to detect any drugs in the patient's system. Garner's blood alcohol content, however, "was up to .075," the doctor testified, near the .10 level that qualifies under Texas law as intoxication for legal purposes.

"How much, now, was that?" a juror asked.

"Well, if you put [it] in mathematical figures," Dr. Winslow said, "this would be, at eight-twenty A.M. on 12-26-'87, he's three-quarters drunk."

The doctor based his findings, he said, on a blood test done locally at Sabine County Hospital. The results conflicted dramatically not only with the Maxies' account of the amount Garner had drunk before his arrest but with the findings of another blood test, which the grand jury would never see.

The second, more sophisticated test of Garner's blood—drawn at precisely the same time as the local test—had been conducted by an independent laboratory in Beaumont, which routinely contracted with the Hemphill hospital and other rural hospitals throughout East Texas to conduct tests too intricate for them to manage on their own. As a diagnostic tool, a sample of Garner's blood had been sent to the Beaumont lab for analysis of blood gases. In addition, the lab routinely had tested the sample for alcohol. There was no trace of alcohol.

It would take investigators months, however, to learn of the existence of the second lab test, the results of which hadn't been available by the time the grand jury was convened. And once completed, results of the independent analysis were either disseminated only in tight, controlled circles, overlooked, or concealed from investigators.

Acknowledging to the grand jury that an autopsy was the surest way of determining the type of injury that killed Garner, Dr. Winslow testified that it was he who had helped preserve the pathological evidence contained in Garner's lifeless body. "That was one of the things that I was very insistent on, an autopsy," Dr. Winslow said. "In fact, I don't know whether . . . We had a report that they were about to release the body to the family. The funeral home, I understood, had already been called and all. And I got hold of the sheriff and all, and I said, 'Under no way should the body be released until you find out totally on these types of things.'"

On New Year's Eve, as Dr. Winslow testified before the grand jury, Justice of the Peace Bill Beaird was planning an inquest in Tyler to determine the legal cause of Garner's death. The Sabine County Grand Jury did not subpoena Judge Beaird as a witness in Hemphill, apparently because he had not yet conducted his inquest and therefore presumably had no facts to offer the grand jury. Had he been called to appear, Beaird undoubtedly would have related the events of only four days earlier in which Sabine County Judge Royce Smith had tried to convince him to release Garner's body *before* an autopsy could be performed. Dr. Winslow did not volunteer—nor did the grand jury know to ask—that he in fact had been in the office when Judge Smith had called Tyler twice to get Garner's body released.

Much later, during another legal proceeding, Dr. Winslow would explain that he had planned to have a private pathologist in Lufkin autopsy Garner's body after it was released from the Tyler hospital. The private pathologist, Dr. Winslow said, previously had performed autopsies for Sabine County.

As he lay unconscious in the Sabine County Jail, the pressure on Loyal Garner, Jr.'s brain intensified by the minute. Just as striking a tethered ball with a fist knocks the opposite side of the ball into a wall, a brutal blow to the right side of Garner's head created a contrecoup hemorrhage in the left side of his brain. The bridging blood vessels between the brain and its covering, the dura mater, had ruptured. The traumatized brain swelled until there was no space left in the skull. Taking the path of least resistance, Garner's brain gradually expanded like a balloon through a keyhole, through the base of his skull and into the spinal column, choking blood vessels and nerves until the brain's functions shut down.

There was no doubt, Dr. Virgil V. Gonzalez told the grand jury, that Garner had died of blows, or "licks" in East Texas parlance, to his head.

Dr. Gonzalez, a forensics pathologist from Tyler who had conducted more than six thousand autopsies in his three-decade career, performed the postmortem on Garner at Judge Beaird's request. Dr. Gonzalez conducted the autopsy at Medical Center Hospital the day following Garner's death, and he discovered "at least two" substantial traumas to the victim's head.

"The blow on the left side, he was still conscious," the Filipino-American pathologist told grand jurors. "He would probably be able to walk. He may be woozy, but not to the extent that he could not stand.

"The one on the right side is the one that knocked him out."

"Was there any mark on the exterior part of the head to indicate any kind of blow having struck him on the right side?" Bill Martin asked.

"No sir. This is one thing, there are no bruises, no contusions whatsoever. And to postulate what kind of weapon was used in this, it must be a soft, smooth object. A fist can do this. A rounded stick can be used. Like a nightstick, hard rubber, rubber stick—you can use this, because these notoriously will not produce any contusion, will not produce any bruises whatsoever externally. But the force is enough, strong enough, to do some damage, and jarring of the brain tissue."

"Could you assume from what you saw," a grand juror wanted to know, "that this was by force rather than by a fall?"

"Yes, ma'am. This is a force rather than a fall. . . . The force to produce the hemorrhage in the brain, the subdural hemorrhage, and to produce the contusion on several places of the brain would indicate that this is a forced injury rather than a fall."

Martin was an experienced prosecutor, and now he sought to tidy up the loose ends from previous witnesses' statements and testimony. "Would what is commonly called a 'slapstick' produce this kind of injury," Martin asked, "and not leave a damage to the outside, on the skin or flesh?"

"Yes sir," Dr. Gonzalez said. "That is very common. I've seen so many cases like that without producing any injury whatsoever to the skin or flesh. Because the object is soft, and that the force is propagated from the head toward the skull into the brain tissue."

Shortly before Dr. Gonzalez was dismissed, a grand juror asked him if Garner had been drinking, the offense for which officers claimed to have arrested him.

"I didn't do any alcohol level because it was too late," the pathologist said. "I didn't do any drug screen because there is no urine. And this is where you get accurate results.

"Alcohol, if you drink one can of beer, within an hour it is all consumed."

The chaotic few minutes in Sabine County Jail during which Garner suffered mortal injuries—however they occurred—appeared sterile and detached when the grand jury reduced them to words on paper. The stilted legalistic wording was straight out of Texas's civil rights statutes.

Thomas Ladner, Bill Horton, and James "Bo" Hyden, the grand jury found, each acting "as a peace officer," did "intentionally subject Loyal Garner Jr., a person in custody, to bodily injury . . . by hitting Loyal Garner Jr. on his head and body with a slapstick and fists and causing Loyal Garner Jr. to fall and strike his head against a wall and door." Further, the grand jury alleged, each of the officers denied Garner "access to reasonable and necessary medical attention after the said Loyal Garner Jr. was injured while in custody."

After each of the two counts, the grand jury added the following phrase: "knowing his conduct was unlawful, and the death of Loyal Garner Jr. occurred therefrom."

The indictments on January 5, 1988, marked the first time in the 151 years of Sabine County that its citizens elected to hold a lawman accountable for brutality in the performance of his job. That the three white officers faced potential life prison sentences under Texas civil rights statutes for beating a black man to death made news in *The New York Times* and on CNN.

"The death of Mr. Garner," wrote Peter Applebome in the *Times* a day later, "has shaken the towns [of] Hemphill and nearby Florien and presented an unsettling glimpse of life and justice in the isolated backwoods of East Texas, where questions of race usually fester below the surface rather than becoming public issues."

Indeed, the news shook and splintered Sabine County like a diesel Caterpillar in a pine thicket.

12

LOYAL

THE OLD BLACK GENTLEMAN wore denim overalls and obvious pain. He was tall and tough to be in his seventies; but in the earliest moments of this January dawn, before the sun would temper the damp and cold, he labored under the weight of a simple shovel and pickax. He left his old pickup truck beside the decrepit frame church on the outskirts of Florien and headed reluctantly across the rutted, one-lane road. When he had walked halfway into the Old Pilgrim Star Cemetery and laid his tools onto the wet grass, the accumulation of mud on the soles of his work boots only added to his burden.

He knew he would have help later, but he intentionally had come early. The Lord told him to. He looked beyond the gravestones to the pines that encircled the tiny country cemetery.

"Loyal," he said in a coarse whisper. "And he *was*, too."

Tears running down his cheeks, Loyal Garner, Sr., turned to the task of digging the muddy hole where his oldest son would rest.

At fifteen, Corrine Holden knew she was too young and too inexperienced to know for sure if love at first sight really existed beyond the movies. Likewise, her teenager's inherent fear of chiding and embarrassment kept her from even broaching the subject with her older sisters. Still, Corrine knew, there was something, well, special about the muscular young man who walked into her sister's restaurant in Many that sultry afternoon in 1971.

He'd noticed her, too, she was sure of that. Out of the corner of her eye, she had caught him staring at her as she carried the plates of home-cooked food to the tables in the tiny cafe. She didn't want to deceive herself, but she was almost certain the look on his face was one of interest. The attention made her self-conscious, and she prayed she didn't do anything that would make her look dumb, like dropping a plate of spare ribs or dumping a glass of tea on the floor.

The stranger, Corrine learned during his increasingly frequent visits to the small cafe, was Loyal Garner, Jr., known simply as Junior to distinguish him from his namesake father. Despite being nearly three years older than Corrine, Junior was quiet and shy, which he modestly attributed to being "a country boy." He lived ten miles to the south, just outside Florien, where he worked in the Boise-Cascade plywood mill.

Junior stood a smidgen over five-foot-nine and carried 155 pounds, packed tight like wet sand in a towsack. There was an efficiency about Junior, who, near as Corrine could tell, didn't have an ounce of fat on his muscularly compact frame; and that efficiency, she discovered, carried over to his conversation. When Junior spoke, it was to say something important, not merely to hear himself talk, like some of the boys who'd tried to impress her before. It was an inherited trait, Corrine discovered after meeting Junior's father. And if the younger Garner appeared serious beyond his years, the phenomenon wasn't that hard to figure.

His parents, Loyal and Sarah Garner, presided over a brood of fifteen children—eleven sons and four daughters. As the oldest child, Junior had grown up at his father's side, helping however he could to scratch out a living. From the time he was big enough to pick up a four-foot length of log, Junior was in the thickets with his dad, loading the pulpwood onto the crippled old bobtail Ford for the trip to the mill. Before he was ten, the only way Junior could move the logs was by "pissanting" them, balancing the logs upright on end, hugging them like big bears, then half-carrying, half-dragging them between his legs to the truck, where his father helped him load them.

Pulpwood paydays were never big enough, and the frequent western Louisiana rain made them few and far between. When the rain turned the red dirt log roads into swatches of impassable mud, Junior had helped his father scrounge up scrap iron, which they sold by the pound to junkyards. In good years—and Loyal Sr. would acknowledge much later there weren't that many—the family of seventeen lived on less than five thousand dollars a year, but "nobody went hungry."

Junior was a product of his environment, and if he ever resented his key responsibility in the hand-to-mouth existence of the Garner family, he never acknowledged it to his family, his friends, or even Corrine. The way his mother saw it, the good Lord had compensated when He made Junior, the same way He had when He gave birds the instinct and resourcefulness to build nests out of nature's discards. "Junior could make do with anything," Sarah Garner would say. "There wasn't anything Junior couldn't fix, build, or grow. He was the best at working with his hands that I ever saw. He was always looking for something better."

At fourteen, Junior was entrusted with the family's tractor, a rusted relic with which he plowed rows straighter than even his father could. The garden, flush with okra, potatoes, greens, tomatoes, black-eyed peas, cabbage, and squash, was as critical to the family's existence as the few thousand dollars a year Junior and his dad earned hauling pulpwood and scrap iron. In the summer, the Garners ate the vegetables fresh from the garden, canning the calculated surplus to get them through the cold months. And always there was a hog or two, maybe a cow, to put at least some meat on the table.

Junior's handiwork was apparent even in the cramped Garner house, which, his mother acknowledged, originally had resembled a shed more than a home for a succession of fifteen children. Periodically, Junior would appear with two-by-fours, linoleum, some carpeting scraps, or a few sheets of paneling stuck in the back of the family pickup. The results of his carpentry weren't always immediately obvious—he never had enough materials at one time to finish a job—but over time, the enterprising teenager transformed the austere structure into a livable, albeit simple, home. Junior even bartered for ceiling fans, which he installed in the living room and bedrooms. The fans, from Sarah Garner's perspective, were the only luxuries in the family's life. They were reprieves from the 100-degrees-plus temperatures that made lighting up the cook stove sheer torture in the summer.

Loyal Sr. had been stunned the first time his oldest son had repaired the decrepit old pulpwood truck. In fact, had Junior asked beforehand, his father would have told him to leave the old truck alone out of fear of aggravating its recurring ailments. Junior had been careful removing the mechanical parts from the engine, placing them on the ground in exactly the order in which he had extracted them. Sitting on the ground, the teenager patiently had reconstructed the pieces, ultimately isolating the

Corrine and Loyal Garner, Jr., approximately 1985

The Garner family, 1989
(Southern Poverty Law Center)

Loyal Garner, Jr., 1974

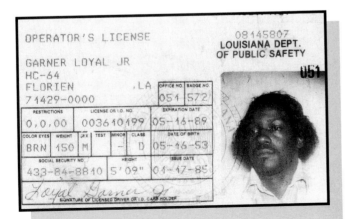

OPERATOR'S LICENSE

08145807
**LOUISIANA DEPT.
OF PUBLIC SAFETY**

GARNER LOYAL JR
HC-64
FLORIEN   ,LA
71429-0000

U51

| | OFFICE NO. | BADGE NO. |
| | 051 | 572 |

| RESTRICTIONS | LICENSE OR I.D. NO. | EXPIRATION DATE |
| 0,0,00 | 003610199 | 05-16-89 |

| COLOR EYES | WEIGHT | SEX | TEST | MINOR | CLASS | DATE OF BIRTH |
| BRN | 150 | M | | — | D | 05-16-53 |

| SOCIAL SECURITY NO. | HEIGHT | ISSUE DATE |
| 433-84-8810 | 5'09" | 01-17-85 |

Loyal Garner Jr
SIGNATURE OF LICENSED DRIVER OR I.D. CARD HOLDER

The defendants:

Thomas Ladner, former Hemphill police chief

Billy Ray Horton, former Sabine County sheriff's deputy

James "Bo" Hyden, former Sabine County sheriff's deputy
(Photographs by Lee Baker)

Special prosecutor John Hannah, Jr. In the rear is a television satellite truck parked outside the Sabine County Courthouse. *(Lufkin Daily News)*

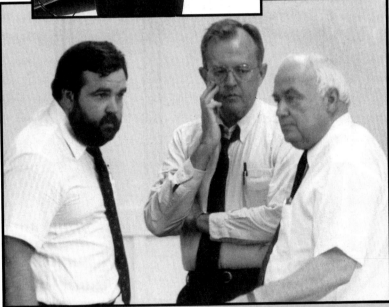

Left to right: Defense attorneys Paul Buchanan, Floyd Addington, and John Seale discuss strategy during a recess in the civil rights trial. *(Lufkin Daily News)*

Thomas Ladner leaving the Sabine County Courthouse with one of his sisters during a recess in the civil rights trial *(Lufkin Daily News)*

The Loyal Garner, Jr., legal team from the Southern Poverty Law Center: (left to right) Morris Dees, Joe Roy, Danny Welch, Pat Clark, Richard Cohen *(Southern Poverty Law Center)*

A sheriff's deputy escorts members of the jury from the Sabine County Courthouse. *(Lufkin Daily News)*

Sheriff Blan Greer (wearing the cowboy hat), Sabine County's chief law-enforcement officer, with Judge O'Neal Bacon taking a break for lunch during the civil rights trial *(Lufkin Daily News)*

Corrine Garner talking with reporters after a Sabine
County jury acquitted three police officers of killing her
husband (Lufkin Daily News)

Smith County District Attorney Jack Skeen talking with reporters after the murder convictions of the three lawmen, Tyler, Texas, 1990

(Photograph by Lee Baker)

faulty part. The proprietor of a junkyard confirmed Junior's findings and traded him a used part that worked. The teenager's success gave him the self-confidence he needed, and he never again was bashful about tearing into machines he didn't yet fully understand.

His oldest son, Loyal Sr. would say with pride, was a "piddler." "Didn't make any difference to him," the old man would say, "Junior could fix just about anything. He had a mind for it, and he picked it up on his own. Lord knows, he didn't learn it from his daddy."

Junior's influence on the family ran deeper than his ability to haul logs and scrap iron and to make repairs on the truck and the house. His ten younger brothers knew him as a strict disciplinarian who, as one recounted, "would get in your face and talk bad to you" if he sensed they weren't carrying their load or treating their mother and father with the appropriate respect.

At sixteen, after his sophomore year, Junior dropped out of the all-black Sabine High School. Making a living, he determined, was eminently more important than finishing his education.

By the time he met Corrine Holden on that rainy, stifling summer afternoon in 1971, Junior Garner had worked nearly two years at the lumber mill in Florien. In the interim, he had managed to take in a welding class at night, which he hoped one day would pay dividends.

Corrine and Junior dated for two years. Almost from the day they met, Corrine realized that the unusually quiet Junior Garner had the commitment and maturity to make a good husband and—someday, she hoped—a father. On August 18, 1973, exactly one week short of her seventeenth birthday, Corrine and Junior, barely twenty, were married.

At the wedding, a girlfriend hugged Corrine and giggled. "I hope you love children, girl, 'cause you're going to have a lot of 'em." Junior wasn't the only one from a huge family; Corrine had five sisters and six brothers.

Eleven months later, Junior and Corrine's first child, Carmica LaShun, arrived. Every two years afterward, almost like clockwork, another child was born—Kimberly Renee, Valerie Denise, Loyal Lynndell, Marlon Cartrell and Corey LaVance—until there were six.

The young couple's first seven years were spent in a secondhand prefabricated home Junior had moved onto the two-and-a-half-acre plot of land next to his parents' house. Loyal Lynndell, the fourth child, had stretched the limits of the small house, leading Corrine to a quiet but firm campaign for an expandable, double-wide mobile home. Her lobbying had to be persistent, she knew, because the quiet-spoken Junior seldom acknowledged he'd even heard her. Finally, one day, she knew she'd gotten through to her husband. "Tell you what," Junior had said patiently. "When I get this place fixed up, you'll change your mind. But if it doesn't look right, we'll get you a mobile home."

As he had years earlier with his parents' home, Junior set out "piddling." Over time, he added on to accommodate his growing family, refinished the inside, put down carpet, and even added an air conditioner. He found rough, unfinished cedar and nailed it onto the outside, adding a rustic look to the old prefab house on cement blocks. The surrounding community adjacent to the unpaved road on which they lived was destitute, but the younger Garner's place stood out as the best in the area. As he told his mother, he'd made the place "presentable," and even Corrine had to admit her remodeled house looked better than a new mobile home.

With Junior living next door, it seemed to Loyal Sr. and Sarah that their oldest child never really left home. On Sundays, Junior frequently barbecued in the yard, not only to give Corrine a day off from the kitchen but because he obviously enjoyed it. Chicken, venison, beef, hot links, it didn't matter; and he always put enough on the grill for his parents.

The proximity of the two families also led to good-natured competition between Junior and his mother. Mrs. Sarah was intensely proud of her garden, and she was known for her ability to coax huge and plentiful vegetables from the tough red clay. One day she gave her son a runner off her potato vine, which he dutifully planted in his backyard. When harvest time came, not only did Junior have more potatoes than his mother, but everyone swore they tasted better—a development that triggered mock indignation from his mother.

Florien was a begrudging benefactor to the Garners and the couple of thousand others who called it home. It was a timber town, its residents and economy sustained almost solely by the miles and miles of pines that surrounded it. Over the years, Junior had watched friend after friend abandon his home for the lure of better-paying jobs in the refineries, paper mills, and assembly lines of Lake Charles, Beaumont, and Shreveport.

Decent wages were tempting, no question, but Junior opted to stay in the pine thickets and red clay where he'd grown up. Florien had been good enough for three generations of Garners, and, the younger Garner reasoned, it'd be good enough to raise a new generation. Corrine had known even before their marriage that Junior attached a high premium to family and what he called "place." He acknowledged that his surroundings were tough, but he took curious comfort in their predictability. He'd eked out a living there since he was a kid and had the confidence to do it as an adult. All a man had to do, Junior would say, was stay busy.

In 1983, after he and Corrine had been married ten years, Junior quit the lumber mill for a job with the Sabine Parish road crew. He'd signed on as a dump truck driver, but Gordon Anthony, his supervisor, had spotted his talents early on. Soon Junior was operating heavy machinery and making minor repairs on the equipment. He earned less than five dollars an hour, but he enjoyed working outdoors and tinkering with the machinery. His gross income for 1984 was $7,957.12—probably more than his father had ever earned, and it didn't have to be spread among nearly as many mouths.

As he always had, Junior tried to be self-sufficient. He chopped wood in the thickets, and in addition to cultivating his garden, he hunted squirrels, rabbits, and deer. Nor was it uncommon for him to drag in a mess of catfish or bass. He also moonlighted at nights and on weekends, fixing friends' cars and trucks or welding pipe and trailers.

"He'd work till it was so dark that he couldn't see anymore, then he'd come in," Corrine recalled. "He'd stay up until one in the morning piddlin' around, knowing he had to get up at five. I'd tell him all the time, 'I don't know where you get all this energy.' "

By 1985, Garner had increased his gross income by almost 50 percent, to $11,632.50—an extraordinary feat in the unyielding West Louisiana economy. Still, there were some things a man couldn't raise, hunt, or improvise for his family, like clothes, and a secondhand car for Corrine to drive to her part-time job as a cook at the small restaurant in Florien.

While some blacks in Sabine Parish grumbled about the restrictive white bankers and their traditional reluctance to loan money to blacks, the officers at Peoples State Bank in Many considered Junior Garner a good risk when he came in in January 1986 and applied for a loan. The bank took out a lien on his house and land and gave him $10,000.

"Anybody who knew Junior Garner knew he was a worker," said John R. Manasco, the proprietor of John's Country Store in Florien. "About the only time I ever saw Junior around was when it was too wet to be working."

John's Country Store isn't the only convenience store in Florien, but the huge log building with the unpaved and pockmarked driveway clearly adds diversity to the word "convenience." Customers can fill up their pickups at the Phillips 66 pumps out front; inside, they can have their deer rifle rebarrelled, buy chicken feed or rat poison, get a thermostat for their radiator, pick out a fishing lure, or order the best hamburger in the parish. And, God forbid, should any of the customers at John's suffer a heart attack in the process, an ambulance awaits beside the building. That's because Manasco, the bearded entrepreneur with the ever-present gimme cap, doubles as Sabine Parish's deputy coroner and paramedic and, for more years than some younger residents can recall, as the mayor of Florien.

Whatever the original purpose of a trip to Manasco's, customers inevitably end up pouring a free cup of stout coffee from the big urn, then sitting a few minutes at the rough wood picnic table in the middle of the sprawling log store. If he had charged for the critical commentary and loose rumors he'd heard traded around the table, Manasco figured he could have retired a wealthy man. "A man can hear anything around this table," Manasco is fond of saying, "and, hell, some of it could be true."

Immediately after Christmas, the mayor and a group had been huddled around the table when a customer came in and announced that Junior Garner had been beaten to death by Texas lawmen.

"The hell you say? What happened?"

"They said he jumped on some white deputies over in Hemphill, and they had to subdue him."

"That's a bunch of bullshit," Manasco replied. "Junior Garner wouldn't jump on no lawman."

As mayor, Manasco had set bonds and levied fines for years in Florien, and Junior Garner had never run afoul of the law. Indeed, when deputies had gone to the elder Garner's house a few years earlier to arrest one of Junior's younger brothers on misdemeanor traffic warrants, the young man had fought off the officers and bolted for a pickup truck. It had been Junior who had grabbed his brother, shaken him like a rag doll, and handed him over to the deputies.

Nor was there a race problem in tiny Florien. The same wasn't true, Manasco had heard, of Hemphill. "Some of the old-timers here are like me, descendants of the outlaws who came here when this was no-man's land," the mayor said. "Now they'll get mad at one another and fight like hell, maybe even kill each other. But that's generally blacks fighting blacks and whites fighting whites. It doesn't have a thing to do with color. We get along with each other pretty well, and everyone looks out for everyone else," said the mayor, who is white. "Race hasn't got a thing to do with it. Hell, when I was a little boy, me and my mother would have starved to death if it hadn't been for the blacks bringing us stuff from their gardens. You don't forget something like that."

News of Junior's death had silenced the cavernous country store.

"No," the mayor finally said, "there's something more to this thing. Junior wouldn't have fought no lawmen."

Heads around the table nodded in agreement.

13

DEATH THREATS AND FREEDOM

JOHN HANNAH, JR., had followed the Garner case in the newspapers and on television. Just as an old football injury can trigger nostaligia about the Big Game long past, the Garner civil rights case carried Hannah back to his days as East Texas's top federal prosecutor. The Garner case, the Tyler defense lawyer knew, represented the kind of abuse of authority that the federal civil rights statutes were designed to prosecute. It was also the kind of case that made his adrenaline flow; being relegated to the sidelines as a spectator was frustrating.

From his days as the U.S. attorney for the Eastern District of Texas, Hannah knew that if the state indictments should actually result in a trial for the three lawmen, the officers probably would never stand trial in federal court. The federal civil rights statutes dated back to Reconstruction, but in recent times, the U.S. Justice Department's normal policy was not to file a civil rights case unless local authorities refused to clean their own houses. And even then, approval to prosecute a cop or a public official normally had to come from Justice headquarters in Washington.

From their inception, the federal civil rights laws guaranteed the federal government the same jurisdiction as local authorities to investigate cases of police abuse and brutality. The law was used at the height of Ku Klux Klan brutality, when some local prosecutors and lawmen in the South were either members of the Klan, sympathizers, or afraid of the Klan's political clout at the polls.

In 1964, federal prosecutors dusted off the statute when Mississippi authorities failed to investigate and prosecute the murders of civil rights workers James Chaney, Andrew Goodman, and Michael Schwerner. It was federal officials, not local or state prosecutors, who ultimately won indictments against nineteen men, including several police officers and members of the Klan. Seven Klansmen, including one who was a deputy sheriff, were convicted in the murders and sentenced from three to ten years in prison.

Hannah had used the federal civil rights statute in the early 1980s to prosecute two undercover Tyler Police Department narcotics agents who had fabricated evidence and committed perjury to indict more than one hundred defendants. The two narcs, Kim Wozencraft and Creig Matthews, were honored as top lawmen by the East Texas Peace Officers Association for masterminding what was then the largest drug bust in Texas history. Despite mounting evidence and a series of front-page investigations by *The Dallas Morning News,* Hunter Brush, the state district attorney at the time, steadfastly refused to investigate the two officers and continued to prosecute the defendants. Hannah assigned the investigation to FBI agents Lloyd Harrell and Ray Meese and ultimately sent Wozencraft and Matthews to federal prison for violating the civil rights of the scores of people they had arrested.

When Sabine County's state grand jury indicted Ladner, Horton, and Hyden, it appeared the locals were cleaning up their own house. News of the indictments left Hannah both surprised and dubious. Hannah had grown up in Diboll, a timber town about sixty miles west of Hemphill, and had spent his lifetime watching justice in Deep East Texas.

That three white cops would be indicted for killing a black prisoner was indeed a milestone in East Texas jurisprudence. On the other hand, the cops' fate would be determined in their tiny hometown by neighbors and friends. Justice, Hannah felt strongly, would best be served in federal court, with out-of-town prosecutors and an impartial judge who didn't have to depend on re-election votes for his judicial future or live in the area after the trial. Legendary federal judge William Wayne Justice, a second-generation native son of East Texas, had been ostracized when he ordered the integration of public schools in Tyler in the sixties. Not only did he receive death threats, but beauticians refused to cut his wife's hair and his daughter was chided and scorned by schoolmates.

That's why federal judges were appointed for life, Hannah figured—

so they could base their decisions, no matter how uncomfortable, on law instead of popularity. It was also why, he knew, the trial of Ladner, Horton, and Hyden should be conducted outside the incestuous confines of Sabine County. Besides, finding unbiased, impartial jurors in tiny Sabine County who hadn't heard the details of Garner's death would be like finding a Hawaiian who hadn't heard about Pearl Harbor.

News, perhaps like beauty, depends on the eye of the beholder. In his offices in Jasper just after New Year's, 1988, lawyer John Seale was looking at the front page of his newspaper and realizing his worst-case scenario. His defense of Thomas Ladner would be conducted beneath a microscope of state and national media scrutiny, with all the inherent and intangible pressures that headlines and sound bites created in controversial trials. Worse, as Seale read on the front page of *The Houston Post*, was the fact that Garner's death already had taken on critical racial overtones. The *Post* reported:

> Garner's death prompted charges from Hemphill's black population of racism and violence on the part of law enforcement officers in this town of 1,300.
> Blacks waited in the courthouse all day Monday while the grand jury deliberated.
> They were outraged when the names of the indicted men were kept secret even though the indictments were not sealed and were delivered in open court.
> "Everybody knows who did it," said an angry Janie Latham as she left the courthouse. "There's no reason to put it under the rug."

Not only did Latham, an outspoken black teacher and gospel singer in Hemphill, allege manipulation and cover-up in Sabine County, but the story also reported a protest rally, sponsored by the National Association for the Advancement of Colored People, scheduled for the next Saturday in Hemphill.

Not that Seale needed confirmation, but his fears were validated the next day by the venerable *New York Times:* "To many blacks, some of whom waited anxiously in the courthouse hallways as the grand jury deliberated Monday, the incident was a reminder that in terms of race, Hemphill remains a throwback to another age."

The stories and fallout were jarring to the small-town lawyer. Overnight, he involuntarily had been thrust from his quiet civil personal-injury practice, one that had made him one of the most respected civil litigators in East Texas, to national scrutiny as a lawyer defending his only criminal civil rights case.

Seale, meanwhile, was hearing another story from Sabine County, one he wasn't reading in the newspapers: if Garner had been white, there would have been no indictments. Secondhand stories were coming out of the grand jury. They indicted, Seale heard, because of the media. "They thought it best to indict," an insider him, "so that there'd be a full-scale trial so that nobody would ever say they had just brushed it under the rug."

John Seale, like Hannah a son of East Texas, had sidestepped the lure of big-city practice, prominence, and money, opting instead to fight his legal battles in his backyard. He had fared well, though, by any standard. He was the senior partner and founder of a law firm that bore his name, and his sprawling complex of modernistic offices with atriums, greenery, and plenty of glass, designed by a Dallas architect, was among the most fashionable in East Texas. His competitors estimated he earned $250,000 a year, probably more, and clearly he was considered wealthy, particularly in a county with an average household income of less than $17,000.

Steadfastly, and against odds that increased proportionately with success, Seale had fought to keep his life simple, in accordance with the pace of East Texas. At noon on weekdays, he drove the few blocks from his office to his comfortable home, also modernistic and designed by the same Dallas architect, for lunch with his wife, Barbara. Their three children were grown and gone (the only son, Steve, also was a lawyer), and the couple planned long weekends at retreats with good golf courses. Barbara, tanned and athletic, loved golf as much as the crosswords in *The New York Times;* John loved the time away from courtrooms and jammed schedules.

Naively, John Seale assumed that even the controversy of *Texas v. Ladner, Horton, and Hyden* would have little impact on the small-town existence he had fought so hard to protect. That, however, was before he saw the black activist preacher from Houston, the Reverend Earnest Charles, interviewed on TV about the Garner case. "What they ought to do with John Seale," the minister said, "is take him up in an airplane and drop him right in the middle of the Sabine River."

The interview stung Seale. He saw his defense of Thomas Ladner as no different from his representing, as he had in probably a hundred cases, injured black workers suing white employers for damages. These were not issues of race, Seale firmly believed, but issues of *law*. Seale considered himself a purist when it came to the law and its canons of ethics. He went to law school in an era when lawyers, particularly small-town lawyers, were respected for their integrity and commitment to the bar. And Ladner, just like the injured black employees, was entitled to the best defense he could muster for his day in court.

Much, much later, Barbara Seale would refer to the Garner case as her husband's "tar baby." "Once he touched it," she said, "he couldn't turn loose of it. It took on a life of its own."

Few developments escaped the attention of the media in the aftermath of the indictments. There were, however, two isolated events that went unreported. The events were important only because they bore testament to the volatility and divisiveness spawned by Loyal Garner, Jr.'s death.

Dr. Grover Winslow, the general practitioner who had testified to the grand jury that Garner's injuries were compatible with his falling, as the officers had claimed, told the Associated Press that he had treated only about six prisoners in the last ten years who had been injured in altercations with police. "It's never appeared to me that we've had any undue amount of trauma administered by police officers," Dr. Winslow said. "I have never felt we have had any police brutality. I've never had any reason to think they were doing anything but a good job." What didn't appear in the account, or anywhere else for that matter, was the fact that one of Hemphill's most prominent citizens quietly had interjected himself into the controversy surrounding Garner's death: Winslow had posted bonds of $25,000 each for Deputies Bill Horton and Bo Hyden, guaranteeing their freedom until they could be tried on charges of killing his former patient.

Nor did the media find out about the letter Corrine Garner received in her mailbox within days of her husband's death. It was crudely lettered, as if written by a child, and was sent to Mrs. Garner in care of Florien, Louisiana. There was no return address, but it bore a postmark that showed it had been mailed in Milwaukee on January 8. The message read:

Dont worry
in a few days
Thomas
Ladner
Bo Hyden
Bill Horton
are going to be
DEAD!

The letter rattled Mrs. Garner. In his lifetime, her husband had never been more than one hundred miles from home, and now someone in Wisconsin felt strongly enough about his death to be making threats. She shuddered; then she called the FBI.

14

"AGITATORS"

VOLLIE GRACE was driving to church with his wife, Alice, and the children on Sunday morning when he first heard that a black man had been severely beaten in the Sabine County Jail. Details on the radio report were sketchy, particularly so because the sheriff's department apparently refused to say anything to reporters. It would be another twenty-four hours before Grace heard the news that Loyal Garner, Jr., had died in a Tyler hospital of severe head trauma.

"I don't really know what happened to me," Grace would tell a stranger three years later, as the two men sat in the comfortable dining room of Grace's home on the outskirts of Hemphill. "The thing that really struck me was, this man was dead, and they were saying that, actually, *nothing* happened. That bothered me more than anything else. That was the thing that really moved me. A man was dead and it didn't look like nothing was going to happen. It wasn't even that he fell on his head, at the time. This man 'just got dead in the jailhouse.' And that there was nothing wrong about how it happened—no explanation was needed about why it happened or anything. 'This man just got dead in the jailhouse.'

"That was just too much. I just didn't know where my 'place' was anymore."

Vollie Grace grew up black in Sabine County, where, he said, generations of blacks "stayed in their place" to avoid confrontations with the whites who controlled government, law enforcement, business, and the economy. Though his growing concrete construction business took him on jobs throughout East Texas, Grace still lived on the old family home site a few miles east of Hemphill. When he built his stylish new brick home, he left standing in the front yard the rock chimney from his folks' old house where he was born. His mother, Mrs. Ura Daniels, lived two houses away on the same farm-to-market road that dead-ended into Toledo Bend Reservoir.

In his more than four decades in Sabine County, Grace appeared to have won the respect of both blacks and, at least until he began challenging the status quo, many of the whites. From outward appearances, he had risen far above the plight of other blacks and many of the whites who lived in the hardscrabble county. The Graces lived in a spacious, white-brick home and drove a new car and pickup truck. Vollie poured concrete foundations for homes, parking lots, driveways, and sidewalks —backbreaking work, unbearably hot in the summer, miserably mean in the winter. Alice Grace supplemented the family income as a teacher's aide for the Hemphill Independent School District. The couple worked hard to be comfortable, a task even tougher with their two oldest children away at college. Wednesday nights and Sunday mornings found the Graces in church, where Vollie's tenor voice contributed joyously to the church's choir.

The death of Garner, whom Grace had never met, had a peculiar impact on a man who never before had considered himself an activist or even, for that matter, particularly vocal. Headstrong and determined, yes; bombthrower, no. The way Vollie Grace figured, he just followed his heart. "It generally tells me what's right and what's wrong," as he puts it.

And something had been wrong when he returned to Sabine County in late 1964 from his tour in the Army.

"Integration had just come in," Grace recalled. "We supposedly had the rights, but it was never tried in Hemphill. I was a country boy. I was raised on a farm and never had much desire to hang around town, and still don't."

One of the first things Grace did upon his return from the Army was look up his lifelong friend and classmate Amos Walters.

"There were three or four little cafes in town then, and that was the thing to do," Grace said. "But I didn't go in there to sit; I went in to eat.

"In the past, blacks had always eaten in the back, near the kitchen. But they had set a big pool table back there, too. People were shooting pool and they were all over your plate, and you were trying to eat with pool cues and everything. So I told the lady who was cooking, 'Serve my food up in the front and I'll go around there and eat it.' So Amos and I ate up front. It wasn't something we'd planned. It just came up on the moment and we did it."

By the time Vollie and Amos returned to the cafe a few days later, word had spread that a couple of blacks were trying to eat with whites. "Two or three whites got locked up about it," Grace recalled. "Since I didn't hang around town, they really didn't know me that well. But they did know Amos. One white guy came over and said, 'Amos, now I know you know better.' Amos took him outside and there was a scuffle, and the whites called the law."

Sheriff's deputies broke up the fight without arresting anybody, but when Amos and Vollie appeared in town, they could feel the tension of being watched. Unwittingly, the boyhood friends had established a precedent for blacks eating with whites. Not surprisingly, though, virtually all the blacks continued to show up in back rooms to eat. That was fine with Grace. He didn't consider himself a civil rights leader, but *he* wasn't going to eat with a pool cue gouging him in the ribs.

Garner's death, though, was different. It was a catalyst.

"It felt like I was suffocating, felt like I couldn't breathe unless I stood up and told what was going on," Grace recalled. "And nobody else was doing anything. It was going to be washed right under the rug."

From Vollie Grace's way of thinking, there had been too damned much debris already shoved under the rug in Sabine County. A black lifetime that he knew and grimly accepted as oppressive suddenly had been jolted beyond the limits of tolerance by what he considered white arrogance, particularly Sheriff Blan Greer's arrogance, in Garner's death.

Grace was a product of the fifties, and Hemphill didn't integrate its schools until 1965, eight years after Grace had graduated. As a child in Sabine County, Grace considered himself an endangered species, ever vigilant about his safety and keenly aware of his "place" in life in tiny Hemphill. Years of pouring concrete and finishing it smooth on his hands and knees had left Grace rugged and wiry, like a marathon runner. It would be difficult for a stranger to imagine that Grace had ever feared for his safety.

"Hemphill was always oppressive," he recalled, ruminating on his childhood. "Back then, you had places and things that you could do and things you couldn't do. You didn't really have any safe place to go unless it was in the black community. You just didn't go in the white community and

feel safe unless you were working. You didn't go into any of the estab-
lishments. You never went to anyone's front door and knocked. You
always go to the back door. You really didn't want to be on the street
alone because you knew you were going to get harassed.

"It was just like being an animal. You know where you can go safely
and not be harmed. You know where the hunting's at and where it's not."

Like her mother, Janie Latham, Barbara Richard was serious about bet-
tering her lot in life. Bright and attractive, Barbara was a product of the
eighties, graduating from Hemphill High School a year before Loyal Garner was killed and almost three decades after Vollie Grace graduated.
Except for the fact that Barbara had attended school with whites and
occasionally had a hamburger with white friends at the Dairy Queen after
ball games, her childhood in Hemphill was amazingly similar to Grace's
of thirty years earlier. "There had been *some* change," Grace conceded,
"but we had so far to come. And you still see these ugly heads rear up
from time to time. We're almost to the turn of the century, and we still
have many of the same problems."

In neither of their lifetimes had Grace or Barbara seen a black elected
to the city council or the commissioner's court. (Pierce Edwards, an older
black man, had been *appointed* to the city council in the eighties, a move
most blacks termed "tokenism" and "window dressing." Those same
blacks noted that Edwards never rocked the boat, and they were skeptical
that he could or would seek election to the post when the term expired.)
Carl Garrett, a member of the Hemphill School Board, was the only black
to hold elected office in Sabine County—and some say in the history of
the county.

There still were no blacks on the local newspaper staff, no black postal
workers, and no black clerks or salespeople in the department store, the
auto parts stores, the drugstores, the clothing stores, or any businesses
around the square. There were no black tellers at the local bank, and
nearly all the checkers at the local grocery store were white. All the more
glaring in the aftermath of Garner's death, none of the men who carried
a badge and a gun for the city, county, or state law enforcement agencies
was black.

When Barbara Richard left Hemphill the year of her graduation, she
left Deep East Texas, humiliated and bitter. Barbara vowed never to
return to Hemphill or Sabine County except to visit her mother, family,

and friends. "Long as they can look down on you and you stay in your place," she said, "it's all right. It's all right *if you stay in your place.*"

Barbara remembered how frequently she and other black teenagers were reminded, sometimes not so subtly, of their "places." Barbara graduated from Hemphill High in the top ten of her class. As a freshman, she was a starter on the girls' varsity basketball team and named a second-team all-district player in her first year. By her senior year, Barbara averaged more than thirty points and twenty-plus rebounds a game and led the conference in every category. She made the all-district team and was named the most valuable player in the conference. But despite her credentials on the basketball court and an impending athletic scholarship to college, when the white coaches in the conference met to name players to the prestigious all-star team, Barbara's name was conspicuously absent.

In her four years at Hemphill High, the young black woman had seen other inconsistencies in the way blacks were treated, scenarios that she could attribute only to racism. "On road games, the best football players, which included many of the blacks, always started the games," Barbara recalled. "But when we played at home in Hemphill, the white players who weren't as good as some of the blacks, they got to start the games because their fathers, who ran the businesses and everything in town, were in the stands. That was upsetting, because most of the black kids, if they had a chance to go to college at all, it had to be on scholarship, and if they didn't get playing time, they didn't get scholarships."

The discrimination, Barbara believed, wasn't limited to athletics. Notwithstanding her academic standing and the fact that she had studied computers in school, Barbara was refused a part-time job by a local real estate agent, who hired a white teenager who, at least in Barbara's estimation, wasn't nearly as qualified.

Shortly before she left Hemphill for college, Barbara recalled, she accompanied a black girlfriend to the bank to apply for a car loan. One of their white classmates had been to the bank earlier in the week and had been approved immediately for a loan. But when Barbara and her friend talked to the banker, the black girl was given additional paperwork with her loan application. "She became upset with the banker's attitude—it was really obvious—and finally we just left," Barbara said. "It just wasn't worth all the effort and heartache."

But perhaps the most vivid scenario emblazoned in Barbara Richard's memory of growing up in Hemphill involved Dean Crockett, a devoted black math teacher who, in his more than twenty years in Hemphill, had gone well beyond his professional job description to keep students interested in staying in school. "Mr. Crockett was never too busy to listen to you," Barbara recalled. "Whether it was help with a math problem or a kid was having trouble at home, Mr. Crockett always listened. And helped. Always. We all depended on him."

In Barbara's last year in school, it was common knowledge among teachers and students that Crockett, upon the retirement of the school's current principal, had been offered the position. The prospect of Crockett becoming principal, which would have made him easily the highest-ranking black professional in Sabine County, was greeted with excitement not only among black and white students alike but also by his colleagues, who believed the black teacher's personal investment in the students certainly had earned him the post.

But one day in 1986, Barbara remembered, Crockett appeared at school uncharacteristically dejected and despondent. Eventually, word spread: Crockett would not be principal of Hemphill High; quietly, he had withdrawn his name from consideration. The black teacher had received several threatening telephone calls. Crockett refused to identify the callers or to describe the threats; for years afterward, he simply refused to discuss it.

"That hurt," Barbara said, "and I'll never forget how sorry I felt for Mr. Crockett and how angry it made me."

Barbara Richard went on to Tennessee State University, a predominantly black school in Nashville, where she majored in criminal justice. Though she suffered a severe knee injury in her junior year, the school continued to honor her basketball scholarship. Before graduating in May 1991, Barbara served an internship in Washington with the Department of Justice's general counsel's office. Perhaps ironically, she worked in the Equal Opportunity Division.

"I'd never live in Hemphill again," she said. "I don't know of any black who's gone off to college and came back."

Vollie Grace, however, did live in Hemphill, as did his wife, mother, brother, and two of his children. And the status quo no longer was acceptable, either for him or for his family. And much of the anger Grace felt, he turned inward, for ever having tolerated without question his second-class citizenship.

"There was a sense that we can't change this, that nothing was going to happen," Grace recalled. "They're always going to keep you like this. And I think that's the way the whole black community felt. If you had a job and were working, making a living and doing all right, well then, you wouldn't want to rock the boat and just go ahead on—as long as you 'stayed in your place,' and you knew where your place was."

Quietly at first, Grace began telling Alice and Mrs. Ura that he had to do something, that *somebody* had to do something, or Garner's death would mean nothing. The Louisiana man's death had to be a precedent, Grace believed, or the next time a black man was thrown in jail it would be even easier for the brutality to go unnoticed. Eventually, Grace was talking openly to a handful of blacks about organizing. He called the group the Concerned Citizens for Sabine County, and he hoped that someday it would contain even some whites who also were fed up with the abuse of authority.

"The tension in Hemphill was such that you could feel it in the air," Grace recalled of the period immediately following Garner's death. "There were just a few people I could talk to, about five or six. And then the whites would go to them and scare them, tell them that the Klan would come in. They didn't try to scare me.

"There was one white guy—we are friends—who came down here and tried to quieten me down and hush me up because his friends were close to the sheriff. The sheriff sent him. There are things in a small town that are mutually understood. The sheriff didn't have to say, 'Now, you go down there and shut Vollie up.' No, he just talked roundabout, and the message would get conveyed. And this guy talked to me in my garage for about two hours one Saturday. I wouldn't bend.

"We agreed that regardless of what happened, we'd stay friends. And we're still friends, because we had sense enough to know at the time that this would pass and we'd still be here. I always felt I didn't have any reason to fall out with somebody over their opinion."

Nor was everyone who was upset over Garner's death black. There were whites, too; but like most of the blacks, they were afraid to oppose a law enforcement community they believed was corrupt and brutal. In opposing the cops, they knew, they also would be opposing the city council, the mayor, the commissioners court, and the county judge who paid them. "There's some decent, hard-working people in Sabine County, just like there are everywhere," Grace said. "But these are the people who never say anything. There was a lot of people against what happened to Mr. Garner."

People in small towns talked, and like the ripples when a pebble is thrown into a lake, each larger concentric circle carried the news of Grace and his Concerned Citizens for Sabine County farther and farther throughout Sabine County. Soon the phone in Grace's kitchen was ringing at all hours of the day and night.

Initially, Grace was surprised that some of the callers were white. "They'd call me on the phone and tell me these horrible things about police and abuse," Grace recalled, "but then they'd say, 'You can't use my name.' After a while, I just stopped them and said, 'Look, you're telling me these things that need to come out, but if I can't use your name to get anything done, there's no use in calling.'

"They had good intentions, but they'd say, 'I can't live here if my neighbor finds out I'm telling you this.' I feel some compassion for them, because there is pressure in the white community. But I'm black and I know where they think my place is supposed to be." A few whites said they feared their houses would be set afire if they spoke out openly. "I told them, 'My house can burn down, too.' "

The Concerned Citizens for Sabine County was an unusual group. While as many as two hundred residents, nearly all of them black, had pledged their support to reforming law enforcement and revamping government, it was virtually impossible to find anyone in Sabine County who would admit to even knowing of the organization's existence. But in small, trusted circles, the Concerned Citizens had people talking. Alice Grace overheard one of those conversations in the produce aisle at Brookshire's Supermarket. "Well, I never would have thought ol' Vollie would have done something like this," a white man told another. "He knows better. We *know* he knows better. He was raised up here all his life."

Which was precisely Grace's point. His life and the lives of other blacks in Sabine County were about to change.

"They began to see I was determined," Grace recalled, "and that I wasn't going to stop. They knew from past experiences that I was an ol' country boy and didn't scare easily. I think they thought, 'We'll have to put up with him or kill him.' And there comes a time when that really doesn't matter. . . . I'm a Christian, and when it comes time to make a decision, I do it.

"Don't get me wrong. I'm not running around here with a death wish."

The Houston Post, in an editorial days after the three officers were indicted, commended the all-white Sabine County Grand Jury for its "seemingly fair handling" of the Loyal Garner, Jr. case. The editorial, headlined
"An End to Savagery," noted:

> Many Hemphill citizens view the indictments as the beginning of
> the end for a dangerous era of police beatings and racial strife. Some
> citizens—both black and white—say police have beaten prisoners
> for decades. Some even say they thought the days of racial prejudices
> and beatings were over, while others expressed delight that the area
> is finally being exposed for what it is.
>
> But race prejudice hasn't been the sole criteria for getting a beating
> courtesy of the Hemphill or Sabine County officers. Although some
> beatings of blacks were probably racially motivated, whites also tell
> of being beaten by the officers in Hemphill.

The narrow back roads that lead to Hemphill were treacherous with ice
that second Saturday in January, but when dawn broke it found the
normally deserted highways unusually heavy with traffic. The people who
traveled them—from Shreveport, Houston, Lufkin, Nacogdoches, all of
Deep East Texas—were black and would say they had traveled rough
roads before.

"Why go to Hemphill?" asked the Reverend Earnest Charles from
Houston. "I go because I'm ashamed that in America today this type of
atrocity could still go on."

And Reverend Charles didn't travel the road by himself. He chartered
a bus and brought along forty-two members of his St. Savior Church in
Houston. Lawrence Jones, a black plumber, drove alone forty miles from
Nacogdoches. Al Edwards, a Texas legislator and chairman of Jesse Jackson's presidential campaign in Texas, drove in from Houston. Echoing
Jackson's campaign trademark, Edwards declared: "I am somebody!" In
all, two hundred blacks gathered early for the rally at the Knox Chapel
Baptist Church on a hilltop outside Hemphill. It was doubtful that any
of the throng had ever met Loyal Garner, Jr.

Glenn Smith, a longshot candidate in his bid to wrest away Blan Greer's
sheriff's star, correctly figured the rally would be a captive audience filled
with potential votes. Even before he stood to speak, he was as obvious

as a vanilla jelly bean in a jar of licorice. "I don't know if you can blame the Loyal Garner death on there being no black law enforcement officials here," Smith said. "It's hard for me to say whether it was a racial incident. But the time has come for blacks to be represented on the force. That's the least we can do."

Even as his challenger spoke, the incumbent sheriff was down on the state highway only a stone's throw from the church, joined by several of Hemphill's leaders and even more state troopers. Sheriff Greer had called the troopers, he said, because half his department—Chief Deputy Bill Horton and Deputy Bo Hyden, and Thomas Ladner, the city's police chief—were suspended (with pay), pending the outcome of their civil rights trial.

Mayor Ronnie Felts drove by the church and the nearby accumulation of law enforcement several times. When he spoke to reporter David Maraniss of *The Washington Post,* the mayor was visibly upset at "all these outside agitators" in his town. "This was not the kind of attention we were looking for," he told Maraniss. "People are trying to make Hemphill something evil, but I don't think race relations here are bad at all. It's no different here than in Georgia, or in New York City, for that matter."

The gathering that next Friday night was a curious one for the Macedonia Baptist Church. During its lengthy lifetime, the old white clapboard church set off the highway on the frayed fringe of Hemphill had witnessed the glories and sadnesses of generations of its black congregants. Weddings and funerals, baptisms of the young and rebirths of backsliders— the old church's wooden floors and high ceilings had witnessed them all.

Those who came that Friday, bundled in coats and hats against an unusually cold night, also came in search of answers and understanding. But unlike any other time at the old church, tonight there were as many whites in the pews as blacks. Vollie Grace had seen to that. He had been on the phone nonstop for days, not only exhorting people to attend but also asking them to phone their own acquaintances with the date and place of the meeting. The rudimentary phone bank had worked. "The only way to change this police situation," Grace had told his family before the meeting, "is to get the whole community together, not just the blacks. Us blacks alone can't get change."

The meeting to discuss police brutality "out in the open and on the table" would be held jointly with the all-white Taxpayer Action Committee. The self-appointed monitoring group, some public officials strongly believed, was a constant pain. It always was critical of officials' spending in the perpetually strapped county, and some of its members, the officials contended, were "radical," even "antigovernment."

Grace had hoped the officials were right. Some of the group's members were among those who called him late at night with guarded confirmations of police abuse. He had especially encouraged them to pass the word about the meeting, hoping that their distrust of law enforcement would outweigh their discomfort of meeting with blacks at a black church.

In Deep East Texas, where blacks and whites historically had never unified publicly on any issue, particularly one involving race, the multiracial gathering at the Macedonia Baptist Church was indeed a historical event. Silently, Grace thought it only fitting that the meeting to air civil rights grievances was being held on Martin Luther King's birthday.

As Grace watched the 125 or so people trickle into the pews, he made mental notes of a few whites who, he suspected, were there for only one reason: to take names of attendees and notes on the meeting and report back to law enforcement. Before the night was over, Grace hoped, the truth would make their ears red.

Whatever was said that night, Grace knew, would be headlines tomorrow. He had watched the reporters come, too, and in fact had solicited them, from the local *Sabine County Reporter* to *The Beaumont Enterprise* and even *The New York Times*. He hoped the outpouring of anger and concern over police brutality from an unprecedented coalition of whites and blacks would force local officials to do the right thing for the right reasons. The media was to be Grace's insurance policy: if Sabine authorities didn't have the integrity to clean up law enforcement, then maybe they'd be coerced by public scrutiny into doing the right things, even if for the wrong reasons.

The atmosphere was delicate, and some of the whites appeared ill at ease. Then the Reverend Will Smith's baritone swept the sanctuary, bringing the controversy head-on to the clusters of white and black faces. "Death came in the midst of us," he intoned, as if it were another Sunday morning of preaching the gospel. "Woke us up. Shook each of us out of our beds. But now we can see, and since we can see, you can't fool us anymore."

The minister's head-first plunge into the Garner death evoked a brief look of pain from Sabine County Judge Royce Smith, who apparently had believed his appearance—and the weight of his office—would temper the outcry. It would only get worse for the aging county judge, who, as the night wore on, became a lightning rod for the crowd's anger.

"We are very reluctant to make the simple statement that this is wrong," Grace told the audience. "But the thing that bothers me the most is that we're in a situation where if a white officer killed a white man we would be even more reluctant to say anything.

"We have grown accustomed to violence. We know it's not right, but we say it's all right. Or maybe it's wrong, but we can accept it. Only when the violence seems to have a racial overtone will the media seem to respond.

"This is a *human* issue," Grace said, galvanizing the whites in the audience.

Chet Cook, a white retired Army officer who had lived in Sabine County the last five years, followed Grace's lead. He rose from the red-cushioned pew and tried to talk through the lump in his throat. "Please bear with me, because I can't help but be emotional under the circumstances," he said, tears in his eyes. "But I don't feel there was anything racial about this."

He looked around the audience until his eyes came to rest on Nora Helms. Pointing his finger toward her, Cook said, "This lady's daughter was harassed by the sheriff's department.

"This man's son," he said, glancing at another white, "was pistol-whipped and had to be taken to the hospital.

"I don't like to see my tax money going to the Gestapo-type operations that we fought wars to eliminate in this country."

The retired officer's testimony, elegant in its emotion, unified the room.

Andy Helms slammed home Cook's point. Law-enforcement officers in Sabine County, local, county, and state, he said from his vantage point as a former officer, were equal-opportunity abusers. Race, even sex, Helms said, made no difference. During the year he worked as a police officer, he'd seen whites and blacks, men and women, victimized by bogus charges, arrests and harassment. Later, his own daughter had been victimized.

"They'll never mess with the people who own businesses or the old-time families in the county," Helms said. "Been all over the world, and I've never in my life seen a town that was run by only a few people. And to continually harass people and do things that didn't even resemble a law officer. The way they treated people and continuously get away with it . . ."

The comments at the meeting established a consensus. Law enforcement in Sabine County was preferential and selective. Those most vulnerable to its abuse were outsiders and the poor and powerless, which included virtually every black in Sabine County.

From the criteria that evolved in the meeting, Loyal Garner, Jr., had been the epitome of targets for abuse: a resident of Louisiana, a minimum-wage laborer supporting six children, and black.

Judge Royce Smith apparently had taken the criticism of his county's law enforcement personally. Before he walked into the brisk night air, he turned angrily toward Vollie Grace. "I'll tell you what," Smith said. "You'll never get us to come to any other meeting you have."

Still, Grace was pleased—and even more so after he read the account of the meeting in *The New York Times*: ". . . When the session ended after two hours, people lingered in the church aisles, like guests reluctant to leave a nice party."

15

LAWYERS FROM ALABAMA

There is little difference between lawless Klan violence, and violence by law enforcement officers. . . .

Many small town Southern police departments think they are above the law. Helpless and powerless blacks are often beaten by white officers and nothing is done. Most of these abused have criminal records and nobody takes their complaints seriously. This time, they killed the wrong person.

—Morris Dees, co-founder, Southern Poverty Law Center, in an April 1988 letter soliciting funds for the Loyal Garner, Jr., lawsuit

---

THE TWO-STORY BUILDING, distinctive in its heavy, tinted glass, stone, and sharp, modernistic lines, seems curiously out of place, like a Mercedes at a garage sale. Surrounding the sleek building for blocks are clusters of aging white buildings made generally unremarkable by their functionalism and institutionalism, everlasting tributes to a score of lowest bidders. Diagonally across Washington Avenue from the chic new intruder, the dome of the Alabama State Capitol rises higher than any of the nearby buildings in the government complex. Atop the dome flies the state's flag, a white background with a red X emblazoned on it, almost identical to the Confederate battle flag.

Three blocks from the new, modernistic building, up the hill on Washington Avenue and virtually unchanged in the hundred years since the Civil War, sits the first White House of the Confederacy. Montgomery, Alabama, was the cradle of the Confederacy, the site where delegates from the South met on February 8, 1861, to form the Confederate States of America and elect Jefferson Davis to guide it on its apocalyptic journey.

There perhaps could be no more meaningful irony, or stronger statement, than Morris Dees selecting the corner lot at 400 Washington Avenue, atop the bedrock of the Confederacy, to build his symbol of civil rights. Just as the building is out of sync with its surroundings, so is its creator. The building and the Southern Poverty Law Center, which it houses, are Dees's manifesto to those in Montgomery who had ostracized him as a "nigger lover" and threatened to kill him. The fact that the Southern Poverty Law Center even needed a new building bore testimony to the contempt of Dees's enemies: in July 1983, the Ku Klux Klan had firebombed his first headquarters, a Montgomery storefront, burning it to the ground.

With the hard-nosed flamboyance that had become Dees's trademark over a decade of civil rights battles, the opulent new building sent a message to the Klan, redneck cops, and old-line law firms: Morris Dees was, by God, here to stay. The five-million-dollar stone-and-glass fortress across from the capital was the kind of unorthodox, in-your-face statement that made Dees and his lawyers loathed—and successful—in courtrooms throughout the South.

And if the message was too subtle, Dees added a constant reminder in front of the building that left no doubt about the political intent of those inside. He commissioned Maya Lin, the architect of the Vietnam Veterans Memorial in Washington, D.C., to design the Civil Rights Memorial. A wash of water perpetually flows over a black granite table inscribed with the names of those who died in the civil rights movement. The design makes the names impossible to read without visitors bending over the memorial, seeing at the same time their own reflections in the water. A curved black granite wall above is inscribed with words from the Book of Amos, made famous in modern days by Martin Luther King, Jr.: *. . . Until Justice Rolls Down Like Waters and Righteousness Like a Mighty Stream.*

Dees, a man who grew up as "Bubba" to his family, and his handful of liberal lawyers and investigators hadn't created a raging river of justice in the South, but they had triggered more than a few flash floods that had sent the proprietors of Deep South ideology and racism scurrying for higher ground. The middle-aged son of a white tenant farmer, the self-made-millionaire entrepreneur-lawyer turned his energy toward civil rights law. His Southern Poverty Law Center became the patron saint of lost legal causes and new precedents.

The center helped engineer the successful defense of Joan Little, a black inmate who killed a white jailer who, she said, tried to sexually attack her in a North Carolina jail cell in August 1974; sued the Alabama State Troopers, forcing the agency to hire its first black patrolman; defended Vietnamese fishermen along the Texas Gulf Coast against attacks by the Ku Klux Klan; rescued a black Marine sergeant from death row in Georgia after proving the man had killed two lawmen in self-defense; exposed inhumane conditions in Alabama mental institutions; and won financial benefits for cotton-mill workers who suffered brown lung disease from cotton dust.

In the first week of January 1988, Morris Dees and the Southern Poverty Law Center were riding the crest of the biggest and most publicized victory in their civil rights careers. Dees, assisted by his top lawyer, J. Richard Cohen, had broken the back of the United Klans of America, disrobing and shaming it in, of all places, Mobile, a citadel of the Old South. Seizing on the gruesome murder of Michael Donald, a young black man from Mobile, and borrowing a tenet of law historically used to sue large corporations, Dees took the lethal actions of two Klan foot soldiers all the way to the doorstep of the Klan's most exalted leader, the Grand Dragon.

Young Donald left his mother's home on a Friday night in March 1981 to walk to a nearby convenience store for a pack of cigarettes. As he walked along the darkened and deserted sidewalk, two Klansmen abducted him, beat him with tree limbs, and, after a violent battle, finally choked him to death with rope. Beulah Mae Donald's son was found the next morning only a few feet from her apartment, hanging by a rope from a camphor tree in the front yard.

In the criminal trial, one of the Klansmen testified that Donald had been chosen "simply because he was black." The purpose, the Klansman testified, was to "show the strength of the Klan . . . to show that they were still here in Alabama."

Dees monitored the criminal trial, during which the defendants were convicted, and was sitting in the spectator's gallery when he hit on a novel legal strategy. "These bastards were agents of the Klan," Dees recounted in his autobiography, *A Season for Justice*. "Why can't we sue the Klan like you'd sue any corporation liable for the acts of its agents?"

In February 1987, four years after the criminal trial, Dees and Cohen convinced a civil jury that the Klan, much like an airline financially responsible for the negligent acts of its pilots, had used its message of racial hatred and violence to cause its agents to kill Michael Donald. The all-white jury returned a seven-million-dollar verdict against the United Klans of America, bankrupting it into extinction and sending tremors through hate groups across the country.

The recipient of the Klan's only financial holdings, a cavernous, $225,000 building outside Tuscaloosa that once had served as its head-quarters, was Beulah Mae Donald, the dead man's elderly mother.

The national media wrote the obituary of one of the South's most notorious institutions. Virtually overlooked in the accounts, though, were two aberrations that separated Dees and his Southern Poverty Law Center from nearly every other law firm in the nation.

While lawyers customarily take contingency fees of one-third or more of all settlements they win for their clients, plus expenses, Mrs. Donald kept one hundred percent of the settlement she won from the Klan. The Southern Poverty Law Center is a nonprofit law firm set up to represent the poor, black and white, who normally couldn't afford lawyers. Instead of charging his clients fees, Dees, who earned his multimillion-dollar fortune as a direct-mail genius, relies on a sophisticated nationwide list of contributors to fund his cases. It was his expertise at direct-mail so-licitation that Morris Dees volunteered to George McGovern, Jimmy Carter, and Ted Kennedy, bankrolling their political campaigns and, at the same time, earning Dees influential friends in liberal Democratic politics.

Another of Dees's modi operandi is one that probably would land most lawyers in front of grievance committees. Unabashedly, Dees solicits clients. In a profession that still debates the ethics of lawyers advertising their services, nearly all state bar associations have strict rules against recruiting clients, a practice critics call "ambulance chasing." The dif-ference, Dees would contend, is that his law firm is nonprofit and doesn't make a penny off the clients it represents.

In the first week of January 1988, the fifty-year-old lawyer wore a furrowed brow as he laid *The New York Times* on his desk and stared through the bulletproof glass at the Alabama State Capitol. Not surpris-ingly, Morris Dees had never heard of Hemphill, Texas, before he read about it in the *Times*. A paragraph buried in reporter Peter Applebome's story nagged at him: "But to many blacks, some of whom waited anxiously in the courthouse hallways as the grand jury deliberated Monday, the incident was a reminder that in terms of race, Hemphill remains a throw-back to another age."

Dees had lived in that age, a white boy picking cotton with black children whose parents, like his own, were poor tenant farmers. That Loyal Garner, Jr., could be beaten to death by white lawmen in the 1980s repulsed Dees. Before day's end, Dees was recruiting a new client for the Southern Poverty Law Center, a widow named Corrine Garner, and en route to Deep East Texas were Joe Roy and Danny Welch, both white former Alabama cops and investigators for the Southern Poverty Law Center.

If some residents of Sabine County blamed big-city reporters for the fallout from Garner's death, it was only because they had not yet met Morris Dees, Richard Cohen, Joe Roy, and Danny Welch. Those "meddlin' bastards from Alabama," in what would become the opinion of many in Sabine County, were lower than a snake's belly in a wheel rut.

Richard Cohen and Morris Dees were merely different packaging for the same product. At six foot two, Cohen was a good three inches taller than his mentor, and at thirty-four, nearly fifteen years younger. And while Dees's deeply tanned and etched face could have been distantly attributable to his days in a cotton field, the handsome Cohen more closely looked the part of a Washington lawyer, which in fact he had been before abandoning a civil practice in favor of litigating civil rights cases in the South. Dees had worked his way through bachelor's and lawyer's degrees at his native University of Alabama, while Cohen had graduated from Columbia University before getting his degree from the prestigious University of Virginia Law School. If Bubba Dees was folksy and casual in his open-collared, blue oxford shirts and khakis, Cohen was eloquent in dark suits and white shirts. If there was any difference in effectiveness or commitment, the lawyers who opposed Dees and Cohen in court couldn't tell. Dees's trip on the civil rights circuit had just logged more miles on his odometer.

Their new client, Corrine Garner, was a widow with six children, so strapped that she had had to accept a stranger's offer of money to get from Hemphill to her dying husband's bedside in Tyler, one hundred miles away. Her only assets were her late husband's old pickup truck and whatever furniture and belongings there were inside her modest house. She owed $8,000 on the $10,000 home loan her husband had gotten a year before his death. But virtually overnight, Corrine Garner had a legal team of two experienced lawyers and two investigators with million-dollar backing from the Southern Poverty Law Center.

Actually, Corrine had to fire one set of lawyers before she could hire the Southern Poverty Law Center. In what Cohen later would describe to the court as "a particularly crude example of solicitation and over-reaching," Corrine had been contacted within days of her husband's death by three lawyers, who ultimately convinced her to sign a contract. Under its provisions, the three black lawyers, Joann Gines-Shepherd and Billy R. Casey of Shreveport and John E. Sherman of Houston, would receive one-third of any settlement negotiated before filing a lawsuit or 40 percent of any settlement or award afterward.

In an affidavit Corrine filed in court to sever her ties with the three lawyers, the widow said that Gines-Shepherd called her repeatedly after her husband's death before she finally agreed to meet with the lawyers four days after her husband's funeral. "Even as I was signing the contingency fee retainer, I had second thoughts about Ms. Gines-Shepherd and the other two lawyers," Mrs. Garner said. "Ms. Gines-Shepherd did not really seem interested in helping me make sure that the people who killed my husband were brought to justice, and I was not just interested in winning some money. One of the men lawyers dropped what looked to be a whiskey flask out of his pocket. This concerned me. . . .

"I started thinking about the fact that the lawyers were going to take a lot of my recovery for themselves. This troubled me because Ms. Gines-Shepherd had told me again and again that she only wanted to help me."

Corrine Garner said she chose Dees and Cohen because she was "a poor person." "They represent poor people without charging a fee or taking any part of what they win," she said. "I felt they were sympathetic with my situation. They were also very interested in seeing that the men who killed my husband were brought to justice."

Gines-Shepherd, Casey, and Sherman asked the court to protect their interest in the Garner case "for the reasonable value of service rendered," a motion U.S. District Judge Robert M. Parker denied during hearings in Lufkin, Texas.

Less than two weeks after Thomas Ladner, Bill Horton, and Bo Hyden had been indicted for the death of Loyal Garner, Jr., Cohen, Southern Poverty Law Center's legal director, filed a civil damage suit on behalf of Corrine Garner, her six children, and Garner's parents, Sarah Lee and Loyal Garner, Sr. The suit, filed in federal court in Lufkin, named not only the three lawmen as defendants, but also the city of Hemphill. Not relying only on the lawmen's limited resources for a judgment, Cohen went for the "deep pockets" of the city's insurance carrier. The lawyer hoped not only to prove that the officers' negligence and/or intent led to Garner's death but also to trace their culpability to the governmental entity that, Cohen claimed, sanctioned the officers' lethal act.

Though the lawsuit was a civil action seeking damages under federal civil rights and Texas wrongful death statutes, it was more damning than the earlier criminal indictments in its portrayal of Hemphill's justice system. While the indictments in Sabine County did not mention race, Cohen, in the first paragraph of the civil suit, claimed Garner died as the result of a "brutal, racially motivated killing." Noting that Ladner, Horton, and Hyden were white and that Garner was black, he alleged that the officers' beating of Garner and subsequent failure to provide the inmate with medical care were results of a racially motivated conspiracy.

Cohen noted there was a "custom or practice of using excessive force and brutality in dealing with persons held in the Sabine County Jail." Then he broadened the web of conspiracy and culpability that he hoped would ensnare the city of Hemphill and, of course, its insurance carrier: "The persistent and widespread use of excessive force and brutality in the Sabine County Jail," Cohen claimed, "is so common and well-settled as to constitute a custom that represents expected, accepted municipal policy." Bottom line, Cohen alleged, the city not only knew about the tradition of brutality by its police officers but, by turning its head and allowing the beatings to continue, actually sanctioned the actions, just as it did garbage pickups on Mondays and Thursdays.

While not specifying the amount of damages this conspiracy had cost its clients, the Southern Poverty Law Center merely asked the court for compensatory and punitive damages "in excess of $10,000," the minimum damages to qualify for federal court jurisdiction.

The news of rabble-rousing civil rights lawyers from Alabama filing a lawsuit against the city and its officers was greeted in local coffee-shop conversations like the re-emergence of the pine beetle. Should the out-of-state lawyers win, speculation had it, Hemphill would be bankrupt. Few of the armchair lawyers mentioned the financial safety net afforded by the city's insurance policy through the Texas Municipal League, which made governmental bankruptcy remote.

16

FORGING AN ALLIANCE

"I DON'T CARE what you stand for," the young mother had told her son, "but stand for something."

John Henry Hannah, Jr., had heeded the maternal advice. "Standing for something" had led him on diverse, sometimes rocky paths, first as a history professor, then as state legislator, state prosecutor, consumer lobbyist, United States attorney, and defense attorney. But as if he had marked the way home with notches on trees, John Hannah always found his way back to East Texas.

Hannah was born in the post-Depression era, "out in the woods somewhere," he says, in Nacogdoches County. Actually, he was born six miles from the county seat in a pine thicket that even the sun and the rural mail carrier had trouble finding. His dad, twenty-two at the time, drove a team of mules, dragging cut pine from the thickets to the nearest rutted road, where trucks waited to haul the timber to sawmills. Velma Hannah became a mother at nineteen and treated her firstborn son "like one of her dolls," he would recall decades later.

Because both parents came from "terribly modest circumstances," they "pushed education hard" on their sons, John Jr. and James, who was eleven years younger. John Sr. could neither read nor write, a situation for which his young wife more than compensated, reading to her young sons constantly and casting an ominous shadow over their shoulders at homework time.

Being dirt poor in East Texas in the thirties and forties meant working in the woods, and many of the men John Sr. worked with were black.

John Sr. couldn't see that the color of a man's skin should make any difference; the only things that mattered to the wood bosses in the thickets were strong backs and sweat.

Probably because the Hannahs shared as much in common with blacks as they did with many whites, John Jr. recalled, his parents "were terribly sympathetic to blacks." Uncharacteristically for the times, Velma Hannah demanded that all the Hannahs show respect to blacks and insisted that her sons would say "sir" and "ma'am" when addressing them.

Before John Jr. was old enough to start school, the Hannahs moved to Diboll, a lumber company town in Angelina County, about seventy miles west of Hemphill. The patriarch of the family had swapped his mule team for a truck, hauling logs from the woods to the sawmill. From the time young John was old enough to pull himself up on the running board, he rode with his father in the truck.

"Dad had a tremendous distrust of authority," John Hannah, Jr., would recall years later, "and he may have had a few scrapes with the law in his younger years. He was always suspicious of authority and he could get pretty short-tempered." Guaranteed to ignite John Sr.'s fuse were the wood bosses, the foremen who determined the order in which trucks were loaded with logs. The bosses' roles were particularly crucial to the drivers, who were paid by the number of loads they hauled. If they didn't get loaded, they didn't get paid.

When John Jr. was four, a woods boss on horseback headed for his dad's truck, a hatchet in his hand, apparently mad at the way John Sr. had parked. Sternly, John Sr. told his son to duck down onto the floorboard. Then he kicked open the driver's door and reached back behind the cab, grabbing a logging hook off a metal rack. Peering over the dash of the truck, young John saw his dad chasing the wood boss and his horse into the timber.

As a teenager, young John, whom the family called "Sonny," would produce a book during lunch breaks in the woods and deposit himself on a tree stump to read. It was a trait he had inherited from his mother, and it appeared to embarrass his father in front of the other loggers, many of whom couldn't read, either.

Years later, Velma Hannah recalled how Sonny would ask a barrage of questions, demanding the most detailed information on a multitude of questions. Hearing the answers, he'd sometimes ask, "Would it change your mind if . . . ?" or "What do you suppose would happen if . . . ?"

"Listen, little boy," she'd say, "you're not a lawyer and I'm not on the witness stand."

Sonny Hannah, who had developed into a muscled six-footer like his dad, was skipping high school frequently during his last two years, adjourning to a local park with an armload of books to read. There were thirty or so members in his graduating class in 1957, and teachers told Velma Hannah her son could have finished at the top were it not for the fact that "appearing smart embarrassed him in front of his classmates."

Never having ventured far from East Texas, the Navy's invitation to "see the world" was particularly enticing to the recently graduated Hannah. After a series of shipboard assignments, he landed a cushy assignment in Okinawa, where he spent a good amount of time snorkeling, playing softball, and eating steak on the beach. "God," the young sailor thought, "I wished I was back in Diboll at the Dairy Queen."

As soon as the Navy would allow, Hannah was back in East Texas, enrolling via the GI Bill at Sam Houston State University in Hunstville, intent on becoming a history professor. He immersed himself in college, taking eighteen hours a semester and trying to make up for time lost to the Navy. But politics became a passion, and in January 1964 he dropped out for one semester to work as a field manager in a congressional campaign.

Hannah's candidate, Benton Musselwhite from nearby Lufkin, was a Democrat, a former Eagle Scout and a football star at Southern Methodist University. Musselwhite had run for Congress four years earlier, losing by only forty-two votes. He was the front runner in his most recent campaign until his opponent ran a series of ads claiming that Musselwhite, a liberal, wanted barbers to cut blacks' hair. Musselwhite was buried at the polls. The defeat stunned Hannah and made him realize, maybe for the first time, that not everyone felt the same as he did about equality for blacks.

After graduating from Sam Houston State University with honors, Hannah won a fellowship, which allowed him to work on his master's degree while teaching history at the university. With only his thesis remaining, Hannah jolted his family by announcing his campaign for state representative.

Once they overcame the shock of the announcement, everyone in the Hannah family hit the campaign trail. John Sr. lobbied every logger he knew, and Velma Hannah knew what hamburgers tasted like in every precinct in the district. Little brother James, only a teenager, ran into a judge in Lufkin who was laboring under the mistaken notion that the near-penniless John Hannah, Jr., had accumulated a large campaign treasury. "Your brother's got so much money it'd burn a wet dog," the judge told young James.

"I don't know about that," James said doubtfully. "Both his feet are on the ground. He's got cardboard in the bottom of his shoes."

There were three other candidates for state representative, and two, like Hannah, were just finishing college. The third, a plumber and Pentecostal preacher, called his trio of youthful opponents "Wink 'Em, Blink 'Em, and Nod." "I don't have the time these boys do," the plumber explained to voters. "When I get up in the morning, I have to shave."

Hannah made it to the runoffs, and late on election night, with one precinct still out, he trailed by nearly fifty votes. The missing precinct was Corrigan, a timber town of less than two thousand in Polk County. Hannah couldn't stand the suspense. He and a carload of supporters drove to Corrigan, where they used the phone at Mamma Essie's Cafe to call the election chairman, Jasper Cockrell, at home.

Cockrell, Corrigan's football coach and school superintendent, answered on about the fourth ring. Hannah knew Cockrell relatively well, but he stammered when he greeted him over the phone. "Uh . . . Mr. Cockrell . . . I was just wondering . . . is there . . . uh . . . something wrong with the vote in your precinct? I mean, it hasn't been . . ."

"No, nothing wrong at all. The ballot box is right here under the bed. Had a long day. I'm gonna get a couple hours' sleep, then carry it into Livingston."

"Well, it's a pretty tight race, and . . . uh . . ."

"How many votes you need?"

"Somewhere around fifty."

"You got a lot more than fifty. Go on and get some sleep, John. You won."

Jasper Cockrell's unofficial tally was validated the next day, and young John Hannah had won the right to represent a major portion of Deep East Texas at the statehouse in Austin. He pulled heavily from the working class, and—what probably tilted the scales for him—he carried virtually all the black vote in his district. It was a formula that worked again in two re-election campaigns.

The young legislator quickly earned a reputation in Austin for com-

petitiveness and doing his homework. He became an advocate for education and the elderly and was the only legislator appointed to the criminal
justice committee who wasn't a lawyer. In 1971, when the Texas statehouse was rocked by an insurance and kickback scandal, Hannah became
a catalyst for the so-called "Dirty Thirty," a maverick group of reform
legislators who revolted against Speaker of the House Gus Mutcher, who
later was convicted in the scandal.

In off hours and when the legislature wasn't in session, Hannah was
"poor-boying" his way through law school. Texas had a law, since abol-
ished under pressure by lawyers, that allowed legislators who had completed two terms in the House and two years of law school to take the
state bar exam without actually having graduated from law school. After
amassing sixty hours of course work at the South Texas School of Law
and the University of Houston Law School, Hannah took the state bar
in 1971 and passed with a score of 85, a better score than many law
school graduates who took the test that year.

A year later, Hannah moved to Lufkin, five miles north of Diboll, and
beat the incumbent district attorney for the prosecutor's job. The job paid
$16,000 a year, a far cry from his $4,800 salary as a legislator. "When
you're starving," Hannah said years later, "that $16,000 seemed like all
the money in the world."

He found his first case in a folder buried in a file cabinet. The son of
a popular local highway patrolman had been killed in a fight over a lover,
and the killer had never been prosecuted for the "crime of passion." The
thirty-two-year-old rookie prosecutor dusted off the file and got an indictment. He stayed up all night every night before and during the trial,
poring over murder statutes and precedents. He had never tried any case,
much less a murder. Like the little boy questioning his mother, he asked
himself over and over again, "What if the defense says . . . ?" And the
young prosecutor convinced a jury to sentence the killer to five years in
the penitentiary, the maximum for murder without malice.

Not long after, Hannah provoked some curious looks in Lufkin when
he announced he would prosecute a young black man for killing an elderly
black mechanic. Law enforcement in East Texas regarded black-on-black
murders as "misdemeanor killings," generally resolved by either overlooking them or allowing their perpetrators to plea-bargain to lesser offenses. The news, however, was warmly received by at least one resident
of Lufkin, a black pathologist from Jamaica. "It'll be the first trial since

I've been here that a black man has been tried for killing another black man," the doctor grinned. "Now won't that be something?"

Like the killer of the highway patrolman's son, the young black man was convicted and sent off to prison. The trials established a precedent: as a prosecutor, Hannah never lost a case.

Hannah's triumphs in the courtroom, his longtime acquaintances noticed, did little to soften the rough edges. There was little about his appearance or decorum to suggest he was an officer of the court. He would never tell a stranger he "practiced" law; he simply "lawyered." When he spoke of his profession, it was with the humility and pride of a man who had fought odds to get his license. He was still East Texan to the core, and while a jury trial might force him into a necktie, he damned well didn't plan to be caught in one outside the courthouse.

More than a few jurors appeared surprised in closing arguments when they glanced at Hannah's left hand resting on the jury rail. An ace of spades was tattooed on the back of the webbing between his thumb and forefinger, symbolic of nothing deeper than a teenage sailor's newly discovered freedom.

Before juries, Hannah was folksy and witty. He avoided legal terms, favoring down-home East Texas analogies that made the same point. Outside the courtroom, he succeeded by listening more than he talked. Beneath the exterior that would have passed as easily for logger as for lawyer, Hannah was sensitive and timid, maybe to a fault.

"Being a prosecutor is the most exhilarating thing I can imagine," Hannah confided. "It's an honorable profession that serves the people. But if you're a prosecutor, winning is a mixed emotion. It's hard to get into celebrating somebody's demise, no matter how evil their crime was. Everybody's got a son, daughter, mother, and they're all crying when Daddy's being hauled off to prison. It's the kind of thing you always think about."

Hannah resigned from his prosecutor's job in 1974 for a post in Austin as head of Common Cause, a consumer lobby group for government reform. A year later, he headed back to East Texas and started practicing law in Lufkin with Claude Welch, a boyhood friend.

In August 1977, an aide for U.S. Senator Lloyd Bentsen, Texas's senior Democrat, phoned Hannah in Lufkin and told him to meet the senator at Houston Intercontinental Airport. "John," the senator wanted to know, "have you ever done anything that would embarrass me or the President?"

"No sir," Hannah responded nervously. "I really don't think so."

John Henry Hannah, Jr., became President Jimmy Carter's appointee as U.S. attorney for the Eastern District of Texas, the top federal prosecutor for forty-one counties that stretched from Beaumont on the Gulf Coast up to Sherman near the Oklahoma state line.

Within months, Hannah had hired the first black, the first Hispanic, and the first female prosecutors in the history of the district.

"This is no longer a white Anglo-Saxon male office," he said. "I used to sit in Lufkin prosecuting cases and there would be a black defendant and an all-white jury, a white judge, two white prosecutors, and a white police officer, and the defendant would probably be represented by a white lawyer. A judicial system not only has to be fair," Hannah maintained, "it has to give every appearance of justice."

FBI agents accustomed to working interstate theft cases, bank robberies, and white-collar crime found themselves juggling a different kind of investigation on their schedules. For the first time since the forties, the United States attorney in East Texas was using federal civil rights statutes to go after corrupt law enforcement officials.

In Bonham, Hannah convicted a sheriff who hauled dope in the trunk of his patrol car and took kickbacks from the operator of an illegal casino. In Tyler, he convicted Wozencraft and Matthews, the two undercover narcotics officers who had planted evidence, used drugs, sold drugs, and committed perjury while engineering the largest undercover drug operation in Texas history. In Longview, he convicted the sheriff of conspiracy to murder and facilitating illegal gambling. For good measure, he added convictions of four of the sheriff's close associates, a local justice of the peace, a county commissioner, and two former sheriff's deputies. "There is nothing more deadly to a society," Hannah told the Longview jury, "than a totally corrupt law enforcement group."

In relatively short order, Hannah had accumulated convictions against thirty-five county officials, mostly on bribery charges. "Corruption isn't new to East Texas," said an FBI agent who investigated some of the cases on elected officials, which the bureau calls public integrity investigations. "Hell, it's been going on here forever. People just looked the other way and accepted it. Until now. It makes Big John mad as hell."

Word spread among law enforcement like ooze in red dirt: good ol' boys with badges who took money under the table, lied on the stand, or beat heads were about to become an endangered species. The mere casual appearance of an FBI agent in a county courthouse created more stomach acid than four-alarm chili.

Prosecuting civil rights and public integrity cases in East Texas, a bastion of status quo conservatism and clannishness, drew statewide attention. *The Dallas Morning News*, whose editorial page at the time paid few compliments to Democrats, applauded Hannah's crusade against crooked cops and officials. "Few ills can endanger the health of a democratic government like corrupt officials," the *Morning News* said. "And law-enforcement officers who misuse their offices are the worst of the bunch. . . . Hannah's prosecution of law-enforcement officers is a reminder that no one is above the law in a democracy—especially those who are charged with enforcing it."

The election of Ronald Reagan in 1980 meant unemployment for virtually every Democratic U.S. attorney in the nation, including Hannah, whose office had amassed one of the highest conviction rates in the country. His Republican successor, Bob Wortham, however, asked Hannah to continue as a special prosecutor, trying about twenty East Texas county commissioners indicted earlier in the year in a widespread kickback scheme. Hannah tried the commissioners the way he had every other official: he convicted them.

Even its most vocal critics, of whom there were a considerable number throughout the South, gave the Southern Poverty Law Center credit for its unorthodox approach to law. The center's civil lawsuit in behalf of Garner's family, angry as it made many residents of Sabine County, was merely a predictable move on the legal chessboard. But quietly, the center's guardians, Dees and Cohen, were evolving a legal strategy that would add an unprecedented footnote in Texas legal history. The Southern Poverty Law Center also would virtually assume—critics would say "usurp"—the State of Texas's responsibility for *prosecuting* the three officers on criminal charges in Garner's death.

A little-known and seldom-used provision of Texas law allows a crime victim or his survivors to hire a lawyer, or special prosecutor, at their own expense to try the alleged perpetrators of the crime. The statute, which requires that the local district attorney agree to step aside, had been used occasionally by family members, but never by an organization or special interest group.

Dees and Cohen, convinced the three officers couldn't be convicted in Hemphill without an aggressive outside prosecutor, would handpick the prosecutor, underwrite his costs, and provide veteran investigators Joe Roy and Danny Welch to help assemble the case, all in an extraordinary attempt to send Ladner, Horton, and Hyden to the penitentiary.

Ever mindful that his intervention even in civil lawsuits branded him an outsider in the community, Dees always recruited local lawyers to assist in cases outside Montgomery. In no case would it be more important to take off the "outsider" edge than in Garner's: he had to find a tough, qualified, *local* special prosecutor to try the cops in Hemphill, a notoriously clannish town even by small-town standards. Dees and Cohen spent hours on the phone calling lawyer contacts throughout Texas, trolling for a tough lawyer with prosecution experience who, they hoped, would be accepted in Hemphill. Virtually every phone call produced the same candidate.

"Call information in Tyler, Texas," Dees told his secretary, "and get me a number for a lawyer named John Hannah."

When Morris Dees phoned John Hannah in late April 1988, he got straight to the point.

"Corrine just doesn't have any faith that justice is going to get done down there, what with everyone knowing everyone else," Dees said. "She'd be more comfortable with someone outside the system. Aren't you from the sticks somewhere down there?"

As was his habit, Dees had done his homework. Sabine County's aging district attorney, Bill Martin, was a lame duck who already had announced he wouldn't be seeking re-election. Martin was returning to his law practice in Newton, just a few miles from Hemphill. Further, ethics would make it difficult for Martin to prosecute Ladner, Horton, and Hyden anyway. As the area's chief prosecutor for twenty years, Martin had been a member of the same law-enforcement team as the three officers. Over the years, Ladner, Horton, and Hyden had made the arrests, and based on their sworn testimony, Martin had tried to put their suspects in prison. The old district attorney would be the first to admit that Ladner and, particularly, Horton had become friends of his.

Hannah felt his blood rush. He'd followed the case in the media and through the lawyer grapevine. He'd built his career on cases like *Texas v. Ladner, Horton, and Hyden.* Damn right, this ol' dog would hunt.

As soon as District Attorney Bill Martin signed the papers, Bubba Dees and Sonny Hannah, sons of a tenant farmer and a mule skinner, were readying to take the battle to the good ol' boys in Hemphill.

17

OFFICIAL SILENCE

JUST AS SURELY as if Sheriff Blan Greer had slapped him in the face, the January 1988 story on the front page of the local *Sabine County Reporter* was an affront to Vollie Grace.

For a month after Loyal Garner, Jr.'s death, the sheriff had continued to pay the salaries of suspended deputies Bill Horton and Bo Hyden—as the city had continued to pay Chief Thomas Ladner—pending the outcome of their trials.

The story, under the headline "No Choice," was apologetic:

Sabine County Sheriff Blan Greer said Monday afternoon that it appears he has no alternative but to halt the pay of two deputies already on suspension, effective January 31.

His budget does not reflect sufficient monies to pay two suspended deputies and also hire replacements, Sheriff Greer said. . . .

"Due to the lack of funds that are available, I have no choice other than to recommend the suspension of Deputies Bill Horton and James 'Bo' Hyden without pay effective of this pay period. . . ."

The Hemphill City Council later elected to follow the sheriff's lead in cutting off Ladner's salary.

The apologetic tenor of the sheriff's announcement jolted Grace, who had been buoyed by the vocal interracial meeting at the Macedonia Baptist Church. The whites who attended had been as critical of Sabine County law enforcement as the blacks. The meeting was a public mandate, Grace believed, to force Sheriff Blan Greer to answer the lingering questions surrounding Garner's death. The trials of Ladner, Horton, and Hyden could be months away; the county was wracked with tension now.

In what surely was the first time a black man ever had gone to the Sabine County Sheriff's Department to demand answers, Grace nonetheless hit a stone wall. From the conversation, it was clear to him that the only mandate that registered with Sheriff Greer was the votes that won him the gold star he wore on his chest. Getting a straight answer from the aging sheriff was like trying to put a handle on Jell-O.

"It bugged me that a white person would just stand there and lie," Grace recalled. "And it's ironic, too. I remember when a white man wouldn't tell a lie to a black man. A white man figured a black man wasn't important enough to waste a lie on. I've been lied to so many times by the sheriff, the judge, and other officials. And I'd be standing there *looking* at them lying to me."

Sheriff Greer, claiming he wouldn't reveal information because it could jeopardize or influence the upcoming trial against the three lawmen, steadfastly refused to answer specific questions about Garner's death. Well, then, Grace wanted to know, how about just explaining the *general* jail policy about providing medical treatment for inmates? Grace was convinced the officers had violated not only local policy but state civil rights laws by initially refusing medical treatment to the fatally injured Garner. Even Grace's request for the department's official policy was denied.

Grace and the Concerned Citizens for Sabine County went public, demanding Sheriff Greer's resignation.

The Sabine County Reporter, in its lead story written on the same day the resignation demand was made, wrote: "Sheriff Blan Greer resign? 'That's not going to happen,' the Sabine County sheriff said. . . . It's in the best interest of the county, the sheriff said, that he not comment on the incident or the investigation at this time."

Unbeknownst to Grace and other residents of Sabine County, Greer and County Judge Royce Smith already were under fire for violations at the Sabine County Jail. A week earlier, the Texas Commission on Jail Standards, without any mention of Loyal Garner, Jr., had notified Sheriff Greer and Judge Smith that they had thirty days to "implement the provisions of the medical service plan, insuring that inmates are provided health care as the circumstances require and are comparable to community standards, [and] provide sufficient jailers and procedures that provide visual, face to face observations of all inmates at least once every hour. These functions shall be performed 24 hours per day. . . ."

Rider Scott, the general counsel for Governor Bill Clements, sent a copy of the commission's findings to District Attorney Bill Martin. "Due to the impact of any remedial action by the Commission and as a courtesy to you, the Governor has asked that I forward a copy of the notification to you."

With the criminal trial weeks away, at least one state agency already had documented half the indictment against the officers—that a fatally injured Loyal Garner, Jr., had been denied the medical treatment required by law.

For too long, Vollie Grace had heard the secondhand quotes attributed to Blan Greer that there'd never be a black deputy in Sabine County as long as he was sheriff. So the black contractor was unconvinced when he saw the story in the *Houston Chronicle*.

The lead paragraph had Sheriff Greer, in the process of interviewing applicants for the two deputy vacancies on his roster, "considering" hiring the county's first black deputy. Noting that none of the "several" black candidates he had interviewed possessed the required police certification, the sheriff nonetheless indicated he might hire one as a jailer, then promote him to deputy as soon as he became fully certified.

The sheriff denied he was reacting to the allegations of racism following Garner's death. "This is something I've intended to do for years," he told reporter Kathy Fair.

Sure, Grace thought as he read the article—just like the now-you-see-it, now-you-don't city council vacancy that surfaced weeks earlier at the meeting between blacks and whites at the Macedonia Baptist Church. After several blacks complained during the meeting that the city council was all white, Dr. Donald Powell, a Hemphill dentist and a member of the council, told the crowd that a recent resignation had created a vacancy. "He said it was a *nonpaying* job," Grace recalled. "He made reference to no black volunteering public service, that without being paid, blacks wouldn't be interested in it."

Janie Latham had been sitting in the front row when Dr. Powell mentioned the vacancy. "Well," Latham said, rising to her feet, "if there's an opening on the city council, I'd be glad to fill the position. I'm ready and willing."

"That's when the crawfishing started," Grace recalled. Within days, Dr. Powell corrected himself, explaining that the council actually had "anticipated" two vacancies. One already had been filled by Bill Barcheers. The other "anticipated" council opening was the post held by Billy Cannon, who had considered resigning to apply for the job of police chief previously held by Ladner. At the last minute, city officials explained, Cannon decided to remain on the council. Dr. Powell had misspoken; there were no vacancies to be had.

A week after the *Chronicle* article quoted the sheriff as "considering" a black candidate for deputy, Sheriff Greer hired Jim Berton, a white, fifty-four-year-old retired Marine and former patrolman for the Port Arthur Police Department who had owned property at the nearby Toledo Bend Reservoir for several years.

Within days, *The Sabine County Reporter* printed a two-column photograph of a young black woman chatting amiably with a uniformed member of the sheriff's department. The accompanying article announced Sheriff Greer's appointment of twenty-two-year-old Yvette Parks as dispatcher. "According to Sheriff Greer," it said, "should she wish to pursue a higher rank with the department after being certified as a dispatcher, the new employee will be sent to a nearby school to receive further training. As for now, Parks has expressed she's eager to get more acquainted with the job. 'I really like it. It's fun. I'm looking forward to learning everything,' she said."

Hiring a black for any job at the Sabine County Sheriff's Department would have been a show of good faith on the sheriff's part, Grace believed, had it occurred *before* Garner's death. Yvette Parks's employment after the racially charged death was tokenism and window dressing, designed to take the heat off the sheriff.

18

MURDER

IN HIS EIGHT years as justice of the peace in Smith County, Bill Beaird had conducted more than eight hundred inquests. In most, he had merely interviewed the police, studied the autopsy findings, and rendered a decision. None, he discovered, had been as difficult or as controversial as the death of Loyal Garner, Jr. Indeed, empaneling a six-member coroner's inquest jury had been an ordeal, pushing the court date to February 9, more than a month after Garner's death and longer than Beaird would have preferred. Many of the witnesses lived in Sabine County, a hundred miles away, and several had attorneys, all of whom had to be officially notified of the court appearance. Dealing with lawyers, Beaird complained privately, always gummed up the works.

And since his public announcement of the impending inquest, the rural justice of the peace had been deluged with calls from the media. Not only did the reporters' interest leave Beaird wondering how his cramped, makeshift offices in the converted mobile home in Noonday would accommodate the throngs of media, but he knew his ruling in Garner's death would be scrutinized, interpreted, and, whatever it was, criticized by thousands.

Four generations before him had been justices of the peace and county commissioners, and Bill Beaird had always figured there was probably a gene among the Beairds that made his hide thick as a mule's when it came to public criticism. That was just politics. But this inquest was different. "There were subtleties I began to notice," Beaird would recall later. "My phone at the office stopped ringing with people who used to call. People didn't drop by for coffee or to chat. I mean, it was like all of a sudden I didn't exist. I saw it happening in the community. I didn't just fall off a truckload of potatoes. The good ol' boy syndrome was alive and well in Smith County, too. White people didn't take kindly to white people defending black people and their civil rights."

People in his rural precinct who tried to brand Beaird as a liberal left the justice of the peace scratching what hair he had left. Not only was he the first Republican justice of the peace in Smith County history, but eight years of no-nonsense rulings and high bonds had established him as the toughest law-and-order justice of the peace in the county. Short sentences and early paroles, Beaird believed, sabotaged good and decent citizens, making them crime victims when they didn't have to be. And with little prompting, the crusty justice of the peace always was quick to volunteer his solution: "The state of Texas buys an island, like Alcatraz. Then you build a five-story prison on it. And when the courts sentence a man to ten years, it *means* ten years. No early outs. Let Mama come and wave goodbye to him. Then you tell her, 'You can pick him up right here in ten years if he's still alive.' "

If Bill Beaird's phone wasn't ringing as much at the office, the number of calls at home was more than compensating. Many of the callers were anonymous. "You need to let that nigger deal alone," one said. "It'd be in your best interest and health." "Why are you spending my tax money on that black?" another wanted to know. "That's Hemphill's business, not ours. You best leave it alone." Ultimately, the Beairds withdrew their teenage daughter from the high school she had been attending and transferred her to an out-of-town school. Beaird could handle the anonymous threats, but he'd be damned if he'd allow his daughter to be taunted, ridiculed, and even threatened at school simply because he was following the law.

As Beaird investigated the Garner case, it became more than a matter of simply following the law. In eight years of listening to a multitude of defenses, rationalizations, and smoke screens, the justice of the peace had developed gut feelings that more often than not had proved valid when all the evidence finally came in. And his gut told him that Garner had been beaten to death. "I don't think they meant to kill him," Beaird told Darla, his wife, one night before the inquest. "They went into that cell to give him a good country ass-whipping. But they went too far and things got out of control. . . .

"If they had got that body out of Medical Center Hospital, nobody in Smith County would have ever known about Loyal Garner, Jr. They'd have hauled him back down there, told people they'd better keep their mouths shut or the same thing'd happen to them. Then they'd have buried him and that'd be the end of it."

After he reviewed the autopsy and discussed the findings with Dr. Virgil Gonzalez, Beaird paid a visit to Smith County District Attorney Jack Skeen in Tyler. He told the prosecutor about the phone calls from Sabine County Judge Royce Smith and how the judge had attempted to take control of Garner's body before it could be autopsied. "The county judge, the sheriff, and good Lord knows who else were trying to get the body, telling me everybody agrees it's an accident. There's a lot here that doesn't add up," he told Skeen. "I think we could be looking at a homicide here."

Beaird always figured he'd been long on common sense, but he didn't fool himself about the law. When he appeared in late January in the Tyler law offices of A.D. and Carol Clark, the justice of the peace was in search of legal help. In addition to being lawyers, the Clarks were friends of his, and A.D. Clark at one time had been the district attorney of Smith County.

"After talking to several of these people, I'm pretty sure there's some kind of cover-up going on," Beaird told the lawyers. "And I'll be honest with you. I basically have become opinionated as to what went on down there. In order for me to be fair and unbiased in this inquest, I think I'll seat a jury and let six good people of Smith County decide the circumstances under which Garner died."

While Texas law is vague in specifying the structure of a formal inquest, it allows anyone "accused or suspected" of foul play in a death be allowed to attend the proceedings, offer evidence, and call witnesses on his own behalf. But it makes no provision for subpoenaing those suspects; their attendance is discretionary.

"Hell, I can see as many as ten lawyers showing up," Beaird told the Clarks. Privately, he envisioned a gaggle of out-of-town lawyers in high-dollar suits, each objecting louder than the other and creating chaos in his converted mobile-home courtroom in Noonday.

The Clarks volunteered to research the inquest statute and to write the charge that would be considered by the inquest jury. State District Judge Galloway Calhoun would be on vacation the week of February 9, and his courtroom in the Tyler courthouse would be appropriated for the inquest. The large courtroom would accommodate all the press, witnesses, and interested parties. The husband-and-wife legal team also would take the day off from their practice and be on call, making sure the proceedings were legally bulletproof.

"I just want to make sure it gets done right the first time," Beaird told the Clarks. "I don't want to have to dig him up later."

Early on February 9, there were more lawyers milling around outside Justice of the Peace Bill Beaird's borrowed 114th District courtroom than many rural East Texas counties had in their entire bar association. And most of the attorneys had an interest in the outcome of the inquest scheduled for ten A.M.

Though the outcome of the inquest ostensibly could lead to additional criminal charges filed against them in Tyler and likewise could be entered as evidence in the Hemphill trial, none of the Hemphill officers showed up for the inquest in Smith County. Suspended deputies Bill Horton and Bo Hyden had retained their own lawyers, but their attorneys had acquiesced to John Seale, Thomas Ladner's lawyer, to represent their clients' best collective interests. Frank Henderson, an assistant Smith County district attorney on Jack Skeen's staff, would represent the state of Texas and therefore present the bulk of the evidence in the death of Loyal Garner, Jr. Barry Abrams, an attorney for a Houston law firm, showed up to represent the city of Hemphill, a target in the civil suit filed by the Southern Poverty Law Center. Morris Dees appeared with two attorneys from nearby Longview, Texas, Glenn Perry and Mark Englehart, whom he had engaged as local counsel in Corrine Garner's civil lawsuit. (John Hannah had not yet formally been appointed special prosecutor in the Sabine County criminal cases against the officers and did not attend.) John E. Sherman of Houston and Billy R. Casey and Joann Gines-Shepherd, both of Shreveport, fired by Corrine Garner in favor of the Southern Poverty Law Center, were there to monitor the inquest in behalf of their new clients, Alton and Johnnie Maxie, who also had lodged a civil rights suit stemming from their incarceration on Christmas night. A.D. Clark, the former Tyler prosecutor, also appeared, primarily to keep his friend Beaird out of legal ambushes by all the high-priced legal talent in the courtroom.

Before entering the courtroom, Beaird summoned all ten lawyers into the judge's chambers. If the only nonlawyer in the proceedings was awed by all the legal talent amassed before him, he didn't show it. As was

Beaird's nature, there was no foreplay in his conversation. He was direct and to the point, reflecting his low threshold for tolerating lawyers and their legal maneuvering. He wanted to make sure everyone understood the ground rules from the "git-go."

"We've researched the inquest statute extensively," Beaird told the throng of lawyers. "The main rule is that there's no rule. We're here to accomplish only two things—to ascertain the manner and means of a man's death. I'm not interested in anything else. Mr. Henderson will present the evidence, and Mr. Seale, you can cross-examine or call any witnesses you need to. The rest of you can confer with whomever you need to.

"This is my ballgame. What I say goes. It's my way or the highway."

Like all good, experienced defense lawyers, John Seale used his opening remarks to cement his clients' case as he spoke to the pool of seventeen prospective jurors, from which six would be chosen to sit on the inquest jury. "What's been on the radio so far has all been one-sided," the Jasper lawyer said. "There has never been any statement that's been given about it by the other side of this. It's all been one-sided."

Seated at the district attorney's table, Dees jotted busily on a yellow legal pad, making notes on what almost certainly would be the police officers' defense when the pending criminal and civil cases against them came to trial. Seale's opening statement to the prospective jurors was a sneak preview before the main feature.

Garner's death spawned a barrage of legal proceedings and possibilities, many of which confused the public and even the reporters trying to explain the process. When the officers were indicted on Texas civil rights charges, the allegations had nothing to do with *civil* law. Violation of a person's civil rights was a *criminal* offense punishable, in the pending case of Ladner, Horton, and Hyden, by a maximum of ninety-nine years to life in prison. Making the criminal prosecution even murkier was the fact that the federal government likewise could file civil rights charges against the officers at any time, exposing them to even more prison time.

The civil lawsuit filed by the Southern Poverty Law Center on behalf of Garner's survivors sought monetary damages in civil court from the individual officers, the city of Hemphill and Sabine County.

The inquest, however, was a particularly high-stakes poker game for Seale. The veteran lawyer didn't want to tip the entire defense strategy for the upcoming civil rights trial in Sabine County, but he had to show enough of his cards in Tyler, if possible, to head off a ruling of homicide. Such a ruling could trigger additional charges of murder in Smith County against the three police officers.

"This case involves a situation where a man was arrested and was taken to jail and refused to take a Breathalyzer test and was obviously intoxicated to the extent that when the blood test was given the next morning . . . he was probably over a .30, which is about three times what it takes to be legally intoxicated in the state of Texas," Seale told the jury pool. "There's going to be other evidence that shows you about the effect of someone being in that extent of intoxication. In addition to the amount of alcohol that was in his system, he had a quantity of Valium in his system at the same time. All of this, I think, is going to be shown in the case."

Seale's claims of Garner's alleged intoxication produced mild discomfort for Frank Henderson and Morris Dees at the prosecution table; they had anticipated some kind of justification for the rough treatment administered by the officers. But the defense attorney's claim of Valium in Garner's bloodstream had jolted them.

"Where in hell did that come from?" Dees whispered to Henderson. Neither had seen any reference in the medical records or autopsy to indicate Garner's body contained Valium. Henderson's blank stare told Dees the assistant prosecutor was as stunned as he was.

Dees scribbled furiously on his legal pad. Richard Cohen, Joe Roy, and Danny Welch had a new assignment: destroy the notion that Garner had been "three times drunk" when he was arrested, and find out where the defense was getting this garbage about tranquilizers.

"He received a situation while in the jail of getting out of control and made an attack on one of the officers," Seale continued. "The evidence [is] going to show that nothing was done except to use the amount of force necessary to handle the situation."

Nine members of the jury pool acknowledged that they had heard or read media reports about Loyal Garner, Jr.'s death, but all of them swore those news accounts would not influence their ability to hear the case impartially. Before the lunch recess six jurors had been chosen—two white women, two black women, and two white men.

Henderson wasted no time in eliciting damaging testimony from the state's key witness, Dr. Virgil Gonzalez. "Would it be your opinion, Doctor, that the injuries that you saw, that you examined . . . could he have died as the result of an accident, maybe slipping and falling and hitting something?"

"Falling, no," Dr. Gonzalez said. "Trauma, yes."

"What does that mean?"

"By falling," the pathologist testified, "the force that would be inflicted on the parts of the body will not be sufficient to really produce a considerable amount of hemorrhage and contusion on the brain. Although you cannot measure the force inflicted on Mr. Garner, I'll say that there is a considerable force to damage the blood vessels underneath the covering of the brain to produce this hematoma or hemorrhage."

"It was your testimony that it was at least two, possibly four, blows that were hard enough to cause that kind of an injury?"

"Yes sir."

Henderson moved quickly to close the loop on a homicide verdict. The doctor had given him the means of death and a pretty good indication of the manner. The prosecutor wanted to crystallize the thought for the jury.

"Again, your findings are consistent with an injury caused by, say, a slapjack?"

"Yes sir," the pathologist replied without hesitation.

On cross-examination, Seale moved quickly to get the expert medical witness to embrace his self-defense theory—that Garner had been drunk, as much as three times the legal alcohol limit, and therefore could have been belligerent enough to have attacked Thomas Ladner in the detox cell and book-in room. Noting that the blood test on Garner in the emergency room of Sabine County Hospital showed a .075 alcohol content, Seale got Dr. Gonzalez to agree that the human body normally disposes of alcohol at the rate of .02 an hour.

"All right," Seale said, "so if this man then were arrested at 7:45 P.M. on December twenty-fifth and if he had .075 at 8:45 A.M. on the twenty-sixth, it would be a matter of extrapolating . . . and you'd add thirteen [hours] times two, which would be twenty-six. So his alcohol would have been .335, wouldn't it?"

"I don't believe I agree, sir," the doctor said, bringing the lawyer up short. "Under normal conditions," Gonzalez explained, "a person or an individual drinking without any injury, that is the usual course of the alcohol consumption and elimination through the body. But once the patient is unconscious . . . the alcohol level of an individual cannot be relied upon. There is a diffusion of hydrochloric acid in the stomach that can be diffused direct to the heart and goes into the circulation. . . . There is a diffusion of alcohol, a diffusion of hydrochloric acid that can be converted to alcohol level into the blood."

Painstakingly, Seale tried to get the doctor to resurrect the theory that Garner had to have been drunk at the time of the altercation in the jail. Gonzalez was unbudging. Seale's questioning finally brought Henderson, the prosecutor, out of his chair. "Excuse me, I'm sorry," the assistant prosecutor interjected, cutting off Seale in mid-sentence, "but I'm going to object to counsel badgering the doctor like that. I mean, that's not necessary. It's not adversary, and I'd ask that he be instructed not to do that."

Beaird, obviously irritated, summoned the lawyers to the bench. From their first meeting earlier that morning, there had been tension between the justice of the peace and Seale. Beaird considered the out-of-town defense lawyer to be obnoxious and arrogant. Seale had had bad vibes about the case even as he drove into Smith County that morning, and Beaird's pretrial demeanor, which he regarded as autocratic, only heightened his fears that Smith County already had its mind made up.

"Any more disruptions," Beaird said in a heavy whisper out of range of the jury, "and I'll clear the courtroom and do this myself. The law doesn't say I *have* to have a formal inquest." When he finished this last comment, he was looking squarely into Seale's eyes. The warning produced a slow burn on the defense lawyer's face, transforming his fair complexion into neon red.

Dr. Gonzalez was still smarting from Seale's questions, and when testimony resumed, he asked Beaird if he could explain his answer. "I didn't testify on the basis of his alcohol," the doctor said. "As a matter of fact, I never, never take the alcohol level, because the alcohol level right after the operation will be of no value. The only time that I find out this alcohol level is when I was subpoenaed to go to Hemphill and that grand jury told me that the alcohol level at that time was .07. I had no idea what they have done. . . ."

Minutes later, when Seale questioned whether his autopsy had revealed any other injuries, Dr. Gonzalez bristled. "I don't distort anything," the doctor snapped. "I don't hide anything, and this is where my testimony is. So that the report as stated there, it's a *complete* report."

If the inquest wasn't going his way, Seale at least gained a firsthand look at his most formidable enemy in the upcoming criminal trial in Sabine County. The doctor, he knew, was the state's most credible witness in the case against Ladner and the other officers. The doctor's credibility would have to be tainted on the witness stand in Hemphill.

While Beaird had subpoenaed twelve prospective witnesses, Henderson called only three others after Dr. Gonzalez—Alton and Johnnie Maxie and Welton Gene Sangwin, a white nineteen-year-old burglar and another of the inmates who had been incarcerated in the Sabine County Jail the night Garner ended up in a coma.

The Maxie brothers reiterated the story they had told the grand jury a month earlier in Hemphill. No one in Garner's pickup truck was drunk when Ladner and Hyden arrested them, they testified, and they signed statements that had been fabricated by law-enforcement officers only because they feared they, too, would be beaten. Additionally, the Maxies testified, officers attempted to cover up Garner's beating by washing his blood-stained shirt and throwing it, still wet, into the cell in the middle of the night. No one heeded their requests to get medical help for their injured friend until the morning after the beating, they testified.

Sangwin, who had been locked down in a cell near the Maxies and Garner, described hearing officers come to the detox cell after the three black prisoners repeatedly had beaten on the cell door. "There was two people there because I heard them both walk up there," Sangwin testified. "The door opened up, and he said, 'Which one of you black sonofabitches is beating on this door?' And he goes, 'I am.' And then I heard *whop, whop, whop* and some wrestling around on the floor. Then I heard him dragging him out down the hall. He said, 'See there, it didn't take three or four of us.' And then they carried him—I heard them when they went up to the front. I heard the door shut, and I heard him scream about two or three times. Then they brought him back, and there wasn't another sound. Nobody said nothing for a pretty good while. Then one of them called up there to the front and said, 'You need to carry this guy to the hospital. He's hurt pretty bad.' "

The four women and two men on the inquest jury deliberated only twenty minutes before returning their ruling. The court's bailiff handed the verdict to Judge Beaird, who cautioned the courtroom about outbursts, then read the jury's ruling aloud:

"We, the jury, find from clear and convincing evidence that Loyal Garner, Jr. died of injuries to his head as a result of homicide."

As Corrine Garner and her in-laws, Sarah and Loyal Garner, Sr., made their way from the courtroom without comment, Judge Beaird and Smith County assistant district attorney Frank Henderson answered questions from the press. "I'm satisfied that the law was carried out," Beaird said, "and that this jury got to the truth."

Then the justice of the peace deferred to the prosecutor. Certainly the inquest ruling paved the way for Smith County to file murder charges against the three police officers, Henderson acknowledged, but the murder charges would be "repetitious" since the officers already faced civil rights charges in Sabine County that carried the same maximum penalty of life imprisonment.

Quietly, as he had throughout the day of testimony, Pearlie Henderson, no relation to the prosecutor, watched the aftermath of the legal proceedings. A month earlier, he had consoled Corrine Garner as she sat at Medical Center Hospital, and as president of the Tyler chapter of the NAACP, he had filed a civil rights complaint with the FBI when her husband died. He had vowed to the widow he would see the case to its end.

Now, he listened as Ernest Deckard, a colleague in the Tyler NAACP, talked with reporters. "I believe justice has been served here," Deckard said.

"Almost," Pearlie Henderson said to himself. "*Almost.*"

Frank Henderson's doubts about filing additional charges against the officers in Garner's death were the kind of impromptu, first-blush statements elicited by the media in breaking news stories.

More pragmatically, filing murder charges against three white police officers for a crime committed against a black prisoner one hundred miles away would be an uphill crawl through broken glass. Frank Henderson's boss, Smith County District Attorney Jack Skeen, knew that, and if he didn't, there were any number of assistant prosecutors on his staff ready to point out the pitfalls of such a potentially ill-fated trip.

Jurisdiction was not an issue. Under Texas's so-called "hitchhiker statute," murder charges can be filed in the county in which the fatal injuries are inflicted, the county where the victim dies, or the county in which the body is found. But almost guaranteed, Skeen's staff reminded him, was a legal free-for-all in an appeals court over the issue of double jeopardy—prosecuting the officers twice for essentially the same crime.

Public sentiment in Smith County, as Justice of the Peace Bill Beaird could have told Skeen, might not necessarily support the county's chief prosecutor embroiling his staff and the county's money in prosecuting a controversial crime rooted in another county. And nobody had to remind Skeen of his backlogged docket of Smith County cases awaiting trial.

Privately, Skeen himself was worried about the message that potential indictments against police officers would send to the law enforcement community in his own county. In January 1983, when Skeen assumed office as a reform candidate, the credibility of the district attorney's office was off the bottom of the chart, primarily because of the Matthews-Wozencraft undercover fiasco. In the five years he had been in office, the forty-two-year-old, quiet-spoken Skeen prided himself on recouping the prosecutor's image in Tyler. Cops discovered that the Democratic prosecutor wouldn't shy away from cases, even when he and police both knew the outcome would be a dice roll. Increasingly, police saw fewer plea bargains and more trials. Likewise, it wasn't unusual for the DA himself to accompany officers on routine patrol, frequently showing up at crime scenes for firsthand inspections of evidence.

Only seven months into his first term, Skeen sent a convincing message to the public, and particularly the county's black population, that the district attorney didn't play favorites. In August 1983, the son of one of Tyler's most prominent businessmen, the white owner of a car dealership, was thrown out of a nightclub. The young man returned with a shotgun, which he fired into a group of young black men who had just walked into the club, and killed one of the bystanders.

A prominent Dallas defense attorney claimed his wealthy young client hadn't intended to kill anyone and, at worst, was guilty only of involuntary manslaughter, a reckless act without premeditation. The novice district attorney, however, refused to budge and tried the man on murder charges. A jury convicted him of murder and sentenced him to twenty-five years in prison.

Pearlie Henderson had monitored that trial, too, as he had many others since in which blacks were involved. Carrying through on his vow as president of the NAACP, he intended to be an ever-present visual reminder that Smith County's blacks, 23 percent of the county's population, expected fair treatment in the courts.

The NAACP leader was seen even more frequently in the Smith County Courthouse after the inquest jury returned its homicide ruling in Garner's death. Henderson and other blacks, including Smith County Commissioner Andrew Mellontree, the county's highest-ranking black official, likewise missed few opportunities to make their feelings known to Skeen. "Sabine County and those others around it are a legend among blacks," Henderson said more than once. "I hear rumors that John Hannah is going to try the case over there, and no question about it, he's a good prosecutor. But I tell you, as long as it's in Sabine County, there won't be any justice, not from those rednecks. Any justice that Loyal Garner, Jr., gets is going to have to come from *Smith County*. That's just the way it is."

By day, Skeen read the autopsy report and the testimony Dr. Gonzalez had given to the Sabine County Grand Jury and the inquest jury in Tyler. He interviewed Dr. Gonzalez and Dr. Ron Donaldson, the neurosurgeon who had performed the emergency surgery on Garner. He got the three officers' written reports from Texas Ranger Roscoe Davis and compared them. By night, the prosecutor anguished over what he knew would be the biggest decision in his five-year career as a prosecutor.

"Because of the number and extent of the blows and the severity of the blows, I believed they were struck intentionally to either cause serious bodily injury or to cause death," Skeen would recall. "Under either one of those theories, the defendants would be guilty of murder in the state of Texas. A lot of people don't understand that in Texas, you can commit murder by intending to cause serious bodily injury and doing an act clearly dangerous to human life. In addition to that, I had written statements from the police officers about the events that simply could not be true."

Cautious by nature, methodical by profession, Jack Skeen was known among his closest associates and friends as the last person to act emotionally or impetuously. Ironically, it was an uncharacteristic sense of outrage that fomented the prosecutor's decision. "What personally offended me was not only the beating, but what happened to Loyal Garner *after* the beating," Skeen recalled. "All through my investigation of this case, it really affected me that, after the beating, they had dragged Garner back to his cell in the middle of the night and tossed him in the cell and, basically, left him to die. To treat a human being like that infuriated me. The actions of those officers were reprehensible."

On March 3, two months after Thomas Ladner, Bill Horton, and Bo Hyden were indicted in their own county on civil rights violations, Jack

Skeen, a copy of the inquest in hand, convinced a Smith County grand jury in Tyler to return a second set of indictments. The three Hemphill lawmen were charged with murder.

Tyler State District Judge Joe Tunnell set bond for Ladner at $50,000; bond for Horton and Hyden was set at $25,000 each. That afternoon, deputies of the Sabine County Sheriff's Department were ordered to arrest their three former colleagues. The attorneys representing Ladner, Horton, and Hyden arranged for their bonds, and the three suspended lawmen walked silently out of the sheriff's office without being mugged, fingerprinted, or jailed.

The decision to prosecute had been anguishing, but when Jack Skeen met with reporters, he was unwavering. "I believe the evidence will show Ladner was the main actor," he said, "but under the law of parties, the other two can also be found guilty. I intend to try to get the cases set for trial as soon as possible."

In Hemphill, Ladner was incredulous. "How in hell can they indict me in Tyler for something I've already been indicted on?" he asked Seale.

"The way I read the law, they can't. I don't think it'll stand up on appeal. It's double jeopardy."

19

FEAR AND ANGER

NOT UNTIL THE INQUEST in Tyler had drawn to a close did Roscoe Davis realize how tenuous his role had become in *Texas v. Ladner, Horton, and Hyden.*

The tall, angular Davis had been an officer for the Texas Department of Public Safety for twenty-five years, first as a decorated highway patrolman, then, for the last twelve years, as a member of the legendary Texas Rangers, the Department of Public Safety's elite criminal investigation division.

As the state's chief investigator into Loyal Garner, Jr.'s death, Davis hadn't been surprised when he was subpoenaed as a witness by Justice of the Peace Bill Beaird. Never having been to the Smith County Courthouse in Tyler, he had allowed more than enough time to make the trip, and he arrived from his home near Jasper well before the ten A.M. proceedings. Milling around outside the courtroom with other potential witnesses and more reporters than he'd ever seen, Davis was approached by a man in a suit whom he immediately figured for a lawyer. "My name's Morris Dees," the man said affably, extending his hand to the lanky Ranger in western-cut suit and cowboy boots. "I'm going to be assisting in the prosecution of this case."

Informal pretrial conferences between prosecutors and police officers to review evidence were customary, and when Dees suggested they adjourn to the district attorney's office on the top floor of the courthouse, Davis fell in behind the lawyer, whom he assumed to be an assistant district attorney. Upstairs, Dees asked him for his investigative files, which he dutifully turned over. He then was directed to a small office, where he sat by himself as the files were being photocopied. Strangely, the Ranger thought, there was no conference and no discussion of his investigation. Only minutes before the inquest was to begin, and still without his files, he was directed to the second-floor courtroom where the proceedings would take place.

Not until the ten lawyers and their client affiliations were introduced in open court did Davis realize that Dees wasn't an assistant district attorney but actually was associated with something called the Southern Poverty Law Center. And while the veteran Ranger had never heard of the Poverty Law Center, he could tell by the context that Dees had some relationship to Corrine Garner and *civil* litigation. Davis, who was there as the state's criminal investigator, unwittingly had turned over his files to a civil litigator whose client had a clear financial interest in the outcome of the case. Though from the looks of things Dees *was*, as he had said, assisting the prosecution during the inquest—his explanation of his role hadn't been an outright lie—the Texas Ranger nonetheless felt duped. He was only a little less angry at the Smith County prosecutor's office for its tacit role in the misrepresentation. During the first break, Davis tersely demanded, and received, his investigative files.

If the preinquest machinations had left Davis confused, the end of the day left him even further perplexed. Both sides had rested and sent the case to the jury, and the state hadn't even called him to testify.

He replayed the day's events in his mind during the two-hour drive home from Tyler, and by the time he pulled into the driveway of his tin-roofed ranch house ten miles outside Jasper, Davis was paranoid. The more he mulled over the day's proceedings, the more he knew how a pariah must feel. Had there ever been any real intention to call him as a witness, or had they subpoenaed him to Tyler merely to get access to his records? And who would end up with those copies of his investigative files?

The Tyler prosecutors had been uncommonly accommodating to the Southern Poverty lawyer—downright chummy, the Ranger thought. It seemed obvious that they too believed that, as the Poverty Law civil suit claimed, there had been a conspiracy to shroud the actions of the Hemp-hill officers in Garner's death. God, had they figured him as a part of the same cover-up?

Ironically, had he been called to testify and asked his opinion, Texas

Ranger Roscoe Davis would have said, well, yes, there could be a conspiracy. He knew he couldn't prove it, not with the evidence he had; but that was his *opinion*. Opinions, he knew, were like relatives: good or bad, everyone had one. But Roscoe Davis hadn't been asked, and since the conspiracy theory was only his opinion, he hadn't volunteered it. Theories and opinions weren't his job; he was paid by the state of Texas to dig up facts—and he had none that conclusively pointed to a conspiracy.

Conspiracies were tough. Generally, the only people with firsthand knowledge were the conspirators themselves. Without a weak link among the participants—someone who, for whatever reason, agrees to testify against his accomplices—conspiracies go unprosecuted for lack of proof.

Actually, the possibility of a conspiracy had crossed Davis's mind as soon as he saw the statements that jailer Clyde Kirk had taken from Johnnie and Alton Maxie, who by the time Davis arrived at the Sabine County Jail, conveniently had been allowed to pay their fines, ensuring their hasty retreat to Louisiana. "Those statements didn't amount to anything," Davis would say later. "Those officers figured out a story they thought would keep their tails out of the fire and then they got the Maxies to give statements to that effect. I knew it just as soon as I saw the Maxies' statements."

Nor did it escape Davis's attention that the statements, as suspicious as he considered them, had been witnessed by one of his colleagues in the Texas Department of Public Safety. Trooper Bill Bradberry, assigned to Sabine County, wore the same Texas Highway Patrol badge Davis had worn for thirteen years before his promotion to the Rangers. Had Bradberry actually witnessed the statements, Davis wondered, or had it been a perfunctory favor to the trooper's friends in Hemphill?

Davis's paranoia on the way back home wasn't without justification. What he feared—that he wasn't trusted—was, in fact, already a reality among some prosecutors and the Southern Poverty Law Center staff. Judge Beaird's recollection of the phone calls from Hemphill in which Judge Royce Smith had attempted to get immediate custody of Garner's body had been repeated to Skeen's staff. The story cast doubt on virtually everyone connected with the Sabine County portion of the investigation.

It had not gone unnoticed by prosecutors that while Davis had interviewed jail inmates and taken their statements immediately after arriving at the jail on Saturday, the Ranger gave the three key suspects, Ladner, Horton, and Hyden, until Monday to submit their accounts of the Garner affair. The similarities in the officers' statements had been so obvious that a Sabine County grand juror had questioned them. The Cop's Code was notorious. How far, prosecutors wondered, did the tentacles of the good-ol'-boy network extend? To the Texas Rangers?

Had there been casual chitchat over a cup of coffee before the inquest, Roscoe Davis might have allayed the prosecutors' skepticism of him. "Those boys got together and put their statements together pat," the fifty-four-year-old lawman would recall later. "And they wouldn't budge. Not one of them. They were going to go together. With most suspects, you can turn one against the other. But these guys were in it together. No way you'd break one from the other two."

Davis actually considered the time he had given the officers to compile their statements as expedient. The officers, he knew, weren't going anywhere. On the other hand, any inmates who might have information about Garner's injuries could be released on bond, transferred to prison, intimidated or coerced in their version of the events, or worse. The inmates were the Ranger's first priority. And because he had major reservations about the authenticity of the statements purportedly given by the Maxie brothers, he had asked Sheriff Greer the next morning, Sunday, to accompany him to Louisiana. The trip validated his suspicions.

On their home turf in Many, Louisiana, outside the confines of the Sabine County Jail and with a state line separating them from the Hemphill officers, the Maxies gave voluntary accounts of Christmas night that refuted the statements they had signed in Hemphill. Indeed, the Ranger had elicited damning first-person accounts that documented the savage beating of Garner and the officers' refusal to provide medical attention.

The inquest, from Davis's viewpoint, was only the most recent chapter in a sorry saga that, he was beginning to believe, would have an equally dubious ending. There was no reason to believe otherwise; the case was out of control even before he inherited it.

That Roscoe Davis even was assigned the case was a fluke. Ranger Don Morris, based in Lufkin and normally responsible for Sabine County, had used the Christmas holidays to schedule an extended out-of-town hunting trip. Davis, who usually covered Jasper, Newton, and Tyler counties to the south, took the call as Morris's backup. The substitution was important only in procedure; Rangers have jurisdiction in all of Texas's 254 counties.

The independent investigation by the Texas Rangers that Sheriff Greer boasted to the grand jury would assure the public that he wasn't "trying to sit on some evidence or something like that" actually was little more than window dressing. By the time Ranger Roscoe Davis walked into the Sabine County Jail there was precious little evidence to support any serious investigation. There was no victim to question: Garner was one hundred miles away in Tyler, unconscious, and alive only because he was connected to a respirator. The Maxie brothers, material witnesses to a potential major felony, had been released. And Davis had to wonder if the Sabine County Jail had ever before been as spotless as he found it, the floors and walls looking as if they'd been freshly scrubbed.

Sheriff Greer, questioned later by Richard Cohen of the Southern Poverty Law Center, acknowledged that when he arrived at the jail Saturday morning, he didn't issue any orders to protect the crime scene or evidence.

Well, Cohen asked, didn't the Sabine County Sheriff's Department have procedures for investigating complaints against officers?

"No sir," the sheriff replied; there had been no complaints "other than this Garner boy, and they were suspended for that." The suspensions, at that time, had been paid suspensions, a point the sheriff hadn't volunteered.

Ranger Davis found no blood on the floors in the detox cell or the book-in room, where inmate witnesses claimed Garner had been beaten. Sheriff Greer, Davis detected, was upset with his deputies. The county's chief law-enforcement officer, the Ranger later would note, "appeared honest and open in every way, but limited in what he could do." The Ranger suspected that whoever cleaned up the floors did it during the night, before the sheriff arrived in the morning.

Davis did find what appeared to be traces of blood in the crevices of the cement-block wall in the booking room. Using cotton swabs and distilled water, he attempted to dig and probe the crevices for enough of the reddish-brown substance to have it analyzed for confirmation and blood type. Weeks later, the Department of Public Safety lab would notify him that his attempts had been futile; there wasn't enough of the substance on the swabs to even confirm what it was.

Virtually the only physical evidence the Ranger was able to collect was a badly worn, leather-shrouded blackjack from Chief Thomas Ladner. "The seam," Davis noted, "had been ripped around the edge." The unraveled stitching allowed the circular piece of lead inside to fall into his hand. Later, however, Ladner surrendered a second blackjack, one that appeared newer and undamaged. It was this newer one, the chief claimed, that he had used Christmas night to deliver the "glancing blow" to Garner's head during the brief scuffle to subdue him in the detox cell.

The cloud of doubt over his integrity in the Garner investigation, Davis would discover, was only forming during the inquest February 9. Before the Garner case was resolved, the issue of his allegiance would become a strong but silent storm that he believed left him marooned and unacceptable to either team of strange bedfellows. The prosecution, the only team for which he had ever worked, was itself a curious alliance of prosecutors and civil rights lawyers who had drafted a defense lawyer, John Hannah, as a special prosecutor. The defendants, all law enforcement officers, were the people he traditionally worked with, not against.

The inquest had left Davis unquestionably unsettled about his investigative role. Weeks later, subpoenaed by Richard Cohen of the Poverty Law Center to give a deposition in Corrine Garner's civil lawsuit, Davis discovered he most certainly had been put in the same camp as Ladner, Horton, and Hyden.

Cohen, a razor-sharp questioner with a penchant for exhaustive detail, had focused Poverty Law Center investigator Joe Roy's skills on gathering phone records and documents for the civil lawsuit. There was little doubt, however, that the same information would be funneled to prosecutors in the criminal trials. Having subpoenaed Sabine County Judge Royce Smith's telephone records, Cohen had confirmed the judge's calls to Medical Center Hospital in Tyler, during which he demanded, according to Justice of the Peace Bill Beaird, that Garner's body be released immediately. Judge Smith, Beaird recalled, had been adamant in his phone calls to Beaird that Garner's death had been an accident. There was no doubt in Beaird's mind that the highest elected official in Sabine County had tried, literally, to bury the evidence.

Cohen got Ranger Davis to confirm that he had walked into the judge's office before the calls to Tyler were placed. Davis recalled that Sheriff Greer had been there, too. The Ranger's memory was vague, but he told Cohen that Dr. Grover Winslow may have been in the judge's office when the calls were placed. (Winslow later acknowledged that he had been present during the calls. He did not, however, admit attempting to bury Garner without an autopsy. The doctor said he had insisted on an autopsy, which he assumed would be performed by a private pathologist in Lufkin who previously had done contract work for Sabine County.) Cohen laid the predicate for a conspiracy that presumably involved not only the Ranger charged with the independent investigation but also Hemphill's most prominent citizens—the county judge, the sheriff, the doctor.

The civil rights lawyer then handed Davis a copy of the custodial death report the Ranger had filed, which had been forwarded to Texas Attorney General Jim Mattox. Such a report was a requirement any time a prisoner died in the custody of police officers. Davis noted in the report that Garner's death had been an accident. In the context of the questions, Davis glanced at the report and winced at how it must have appeared to everyone, particularly the prosecution and the Southern Poverty Law team.

How, Cohen asked, had the Ranger determined that Garner had been killed *accidentally*?

Davis's explanation was subjective. It was based, he believed, on a dearth of documentable evidence. Worse, the Ranger knew his response was rooted in gut instinct and semantics, a dangerous reply to a lawyer who made his living with words. "I didn't feel that there was any *intent* on the part of the officers to cause Loyal Garner's death," he replied. "I'd say that they had no intent to do *serious* bodily injury to him. That was my feeling."

Like a rabbit trapped in the glare of headlights, Roscoe Davis knew he was caught. "They had their minds made up that there was a cover-up," Davis said later of the prosecution team. "And they actually wanted it to appear that way. And that's where they put me."

Davis had been proud of his twenty-five years in the Department of Public Safety, and he knew his personnel file documented his conscientiousness. He had been commended for working on presidential protection teams, bribery cases, shootings, and bank robberies. As a trooper in 1972, Davis had saved a truck driver's life, winning the Texas Police Association's highest award for bravery. In twenty-degree weather, Davis had dived into a rain-swollen creek alongside Interstate 35 to where the driver was trapped in the twisted, almost wholly submerged cab of the truck. For more than an hour, Davis held the man's head in a small pocket of air while wrecker crews tore through the wreckage to free him.

Roscoe Davis always envisioned staying on with the Texas Rangers until mandatory retirement at age sixty-five forced him out. But as Bill Beaird had discovered before him, the Garner case was taking his career into strange and uncharted directions. Early one morning, the disenchanted Ranger phoned Department of Public Safety headquarters in

Austin and asked for the personnel department. On a pad of paper beside the phone, he jotted down several figures. He analyzed the numbers for several minutes and shrugged. His retirement would be considerably higher if he hung on another eleven years until he was sixty-five, but the pension figures scrawled on the paper would ensure a decent, if modest, living for him and his wife.

He had been thrust unwittingly into a no-win investigation, Davis concluded, one based less on fact than on race, police, and politics. The pressures were too intense for the facts to ever prevail. Every lawyer in the case was putting his own spin on the facts, ultimately—and erroneously, Davis believed—ascribing motivations to everyone involved, himself included. And he damn sure didn't appreciate the whispered assault on his integrity.

Roscoe Davis was known among colleagues in the Department of Public Safety as an uncommonly quiet, even withdrawn lawman. He had prided himself on dodging politics during his twenty-five years with the DPS. He despised politics; it got in the way of professionalism. He knew he had had enough; he would be retiring in the next few months. The damn lawyers could believe what they wanted to believe. Just the thought of throwing the Garner case up in the air gave him immediate peace of mind.

Traffic was light on Louisiana Route 175 during the first two hours after daybreak on March 4. Louisiana State Trooper Lee R. Isgitt saw the old Volare station wagon in his mirror before he noticed it on the radar screen. Instinctively, the trooper glanced at the radar meter. Fifty miles an hour. A law-abiding citizen driving the speed limit. As the station wagon passed the black-and-white patrol car parked beside the highway, the two black men in the front seat waved casually at the trooper.

As Alton Maxie lowered his hand, he wondered if he'd ever get his life back. The mere sight of the state trooper made him literally sweat. It was an involuntary reaction, like the graphic mental replays of that Christmas night in Hemphill that seized him every night when he fought for sleep.

Only a day earlier, Alton and his older brother had been subpoenaed to Tyler, Texas, bound by law to relive another time for a second grand jury the horror of watching their friend die. Short of an official subpoena, Junior Garner's death was a topic the two brothers didn't discuss anymore. They had owed Garner's widow, parents, and brothers a full accounting of their loved one's last hours alive. Recounting the story left Alton feeling less a man. The recollections—to Garner's family, to a grand jury in Hemphill, to an inquest in Tyler, and, finally, to another grand jury in Tyler just the day before—wracked Alton with guilt. No one had ever asked, but always he imagined that people were wondering the same thing: *Why didn't you do something to stop it?*

At times, Alton became so immersed in the question that even he forgot about Deputy Bo Hyden placing his hand menacingly on the grip of his pistol, motioning him back onto the cement ledge in the detox cell as Thomas Ladner slammed the blackjack onto Garner's head.

A mile and a half past the point Trooper Isgitt chose for his speed trap, Route 175 veers sharply to the right, as if highway engineers had intentionally chosen to spare the thicket of towering pines to the left. The old Volare station wagon, with Johnnie Maxie at its wheel, made no attempt to negotiate the curve. Instead, it headed straight, across the oncoming left lane, then ninety-nine feet and ten inches along the left shoulder and over a cement drainage culvert. The station wagon traveled another thirty feet before it slammed into a ten-inch pine tree, shearing it four feet from the ground. Like a fighter staggered by a haymaker, the old car spun slightly sideways and careened another twenty feet before a second pine finally ended its momentum. The second impact embedded the car's right front door post and windshield in the pine bark, just inches from Alton Maxie's face.

His head bleeding profusely, Alton miraculously freed himself from the wreckage. Johnnie was trapped beneath the steering wheel, wedged tight and bleeding like a stuck hog. Alton didn't need to be a doctor to know his older brother had suffered major head injuries. He was afraid to try to move him. Staring at his unconscious brother pinned in the driver's seat, Alton panicked. The familiar feeling of helplessness, first felt in a jail cell in Texas, swept him as he himself stood battered and bleeding in the thicket. He wondered if he was about to witness the second death of someone close in barely two months.

The young black man was diverted by the sound of the black-and-white trooper's car he and Johnnie had passed only minutes earlier screeching to a halt. Trooper Isgitt radioed for a rescue unit and ambulance even before he sprang from his car.

The impact with the first pine tree had crinkled the old Volare like aluminum foil around its driver, rendering Johnnie Maxie helpless and probably unconscious in the seconds before the second impact. Rescue teams pried and beat on the wreckage, finally resorting to the "jaws of life," a mechanical-hydraulic apparatus, which finally ripped an opening in the metal big enough to pull the large man out.

After the ambulance sped away with the Maxie brothers, Trooper Isgitt retraced the errant car's path from the highway into the pine thicket. The accident was curious. It had been a clear morning, with nearly two hours' sunlight. When the Maxies had passed his patrol car, they were driving fifty, the speed limit. Yet the trooper found no skid marks, no pressure marks, no scuff marks, and no rim cuts on the pavement—nothing to indicate that Johnnie Maxie had tried to stop or that a blowout had knocked the car out of control. Nor was there any evidence that once the Volare left the highway its driver ever attempted to stop.

"Tires were worn on the vehicle," the trooper noted in his report, "but did not cause the accident. From evidence at the scene, it appeared that the driver had tried to straighten out the curve."

Alton Maxie, the only occupant of the station wagon physically able to answer any questions, was no help. Shortly before they entered the curve, Alton told the trooper, he had bent over the floorboard to retrieve a cigarette lighter he had dropped. The impact with the first tree occurred so quickly, Alton said, that he only had time to brace himself. He hadn't glanced at his brother in the driver's seat.

Trooper Isgitt, left with no cause for the wreck, called Trooper Charles Seaverson, a safety expert, who examined the wreckage. The steering and brakes, Seaverson discovered, apparently were in working condition. And there was no evidence to indicate that either the driver or passenger had been drinking.

When it came time for Trooper Isgitt to write his report, he could only infer the cause of the crash. On the standardized accident report, he chose the block marked "fatigued" to describe the driver. In his narrative, the officer wrote: "Both the driver and the passenger had gone to a court hearing in Tyler, Texas on Thursday (03-03-88). Upon coming home late on Thursday, they did not get any rest. They went to work and worked all night."

If Johnnie Maxie dozed off at the wheel, he did so in the two minutes it took the Volare to get from the trooper's cruiser parked beside the highway to the crash scene in the thicket. And both brothers, as the trooper noted in his report, clearly had been awake when they passed his cruiser, waving as they drove by, right before before the crash.

Johnnie Maxie was in critical condition with massive head injuries, and doctors transferred him from the small rural hospital in Many to the regional trauma center in Shreveport. They estimated he'd be hospitalized for weeks, maybe months. He was lucky to have even survived. Alton was more fortunate, suffering only lacerations, bruises, and a precariously close encounter with death.

The mysterious accident was not received well in Texas. Practicioners in a profession more familiar with skepticism than coincidence, prosecutors John Hannah and Jack Skeen were more than a little dubious about the "accident" that almost killed their only two eyewitnesses. The Maxies, fearful of retaliation from Texas law enforcement authorities, had been escorted by Louisiana sheriff's deputies when they had been subpoenaed to Tyler, as they had been on their previous trips to Hemphill. Now, a day after their testimony in Tyler, they had almost been killed.

Neither Hannah nor Skeen liked the pattern; but phone calls to the Louisiana Highway Patrol hadn't produced any evidence of tampering with the Maxies' station wagon. The phone calls hadn't assuaged the gut feelings of either of the prosecutors. Both vowed that when the Maxies returned to Texas to testify in the trials, they would make the trip under heavy protection. With no evidence, Hannah and Skeen reluctantly chalked up the mystery to a quirk of fate.

Temporarily at least, the inquest and the ensuing murder charges in Tyler shifted the spotlight of scrutiny off Hemphill. For a while, stories in the papers bore Tyler datelines and the live-at-five reports used the Smith County Courthouse as a backdrop instead of the antiquated building that was the seat of government in Sabine County. One old gentleman in Hemphill, undoubtedly speaking for many of his friends and neighbors, likened the reporters to cattle. "They moved on to greener pastures, all right," he said, "but not before they left their shit in our backyard."

In Sabine County, the Garner death became a lightning rod for public opinion, *the* single issue that determined whether friendships would be ongoing, even whether residents supported their community. The few who spoke out publicly in favor of prosecuting the lawmen became "outsiders" and "troublemakers" who didn't have the best interests of their town and county at heart.

That Garner's death was a catalyst was apparent not only in the early-morning coffee gatherings at Twitty's Restaurant but also in the weekly *Sabine County Reporter*'s editorial pages. When the county's only newspaper editorialized on Garner's death, it condemned neither police abuse nor racism. The real culprit that had splintered this "peaceful, small East Texas town," the paper said in an "open letter" to the media, was, in fact, the media. And the *Reporter* assessed the damage in an economic bottom line—loss of tourism.

Although you don't seem to believe it, there's been no racial problems here and none exists today, according to most everyone—both blacks and whites. . . .

The effort on your part to make the incident racial, which was noticed nationwide, implied to the nation that Sabine County folks take the law into their own hands and pay little attention to the laws which govern our actions. . . .

While in search of a racial story, one that didn't exist, the big circulation daily newspapers and TV stations threatened the local economy by weakening the attractiveness of Sabine County in the eyes of potential tourists—customers. . . .

Through your effort to tag "racial" on the Garner death, so Sabine County could then be "fixed" and racism erased at least to the point of the remainder of the nation, metropolitan-area folks with recreation dollars to spend may now go elsewhere.

The weekly's view of the media coverage in the Garner death was one widely shared, making out-of-town reporters about as popular as IRS agents and door-to-door solicitors for Jehovah's Witnesses.

While waiting in the doctor's office for her appointment, Mary Collis, a longtime resident of Sabine County, had browsed through a *Reader's Digest*. She stopped at a piece called "Can We Trust the News?," reprinted from *The New Republic*. The focus of the article—that reporters weren't always objective in their reports—was strikingly apparent in the coverage of the Garner case in her own county, Collis believed. Two sentences she found particularly applicable: "Reporters often allow their political views to shape what they cover and how they cover it. They treat America's political, business and social leaders as targets."

The article was the basis of Collis's letter to the editor of *The Sabine County Reporter*. "Isn't this the very thing that has happened in Hemphill, Texas?" she wrote, and continued:

The media has created a monster in our town.

There is not one person that has read *The Houston Post, The Houston Chronicle, The New York Times, The Lufkin Daily News* etc. regarding the death of Mr. Loyal Garner that can truthfully say they did not find certain statements questionable.

It is really upsetting to read derogatory statements about men of Hemphill who have been our leaders and protectors. . . .

The people of Hemphill, Texas have got to be saddened by what the media has done to our town. There have been friendships, careers and innocent people damaged beyond repair.

Collis may have spoken for the majority, but another letter to the editor in the same edition made it clear her viewpoint wasn't unanimous.

A woman named Dorothy Stoner had heard about Janie Latham volunteering during the January 15 town meeting to fill the elusive city council vacancy, which suddenly was no longer open to the black woman. Stoner's letter to the editor was underscored in cynicism:

"Well now, the good citizens of Hemphill have just witnessed the biggest shell game of all time; 'Now you see a vacant seat on the city council, and now you don't.' I imagine Billy Cannon changed his mind about resigning at about 9:45 P.M. on Friday night, January 15, don't you think?

"This is only a temporary setback in the battle for equality and justice for all."

The Garner incident was a volatile issue in Hemphill, and as Collis noted in her letter, it had indeed splintered friendships. And while Garner's death consumed casual conversation, most feared putting their views in print for everyone to see.

The only other letter to the editor in that issue was a seemingly innocuous plea for help from the Hemphill Garden Club. Thirteen ladies from the Garden Club had picked up twenty-eight garbage bags of trash beside the highway leading into Hemphill from Pineland. Rhonda Berry's letter beseeched the public for help in reducing litter on the county's highways and invoked the state's popular antilitter slogan: "Don't mess with Texas."

By March, cars and pickup trucks throughout the county began sporting bumper stickers that broadcast Sabine County's defiance against outsiders who would criticize or meddle with its affairs or its residents.

DON'T MESS WITH HEMPHILL! cautioned the white stickers in blue capital letters. Already known throughout East Texas for its clannishness—and some would say social and political incest—Sabine County was going public with its attitude toward the outside world. Overnight the bumper stickers became a referendum, publicly pronouncing the car owner's support of Chief Thomas Ladner, Chief Deputy Bill Horton, and Deputy Bo Hyden.

Hemphill and Sabine County, its residents wounded by public perception, were closing ranks like an extended family protecting a beleaguered relative. They shunned those among them who didn't share their "us against them" perspective, berated visiting reporters, and organized to support their embattled police officers.

The Pineland Volunteer Fire Department, in the southwest corner of Sabine County, was known for civic contributions that went well beyond fighting fires. Volunteers solicited donations and held fund-raisers not only for fire equipment but also for sick children who desperately needed organ transplants and, most recently, to help Pineland's own Teresa Weatherspoon defray her expenses as a member of the U.S. Olympic women's basketball team, which won the gold medal in Seoul, South Korea.

Though it wasn't announced in the *Reporter* like most of its fund-raisers, word of mouth attracted more than two hundred people to what was perhaps the volunteer fire department's most unusual civic enterprise. Cars and pickup trucks, many bearing DON'T MESS WITH HEMPHILL! stickers, packed the grassy parking lot on a Saturday for a benefit fish fry. Nearly one thousand dollars was raised for the defense fund for the three indicted lawmen.

Much as the bumper-sticker campaign "appeared" one day, so had the fund-raiser; no one would claim credit for the ideas.

20

PATTERNS AND CIRCLES

History is little else than a picture of human crimes and misfortunes.

—Voltaire

History repeats itself.

—Anonymous

THE DEATHS OF Loyal Garner, Jr., and Woodrow Wilson Daniels spanned twenty-nine years and four hundred miles. Though a generation apart, their lives and deaths were so chillingly similar they could have been scripted. Together, they bear grim testimony to how little years have changed the plight of black prisoners in the hands of white cops.

On June 21, 1958, the thirty-seven-year-old Daniels, a black man, was arrested by sheriff's deputies on charges of reckless driving, drunkenness, and possession of whiskey. The deliveryman and father of five was locked in the Yalobusha County Jail in Water Valley, Mississippi. Nine days later, Daniels lay dead in a Memphis hospital of massive brain damage he suffered during an altercation with Sheriff J. G. "Buster" Treloar, who was described at the time by United Press International as a "family man and churchgoer."

A white couple at the Yalobusha County Jail to post bond for an inmate testified they saw the sheriff repeatedly hit Daniels in the head with a blackjack. Dr. Maubry McMillan, a white doctor in the rural north Mississippi town, was summoned to the jail to care for the unconscious inmate. The doctor testified that Sheriff Treloar told him: "I had to tap him on the head." While he was attending to the black man, the doctor said, the sheriff kicked and cursed the inmate. At one point, Dr. McMillan said, the sheriff kicked Daniels's leg and yelled, "You sonofabitch. There's nothing wrong with you."

Under oath, Sheriff Treloar said that when the cell doors had routinely been opened during the day, Daniels had gone from the colored cells to talk to a prisoner in the white cell block. The sheriff said he was escorting Daniels back to his own cell when the inmate grabbed hold of the bars. As the sheriff tried to wrench Daniels's hands loose, he said, the inmate fell to the floor, and the sheriff hit him once as he fell and "three or four times" as Daniels lay on the floor. None of the blows, the sheriff swore, hit Daniels in the head. It was possible, the sheriff speculated, that Daniels could have struck his head on a piece of metal connected to an elevator shaft.

An all-white jury of farmers and mechanics took twenty-eight minutes before acquitting Sheriff Treloar on manslaughter charges. Upon hearing the verdict, the husky sheriff walked to the evidence table, picked up the blackjack in question, and tucked it in his back pocket as he left the courtroom.

Just as the sun was lighting up Cleveland, Texas, on an unusually chilly morning in March 1988, two officers found Kenneth Simpson's body sprawled facedown on the cement floor of the Cleveland City Jail. He was trussed like a hog-tied wild animal, his hands cuffed behind him and his ankles bound with disposable plastic restraints called "flex" cuffs, and his pants rested mid-thigh, exposing his naked buttocks.

Simpson had been a big man, his six-foot frame bearing nearly 250 pounds, and his bulk and rigor mortis played hell with the emergency technicians as they tried to position the corpse on the gurney. Moving one of his arms or legs moved his entire body. The death was not fresh.

"Hambone" Simpson, thirty-one and black, was one of Cleveland's characters, the kind of hell-raising hustler indigenous to virtually every town in America, no matter how small. For most of his life, he had walked the edge. There wasn't a cop in Liberty County who hadn't heard about the perpetual wad of illicit money in Simpson's pocket from rolling dice or dealing cocaine, or about his explosive and unpredictable temper.

The ninth-grade dropout was much bigger and certainly more glorious in death than in life. Within days of his death, the Department of Public Safety teletype moved a terse message to outposts throughout the state about a rally held in Cleveland to protest Simpson's death. The rally was Simpson's fifteen posthumous minutes in the limelight. Few of the black marchers actually knew Simpson or his proclivity for society's outer fringes. Not that the knowledge would have changed their course of action. Simpson was an example, symbolic of the larger issue of blacks needlessly killed by police. He died less than two weeks after three East Texas lawmen had been charged with murdering Loyal Garner, Jr. And for all the criminal offenses Simpson had been suspected of committing, his final arrest had been an ironic and fatal mistake.

Word in Cleveland's black community was that Hambone was beating the bushes trying to raise four thousand dollars so he could pay two cops "protection money," the price of doing business when you're a dope dealer and gambler. The normally flush Simpson was experiencing a cash flow problem, and at about eleven P.M. on March 15, 1988, he boldly appeared at the Cleveland Police Department. Whether he was concocting an imaginative ploy to take the pressure off his past-due debt or whether he truly was about to blow the whistle on crooked cops, Hambone loudly inquired of the dispatcher the telephone number of the United States marshal in Houston. Anticipating he'd need a pen to write down the number, Simpson borrowed a metal Cross pen from Tom Yates, a white Cleveland patrol officer. The dispatcher said she couldn't locate the marshal's number, and Simpson left the station. On his way out, he dropped the Cross pen on top of a vending machine.

When Officer Yates realized Simpson had left without returning his pen, he drove to Simpson's mobile home in the Quarters, Cleveland's black section, to confront Simpson. Yates demanded the return of his pen; Simpson belligerently claimed he didn't have it. Spontaneously, a disagreement over a twenty-dollar mechanical pen escalated.

Using the portable radio attached to his belt, the young white officer summoned virtually every police, sheriff's, and Department of Public Safety officer on duty. A crowd of about twenty of Hambone's black neighbors clustered around the yard, watching the proceedings.

Gone apparently unheeded in the chaos of the moment was one transmission from the dispatcher at the Cleveland Police Department: she had found Officer Yates's pen atop a candy machine at the station. But even if the transmission had been acknowledged, the confrontation no longer was about an arrest for petty theft; it was about the authority of the system and a black suspect challenging a white officer. It was about egos, Yates's and Hambone's.

A black sheriff's deputy finally coaxed Simpson into his squad car, but not before Simpson continued his diatribe against "redneck cops." Wary of Simpson's size and his current temperament, officers violated a cardinal police procedure when they got him to jail: they booked and jailed him without searching him. Minutes later, when they checked him in his cell, Hambone Simpson was in the process of creating what would be his last act of defiance against the system: he was smoking a joint of marijuana in the middle of the Cleveland City Jail.

Two state troopers, who were among the veritable platoon of officers gathered in the Cleveland Police Department that night, later recalled that Police Captain Ike Hines was mad as hell at being called back to the station during his off hours. And both recalled his remark as he eyed the ten officers scattered around the duty room. "Captain Hines seemed to be upset because he was called out," Trooper John B. McDaniel wrote in his official statement, "and said to the effect that one person could go in with a nightstick and whip his ass, then take him to the hospital and get him sewed up. No one took him seriously."

McDaniel clearly didn't speak for his junior partner, twenty-seven-year-old Trooper Donald Lee Smith. The young trooper assumed the burly captain was serious as a heart attack when he made the comment. "I was somewhat amazed at what he said," Trooper Smith said later, "and wanted to leave, but stayed for the safety of all concerned. I decided not to go into the cell if a baton or flashlight was taken in."

Eight whites and three blacks, all patrolmen, deputies, and troopers, stormed Simpson's cell. As was his habit, one of the city patrolmen carried a concealed tape recorder in his shirt pocket, which he later explained was used to "cover [his] ass" against unwarranted complaints from citizens. The device recorded more than a half-hour of uncontrolled chaos. It may also have been Kenneth Simpson's last half-hour of life.

The tape is guttural, raging, pleading, screaming, and whimpering, recording a godawful battle that apparently spans the entire cell: A platoon of cops lifting Simpson into the air, then depositing him prone on the cement floor. Captain Hines grabbing Hambone in a headlock. A 240-pound black cop sitting on the prisoner's chest to subdue him. Cuffs going on his hands. Simpson alternately pleading for mercy, then yelling "Redneck . . . Redneck!" and threatening, "Black folks, kick those white folks' ass." A cop yelling, "Crack his fucking head open! That'll get some respect from him!" A black deputy saying, "I doubt if we can leave him like this." Yates replying, "Go ahead and cuff those feet with flex. . . . Then we won't worry about him in the morning."

Two officers found Kenneth Simpson's body at 5:30 A.M. the next day. Every officer who had been in the cell the night before swore Hambone had been alive when they left him.

The autopsy showed Simpson died of "asphyxia due to trauma to the neck." Exactly how he died wasn't nearly as obvious. The forensics pathologist in Houston said he couldn't determine if Simpson had been choked to death or if he somehow had managed to strangle himself.

After nearly four days of testimony, a Liberty County grand jury declined to indict any of the eleven officers who had been the last to see Kenneth Simpson alive.

Shortly afterward, Jan Jarboe, a writer for *Texas Monthly* magazine and a native of Cleveland, returned home for the twenty-year reunion of her high school class. The story of Simpson's death intrigued her, and while in Cleveland, she interviewed several people about it. One of her classmates was a Cleveland police officer—one of the eleven who were in Simpson's cell the night of March 15—and he approached her at the reunion, surly and curious about why Jarboe hadn't interviewed him about Simpson's death. Actually, the question was more an excuse to express his point of view. "I know what happened," the cop told Jarboe. "The nigger killed hisself."

Pearlie Henderson knew that little had changed in rural pockets of the South in the nearly thirty years since Woodrow Wilson Daniels's confrontation with white police in Water Valley, Mississippi. Loyal Garner, Jr., and Kenneth Simpson bore testimony to that. But what bothered the East Texas civil rights leader almost as much were the confrontations he *didn't* know about.

Troy Starling, for example, had been shot to death by a white trooper only fifty miles from Tyler in adjoining Rusk County, yet the young black man already had been buried and the officer acquitted by the time Henderson heard about it. After the fact, there was little the NAACP could do.

And there was a whole other category of deaths and injuries that Henderson attributed to police abuse, one even he acknowledged was tenuous in documentation: high-speed police chases.

"You know, families talk, and fathers tell sons about what white cops do to them beside the road at night," Henderson said with a bitter edge to his voice. "The fathers are trying to help their sons, see? But then the teenager borrows the family car, looks in the mirror, and sees flashing red lights. He's just a kid, right? He floorboards it. He's not really worried about a ticket for running a red light. He's worried as hell about what the cop's gonna do to him once he catches him. He's going ninety around a turn, loses control, hits a guy wire off a phone pole, rolls Daddy's car, and kills himself. It happened here in Tyler a couple of months ago. When it makes the newspapers, see, the cop says the kid was evading arrest. Really, the kid was trying to save his ass. And you don't have any idea how many times that happens."

On futile days, Henderson figured it was probably a blessing that he *didn't* know the actual numbers of blacks killed by white officers. He already was pushing the tenets of the "Serenity Prayer," particularly the verse about "accept[ing] the things I cannot change."

21

THE RACE TO THE COURTHOUSE

THOMAS LADNER, Bill Horton, and Bo Hyden had been free on bond since January 5, when they were indicted on the civil rights charges in their hometown of Hemphill. Their trial still had not been scheduled by March 3, when the Smith County Grand Jury in Tyler indicted them a second time, accusing them of murdering Loyal Garner, Jr.

Acting autonomously, as all state judges do in scheduling their dockets, State District Judge Joe Tunnell routinely set the murder trial for July 11 in his courtroom in Tyler. The five months between the officers' indictment and their scheduled trial was about average for Judge Tunnell's backlogged docket.

Three weeks after Judge Tunnell announced the Tyler trial date, State District Judge O'Neal Bacon, who for twenty-nine years had presided over the First Judicial District, which includes Sabine County, made an announcement of his own. The three officers would be tried in Hemphill on the civil rights charges May 16—almost two months *before* the murder trial just scheduled for Tyler.

Judge Bacon's decision to hear the civil rights case in Hemphill first, after allowing the case to lay dormant for more than three months, ensured that *State of Texas v. Ladner, Horton, and Hyden* would be more than an adversarial proceeding between the state and the defense attorneys. It would pit one jurisdiction against the other to determine which one dispensed justice.

Among themselves, Dees, Cohen, Hannah, and Skeen and his staff in Tyler saw it as another piece in the conspiracy to exonerate the three officers, trying them first in their biased hometown and no doubt winning an acquittal. With an innocent verdict behind them, the officers' attorneys would surely fight to kill the second trial in Tyler, one in which they had a chance at a fair jury, claiming that their clients were about to be tried twice for virtually the same crime.

John Seale, Ladner's lawyer and the lead attorney of the officers' defense team, was unabashedly pleased both at getting the earlier trial date and at getting the case heard in Hemphill in Judge Bacon's courtroom. He knew that if his interpretation of double jeopardy was accurate and he played his cards right, there would be no murder trial in Tyler. In addition to his "home court" advantage, Bacon and Seale virtually had grown up together. For almost as long as Seale had tried cases in East Texas, the somber Bacon had been the presiding judge in the First Judicial District. Perhaps more than any other lawyer in the state, Seale was familiar with Judge Bacon's demeanor, his likes and dislikes, his quirks and soft spots. Indeed, much of Seale's considerable success as a lawyer had been achieved in front of Bacon's familiar bench. The lawyer considered the judge a friend and respected him, enough that his firm contributed $300 to Bacon's most recent re-election campaign, which by the judge's own account would be his last. The contribution was a piddling amount by urban standards, but it nonetheless totaled about half of the judge's campaign treasury in the sparsely populated district.

Still, when criticism trickled in from Tyler that Judge Bacon had intentionally scheduled his trial in Hemphill to interfere with the previously scheduled murder trial, Seale discounted it out of hand.

"After the officers were indicted in Sabine County, Judge Bacon let it be known that he wanted to get the case up for trial and try it as quickly as possible so that justice could be done," Seale recalled later. "If they were guilty, let them be found guilty, and if they were innocent, let them be found innocent and put an end to this." Later on, John Hannah and some others widely criticized Judge Bacon and accused him of trying to win a race to the courthouse, getting the case tried in Hemphill first. There wasn't any need for a race to the courthouse.

"The judge's statement that was made at that time, which I always considered a very admirable one, followed two other situations that I personally had been involved in: one in Sabine County where an assistant tax collector was indicted for misappropriation of funds, and one in Newton County where the tax collector was indicted and charged with getting away with some funds. Both cases were set for trial the very first term of court afterward. We tried them, and fortunately"—Seale grinned modestly in anticipation of the punch line—"both of them were acquitted.

"But the judge's attitude in both of those . . . [was] that any time a public official is charged with wrongdoing . . . it should not linger there and fester. All sides should get ready and try the case and let it be decided one way or the other. There was a precedent, and both these cases would have been within two years preceding the Garner situation. He tried that case no differently than he had treated the others that I've been directly involved in."

Lawyers are about as fond of surprises as mongooses are of snakes, and Hannah, Skeen and Christian Bryan, a Skeen assistant, and everyone else in the Smith County prosecutor's office had anticipated the defense team's long-range strategy of double jeopardy. In a perfect world—and it was John Seale's sincerest hope that he could deliver precisely that scenario—the officers accused of killing Garner would face *one* trial, in Hemphill, be acquitted, and be wearing their old badges twenty-four hours later, like Sheriff Buster Treloar thirty years earlier in Water Valley, Mississippi.

In its purest context, the issue of double jeopardy is as thoroughly American and fair as the right to vote. If Mama suspects, for example, that Junior has had his hand in the cookie jar, she gets one shot at disciplining him. Having faced the music, Junior moves on with his life. And so it is with the Fifth Amendment. Once a person has been tried, the state can't lurk in the wings, vindictively gathering new evidence to drag him back into court for the same crime. In short, fairness and the law dictate that, as lawyers put it, the state gets "one, and only one, bite at the apple."

The bedrock principle of double jeopardy was spelled out in 1957 by the U.S. Supreme Court in *Green v. United States:* "The underlying idea, one that is deeply ingrained in at least the Anglo-American system of jurisprudence, is that the State with all its resources and power should not be allowed to make repeated attempts to convict an individual for an alleged offense, thereby subjecting him to embarrassment, expense and ordeal and compelling him to live in a continuing state of anxiety and insecurity. . . ."

Bryan, Skeen's appellate lawyer, was dubious of the new court setting in Hemphill, but not surprised. "Our trial was set for July 11 way back in March," Bryan said later. "They, much later, set their trial. We think it was a conscious effort to try their case before ours. . . . It's real hard to show on the record that they procured it for a purpose, but we think that's an inference that can be drawn. They're saying, 'It just happened to be set then—what a coincidence!' "

If the earlier date set in Hemphill wasn't part of a larger plan to shield the officers from being tried by an out-of-town jury, Skeen and Hannah believed, it at least smacked of the same kind of hometown favoritism that had worried them all along about trying to extract justice in Sabine County.

Even before there were pretrial motions heard in Hemphill, Seale and his colleagues on the defense team—Paul Buchanan, who represented Bo Hyden, and Floyd Addington, Bill Horton's lawyer—predictably argued that the murder charges in Tyler violated their clients' constitutional protection against double jeopardy. The defense lawyers promised that they would go to the Texas Court of Criminal Appeals, and if necessary to the U.S. Supreme Court, to cancel out the murder trial in Tyler, which they contended would give the state two bites at the same apple.

Christian Bryan already had briefed the issue of double jeopardy. The legal dilemma was an unprecedented one for Texas courts; the young prosecutor couldn't find a single case in which prosecutors had tried a law enforcement officer first for civil rights violations, then for murder in the same death. In his thirteen-page briefing memo, which he sent to both Skeen and Hannah, Bryan believed he found sufficient case law to allow prosecutors to dodge the double jeopardy bullet.

The issue, Bryan believed, hinged on the different elements of proof required by the two laws. "Simply stated," Bryan wrote in his memo, "where each statute requires proof of a fact that the other does not, two prosecutions are not precluded by double jeopardy." So, should Junior break the lid to the cookie jar in the process of stealing a cookie, ostensibly Mama should be entitled to spank him twice—once for stealing the cookie and once for breaking the lid.

Bryan found several cases that he hoped would support his thesis. Appeals courts determined, for example, that it had not been double jeopardy when a man was convicted for both aggravated kidnapping and aggravated robbery stemming from one criminal act. Similarly, the courts had found no problem in a man convicted of robbery and murder with malice in the same scenario. "Conviction of each offense requires proof of an additional fact which the other does not," Bryan summarized.

The briefing lawyer found a 1984 case from Waco, *Lozano v. State of Texas*, in which a man was prosecuted, as a result of one arrest, for both possession of marijuana and delivery of marijuana. "A single act may be an offense against two statutes," the appeals court ruled. "If each statute requires proof of an additional fact which the other does not require, an acquittal or conviction under either statute does not exempt the defendant from prosecution and punishment under the other." When Lozano was arrested with marijuana, he was violating the law against a citizen possessing an illegal substance; when the state showed the reason Lozano had the marijuana—to sell it—Lozano violated a different law "against the peace and dignity of the State of Texas."

Prosecuting Ladner, Horton, and Hyden for both civil rights violations and murder, Bryan theorized, wouldn't constitute double jeopardy because prosecutors had at least two separate burdens of proof. Because the Texas civil rights law focused exclusively on law enforcement officers and prisoners in their custody, Hannah would have to prove that Ladner, Horton, and Hyden were, in fact, officers; that Garner was a prisoner in their custody; that the officers knew their conduct in beating and/or depriving Garner of medical treatment had been unlawful; and that Garner died as a result of their actions.

In the murder case, Skeen, on the other hand, would have to prove *intent*: that Ladner, Horton, and Hyden intended either to kill Garner or to cause the prisoner serious bodily injury which led to his death. Unlike the civil rights charges, the murder charges, from a legal viewpoint, made irrelevant the fact that the three assailants were peace officers and Garner was their prisoner.

Finally, Bryan found a degree of comfort in a portion of the Texas civil rights statute, the law under which the cops had been indicted in Hemphill: "This section shall not preclude prosecution for any other offense set out in this code." And certainly that included murder.

Law, like beauty, is in the eye of the beholder. Seale didn't argue with Bryan's reading of the law; he merely believed the law was unconstitutional. "Even if the legislature wanted to, it doesn't have the power to create two statutes in order to try someone twice for the same offense," he said. "Even if they try and call it by two different names, it's still double jeopardy."

Prosecutors and defense attorneys could, however, agree on at least one thing. At some point, the issue of double jeopardy was going to lead them to appeals court.

Trial delays in Texas courts are common as twang in country music. Their perfunctory approval by judges, in fact, has littered the legal system with cases that won't go away, backlogging fresh cases behind some that originally appeared on docket sheets long since yellowed.

But if Special Prosecutor John Hannah believed he would be beneficiary of such a routine continuance in Hemphill in *Texas v. Ladner, Horton, and Hyden*, District Judge O'Neal Bacon sorely disappointed him.

The anger and contempt underlying the opposing lawyers and warring jurisdictions reached ground zero in a hearing May 10, just six days before the civil rights trial was to begin in Hemphill. Hannah had announced on March 25, as had the defense lawyers, that the state was ready for trial. While Johnnie Maxie remained hospitalized after the bizarre car wreck in Louisiana, the veteran prosecutor assumed that by the time the trial date was set, he would be well enough to testify; if he wasn't, Hannah would merely ask for a continuance.

Now Hannah was in court asking for a delay. Maxie had been hospitalized for two months and had been discharged only a week ago, the prosecutor told Judge Bacon. He had visited Maxie a day earlier, and the man had been "confused and addled and . . . very sick"—obviously "in no condition, mentally or physically, to participate in a trial within the next few weeks."

Hannah offered as evidence sworn affidavits from Maxie's doctor and attorney. "I feel that under no circumstances would he be able to undergo questioning," wrote Dr. David A. Cavanaugh of his patient. "When I reevaluate him in one month, I will better be able to determine when he may be able to do this." Maxie's medical condition was reiterated in a sworn statement by his lawyer, Billy Casey. "I will resist all efforts to subpoena him to any trial or hearing prior to his doctors saying that he is physically and emotionally able to testify," Casey wrote of his client.

Johnnie Maxie, Hannah argued, was critical to his case. "Other than defendant Ladner and defendant Hyden, both white law enforcement officers, the eyewitnesses to the beating were two black inmates, Johnnie Maxie and Alton Maxie," Hannah said. "I do not believe the state of Texas could receive a fair trial in this case without the testimony of Johnnie Maxie."

John Seale had the right to cross-examine Hannah in the hearing for continuance, and he performed the task with a vengeance.

"The implication is clear that it appeared to you that Mr. Maxie will be able to testify by July 11, so that he'd be able to testify in Tyler, but he's not able to testify in Hemphill?"

"That's not clear to me at all," Hannah replied. "I think my affidavit, Mr. Seale, indicates he's supposed to see his doctor again around June the first. Hopefully, his doctor will say that he is able to testify at that time. Hopefully, you and I can try this case here. That's what I want to do."

"Without getting into arguing the merits of it right now," Seale plodded on, "you know that there are going to be some contentions made, in whatever place the case is not tried first, relative to double jeopardy. . . ."

"Based on my opinion, I would expect those contentions to be made."

"All right, sir. So, then, it can become very crucial where this case is tried first, can it not?"

"As far as the State is concerned, yes," Hannah agreed.

"And it's your testimony," Seale hammered in, "that you don't know anything about the fact that the Southern Poverty Law Center, along with the NAACP, has been making a concerted effort to see that this case is tried in Tyler before it's tried in Hemphill?"

The special prosecutor wasn't sure how the NAACP or the Poverty Center could have gone about such an action. He shrugged. "No, sir." He paused a minute more, then convinced himself he didn't want Seale to get away with implying he was merely trying to stall. "Excuse me, let me continue," he said. "As a matter of fact, Mr. Seale, I get paid more if the case is here. So that's where my bias is." It was true. If the murder trial was tried first in Tyler and the officers were convicted, there was no certainty of a second trial in Hemphill. And no trial, no legal fee.

John Seale nonetheless argued strenuously against granting a continuance. Contrary to Hannah's claims, Seale argued to Judge Bacon, Johnnie Maxie's testimony wasn't that critical to the state's case, because his brother, Alton, could testify to the same events. Beyond that, the defense lawyer noted with cynicism, "in the event that we go to trial on the sixteenth, we'll see Johnnie Maxie. I'm convinced of that."

Seale paused long enough to determine whether he should say what was on his mind. Customarily calm and reverent in a courtroom, he nonetheless plunged headlong, taking the bull by the horns. If prosecutors believed there was a conspiracy in Sabine County to protect Ladner, Horton, and Hyden, well, by God, there was another conspiracy afoot, too. "Your Honor, I can't help but vent my feelings about this," Seale intoned, his face reddening. "This is a case that needs to be tried in Sabine County. Whatever happened in this case happened in Sabine County. It did *not* happen in Smith County. Smith County has no business being involved in this case, and Smith County is involved in this case for one reason—and that is because of the actions of Mr. Hannah's employer, the Southern Poverty Law Center, that urged them to push up there for an inquest and then urged them to push up there for an indictment.

"I have been in this case throughout, and I've been at every hearing that's been in Tyler, and nothing could have come through any clearer to me than it's the idea of these organizations that they want this case tried in Tyler rather than in Hemphill because they seem to think that they can't get a fair trial in Hemphill, and I would respectfully represent to the court that the idea of where these men get tried should not be orchestrated by some organization from Alabama. I think that's exactly what's going on in this case."

Seale's emotionalism was contagious and spread to the other side of the courtroom. John Hannah was on his feet, reiterating his reasons for a delay. The special prosecutor looked Judge Bacon squarely in the eyes as if it would make a difference. "And you've also heard Mr. Seale say, Your Honor, that he was looking forward to seeing Johnnie Maxie on that stand, and indeed he is, because Mr. Seale says, 'Why, he's made three or four statements three or four other ways,' and Mr. Seale intends to grill Johnnie Maxie, who has spent the last two months in the hospital, Your Honor, and who's only been released last week.

"Mr. Seale, as he admits, intends to work Johnnie Maxie over—a sick man. And I submit to this court that Johnnie Maxie needs some more days and more time so that he can testify for the State and that he can withstand Mr. Seale's admitted onslaught of a sick man. That's all I have to say."

Hannah didn't have a chance to swallow before Judge Bacon announced his ruling. "Motion for continuance denied," he said impassively. "The case will proceed to trial on May 16 at nine A.M."

Bill Martin, the district attorney who agreed to acquiesce to John Hannah in the prosecution of Ladner, Horton, and Hyden, graciously stayed on to assist the out-of-town lawyer. In his twenty years as chief prosecutor in Texas's easternmost counties, Martin, like John Seale, had spent considerable time before Judge Bacon's bench. But unlike Seale, Martin neither considered himself one of the judge's friends nor particularly respected the judge's judicial abilities. The strained relationship between judge and DA perhaps was more pronounced since both lived in Newton, a tiny timber town of sixteen hundred a good rock's throw from Louisiana.

"Let's just put it this way," Martin later said, "it's pretty common knowledge that I'm not one of Judge Bacon's biggest fans."

Being coy was not normally Martin's nature. Agreeing with a stranger, for instance, about the inherent beauty of his native East Texas, Martin noted, "Yeah, it's beautiful country—but we could use a better class of people." He was as deliberate as he was big—well over six feet—and while age had turned his hair a distinguished gray, the years had been kind to his midsection: even beyond sixty, Martin still bore traces of the star football player and champion boxer he once was. His hands were the size of softball gloves, and he still looked like he was good for a few rounds. Like Hannah, his new protégé, Martin had been an enlisted man in the Navy, later using the GI Bill to earn his law degree from Baylor University.

Within minutes after Judge Bacon had denied Hannah's request for a delay in the trial, the special prosecutor informed his older ally he intended to ask the circuit court of appeals in Tyler to force Bacon to postpone the trial. "Yeah," Martin told him, "you could probably do that. But make sure that's what you want to do, because you'll pay a price for it."

The law makes provisions for all sorts of remedies and appeals when lawyers believe judges aren't treating them fairly. But most lawyers, aware of the axiom that you can win the battle and still lose the war, tread lightly in availing themselves of options to overrule, and therefore embarrass, judges. A judge's goodwill, most believe, ultimately is worth more than a technical victory over a point of law—unless, of course, the technical point is critical to the case.

Hannah was madder than hell with Judge Bacon's ruling, and he was damned, he told Martin, if he was going to take it lying down. "I'm sure as hell not going to trial in Hemphill without both of my only two living eyewitnesses," Hannah said. "I'm getting a goddamn writ of mandamus."

A day after Judge Bacon returned the ruling against him, Hannah was in the Twelfth Court of Appeals in Tyler. Before he finished, he got a writ forcing the postponement of the trial in Hemphill. And on June 2, the appeals court further ruled that Judge Bacon had been "under a clear legal duty to continue and postpone the three criminal cases from their trial setting on May 16." Judge Bacon, "being without discretion to do otherwise," the appeals court noted, "failed to carry out his ministerial duty to continue the cases from their May 16, 1988 trial setting."

Hannah had won his postponement, and he wouldn't have to prosecute his case until Johnnie Maxie had recuperated. The victory had been significant, Martin knew, but it had only been a battle. The war had barely begun.

22

PRECARIOUS POSITIONS

EVEN IF BO HYDEN hadn't already been appreciative of the gravity of the charges facing him, the sepia photograph hanging prominently in the lobby of Paul Buchanan's law office in Beaumont would surely have had a sobering impact. The photograph depicts a twenties-era jury seated behind a courtroom railing. The grim-faced jurors look conspicuously aggravated, as if they'd all swallowed something foul. Beneath the photograph is the caption *Some day, 12 wonderful people could destroy you.*

On the receptionist's desk were Buchanan's business cards, fold-out affairs that opened to the defense lawyer's own version of the Miranda warning. Under the heading "You and the officer . . . what to do," the cards cautioned clients to remain silent, to speak only after they had called their lawyer (i.e., the name listed on the reverse side), and to resist any kind of search until they've spoken with him. The card also included some common-sense etiquette should the client be unfortunate enough to fall into the hands of the police. *"Be respectful,"* it advised. "It's only you and him, and you don't need any more trouble than you already have. Now, CALL YOUR LAWYER AS SOON AS POSSIBLE!"

Paul Buchanan's office was clearly alien territory for a suspended cop. But as unorthodox as the situation may have been for the sheriff's deputy, so it was for Buchanan to count cops among his clients. At thirty-four, Buchanan was of average height, maybe fifteen or twenty pounds overweight, and wore a bushy beard that made him look like a five-foot-ten muskrat. Recently, an ongoing and bitter divorce had left his expression not unlike those of the jurors depicted in the photograph in his lobby.

Attorney Paul Buchanan's name was spoken frequently and appeared prominently in newspapers in Beaumont, about one hundred miles due south of Hemphill and the closest major metropolitan area. Beaumont is a steamy, raucous Gulf Coast port of about 125,000 whose existence hinges on shipbuilding, refineries, steel mills, and other industries whose products depend on blue collars and sweat. Those who knew Buchanan figured Beaumont, a tough, sometimes coarse city, was an ideal place for his style of law.

Buchanan commanded growing attention in southeastern Texas on two counts: he was a fierce and emotional competitor in a courtroom, and, belying the image as the well-dressed redneck, he was an equally fierce and emotional *liberal*. Dressed in his ever-present western-cut suits and cowboy boots, Buchanan had argued his way to enviable success, returning more than his share of clients to the sidewalks and out of the grasps of prosecutors and the Texas Department of Criminal Justice.

Unlike co-counsel John Seale, whose demeanor before the bar appeared almost courtly, Paul Buchanan made every criminal defense a gut issue, as if someone had commented publicly about his sister having nose hair. The burden of his clients' threatened liberty frequently reduced Buchanan's demeanor to that of a wet bantam rooster, attacking whatever and whoever most jeopardized his client's continued freedom. His tactics in the courtroom, while admittedly successful, hadn't earned Buchanan friendship, particularly among police officers. "If I can't find anything else," Buchanan would explain of cops, "I can generally show they were at least sloppy in something they did."

Buchanan wasn't paid to make friends. Friends, by his reckoning, were people you *chose* to meet for a few shots of whiskey after work, not the people you were paid to impeach, discredit, and undress on the witness stand. If he made some of them—cops included—mad as hell, well, he'd probably had a good day. He made allowances, of course, for those lawyers "on the other side" who were paid, too, to do the same thing in behalf of their clients. It wasn't personal; it was professional. "I like to think I'm one of those lawyers you can call a sonofabitch in a courtroom, then go have a drink with after the trial," he explains.

In October 1975, when the state bar licensed Buchanan, he was twenty-two, the youngest lawyer in the state and barely old enough to drink or vote. Even before he graduated from Baylor Law School, he had dreamed of becoming a criminal defense lawyer. Like a spy scouting the enemy,

Buchanan had joined the Jefferson County District Attorney's Office and stayed only long enough to learn how the enemy thought. He threw in with a former county judge briefly and later ended up working for Joe Goodwin, a legendarily tough defense attorney cited by *Texas Monthly* magazine as one of the top ten defense attorneys in Texas. Working for Goodwin, Buchanan said, taught him to be "passionate instead of some namby-pamby wimp with a checklist."

While defense colleagues John Seale and Floyd Addington were general practitioners in Jasper, Buchanan was certified by the State Bar of Texas as a criminal defense specialist. "I love criminal defense work, but it's not as fun as it used to be," Buchanan said, attributing the demise of his profession to the Reagan era and the throngs of Republican appointees Reagan put on the benches. "With Reagan, everything you come up with, they just blow off. And now there's this awful move to try to indict the lawyers. There's not a criminal defense lawyer I know who hasn't had his clients asked questions like 'How much did your lawyer know about this?'

"I don't like to brag, but I'm as straight an arrow as they come. I drink a little whiskey, but I don't do dope, never done dope, and won't do dope. If anybody comes into my office with a big cash fee, I'll promptly take it, deposit it in my account, and fill out the IRS forms and claim it. But woe be to anyone who comes in here with dirty money. They'll leave with it."

When Bo Hyden appeared in his office, the suspended deputy presented a distinctively different challenge for Buchanan. Cops traditionally were redneck conservatives, not the kind that evoked natural empathy from Buchanan. Under normal circumstances, Buchanan would have viewed the wiry deputy as the enemy. But Buchanan liked the quiet-spoken Hyden from their first meeting. "Here's Bo Hyden, he's making eleven hundred dollars a month, working on Christmas Day—probably rather be home with his family, but he's out there doing his job," Buchanan recalled. "And all of a sudden he's on the front page of every newspaper. He's in *The New York Times;* he can't watch ABC, CBS, NBC without seeing his picture. He goes out to lunch, and it's like the Scopes trial." With all the media exposure, Buchanan viewed his new client as a victim of the First Amendment.

Buchanan's liberal friends looked askance when they learned he was representing a deputy sheriff accused of beating a black prisoner to death. The young lawyer's stock defense was to paraphrase Alan Dershowitz, the Harvard law professor who successfully defended Claus von Bulow on charges that he tried to kill his millionaire wife. "When you sign on to the First Amendment Club," Buchanan would say, "you don't earn your credentials by representing popular people. People don't test the First Amendment by defending popular people."

Nonetheless, Buchanan's highly publicized defense of an embattled cop was changing his life, and, as a liberal, the white lawyer was particularly pained by the fallout.

"You know," he pondered later, "I guess you're going to get called a racist occasionally just because somebody's skin is black. I got some awful things on my answering machine. I got some nasty, nasty messages, saying I'd never represent another black client as long as I lived."

One day at the federal building in Beaumont, a black female prosecutor told Buchanan, "I don't think I like you anymore." He sat down that night and wrote her a three-page, single-spaced letter. "I said, 'You can't believe everything you read,'" Buchanan recalled. "I said, 'Here's the evidence,' and that 'your perception of me is something I really value.' It didn't help. She used to refer me a case occasionally, but no more. She's been nothing but unpleasant to me ever since. I find that real damn unfortunate. To me, that's just reverse damn racism. She should have understood that even if they beat the hell out of Garner that they were entitled to a fair trial. Being a black lawyer, she should know that the downtrodden, the good, the bad, and the ugly all are entitled to fair justice.

"I read where the American Civil Liberties Union lost a lot of membership when it decided to defend the Nazis in Skokie," Buchanan said, refering to the Illinois city's refusal to issue the American Nazi Party a parade permit. "It really pissed me off. I said, 'How dare you call yourself a member of the American Civil Liberties Union and not understand that that defense was proper?' They were defending the First Amendment *period*. It offended me. I'm not a closet liberal. I'm a real liberal. I believe in the first ten, especially the first eight, amendments."

As the trial in Hemphill neared, Hyden, for the most part, believed in God and in Buchanan—maybe not necessarily in that order. "Bo was philosophical about the whole thing," Buchanan recalled. "He never really worried about it too much and felt like he didn't do anything wrong and that God would take care of it, so to speak. He had a lot of faith in the system and that he wouldn't get convicted."

While the three lawmen had accounted for the most controversial chapter in Sabine County's history, Hyden, like Ladner and Horton, had become a virtual phantom in Hemphill after the indictments in January. All three lived in the country outside of town, and they had immersed themselves in what they hoped would be only temporary jobs following their suspensions as cops. Residents of Hemphill, happening occasionally to pass the time of day with one of the accused ex-lawmen, would make reports to others. Ladner, word had it, was operating heavy machinery for a local construction company, a job he'd held as a young man fresh out of the Army. The company's owner, Billy Joe McGee, a longtime and sympathetic friend, had volunteered the job immediately after Ladner was suspended. Townspeople heard that Horton, despite being fifty-eight, was breaking quarterhorses and occasionally working as a truck driver, a job he'd had before going into law enforcement. Hyden, local gossip held, had "gone to the woods," cutting timber in the thickets. Periodically, people heard that the youngest of the indicted officers had appeared as a lay witness at fundamentalist churches, apparently deeply moved by the troubles that beset him. But whatever Ladner, Horton, and Hyden were doing since their suspensions, they were doing it quietly, and well away from the scrutiny focused on Hemphill.

The tiny town had become a circus even before July 5, when the trial finally was scheduled to begin. Paul Buchanan drove up from Beaumont for a pretrial hearing and discovered minicams, satellite trucks, and more reporters than he could shake a stick at. And most of them were clustered around John Hannah, who, it seemed to Buchanan, was forever extolling the virtues of Loyal Garner, Jr., to the press. "It was a carnival even before trial," Buchanan recalled. "The only thing missing were corny dogs."

Public perceptions immediately before trial were a concern to the feisty lawyer from Beaumont. Buchanan practiced rough-and-tumble law; and biting his tongue—a course he, Addington, and Seale had agreed upon and imposed on their clients—was alien to everything his gut told him, particularly when he saw Hannah swaying public opinion against the defendants.

But the prosecution's proclivity for speeches on TV and in the newspapers didn't make Buchanan nearly as mad as his mail. As a card-carrying liberal, his name appeared on countless mailing lists that targeted liberals, from groups that needed money to save the whales, clean up toxic waste, or monitor acid rain to protecting the rain forest.

He was in his office after an exhausting night and morning spent preparing for Hyden's defense when he finally got to the mail his secretary had stacked on his desk. He ripped open the envelope without paying attention to the return address. The two pages he held in his hands triggered a tirade heard throughout the office.

"The nation is outraged by the death of Loyal Garner, Jr.," the letter read. "The United States Justice Department is investigating the case. Your prompt support today may be helpful in making a national example out of this gross abuse of police power."

Buchanan grew madder with each line. "Nothing we do will ever return this good man to his family, but we can see to it that the family he loved can face the future with some measure of dignity and security.

"Please show them you care by sending as generous a donation as you can today."

The letter was from the Southern Poverty Law Center and signed by its chief counsel and co-founder, Morris Dees.

"This sonofabitch is asking me for money so he can kick my ass in a courtroom?" Buchanan yelled. "Bullshit!"

His gut tightened. Now Paul Buchanan was ready for trial.

If there was a race between Sabine and Smith counties to be first to get the indicted officers into court, it appeared by late June that it could be a dead heat. Finally, before the end of the month, Johnnie Maxie's doctor verified that his client had sufficiently recovered from his car wreck to testify.

Judge Bacon immediately set the civil rights trial in Hemphill for July 5, six days before the murder trial in Tyler was scheduled to begin. No attorney in the case figured the Hemphill trial would take less than two weeks; the Tyler trial would have to wait.

"I think everyone is entitled to a trial by their peers," Judge Bacon said, "and their peers are in *this* county."

The judge undoubtedly was aware of the controversy and speculation surrounding the setting of the officers' trial dates. But if he was sensitive to the inference that he, too, was a part of some kind of "conspiracy" to afford the embattled cops a home-court advantage, his decisions didn't reflect that concern.

O'Neal Bacon, graying, balding, and distinguished, was old school. He was elected and paid to make tough decisions, and he had done so with unflinching authority for thirty years. His decisions, he believed, were a matter of public record and spoke for themselves. He felt compelled neither to explain his rationale nor to defend it. Should an appeals court find a problem with his rulings, it was empowered to reverse him. So be it; that was the system.

Lawyers are quick to categorize judges, frequently lumping them into one of two groups: hand wringers and decision makers. Hand wringers listen to arguments, take them "under advisement," and return their decisions later. Decision makers rule from the bench. By acclamation among lawyers who practiced in his court, O'Neal Bacon was a decision maker. "Hand wringers make decisions without having to look the lawyers in the eye," said one attorney who practiced in Bacon's court. "That never bothered Judge Bacon. Sometimes, you could tell he really enjoyed it, too." And once he rendered an opinion, the quiet, reserved Judge Bacon expected lawyers to live with it. Until an appeals court determined otherwise, his opinion was the law.

"The only time Judge Bacon ever got really testy," the same attorney said, "was when a lawyer didn't follow the spirit of his rulings, or tried to continue his argument. The judge had no appreciation for that kind of behavior."

The six months since her son's death had left Sarah Garner feeling like a pendulum, swinging from lethargic numbness to the most intense mental and physical pain the elderly woman had ever known. She had always heard it was a curse to live long enough to see a child die, and now she knew it was true. Through the bountiful goodness and grace of God, not the kind of material rewards you could carry in a wallet or take to the bank, Sarah and Loyal Garner, Sr., had raised fifteen children. The devoutly religious couple wasn't the kind to pick favorites, but Loyal Jr. was the oldest, and as such, he held a special place in his parents' eyes.

Since Junior's death, Sarah and Loyal Sr. spent even more time next door with Corrine and her kids. Occasionally, Sarah would recall aloud a story she thought Junior's children should know about him. The old woman worried that the children, particularly three-year-old Corey and five-year-old Marlon, might not remember much of their dad. At least Corrine hadn't had to scrounge since Junior's death. The Southern Poverty Law Center had arranged for a $12,000, interest-free loan pending the outcome of her civil lawsuit against Hemphill and Sabine County.

Now, with the criminal trial coming up in only a few days, thoughts of returning to Hemphill intensified for all of Junior Garner's survivors. "My heart just sank when they called and said the trial was going to be in Hemphill," recalled Corrine, who until the end had prayed the officers would stand trial first in Tyler. The trips to the grand jury and for pretrial hearings had been unnerving. "Every time I went to Hemphill, I could just feel what those people were thinking about me."

One man, one of the old timber cutters who whiled away his days playing dominoes on the courthouse square, delivered the cruelest blow of all. Corrine had walked past the group en route to the grand jury when the old man yelled after her: "Your husband got exactly what he deserved!" Behind her, several others grunted in agreement.

"I wish," Corrine had told her children, "that it would have been someplace else. But we'll just have to turn it over to the Lord."

"Mama," one of the boys said, "when I get big enough, I'm gonna go over there and kill those white men just like they did my daddy."

"Me, too," volunteered his brother.

The childish threats frightened Corrine. She hadn't raised her children to be racist or violent. The next Wednesday night, and every church day thereafter, she hauled the boys to her pastor, who, she prayed, would help them deal with their anger.

News of the impending trial in Hemphill had hit hard next door, too. Sarah and Loyal Sr., said one of their sons, were "down in the dumps." Sometimes they were calling on the good Lord hourly for help. "I prayed and prayed," said Loyal Sr. "I wasn't afraid to go over there to Hemphill for the trial. If they wanted to take my life, that was up to Him."

The old man pondered a moment before he spoke again.

"I wouldn't have no business over in Hemphill, but that's where they killed my son."

John Hannah and Glenda Shelton, his legal assistant, had made the trip from Tyler to Hemphill many times, interviewing witnesses and conducting research. Now, as they loaded three boxes of legal files, which Shelton meticulously had cross-referenced by name and chronology, into the trunk of Hannah's car, they both faced the trip to Hemphill with anticipation and dread.

"It was like driving into a time capsule," she recalled later. "Hemphill reminded me of old days. There was something I couldn't put my finger on, but it really made me feel eerie and weird."

Hannah could put his finger on it, and did. "If you weren't from Sabine County," he said, "they resented hell out of you. And they damn well made you feel it."

On his trips to Hemphill, he marveled at having grown up only seventy miles to the west. Hemphill and Diboll shared things in common—the most important thing, as a matter of fact: timber. The residents of both towns generally either hauled timber, as Hannah's father had, or cut it, or sawed it, or milled it. Seventy miles, Hannah thought, couldn't change people that dramatically—not economically, socially, or politically. The sociology intrigued him. Had Diboll been as backward as he knew Hemphill to be, and had the years just smoothed out the rough edges in his mind? Five minutes in Hemphill gave him his answer. Hell, no. Forget Diboll. The way people looked at Hannah in Hemphill, he just as easily could have parachuted in from Philadelphia.

The special prosecutor had devised a plan he hoped would minimize the discomfort of having to live in Sabine County for at least two weeks. He'd found a picturesque fishing and hunting lodge, the Fin and Feather, about twelve miles east of Hemphill on Toledo Bend Reservoir. Situated on a hillside overlooking an inlet, the resort was built in small clusters of rooms interspersed among stately pines. At the bottom of the hill, across from a huge dock, was a small restaurant where Hannah and Shelton could take breakfast and dinner.

The two colleagues discussed the prosecution strategy as they drove eastward. Hannah knew his open battle with Judge Bacon, and his subsequent and successful trip to an appeals court to win his continuance, hadn't won him points with His Honor. As they drew closer to Hemphill's city limits, Hannah wondered aloud how the state of Texas would ever get a fair trial in the town. Between word of mouth and the avalanche of news coverage, he'd bet, there wasn't a soul among the four thousand registered voters in Sabine County who hadn't heard about Ladner, Horton, and Hyden being accused of killing a black man.

Asking to move the trial to another Texas city, Hannah's overwhelming preference, was pretty much out of the question. He'd already heard the judge say he wouldn't consider granting a change of venue. Moreover, Texas law doesn't allow a prosecutor to appeal a judge's refusal to move a trial. To attempt to move the trial and fail, Hannah surmised, would make Judge Bacon even more prodefense that he already appeared to be. And after getting the judge overruled on the continuance, the special prosecutor figured an almost certainly doomed attempt to move the trial would be merely throwing kerosene on the fire.

Jury selection is critical in any trial, but Hannah knew a mistake in selecting a jury could be fatal to the state in this case. His new assistants, Bill Martin and Charles Mitchell (soon to be Martin's replacement as district attorney), lived in the district. They knew these people, and Hannah would rely heavily on their judgment.

Enough prospective jurors had been called for jury duty to equal about 25 percent of Hemphill's entire population of fifteen hundred. The day before jury selection was to begin, Hannah noticed that one of his opponents, Floyd Addington, Horton's lawyer, was quoted in *The Dallas Morning News*. Addington, a genuinely smooth and talented lawyer from Jasper who knew the adjacent Sabine County about as well as John Seale did, told the reporter that selecting an impartial jury shouldn't be a problem. Yeah, not for the defense, Hannah thought as he read the article.

"The only way to find out is to try," Addington told the *Morning News*. "This being a rural area, we think a jury can be seated out of the several hundred prospective jurors who will be there. And really, in something that has become this complicated, a change of venue now makes no sense for the defense or prosecution.

"The only thing that makes any sense is to go to trial in Hemphill and see what we can do," Addington said, "and then go on to the next one in Smith County. There's no use trying this case for the rest of the 20th Century. This has been a nightmare for a lot of people. It can't go on forever."

Not even old-timers know which came first, the Sabine County Courthouse or the stately native pecan tree on its south side. Many surmised that the pecan tree, Texas's official state tree, was planted at the same time the courthouse was built, about eighty years ago. If that was so, Mother Nature's creation had fared better than man's.

July 5, 1988, was hot and humid, pushing one hundred degrees. A soft wind, hot as car exhaust, rustled the pecan's highest limbs against the glass window outside the garish blue courtroom on the third floor. Seating was at a premium, and every opening on the antiquated benches had been filled as soon as the deputies opened the doors. Two floors below, hundreds of Sabine County residents milled around listlessly like penned cattle. There were more prospective jurors than the system could accommodate, and overwhelmed bailiffs and deputies resembled too few cowboys for too large a herd. Few of the potential jurors spoke of the impending trial. More often than not, they remarked about the throng of reporters and satellite uplinks that littered the tiny town square. One woman mused that the reporters resembled locusts.

As John Hannah plopped his briefcase on the floor beside the prosecution's table, his eyes took in the aging courtroom. Immediately, he was reminded of *To Kill a Mockingbird*.

23

A JURY OF PEERS

If GLENDA SHELTON ever needed to defend her belief that Hemphill was locked in another era, she needed only to introduce into evidence Judge O'Neal Bacon's courtroom. Except for a huge 1988 wall calendar behind the judge's bench, courtesy of the friendly folks at Starr Funeral Home, there was nothing to indicate that it wasn't 1930.

The stairs that led to the third-floor courtroom creaked even under a child's weight, and the water stains on the ceiling bore testimony to decades of unchecked rains. The jurors' straight-backed wooden chairs were sadistic even with the green foam inserts on the bottom. They were lined in two rows along a wall to the judge's right, behind an ornate dark oak railing. The judge's bench, probably handcrafted from the same oak, stood regally at the front of the cavernous room. Watching justice dispensed in Sabine County was a painful ordeal; spectators sat on hardwood slats bolted to sides made of black ornamental iron, which in turn were anchored in the cement floor.

Even early on July 5, before the sun reached its zenith, heat had registered its toll on the six lawyers seated at the front of the room, soaking their shirts with sweat. It wasn't that Judge Bacon's courtroom wasn't air-conditioned. It was more that 265 prospective jurors were packed armpit to armpit on the hard benches, overwhelming the feeble air-conditioning system.

Before the voir dire, or jury selection, began, the judge remarked that in a rural area, "everybody knows everybody else." John Hannah nonetheless winced when he asked for a show of hands on how many of the potential jurors knew Thomas Ladner, Bill Horton, or Bo Hyden. Virtually every person in the courtroom raised his hand.

Local prosecutors Bill Martin and Charles Mitchell were seated at the state's end of the table, and even their cursory scan of the audience revealed a score of people they didn't think would take kindly to the prosecution. And those were just the faces they knew. There was, for instance, the husband of one of the defense's key witnesses; Hemphill's city manager; a sheriff's dispatcher; three or four who contributed to the officers' defense fund; in-laws of the defendants; and God only knew how many people who considered themselves friends of the three accused officers.

John Seale is meticulous by nature and organized by habit. In real life, he knew, trials weren't won by Perry Masons and Ben Matlocks browbeating confessions from the witness stand, thereby shifting the blame away from their clients in the final hour of testimony. Rather, trials were won by encyclopedic knowledge of the evidence, smart questions, and methodically selected jurors. And when it came to juries, Seale knew he had a leg up on his out-of-county competitor, John Hannah. It was an advantage that no big-city lawyer could ever match. In more than three decades of trying cases in Sabine County, Seale diligently had recorded a brief biography of every potential juror he'd questioned. Since prospective jurors came from the lists of registered voters, the jury pool in the small county remained fairly constant. Transferred to three-by-five-inch index cards, the information was a ready reference on spouses, children, jobs, political and religious preferences, and civic affiliations of prospective jurors. Seale knew that this information, coupled with experience and, finally, gut instinct, should provide the defense a decided advantage even before the first witness was heard. And the odds were good, he figured, that if a potential juror had escaped his card file through the years, his co-counsel from Jasper, Floyd Addington, or, more likely, the defendants themselves, could provide a quick read on the individual. Buchanan, the out-of-towner on the defense team, would defer.

In the voir dire, the prosecution and defense question the potential jurors, poking and probing for intangible factors that might make them a favorable juror for their side. (As the lawyers' axiom goes: "Objectivity be damned—the best juror is the one who believes whatever the hell I tell him.") The lawyers also try to hone in on any close relationship, moral belief, or presupposition among the potential jurors that would taint their ability to render a fair and impartial verdict. Those jurors the lawyers try to convince the judge to strike "for cause." Should the judge refuse, the prosecution and defense each have eighteen peremptory, or discretionary, challenges with which they may remove, without giving a reason, any member of the panel they consider suspect.

The lawyers' strategies became apparent with their questions. Seale, Buchanan, and Addington were looking for business owners, civic leaders, and prominent people in the community with strong roots. Community pride, they hoped, would be strong enough to shield the three local lawmen who sat at the defense side of the table from the out-of-towners who would attempt to put them in the penitentiary. Blacks, of course, were to be avoided at all costs. They likely would be sympathetic to the state, because Texas blacks traditionally have been leery of white law enforcement officers and, more specifically, because the victim was black. On more than one occasion in the questioning, Seale found a way to mention the Southern Poverty Law Center and the fact that the out-of-state group was footing Hannah's fees. Likewise, he pointed out that two key witnesses, Alton and Johnnie Maxie, like Corrine Garner, had filed a civil suit against Hemphill and Sabine County. The implication was obvious: the state's two key eyewitnesses were trying to take the county's tax money back to Louisiana with them. The defense strategy clearly was headed, like the DON'T MESS WITH HEMPHILL bumper stickers, toward an "us against them" affair.

Hannah, Martin, and Mitchell, by comparison, were searching for any juror who might be antiestablishment, if in fact there were any fringe elements in Hemphill. Hannah's investigation, supplemented heavily by the Southern Poverty Law Center, showed that there had been beatings in the Sabine County Jail before Garner's. His hope was to get a father or mother whose child had been victimized, or at least to find someone who knew someone who had left the Sabine County Jail less healthy than he'd been when he entered. The special prosecutor needed free-thinkers, people who balked at following the pack. Obviously, an all-black jury would be a coup for the prosecution.

Only briefly into the selection process, John Hannah knew he would be dipping heavily into his peremptory challenges. He also suspected that he'd run out of them before he ran out of potential jurors with prodefense sympathies.

One of the prospective jurors admitted under questioning that he was a "close friend" of Bo Hyden's. "It'd be hard," the man confided, "to sit on the jury and help send Hyden to the pen." Hannah asked the judge to strike him for cause. Judge Bacon, however, called the man to the bench, reiterated the standard jurors' responsibility, then asked the man if he could be fair and impartial. Hyden's friend, of course, said he could; the judge refused to strike him for cause. Hannah objected, but ultimately was forced to use one of his precious peremptory challenges to oust Hyden's friend from the jury.

Another prospective juror, Woodrow Russell, the husband of Mary Russell, the sheriff's dispatcher on duty the night Garner was injured, swore to Hannah that neither his wife's firsthand knowledge of the case nor her employment with the Sabine County Sheriff's Department would affect his fairness as a juror. Russell's claim of impartiality taxed even the judge, who excused him from the jury.

Hannah was successful in getting Judge Bacon to strike a potential juror who admitted he had attended the fish fry that raised funds for the three lawmen's defense. When Hannah discovered another patron of the fish fry, John Seale asked for a conference at the bench. The defense attorney argued that not every person who had attended the fish fry had gone to express his support of the three accused lawmen; some, he maintained, had gone merely to "socialize." Mere attendance, Seale argued, wasn't enough to disqualify a person as a juror. Judge Bacon agreed. He refused to expel the juror—or anyone thereafter who acknowledged attending the officers' fund-raiser.

Dorie Mae Handy, Seale knew, was a gamble for the defense. Notwithstanding the fact that she was black, Seale found himself seriously considering Handy for the jury, a possibility that panicked cocounsel Paul Buchanan. The strategy, defense attorneys had agreed, was to pack the jury with people who would rally around, and defend, their embattled community. Yes, the forty-year-old woman appeared docile enough, and certainly not a leader; but there were some abstract factors, Buchanan suggested, like skin color, cultural background, and historical legacy, that were more basic to the formation of viewpoints than where people lived. Adding a black, *any* black, he argued, was a needless risk that could backfire. Seale, who could imagine the appearance of an all-white jury hearing the case, wasn't swayed by Buchanan's argument.

Bill Horton broke the stalemate. "She's okay," the former chief deputy whispered. "They're not fussers or complainers," he said of Handy and her husband.

Horton had information that even the defense lawyers later claimed not to have had. The Handys were known to drink a little—a habit that had accounted for Horton's sporadic appearances at the Handy house and, on occasion, had necessitated trips to jail for the Handys. Horton always had treated the couple fairly, and he knew Handy would remember. Just as important, Handy was a domestic worker who owed her livelihood to another member of the jury. Wilma Dean Hinson, who already had been chosen, owned the nursing home where Handy had worked for years.

Seale announced the defense had no problem with Handy. Hannah, proud to have even one black, certainly had no objection.

By the end of voir dire, the twelve chairs in the jury box were filled with six men and six women. Eleven were white. They were housewives, three business owners, a telephone company employee, a manager, a county employee, and a cleaning woman. By day's end, Seale left a contented man, certain he had done the best he could with the jury.

The same jury left the normally placid Sarah Garner with a sense of impending doom. "They're going to do what they want to do," said Sarah, who normally avoided talking with the media. "They are all white and one black. That's unfair. It seems like there is a racial problem over here."

The problem transcended race, from John Hannah's point of view. Bill Martin, Hannah suspected, had been right in his grim warning about Judge O'Neal Bacon. Twice Seale had moved to dismiss potential jurors, and twice the judge routinely had granted his requests. Hannah had made twenty-three motions to dismiss, twelve of which Judge Bacon summarily had denied. Hannah felt like he'd just witnessed a car wreck.

"I've got a feeling this isn't going to be pretty," the special prosecutor told Glenda Shelton. "We got no choice. We play what we're dealt."

24

PROSECUTION

REPORTERS MAY DOZE, go for coffee, or phone the office during witnesses' testimony, but, guaranteed, they'll be in the front row for the opening and closing arguments. Unfettered by the strict courtroom discipline that requires predicates, foundations, and adherence to evidence, lawyers are most quotable during opening and closing statements, in which they "interpret" for the jury what *they* believe the evidence will show or has shown. The process actually has little to do with law and sometimes even isn't that akin to fact. Employing sometimes shock or poignancy, but always oratory and drama, the lawyer hopes to project enough sincerity and credibility with the jurors that they'll take his perspective with them behind the closed door to the jury room.

If anyone in the courtroom had possessed the credulity or the gullibility to believe the opening remarks of both John Seale and John Hannah, he would have to have assumed Loyal Garner, Jr., was a split personality of extraordinary proportions. Garner, as portrayed by the special prosecutor, was a hard-working, difficult-to-rile family man, a loving husband and doting father of six who never before had been arrested for so much as even a traffic infraction. He was a Good Samaritan who had given up a portion of Christmas Day to help a friend with a car problem. That same Loyal Garner, Jr., as depicted by the lead defense counsel, actually was a belligerently aggressive assailant who, high on a mixture of alcohol and Valium, had attacked a police officer in the performance of his job. Indeed, at the time of Garner's arrest, the defense lawyer contended, Garner had been on a clandestine trip to pick up a load of illicit methamphetamines.

The country lawyer, Hannah observed from the counsel table, was damn good. He was conservatively tailored and humble in the way he addressed the jurors and judge. He wasn't nearly as homespun as the late Senator Sam Ervin of North Carolina when he won over a nation during the televised Watergate hearings, but Seale possessed some of the same charm. Beneath the small-town veneer, the prosecutor suspected, was an astute lawyer whose talents would command six figures and a penthouse office in the big city. Jurors, the competitor suspected, would equate the Jasper lawyer with sincerity, a real problem for the state of Texas.

"Testimony will show," Seale predicted, "that the blows were two to one—two for Garner and one for Ladner." The only reason Ladner and Horton had gone to the cell was to "calm [Garner] down and allow him to use the telephone." Once in the booking room, where the phone was located, Garner inexplicably changed his mind about the call. There was a brief scuffle when Garner tried to attack the officers, got caught up in a chair, and bumped his head on the wall. The officers "walked" Garner back to the cell.

Seale's rendition of the events produced a dull roar of approval through the courtroom, with the single exception of the blacks who sat clustered at the back, near the door. Judge Bacon either didn't hear the vocal reaction or, more likely, didn't believe it was disruptive enough to warrant a warning to the crowd.

Seale's contention that Garner was a drug trafficker, Hannah admonished the jury, was "part of a cover-up, because the officers knew there would be accusations against them after Garner was beaten. They thought the drug trafficking thing would make Garner sound bad before a jury."

Ladner and Hyden had gone to the detox cell "not on a peaceful mission" to offer Garner a phone call, the prosecutor contended, "but to show who's boss in the Sabine County Jail."

That afternoon, Hannah called Garner's widow, Corrine, and his former supervisor, Gordon Anthony, as witnesses. Occasionally through tears, Corrine Garner emotionally recalled her life with Loyal, leading up to Christmas 1987, the day she last saw him alive. Garner emerged as a dutiful husband and father whose only priority had been his family. Seldom, Mrs. Garner testified, did her husband drink, and when he did, it was "only a beer now and then."

Gordon Anthony, head of the Sabine Parish road crew in Florien and Garner's supervisor for five years, described his former employee as his "right-hand man." Garner was the most dependable and capable of all his employees and the first to whom Anthony turned during emergencies when roads were flooded or blocked by trees. Anthony, a white man, said he never had seen Garner when he appeared to be drunk or under the influence of drugs.

Seale's criticism of the media coverage was no secret, but his stunning contention in opening remarks that Garner was a drug smuggler helped even the score in the media. The next edition of the *Houston Chronicle*, the biggest newspaper to circulate in southeastern Texas, carried a banner headline on the front page that read: GARNER WAS DRUG TRAFFICKER, ATTORNEYS SAY.

"Damn it, turn that damn fan a little more this way so we can *all* get a little of it."

Floyd Addington and Paul Buchanan shot surprised glances at Bill Martin, the sturdy district attorney wedged at the single fifteen-foot counsel table between John Hannah and first assistant prosecutor Charles Mitchell on one side and the three defense attorneys on the other.

"I'm not kidding," Martin said, his voice as menacing as his size. "Hell, I brought fans from my office up here. Least you boys can do is turn the damn things around this way a little. Don't make me get up."

Texas v. Ladner, Horton, and Hyden was heated enough; the suffocating courtroom only made it worse. Quickly, though, the cool breeze was turned toward the prosecution side of the table.

It was fitting that Bill Martin was seated in the middle of all the lawyers, literally bumping knees with both the prosecution and the defense. His allegiances had been split down the middle from the beginning. The prosecutor hadn't known Hyden that well, but Ladner and Horton were more than merely former colleagues of his; both had been good friends. The modest and self-deprecating Martin had been honest enough to realize his conflict long before the Southern Poverty Law Center had suggested that he step aside to allow John Hannah's appointment as special prosecutor. In fact, Martin already had tried unsuccessfully to get Texas Attorney General Jim Mattox to provide one of his lawyers to prosecute the three lawmen.

Martin's reluctance about trying the three cops wasn't about politics;

it was about personal feelings and integrity. "The question arose in my mind whether I could put the proper perspective on this case, not whether I approved or disapproved of what happened," Martin recalled later. "The problem in my mind was whether I could give Garner's family a fair shake. You can understand that I felt they ought to have a fair shake as well as the other people. I felt like I'd follow the proper procedures, but would I put my heart and soul into it?

"It was a heart-rending time. Here was a man who'd lost his life, and I didn't know anything about him. . . . This was just another incident in my life. It just so happened that it involved three what I consider good men who may have been just a little too strong in their efforts to correct something."

As the district attorney watched the three officers at the other end of the room, Martin couldn't help focusing on his old friend Bill Horton. The fifty-eight-year-old former chief deputy, the oldest of the defendants, steadfastly had refused plea bargains offered by Hannah and, later, by Smith County District Attorney Jack Skeen. The grandfatherly Horton didn't have to be in the courtroom, at least not as a defendant. "I'll bet he felt, 'Well, I'm not deserting my friends,'" Martin tried to explain. "He'd rather take the rap than take the clean break. That would mean he'd have to testify, and he wouldn't do it. That was part of the deal, and he wouldn't do it.

"In my opinion," Martin said, "there were no winners. Everyone was a loser."

There was no question among John Seale, Paul Buchanan, and Floyd Addington: Dr. Virgil Gonzalez had to be destroyed on the witness stand if their clients stood a chance of acquittal. The Tyler pathologist, even more than eyewitnesses Alton and Johnnie Maxie, posed the greatest single threat to Ladner's, Horton's, and Hyden's liberty. Gonzalez's testimony already had been devastating for the three ex-lawmen, accounting for two grand jury indictments and an inquest jury's finding of homicide. Thursday, July 7, the defense lawyers knew, would be an acid test for their case.

Judge Bacon, by John Hannah's way of thinking, already had taken away much of Dr. Gonzalez's effectiveness as an expert. Over Hannah's strenuous objections, the judge had ruled with the defense, agreeing that the photographs of Loyal Garner, Jr.'s autopsy were "inflammatory and prejudicial." The jury, he said, would not see them. The doctor would have to draw his illustrations on a portable blackboard. Dr. Gonzalez's qualifications as a pathologist were documentable; his ability as an illustrator, however, required some imagination. Likewise, Hannah knew, the doctor's English occasionally required keen concentration to follow, a problem compounded by his use of medical terminology. Privately, Hannah feared the jury might see the doctor as part of the defense's web of out-of-town agitators, or, even worse by East Texas standards, as a "foreigner."

Hannah painstakingly took Dr. Gonzalez through virtually the same testimony he had provided to the grand juries and the inquest trial. Yes, Gonzalez testified, Garner had suffered at least three blows to the head. Indeed, he said, it was the thunderous force of the blow to the right side that caused the brain to hemorrhage and swell, cutting off the man's blood supply and killing him. And yes, the blows were compatible with damage inflicted by a blackjack.

Defense lawyers had used the doctor's previous testimony to prep for their cross-examination. Seale repeatedly attempted to get the doctor locked in on Garner's purported alcohol level the morning after he had been arrested, a critical factor in attempting to portray the dead man as a belligerent assailant. The doctor was unbudging. He didn't take a blood alcohol level during his autopsy and had seen no authentic evidence that Garner even had alcohol in his blood. Nor would the doctor cooperate in Seale's attempt at hypothetically extrapolating backwards to show that at the time of Garner's arrest, his blood alcohol level would have been in excess of .335, or more than three times the legal limit for intoxication.

Hannah's repeated objections, nearly all of which were overruled, provided no reprieve for the doctor under Seale's attack. The unyielding sparring was fraying both men's patience.

Finally, the doctor noted he couldn't explain how much a person would have to have drunk to be as intoxicated as Seale suggested Garner was because there were too many factors to be considered. And beyond that, Dr. Gonzalez testified, he couldn't conjecture, because "I've never been drunk."

The doctor's response brought an outburst of laughter from the audience. Hannah was furious. He had complained earlier to Judge Bacon that the prodefense spectators were influencing the jury, inevitably expressing their approval when the state's motions were denied or laughing cynically when the state made a damning point against the defendants. Something needed to be done about the outbursts. The judge cautioned the audience that he'd clear the courtroom if the noise continued.

There was no defense strategy that scripted Paul Buchanan as the heavy; it was a role to which he aspired. He'd watched the doctor's testimony and found him to be complacent and smug. Toward the end of his questioning, the feisty Buchanan deliberately provoked Dr. Gonzalez. For thirty years, the pathologist had lived comfortably in a world of scientific certainty. A tumor was either benign or malignant; an organ was unremarkable or fatty. He was ill equipped to handle innuendo, particularly about his integrity.

How much, Buchanan wanted to know, was the doctor getting paid for the autopsy and for testifying for the state of Texas? The doctor clearly regarded the information the way he would his tax returns, and refused to answer. Buchanan was relentless, pushing the doctor for an answer. Finally, the lawyer struck the nerve he'd been probing. "You tell me how much *you* charge and I'll tell you," Dr. Gonzalez erupted. "I'm here to testify about Loyal Garner's autopsy, not to be scrutinized about how much I charge." Cautioned by the judge to answer the question, the doctor acknowledged he charged $200 an hour, nearly two-thirds the average *weekly* income in Sabine County—a fee the lawyer hoped the jury would regard as extravagant.

Buchanan hadn't been any more successful than Seale at eliciting testimony to shore up their drunk-and-belligerent theory, but he had exposed an angry personal side of the doctor for the jury. At least they knew this "expert" was as human as everyone else. Buchanan returned to his chair a contented man.

Hannah called several inmates as witnesses, but he used a combination of two, both young and white, to provide a beginning-to-end glimpse of Garner's brief stay in jail.

Weldon Sangwin recalled hearing, but not seeing from his vantage point down the hall, Thomas Ladner yelling for someone to open the detox cell, then menacingly asking, "Which one of you black mother-fuckers is banging on that door?" The challenge was followed in short order by three dull thuds, Sangwin testified, "*whop, whop, whop.*

"I heard Thomas say, 'See there, it doesn't take three or four of us.' "

Twice after Ladner and another officer took Garner to the front of the jail, Sangwin said, he heard Garner scream. After the officers returned to the cell with the prisoner, according to Sangwin, "I heard one of the prisoners say, 'You need to get a doctor. This guy's hurt pretty bad.' "

Trent Taylor confirmed what Texas Ranger Roscoe Davis had suspected early on. Taylor had cleaned up the detox cell early the morning of December 26, hours before the Ranger arrived. Taylor confirmed Sangwin's testimony about Garner being beaten and recalled hearing Ladner ask Bo Hyden for a blackjack.

After Garner had been returned to detox, Taylor testified, Ladner appeared at his cell next door. "He told me he had some stuff he wanted me to clean up," the thrice-convicted Taylor told the jury. "He said, 'If you see anything that needs cleaning up, clean it up.' " The former trusty said he found "four or five" drops of blood in the hallway leading to detox, which he removed with a mop. In the jailer's office, Taylor recalled, he saw a frayed blackjack lying on the desk.

Hannah bore in closely, using his witness to emphasize that the officers not only knew how seriously they had beaten Garner but had refused to call a doctor and tried to cover up evidence of the beating.

Taylor confirmed that Ladner tried to get him to remove Garner's bloody shirt and jeans and replace them with clean jail clothes. The young witness visibly cringed at the recollection, and said he had refused.

One of the other men in detox, Taylor testified, either Alton or Johnnie Maxie, told Ladner that the unconscious Garner needed a doctor. "Ladner didn't say anything," Taylor recalled.

The next morning, after Garner and the Maxie brothers had been removed from detox, Taylor said, he cleaned up the detox cell. He said he found a twelve-inch pool of blood on the cement floor below the ledge where Garner had lain.

The cross-examination of Johnnie Maxie was as intense as the defense's attack on Dr. Gonzalez. Repeatedly, Seale, Addington, and Buchanan alluded to the original statement Maxie had given to jailer Clyde Kirk. Nowhere in the statement, they pointed out, did Maxie make any reference to Junior Garner being beaten. Quite the contrary, the lawyers pointed out: Maxie had said the officers were "kind and gentlemanly." And now he was recanting the statement? Which of his versions of the "truth," the lawyers demanded, was in fact the truth?

Johnnie Maxie, still recuperating from the head injuries he had suffered in the car wreck in March, was more addled and uncertain than he'd been in his previous testimony to the two grand juries and at the inquest. Maxie's slow and sometimes hesitant responses to the barrage of questions, Hannah believed, stemmed from his critical head injuries. To the jury, however, Hannah feared Maxie would appear reluctant and less than candid.

Hannah tried to bolster his eyewitness, asking him if he "would have signed the Constitution if they had shoved it before you that morning?"

"Yes," Maxie replied.

Asked why he signed the statement if it wasn't true, Maxie feebly replied, "I didn't have no choice. I was told to sign it. Yeah, I was afraid. I signed it."

Junior Garner, Johnnie Maxie reiterated under Hannah's questioning, was neither drunk nor trafficking in drugs on Christmas Day. In fact, the elder Maxie said, Garner had been a lifelong friend and he'd never seen him use drugs or drink heavily.

Hannah correctly anticipated that the defense team would bludgeon inmate-witnesses Taylor and Sangwin on cross-examination, dragging up their considerable arrest records to undermine their truthfulness. But he had pigeonholed what he considered his best "jailhouse" witness for use later in the trial.

Jimmy Earl Moore was from nearby Pineland. He was seventeen, clean-cut, and had been arrested only once, for burglarizing a school. Hannah hoped the jury would embrace his own assessment of Moore: a good kid who fell in with the wrong crowd but now wanted to do the right thing. On Christmas night, Moore was locked in the cell directly across from detox. He, like several other inmates, had heard the bloody confrontation between Garner and Ladner and Hyden. But Moore, by stooping to his knees and peering through the rectangular "bean hole" in the metal door, was the only inmate who actually *saw* portions of the confrontation.

Moore's testimony would be explosive and credible, Hannah knew. His recollection would be critical in refuting the officers' claim that Garner was in good shape when he was returned to the cell from the book-in room.

Moore, whose cell was closer to the book-in room at the front of the jail than the other inmates', had told Hannah in a pretrial interview that he heard Garner pleading, "I've got a wife and kids." Ladner, he said, had replied, "I don't give a damn." Moore recalled Ladner yelling, "Get in there, you black bastard." The teenager said he heard two more blows before the door to the book-in room slammed. Minutes later, according to Moore, he had been looking out the bean hole and saw Ladner and Hyden return Garner to detox. "The whole side of Garner's head was covered with blood," Moore told the prosecutor.

But before Hannah could call Moore to testify before the jury, another witness accused Moore of violating the rule that prohibits potential witnesses from discussing the case. Moore's chief, and only, accuser was Holton "Bubba" Johnson, the Newton constable whom Horton had allowed Johnnie Maxie to call Christmas night from the Sabine County Jail. Constable Johnson, in his appearance before the Hemphill grand jury in December, had testified that Johnnie Maxie was a snitch who sometimes passed him information. Johnson likewise was the only witness who alleged that Garner was on a "methamphetamine run" at the time he was arrested on Christmas by Ladner and Horton.

The constable, who was to appear as a witness for Ladner, Horton, and Hyden, told Judge Bacon that while sequestered in the witness room, he overheard Jimmy Moore discussing the case. Actually, Hannah discovered, a witness who already had testified had mentioned to Moore that lawyers were "trying to show how drunk Garner was." It was far from a "discussion" in which details of testimony supposedly were revealed, Hannah argued.

Judge Bacon struck Moore as a witness and dismissed him; the jury would not hear the teenager's recollection of the events.

Hannah was furious. And his anger was only intensified when he learned that Bubba Johnson, who also had been privy to whatever was discussed in the witness room, nonetheless wasn't being disqualified as a witness for the three officers. If the conversation had been so pejorative as to taint the objectivity of the state's witness, Hannah demanded to know, how come it hadn't tainted the witness for the defense? The constable had heard it, too.

"We ought to just go across the street and pack up our crap and go back to Tyler. This is the goddamnedest railroad job I've ever seen in my life. It's not even a trial."

John Henry Hannah, Jr., spoke in an angry whisper, mad enough to be yelling, but stubbornly refusing to give the lunch-hour patrons of K-C Drug the satisfaction of knowing how badly things were going for the prosecution. Most days during the lunch break, Hannah and his paralegal ventured to the old-timey soda fountain across from the courthouse for a sandwich. And most days, Glenda Shelton noticed, they got their sandwiches only after every local had been served, no matter how much later the locals showed up.

"We're losing and we shouldn't be," Hannah said. "We've got a case. Everybody in this town knows what these bastards did, and they're damn sure gonna walk. They don't give a damn. The jury's packed with good ol' boys, and the judge won't let me put on any evidence. Every time the judge beats up on us—which is *all* the time—the audience snickers and gives us hell."

Speaking of hell produced a fleeting grin on the prosecutor's face as his thoughts turned to his father. Velma and John Henry Hannah, Sr., had driven over from Diboll and spent every day in the courtroom. Almost by the hour, the senior Hannah was becoming more the mule skinner who had chased the timber boss through the woods forty years earlier. And the judge didn't seem predisposed to stop the prodefense snickering and giggling. "I'm afraid Dad's gonna hear some of that crap and throw a punch at somebody," the younger Hannah said. "Then all hell *will* break loose, I guarantee you." He was only half joking. He remembered well the phone call for legal advice when his father, well past sixty, had knocked a young truck driver over a desk at the Temple-Inland mill.

A fistfight wasn't out of the realm of possibility. The younger Hannah himself already had warned the judge that if Seale didn't stop poking his finger into Hannah's chest, he planned "to knock him on his ass."

But nothing was more offensive or pathetic, Hannah thought, than the small and docile huddle of blacks in the back of the courtroom. "They're so beaten down they're afraid to even be seen in the courthouse," he told Shelton. "They're scared, and I don't blame 'em—not for a minute."

Vollie Grace, who for the last several months had been busily recruiting members for his Concerned Citizens for Sabine County, also had noticed the blacks' reluctance to sit in on the trial. Eyeing the spectators, Grace saw almost no young black men. He'd experienced the same problem recruiting members for his group; the younger men, most of whom depended on white employers, were afraid of losing their jobs, or maybe worse. Grace owned his own business and had canceled jobs during the course of the trial. Except for Garner's family, seated, as he was, near the front, the contingent of blacks—overwhelmingly women and retired men—sat clustered in the rear of the courtroom. It fell to them to monitor the trial and carry the word back to East Mayfield, the rutted, unpaved "black section" of Hemphill. There no longer were separate drinking fountains in the Sabine County Courthouse, but Grace had seen living proof, in a courtroom of all places, that segregation was still alive and well.

The courtroom had had a profound impact on Hannah and, as he sat in the drug store, he had no appetite, leaving most of his sandwich on his plate. Glenda Shelton reminded her boss of one of his favorite clichés: "It ain't over till it's over."

Peripherally, the paralegal noticed two black boys approaching from the door of K-C Drug. The older, maybe eleven, stopped about six feet from their table, uneasily surveying the white faces in the dining room. The smaller one—Shelton guessed he was about eight—came closer until he was within reach of Hannah. Saying nothing, the little boy reached over and squeezed, then patted, the prosecutor's arm. Embarrassed, he turned and walked quickly back to his friend. Together, they bolted from the soda fountain like jackrabbits.

John Hannah's eyes turned red and watery.

Curiously enough for the prosecution's case, Hannah called only two Texas law enforcement officers as witnesses; the others would testify in behalf of the defense.

Refuting Johnnie Maxie's recollection of the affidavit he took, Sabine County jailer Clyde Kirk testified he wrote the elder Maxie's account almost verbatim as Maxie recounted the arrests. Under Hannah's direct examination, however, Kirk acknowledged that he had questioned both Maxies only after an early-morning phone call to the jail on December 26 from Chief Deputy Bill Horton. Horton, the jailer testified, told him to go check on the prisoners in detox. Told he couldn't rouse one of the inmates and that he was calling an ambulance, Kirk testified, the chief deputy instructed him to take statements from the other two prisoners in detox and to focus the statements on drugs.

Hannah, trying to drive home for the jury that the phone call was part of an evolving cover-up, got the old jailer to admit the phone call was uncharacteristic of the chief deputy. In fact, Kirk admitted, he'd never before been asked to check on the welfare of any inmate, much less take a statement from one.

Later, trying to discredit in advance Ladner's anticipated defense that he'd used "only that force necessary to subdue" an unruly Garner, Hannah asked Texas Ranger Roscoe Davis if in his opinion the three black prisoners had posed a threat to Ladner and Hyden in the detox cell. No, the Ranger said, it did not appear that deadly force had been warranted. Garner, Davis testified, weighed about 155 pounds, compared with about 270 pounds for the chief of police. The chief had admitted to hitting Garner with a blackjack, Davis said. "I asked him to give me the slapper he used during the disturbance," the Ranger said. Ladner actually gave him two blackjacks, one of which had come unstitched, exposing the lead weight in the end. The Ranger said Ladner told him he used the newer one and kept the damaged one in a file cabinet.

Hannah was unable, however, to introduce the older, frayed blackjack into evidence. The Texas Ranger testified he no longer could find it. The blackjack had been among the evidence he had seized in the case, Davis said, but apparently it had been misplaced.

The courtroom was packed Friday afternoon, the fourth day of testimony. Several regulars who had returned from lunch too late to retrieve their seats lined the walls along the third-floor landing outside the courtroom. The half-glass swinging doors allowed them to see, if not hear, everything that transpired inside.

The six lawyers had their backs to the audience, and none of them actually saw the incident that created the low roar and shuffling behind them. Hannah turned to the audience just in time to see a deputy sheriff reaching over several spectators. The lawman had a black man by the arm, pulling him awkwardly toward him as he stood in the aisle. An obviously pregnant white woman in the row in front of the black man was turned sideways in her seat, staring at the man and gasping as if she were crying.

The black man was Willis Garner, one of Junior Garner's brothers. He had a perplexed, frightened look as the deputy moved him rapidly toward the swinging doors and out of the courtroom. The whispers turned to outright conversations among the startled spectators. Hannah approached the bench and Judge Bacon ordered a recess.

By the time the prosecutor pushed his way through the gallery to the back of the courtroom, he had picked up bits and pieces from the spectators. From what he gathered, Willis Garner had been arrested and hauled off to the Sabine County Jail. A white woman muttered that the black man had "blown on the woman's neck" and had "brushed up against her arm."

Liz Green, a black woman who had been sitting not five feet from him, said Willis Garner "didn't do nothing. He was just sitting there. He said he felt sick. The white woman turned around and pointed her finger in his face and said he was breathing on her."

Loyal Garner's brother had been arrested for "breathing" on a white woman? Hannah's pace quickened, carrying him across the courthouse lawn to the Sabine County Jail. "I was damned if I was going to let them take Loyal's brother to the same cell where they killed him," Hannah said later. Sheriff's deputies said they merely planned to question Willis Garner, not necessarily jail him. Hannah refused to leave, and the deputies later released Willis Garner without charges.

As outrageously insensitive as the arrest was, Hannah discovered, it also could have a devastating impact on the state's case. The sobbing pregnant woman, who later had locked herself in the women's restroom, was Lydia "Dollie" Turner, the daughter of juror Mary Pritchard. The incident, Hannah was convinced, had to have infected the jury.

He already was considering a motion for a mistrial when he learned thirdhand during the weekend that a radio reporter, one of the pack that followed the jury every time they left the courtroom, had attempted to interview Mary Pritchard the night of the incident. The jurors were bound by oath not to discuss the case with anyone.

Pritchard, a congenial forty-eight-year-old divorcee, owned Mary's Pines Snack Bar ten miles away in Pineland. The cafe was a popular gathering place in the tiny timber town, catering mostly to the timber haulers who trucked logs to the Temple-Inland mill across the tracks behind the cafe. Unbeknownst to Hannah, it also was a popular coffee stop for many of Sabine County's police officers. Not surprising, then, was the wall calendar from the Sabine County Sheriff's Department, picturing the sheriff and all his staff, hanging in the coffee shop.

Following the incident between Pritchard's daughter and Willis Garner, the enterprising radio reporter drove out to have a milkshake at Pritchard's place and, apparently, tried to interview her.

Hannah tried to convince Judge Bacon to declare a mistrial. The courtroom outburst alone, involving a brother of the deceased and the daughter of a juror, could have tainted the jury against the state, Hannah contended. Judge Bacon denied his motion without elaboration, apparently not convinced the jurors had seen the incident.

The incredulous special prosecutor tried again for a mistrial, this time based on the reporter's purported interview with Pritchard. The hearing occurred in open court, but after the jury had been removed.

"Mrs. Pritchard, it's my understanding, expressed some concern to the reporter and also expressed fully that she knew about the incident," Hannah argued. "Based on that, I would renew my motion for mistrial and, secondly, strongly, if that motion is denied, strongly urge the court to allow us to question Mrs. Pritchard alone to see if she indeed knows about the event that transpired in the courtroom between her daughter and the victim's brother, and whether or not that might affect her in any way, and whether or not she's communicated that to any other juror."

Seale was on his feet. "Of course, if these reporters are following their usual thing of running and putting the microphone in front of you . . . that's something we certainly have no control over," he told the judge. "In answer to the second part of that, to take a juror out and put them under questioning and cross-questioning back and forth like that is completely unfair to the juror to the effect that it coerces the juror or whatever."

Bill Horton's lawyer, Floyd Addington, not only argued against granting a mistrial but used the forum to emotionally express the widespread contempt in Hemphill for the media. "From late December 1987 until the present time," he told the court, "I don't think anyone has seen reported an accurate statement of the facts that have developed. . . . The media has elected, for whatever reason or another, to side with the prosecution in this case and condemn and convict three Sabine County officers without a trial. And for all I know, this is a conspiracy among the press to cause a mistrial here, because I have seen reported statements from the Houston preacher [Earnest Charles] and from the Sabine Parish [Louisiana] people that there could not be a fair trial granted in Sabine County, Texas. Now, to destroy or to attack the integrity of this jury by second- or thirdhand hearsay of a . . . reporter is one of the most ridiculous things I have heard and is extremely prejudicial to my client, Bill Horton. . . ."

Addington's soliloquy elicited a low roar of approval from the audience, who obviously shared his opinion. The proceedings, Hannah surmised, were becoming a pep rally.

"I think we need to move ahead," Addington continued. "We're ready to proceed and get the case over with, and then let's go to Tyler."

Hannah pointed out that the reporter who told him of the attempted interview of Pritchard also claimed to have told the judge. He again urged his motion to declare a mistrial.

Addington, however, wasn't through, and his remarks clearly were tailored to ingratiate himself to Judge Bacon. "Your Honor . . . I know of my own personal knowledge not about judges elsewhere, in Tyler, Houston, or whatever, but I know the position of the judges in the First Judicial District—Judge Smith, Judge Bacon, Judge Lawless—and they do not listen to the press nor do they talk to the press," Addington said smugly. "Mr. Hannah's assumption that a reporter talked to you, I think, is false to start with. . . . I would like the record to show that is the court's policy as I've known it to be as a member of the bar for many years."

"That is the court's policy," Judge Bacon reaffirmed, without saying if the reporter had indeed told him of the incident, ". . . the motion is denied and the request is denied."

Actually, the potential taint to the juror was far more extensive than even Hannah had imagined, but the damage wasn't attributable directly to what Pritchard saw in the courtroom or to the reporter who tried to interview her about the incident.

Pritchard later would say she hadn't noticed the incident in the courtroom. With "people coming and going all the time," she explained later, she had not noticed any unusual commotion. Further, she said, she didn't realize her pregnant daughter was even in the courtroom. On her way out of the courtroom, however, a friend touched her on the arm and said, "Mary, Dollie's okay."

"But I thought she said, 'Mary, *is* Dollie okay?'—Dollie was expecting—and I said, 'Oh, yes, she's doing fine.' My friend had a funny expression on her face and said, 'Oh, you didn't know?' She said, 'Well, she was feeling a little faint in the courtroom, but she's feeling all right now.' "

After court, Pritchard drove back to her coffee shop in Pineland and was clearing coffee cups from the tables when Sheriff Blan Greer and District Attorney Bill Martin walked in.

Greer asked her the whereabouts of her daughter. Pritchard has four daughters—Stacey was the only one still at home—and it took the juror a while to figure out he was inquiring about Dollie.

"Mr. Blan said, 'I can't tell you, but she's okay,' " Pritchard recalled.

The sheriff's cryptic remarks left the juror with an ominous feeling. Pritchard knew something had happened to her daughter, but she didn't know what. Because the sheriff had been accompanied by the district attorney, she ruled out the possibility that Dollie had been in an accident. "The first thing I thought was that somebody had done something to her," Pritchard recalled. "I went home and told Stacey, 'Something has happened to Dollie, but Mr. Blan said she was okay. Call her.' "

Remembering the judge's order that jurors not discuss the case or listen to anyone who did, and fearing that Dollie's dilemma, whatever it was, might involve the trial, Pritchard told Stacey to go to a phone outside the house. Pritchard wanted to follow the letter of the law. "I want you to go to a pay phone and call her and make sure she's okay and see if you need to go and stay with her or if y'all need to go somewhere and stay in a motel. But don't tell me what it is."

By Pritchard's own account, she could only have wondered through the rest of the trial what actually had happened to her pregnant daughter.

For Willis Garner, the bizarre incident in the courtroom brought him face to face with the same system that had led to his brother being beaten to death. He was stunned, he said, when the white woman suddenly turned and told him, "I wish you'd quit breathing on me." He wasn't aware he had been.

"They made me look small," he said later in the day when he was released from the Sabine County Jail. "One of my brothers is already dead and gone. I'm going back to Louisiana and I ain't coming back no more."

Having lost one son in Hemphill and watched helplessly as another was forcibly evicted from the courtroom, old Sarah Garner was physically ill. "I'm so sick of this I don't know what to do," she told a reporter for the *Houston Chronicle*. "I already had one of my boys killed over here."

The state's final witness was the chief of detectives for the Sabine Parish Sheriff's Department in Many. Chief James McConnic had done a background check on Junior Garner and a computerized search of local and Louisiana crime records. Before Ladner and Hyden arrested him on Christmas beside Texas 87, Loyal Garner, Jr., had never been arrested.

25

"WILD MAN"

DEFENSE ATTORNEY Floyd Addington's criticism of the media, including his speculation that a conspiracy existed among reporters to convict the three lawmen, was as prevalent in Sabine County as pine beetles and pickup trucks. Addington's antimedia sentiment, recorded in the trial transcript, crept openly into the streets in Hemphill.

One television technician, whose only link to reporting was operating the maze of electronic gadgets that transmitted the signal, was stunned when an angry man appeared at the satellite uplink van parked near the courthouse. "Why don't you take your cameras and whatnot and just get the hell out of here," the man told the technician. "We're just pretty sick of it. I mean it—we're tired of y'all and all this mess y'all brought."

"We can't help but be upset with the press," a woman told reporter Mary Flood of *The Houston Post.* "This courthouse and town look so bad, but we have fond memories of this place. I wouldn't live anywhere else." The woman's perspective was alien to metropolitan reporters, who had come to view the decrepit old courthouse as somehow symbolic of everything that was wrong with this backward county. But the local woman saw the same courthouse as the place where she had adopted her children, whom she later took to country festivals held on the courthouse lawn beneath the tall pecan tree.

If reporters found symbolism in the courthouse, so did the townspeople in the satellite trucks and the reporters. *They* were the embodiment of the ills that beset the forgotten little town. The media were from out of town, and there weren't any problems in Hemphill that didn't involve out-of-town people. Loyal Garner, Jr., was from out of town, and though it was less than forty miles' distance to Louisiana, he was from out of state.

"What business did he have over here on Christmas anyway?" posed one middle-aged woman, as if passports were required to travel through Sabine County, particularly on holidays. "That's what started this whole thing. We wouldn't have all this problem if he'd stayed home." The simplistic rationale, prevalent in coffee shops and stores, appeared to be that Garner brought about his own death by not staying where, local consensus had it, he *should* have stayed—at home in Louisiana, particularly on the most significant family and religious day of the year. Once Garner breached this dictum, it seemed, he was responsible for anything that happened to him, like a child who disregarded his parents' warning to play in his yard, ventured into the street, and was hit by a car. Under prevailing local opinion, then, Hemphill would have performed a public service by erecting a sign that said, ENTER AT YOUR OWN RISK—HEMPHILL WAIVES RESPONSIBILITY.

The two eyewitnesses, the Maxies, were out-of-town, John Hannah was out-of-town, the pathologist was "a foreigner," the Texas Ranger was out-of-town, that "civil rights group is out of Alabama or somewhere like that," and certainly the media were out-of-town.

In the midst of the trial, hometown allegiances and the First Amendment clashed one afternoon on the courthouse lawn. As the attorneys and defendants emerged from the courthouse after a trial session, a Hemphill police officer yelled to photographers that anyone filming people coming out of the building would be arrested. The photographers knew that any arrests for shooting film outside a public building wouldn't withstand a court's scrutiny. But they also were aware of Willis Garner's unprecedented arrest for breathing on a white woman, undoubtedly forcing them to weigh the plethora of bizarre charges Hemphill police might concoct against them.

When the courthouse door opened, there was a momentary lull of apprehension before first one camera, then others, clicked and whirred.

Tenuously, the First Amendment prevailed. There were no arrests, only more tension.

The foundation for the defense of Thomas Ladner, Bo Hyden, and Bill Horton, apparent since John Seale's opening remarks to the jury, was self-defense. The brick and mortar, the defense hoped, were Loyal Garner, Jr.'s purported alcohol-and-drug-induced rage and the fact that the Louisiana man was a drug dealer. The chief architects of those two theories were Hemphill's physician, Dr. Grover Winslow, and the constable from a neighboring county, Holton "Bubba" Johnson.

Before the defense called its first witness, Paul Buchanan primed jurors for what they would hear. "We will attempt to show you . . . beyond any doubt that the blood alcohol of this human being was somewhere between .26 and .335," Buchanan said. "We will show you that this man had a sufficient amount of Valium in his bloodstream when he got to the hospital before anything was administered to him such that the expert testimony will be that this man could very easily have been a wild man, that between the combination of Valium and the high intoxication level, there was not one inhibition left in this human being, that whatever normal inhibitions that we call upon in our daily life that constrains us from being an out-of-control person would have been—between the drugs and the alcohol—totally and completely subdued.

"We will attempt to show you that there was, in fact, a dope deal that night contemplated by one or more individuals in that pickup truck. . . ."

Dr. Winslow's testimony, Seale, Buchanan, and Addington hoped, would do for the defense what they had been unsuccessful in getting Dr. Gonzalez to do—extrapolating from a controversial blood test to show that Garner, at the time he was arrested, was triple-drunk by legal standards.

The defense's hypothesizing about Garner's blood alcohol level, as reflected in local testing at the Sabine General Hospital, would occur in a vacuum. While Hannah and the Southern Poverty Law Center were aware that a sample of Garner's blood also was sent to a private lab in Beaumont to test for blood gases, they did not yet realize the lab also routinely performed a blood alcohol test. That test revealed no trace of alcohol in Garner's blood.

Establishing that Garner was drunk at the time of his arrest was crucial to the defense's "wild man" theory.

Seale wasted no time in extracting from Dr. Winslow that blood drawn from Garner at 8:30 A.M. on December 26 in the emergency room at Sabine County Hospital revealed a blood alcohol content of .075, just under the .1 legal definition of intoxication.

Hannah anticipated the strategy and objected: "This would be a scientific test requiring a strict chain of custody showing how the blood sample was handled, who handled it, who did the testing, and what the test results were." Dr. Winslow said the blood had been drawn by a lab technician, then picked up by a courier for the independent lab in Beaumont, ninety miles to the south, where it was tested.

Hannah asked for permission to question the doctor outside the presence of the jury before Seale continued questioning the defense witness. The judge agreed. Granted, the chain of custody of the blood was a legal argument, but Hannah knew he had to fight any perception that Garner had been drunk and therefore, according to the defense, belligerent and aggressive. He had to leave the possibility with the jury that the blood sample could have been tampered with.

"Doctor, do you know who handed the blood to the person who picked it up?" the prosecutor asked.

"I'm sure it would be the lab technician," Dr. Winslow replied. "I did not witness it."

"So you don't know who handed—"

"She always does it. She is the only one that handles it."

"Excuse me, Doctor, you don't know?"

"The lab technician handled it."

"Did you see the lab technician hand it to the person—"

"She's the only one—"

"Excuse me, Doctor. We'll get along better if you will just answer the question."

"I did not personally see the lab technician put her hands on it and hand it to another person."

"When that person, who you do not know the name of, got there, who did they give it to?"

"I do not know."

Judge Bacon overruled Hannah's objection to the blood test.

Seale moved quickly to reestablish his rhythm with the witness.

"With reference to alcohol in the blood, that didn't have to go to Beaumont, did it?. . . . That testing that showed the .075 showed up and came out here?"

"Yes."

"Now in addition to what that showed, then the test that did come back from the lab in Beaumont . . . [did it] make a showing of any other substances in his body, particularly Valium?"

"They did."

Dr. Winslow confirmed under Seale's questioning that the body normally disperses alcohol at the rate of .02 percent an hour.

"If you wanted to find out what the alcohol content had been at a given time, for example, thirteen hours previously," Seale suggested, "you would multiply .02 times thirteen?"

"That's correct."

"And you get .26. And you add that to the .075, and then in that case, would you get .335?"

"Correct."

"Which would be over three times the normal amount of legal intoxication?"

"That is right. . . . There's no question whatsoever that he was more than legally drunk."

"Dr. Winslow, are you familiar with the effects of mixing large amounts of alcohol and large amounts, or just amounts, for that matter, of tranquilizers?"

"It can have side effects from comas, convulsions, hallucinations, agitations, mental confusion—multiple things can happen from it," the doctor said. "On the other hand, you could go to sleep from it. But it could have multiple things happen."

"Can the mixing of tranquilizers and alcohol have an effect on the way a person acts?" Seale asked.

"It can. It can make them wild."

Before Seale surrendered his witness to Hannah for cross-examination, he elicited the doctor's agreement that "head injuries are frequently fatal in cases of intoxication," and "in the later stages of acute alcoholic intoxication, the intoxicated individual . . . becomes stuporous and eventually lapses into coma."

"Doctor, the way you've been testifying," Hannah challenged, "you would think you're on these people's bonds. Are you?"

"We object to that, Your Honor!" Buchanan yelled.

Judge Bacon spoke over the low roar of disapproval from the audience, sustaining Buchanan's objection and instructing the jury to disregard Hannah's comment.

The prosecutor, however, had no plans to finesse this witness. He was indignant and it showed. "Are you on these people's bonds?" Hannah asked, this time withholding any comment.

The doctor didn't answer.

"Speak up, Doctor."

"Just give me time, I'll speak," Dr. Winslow shot back. "I'll speak just the same as you can. Yes, I signed a bond."

"More than one of them?"

"I cannot be positive, because I went over there and I signed the bond and, as far as I know, it was only one, Mr. Horton's, and I believe that's all."

"If I told you that you were on another one's bond, would you believe that?"

"I signed my signature one time," Dr. Winslow maintained, "so I won't tell you, because I sign bonds—it's not an unusual thing for me to go by and sign bonds for someone. This is not an unusual practice."

"After you saw the condition of Mr. Garner in your hospital, did you go over there and bond the Maxies out, the Maxie brothers?"

"No, I did not bond them. I was not requested or asked to."

"You don't think your relationship with these people," Hannah asked, pointing toward the three officers, "would affect your testimony, do you, Doctor?"

"I know it would not," Dr. Winslow replied tersely.

"Doctor, when Loyal Garner, Jr., got there, was he basically as good as dead," Hannah asked, referring to the Sabine County emergency room.

"Yes. . . ."

"You're not telling this jury that this man died because he had too much to drink, are you?"

"This man died from a bleeding inside his head, intercranial bleeding, subdural hematoma, pressure, expanding lesion that affected him and made it that there was no way a fellow could live with this type of lesion. Contributing causes, exact causes, I'm not testifying as to that."

Dr. Winslow noted later, however, that the officers' delay in getting Garner to the hospital probably didn't matter. "In looking back," he said, "it's very doubtful that he could have been saved if he had been brought in immediately. . . . I don't think he could have been saved if he had been carried to the largest hospital with all of the facilities in the world."

Hannah pulled out the medical records and walked toward Dr. Winslow. "And y'all did a blood test early that morning and found .075 percent alcohol in Mr. Garner, I believe?"

"That is correct."

"And *then* you prescribed Valium for him?"

"If you check the records, Valium was given after twelve o'clock that day."

"Yes, *after* you found the alcohol?"

"Yes," the doctor said, "he was going into convulsions and Valium is a drug for convulsions."

"Even with alcohol in the body? What I was trying to clear up, Doctor, is the fact that you talk about the horrible effects people that have had alcohol and took Valium or had Valium and took alcohol. You did do that, didn't you?"

"Yes. . . . I administered it some *four and a half hours* after that, so it [the blood alcohol content] naturally would be lower. If it was initially at the regular rate, he would be relatively free of alcohol at that particular time."

The doctor and prosecutor continued to spar, from the size of a blood stain on Garner's pillow to whether the nose actually is part of the face.

The significant difference in size between Ladner and Garner had come up earlier in Ranger Roscoe Davis's testimony, and on redirect examination of Dr. Winslow, Seale tried to erase any problems jurors might be harboring about the differences in size of Ladner and the prisoner. Recalling the purported mixture of Valium and alcohol in Garner's body, Seale asked the doctor if a person with such a mixture of chemicals would "gain strength that they never would have otherwise or lose whatever inhibitions they would have had?"

"Under anxiety and hallucinations, et cetera," the doctor said, "people have been known to gain unusual strength. That's why we hear of persons, as a result of excitement, lifting weights maybe to free a person or lifting maybe a log off of a person. . . . It's nature's method or God's method that is given to us as a protection."

Holton "Bubba" Johnson lived in the northern portion of Newton County, a leg-shaped county just south of Sabine. He was employed by the United States Army Corps of Engineers, the builders and upkeepers of the Toledo Bend Reservoir, and he was the duly elected constable for the Third Precinct in Newton County. More importantly from the defense attorneys' point of view, Bubba Johnson was the one person on whom they could pin their efforts to portray Loyal Garner, Jr., as a drug trafficker.

Johnnie Maxie, Johnson testified, was an informant who, in the three months prior to Christmas, 1987, had passed on tidbits of information that had allowed the constable to solve a burglary case. On Christmas night, he said, Sabine Chief Deputy Bill Horton called him, saying a prisoner in his custody, Johnnie Maxie, claimed to be working for him and wanted to talk to him.

"How would you describe what Johnnie Maxie did for you?" Seale asked.

"I think the term that we normally used is that he was a snitch," Johnson said.

"In other words, he told on other people that were about to commit a crime to help you make an arrest, is that basically correct?"

"Basically, I think, in order to save his own hide—I think that's basically what a snitch is."

Though the scenario wasn't specific, Johnson apparently met the elder Maxie when Maxie was drunk. "I have seen him on one occasion," the constable said, "[when] his vehicle was setting beside the road and he was passed out in it."

On Christmas night, Johnson recalled, Johnnie Maxie talked "very openly, calm" during the phone call from the Sabine County Jail. "Johnnie and I had been working a drug deal earlier, and he was telling me that the deal . . . was supposed to go down the next day, the twenty-sixth of December, between ten [A.M.] and two P.M., and the subject he had told me about earlier, Jay Brown, was supposed to be running methamphetamines."

"Methamphetamines?"

"From Houston, and he was going to make a drop at the Louisiana lookout tower over in Sabine Parish, between ten and two."

"Did he tell you who was to make the pickup?" Seale asked.

"He gave me the name of Loyal Garner, and he gave me a vehicle that he was supposed to be driving, a 1978 black Chevrolet pickup with a Louisiana registration, T-Tom-222494." (Actually, Garner's pickup truck, the one in which he and the Maxie brothers were arrested, was not a Chevrolet but a Ford Explorer. Seale, however, made no attempt to correct the constable.)

"And did he tell you that this would now be deflected because Garner was in jail, as he was?"

"Yes, he did."

Of the phone call from the Sabine County Jail, which would have been after the confrontations in the detox cell and the book-in room, Seale asked Johnson if Maxie said "anything . . . about any concern over Garner's physical condition."

"No sir, he did not."

"Did he say anything was wrong with Garner?"

"No sir, he did not."

Even before Johnson took the witness stand, he had stung the prosecution's case by reporting potential witness Jimmy Moore's violation of the oath of silence in the witness room. And neither Hannah's nor the Southern Poverty Law Center's investigations of Garner's background had revealed any remote indication of drug involvement. The prosecutor was doubtful of the constable's testimony for multiple reasons—a skepticism Hannah hoped to pass on to the jury during his cross-examination.

Hannah asked the constable to detail Johnnie Maxie's contributions as an informant. Johnson said they amounted to two arrests for one burglary. "I don't think we've had any more convictions on stuff," he added. "He's given me a lot of information on who does what, where they do dope, where they don't do dope."

"Okay," Hannah said. "And you don't know if that stuff is true or not true, do you?"

"As long as I'm holding a warrant over him," Johnson said, referring to Johnnie Maxie, "it's true. He's going to spill his guts as long as I've got a warrant, and I've got two on him now."

"What kind of warrant?"

"Theft by check."

"And as long as you've got that warrant on him," Hannah said, "he's going to tell you anything you want to hear?"

"He'll tell me anything I want to hear to save his hide. That's what a snitch is."

The mysterious methamphetamine deal, Johnson acknowledged to Hannah, was the first to be set up by Johnnie Maxie. There had been three conversations between the informant and the constable, he said, about the drug bust.

"The very first time that Loyal Garner, Jr.'s name was mentioned was late on the night of the twenty-fifth?" Hannah asked.

"That was the first time of which I wrote it down on my book," Johnson said. "I don't recall it, that name, earlier than that. We had discussed names, but I don't recall that. . . ."

Hannah pressed Johnson on why Johnnie Maxie would have tried to barter information for freedom on the misdemeanor public intoxication charge for which he was jailed Christmas night. "There must be something you know about Johnnie Maxie that I don't," Hannah told the constable, "and I would like for you to tell me. I don't understand how a person facing a $22.50 fine would confess and put his brother and very good friend facing a first-degree felony. You explain that to the jury."

"I can't explain what Johnnie Maxie thinks. All I can explain is from my previous experience, he spills it out. When he has a little bit of something on his back, he'll turn somebody else down the road to save his hide."

"In other words . . ." the prosecutor said, "isn't it, Constable, that Johnnie Maxie is extremely afraid of law officers?"

"I think he's intimidated by the uniform. I don't know if I would say that he's afraid, but I think he's afraid of what he has done when he gets around a uniform."

Since Johnson had testified that Maxie was an informant whose information had proven reliable, Hannah asked him if he had tried to intercept the delivery of methamphetamines December 26 as it moved through Newton County from Houston en route to the lookout tower across the Louisiana line.

"After he gave me that information that night," Johnson said, "yes sir, it was set up."

"And since Johnnie's information was so good, do you have a conviction on that now?"

"No sir, we do not."

"Did you get an arrest that day?"

"No sir, we did not. . . . We didn't intercept it."

26

"PSYCHOTIC BULLY"

BEFORE THE TRIAL of her husband's death, Corrine Garner had never seen a trial except for the fictionalized accounts on television. But as if the disgusted look on John Hannah's face weren't ominous enough, Corrine also sensed trouble in the judge's attitude and the jurors' reactions to the witnesses. The possibility of her husband's attackers being set free immersed her in her own thoughts as she and her sister resumed their daily shuttle along Texas 87 to Hemphill for another day in court.

Corrine had only casually glanced in the rearview mirror, but the rapidly approaching pickup truck jolted her from her private thoughts. As the white pickup loomed larger in her mirror, she could tell its driver was a white man. It came up fast, followed closely for a while, then accelerated, slamming heavily into her rear bumper. As she screamed at her sister, Corrine held tightly to the wheel and watched helplessly as the man swung the pickup out of the lane and pulled alongside, screaming and pointing at her. The pickup veered closer and closer into her lane, finally forcing her car onto the shoulder and then swerving into the dirt driveway of a closed service station. Neither Corrine nor her sister was injured, but both were rattled and unnerved.

With no license plate number or even a good description of the driver—it all had happened so fast—John Hannah knew there was precious little he could do, particularly since he didn't trust any law-enforcement officer in Sabine County. Nonetheless, Corrine Garner's information deeply concerned him.

There was little doubt in Loyal Sr.'s mind when he heard of the incident later in the morning: "Somebody wanted to kill her," the old man said. Corrine's father-in-law, as he always did in times of crisis, fell back on his religion. "The Lord just wasn't ready to call her," Mr. Garner said. "He wants us to see this through."

The incident, Hannah knew, wasn't unlike the mysterious crash five months earlier that almost killed Johnnie Maxie. The special prosecutor knew this most recent near miss would be like the first, written off as a freak accident. In the aftermath of Willis Garner's arrest in the middle of the packed courtroom, the incident on the highway only confirmed what Hannah already suspected: somebody was trying to send a message. Feelings were running high, and, worse, there was an almost tangible undercurrent of violence in the air. Sabine County was a tinder box, and he worried what it would take to ignite it.

Certainly, a guilty verdict against the town's three officers could be a catalyst. But Hannah didn't delude himself. The chances of getting a guilty verdict against them in this environment were about as likely as Judge Bacon inviting him home for dinner to meet the wife.

Unlike Loyal Garner, Sr., Hannah couldn't find comfort in religion. He had to rely on the law. He had tried more civil rights cases than anyone else in Texas, and never had he seen such a prejudiced and biased courtroom. Indeed, one night, after what he considered a particularly brutal bludgeoning at the hands of Judge Bacon, the special prosecutor drafted a motion to disqualify the judge. "Judge Bacon is so biased and prejudiced against the State of Texas," Hannah's motion read, "that a fair trial cannot be had by the prosecution."

Noting that he already had to go to the court of appeals to get a continuance, the special prosecutor wrote in his draft: "Since the beginning of this trial, the judge has continued to make rulings that are in direct contradiction to established law and procedure of this country and state. His actions have included refusing to strike members of the jury panel who have contributed to the defense fund established for the benefit of the defendants; prohibiting voir dire questions by the prosecution which have been specifically approved by the Court of Criminal Appeals; failing to control the courtroom spectators from expressing its pleasure or disapproval of testimony being given on the stand; [and] failing to control the defense attorneys from making gestures and sidebar remarks.

"Moreover, Judge Bacon has excluded from evidence highly relevant and admissible evidence, such as autopsy photographs explaining the medical evidence . . . in an obvious attempt to aid the defense in this case. . . . In total, Judge Bacon has demonstrated such bias and prejudice against the state and in favor of the defendants that a fair trial and verdict cannot be rendered in this case."

The motion was explosive, particularly considering that it had to be presented and argued before Judge Bacon himself. No way in hell, Hannah knew, the judge would disqualify himself, and the impact would be nuclear fallout on what was left of his case. Biting his tongue was not one of John Henry Hannah, Jr.'s most notable traits. Filing the motion at least would make him feel like he was fighting back. But it also, he realized, wasn't in the best interests of his clients, the state of Texas and, in a very personal way, the Garner family—at least not now. The potential for angering Judge Bacon even more was too great.

Hannah tucked the motion in his briefcase, carrying it with him into the courtroom every day. He meant every word he had written, but he dreaded the magnitude of such an event that would force him to file it.

For most of a week, the prosecution had presented a series of witnesses whose recollections and opinions were designed to send Thomas Ladner, Bill Horton, and Bo Hyden to the state penitentiary for up to ninety-nine years or life. But none of the witnesses, not the tearful Corrine Garner or the authoritative Dr. Gonzalez, had produced any readable expression on the faces of the three accused former lawmen who sat just inside the courtroom railing. At dramatic junctures in the testimony, reporters studied the men's faces for reaction and found none. A stranger to the case would have mistaken the three officers for disinterested witnesses, not defendants whose futures hung on the testimony they were hearing.

During recesses, Bo Hyden retreated to a spot in a courtroom hallway, lighting Marlboros and occasionally nodding to an acquaintance or agreeing with a friend that, "yeah, that heat and humidity are pretty rough." Bill Horton, more accustomed to outdoors than to trials, welcomed the reprieves to stretch his legs and escape, however briefly, the confining courtroom. Thomas Ladner, though, was surrounded by his family, shrouding him in a protective insulation. Wife, mother, sisters, in-laws, nieces and nephews, they all spent every spare moment with him.

On July 12, the day Ladner was to testify, court hangers-on and reporters arrived even earlier than usual, not leaving to chance a good seat at the front. Ladner was the leading character in the best drama in Texas, and there had not been a single quote from him, or his two colleagues, in the newspapers or on TV since Garner's death. The six-foot-one, two hundred seventy-pound former lawman commanded everyone's attention.

John Seale had barely allowed his client to state his name and address when the attorney feigned forgetfulness.

"Now, Thomas, before I forget it—I'm bad about that," Seale said— "who signed your bond in this case?"

"John Seale and Sid Stover."

"Sid Stover is a law partner of mine?"

"Yes sir."

Hannah had made an issue of Dr. Winslow's signing bail bonds for Horton and Hyden, and if the doctor had spoken favorably in Ladner's behalf, Seale wanted to make sure the jury knew it wasn't because the doctor had posted his bond, too. Satisfied he hadn't left the issue hanging, the lawyer moved on meticulously, leading Ladner through his Sabine County roots, high school, his tour in Vietnam, his family, and his fifteen-year career in law enforcement, first as a constable in Yellowpine, and since 1978, as chief of police in Hemphill.

Seale's questioning was adroit, barely hitting the tops of some issues and burrowing in on others that, at face, appeared unimportant. But like most tasks John Seale undertook, the strategy was well thought out and effective. In asking about his client's military experience, for example, Seale asked only one question about his tour in the Army: "Was any of that time spent in Vietnam?" Ladner nodded affirmatively. Then the lawyer moved on without eliciting that, in fact, Ladner had been honored with the Bronze Star for bravery.

When he asked Ladner what he had been doing before that fateful Christmas shift, the former chief replied: "We had been camping for a week or so at a deer camp."

"Who had been camped at the deer camp?" Seale asked.

"Me and my wife and my kids and her daddy and mother."

"So," Seale said, "this wasn't a *stag* deer camp or out with the boys or anything?"

"No sir."

"It would have been your family, is that right?"

"Yes sir."

Skillfully, Seale had dodged the public's doubts not only about the controversial war in Vietnam but also the perception among many that Vietnam veterans were violent and had problems readjusting to civilian life. Being a hero in that war could be interpreted as merely being more violent—certainly an issue Seale wanted to dodge. Instead, the lawyer honed his client's image as a caring family man. Ladner hadn't been stalking Bambi with a bunch of hunters; he had been camping out during the Christmas holidays with his family and in-laws. The strategy was subtle, but Seale knew that cases sometimes were won or lost not on the evidence but on the subtleties that shaped human perceptions.

Ladner's testimony was plodding and delivered in a drawl that left no question about his Deep East Texas roots. He and Bo Hyden had been up north of Hemphill, near Milam, to help a man who had locked his keys inside his pickup. On their return trip, they encountered Garner's pickup on Texas 87, heading toward Hemphill.

"I told Bo, I said, 'Bo, looks like there is a vehicle yonder, possibly something could be wrong with it,' I said, 'you know, driving bad.' He said, 'Well, let's go on up there.' And we did, and we got to what we call Drag Strip Hill. It's about, oh, a quarter of a mile from the city limit, three lanes there—one lane going north on 87, two lanes coming south on 87. We got on up pretty close there and the gentleman pulled over. Bo said, 'Well, go ahead and pass him.' And I said, 'No, I don't think I need to pass him right now.' I said, 'Let's wait and see.' So he pulled back over in the right lane, in the lane he was supposed to be in. The lanes narrowed down and he got back in front of me. We came on in and hit the city limits, and I guess after we got a quarter of a mile inside the city limits, Bo said, 'Well, you need to go ahead and stop him.' "

"What was he doing that caused you to stop him?" Seale asked.

"He was driving over the center stripe."

"All right."

"Long ways."

"What did the vehicle do immediately when you put your lights on?"

"It left and went across the road, nearly off the road, and came back."

According to Ladner, Garner "was intoxicated from his appearance." Asked if he had been drinking, the ex-chief testified, the driver replied, "Yes sir, I have."

Inside Garner's pickup truck, Ladner said, he saw a .30-30 rifle, some empty beer cans, a half-pint bottle of Crown Royal bourbon, a half-pint of Bacardi rum, and a six-pack of Budweiser. He said he told Garner he would be charged with driving while intoxicated, and that he told Johnnie and Alton Maxie they would be charged with public intoxication.

The suspects, who were not handcuffed, were instructed to get in the backseat of the patrol car and were taken to the Sabine County Jail, arriving about 7:55 P.M. The arrest and book-in were uneventful. They were offered phone calls, the former chief recalled, which they declined because they wanted to wait until a judge set their fines. Likewise, Ladner said, Garner refused a Breathalyzer test he offered. Johnnie Maxie, Ladner said, told him he was a snitch and "needed to talk to somebody," but Ladner said he didn't have time to listen. "I said, 'This is Christmas and we need to be out on the road working.'" The prisoner could talk to Chief Deputy Bill Horton when he arrived. The three black men were booked into the jail, and Ladner drove Hyden to pick up Garner's truck beside the road.

When Ladner and Hyden returned to the jail, Horton was walking in right before them. According to Ladner, Horton stopped by dispatcher Mary Russell's office and learned the three new prisoners in the detox cell were beating on the cell door with enough force to activate the "door ajar" warning on the dispatch console. Horton, according to Ladner, went down to the cell to quiet the prisoners.

"And then when he came back," Seale asked, "did they keep on making noises? Did they keep on making the red light come on in the dispatcher's office?"

"Yes sir, they did."

"And did you say something to Mr. Hyden about going back there?"

"I told Bo, I said, 'Bo,' I said, 'Let's go back there and get those boys out and let them make the phone call and see if we can get them to quiet down.'"

"Were you mad at anybody?"

"No sir."

"Did Bo Hyden ever have his gun on in the jail that night?"

"No sir, he did not."

Seale asked Ladner to describe the scenario in the jail cell.

"The door came open," the former chief said. "Bo pulled it open. I stepped inside the detox and I asked, I said, 'Who is doing all of this beating back here?' Mr. Garner, he was sitting on the ledge there. He jumped up and he said, 'I am, motherfucker.'

"And I started to move on forward just a little bit. He run at me. Bo

grabbed him around the waist. I turned around. When I turned around
. . . his right fist hit me here in the left ear. . . . After that, he hit me
with his other hand on the side of my neck."

"And what did you do then?"

"I had my blackjack in my pocket," Ladner recalled. "I jerked it out
and I came down with my left hand to hit him. He partially blocked my
hand and I did hit him, and my blackjack flew out of my hand and went
out into the hall."

The blow with the blackjack, Ladner testified, was delivered with his
left hand, though he normally was right-handed. Seale made sure the
distinction was made; the blow to Garner not only had been glancing but
had been delivered with Ladner's weaker hand.

"And where on his body did you hit him, in your opinion?"

"Somewhere on the head."

"How many times did you hit him?"

"One time."

"And why did you hit him, Thomas?"

"Because when he hit me in the ear, it hurt," Ladner said. "Then he
hit me beside the neck. I knew I was in trouble. . . ."

"Did you hit him to defend yourself?"

"Yes sir."

Ladner continued his recollection of Christmas at the Sabine County
Jail. "I grabbed Mr. Garner around the neck and held him. And he said,
'That's enough.' I said, 'Son, do you want to make that phone call?' and
he said, 'Okay.' That was all."

On the prosecution side of the table, Hannah was having trouble con-
taining his cynicism. Ladner's foul mouth was legendary among the
witnesses he'd interviewed, and throughout his testimony, the former
chief consistently referred to the three blacks as "gentlemen," careful to
call them "Mr." Garner and "Mr." Maxie. The prosecutor made a note
on his legal pad and underlined it.

Garner turned belligerent again when he and Hyden got him to the
book-in room to make the phone call, Ladner testified. "I tell Mr. Garner
to go ahead and make his phone call. And he said, 'No, I'm not going to
make that phone call.' I said, 'Mr. Garner,' I said, 'we're going to have to
put you back up in your cell. This is Christmas night and we need to be
out on the roads working.' And he said, 'No, you three white mother-
fuckers ain't going to put me nowhere. . . .'

"Well, he was standing behind the desk where the telephone was," Ladner continued. "And there was a flashlight setting on the desk. He made a run for that flashlight. . . .

"And Mr. Horton grabbed it, took it away from him. Mr. Hyden grabbed him from behind. And there was a swivel chair there between me and Mr. Garner. I tried to grab him and I couldn't get a hold of him. I got tangled up in the swivel chair and he stumbled and fell. . . . Well, I say he hit the wall. I seen him when he got up from over there. I can't swear that he hit the wall."

"After he hit the wall," Seale asked, "was he bleeding?"

"Yes sir."

The blood appeared to be coming "from back here on the edge of the head here, somewhere," Ladner testified, pointing to the back of his own head.

"When I saw the blood, I asked Mr. Garner, I said, 'Son, do you need to go to the doctor?' and he said, 'You three white motherfuckers ain't going to carry me nowhere.'" Part of the indictment alleged that the three officers deprived Garner of medical treatment. This was an important point for Seale.

"And . . . when he got up there," the lawyer asked, "did he get up and get onto his own two feet and did he walk back to the cell?"

"Yes sir, he did."

"Was he walking on his own?"

"Yes sir."

In fact, Ladner testified, he followed Garner as Horton and Hyden escorted him back to the cell. En route, the former chief said, he stopped to pick up the blackjack that had flown from his hand earlier. The point was important, Seale knew, and he hoped the jury picked up on it: Ladner wouldn't have had his blackjack in the book-in room.

Ladner acknowledged later telling trusty Trent Taylor to get Garner to change into jail-issue clothes, but he said he intended for all three prisoners to put on the clothes. He decided against the change of clothes, he said, when Alton Maxie told him, "If you wake him [Garner] up, you're going to have to fight him again."

Anticipating Hannah's cross-examination, and trying to take the edge off earlier testimony from jail inmates, particularly Angus Bozeman, Seale asked Ladner if jail inmates had anything to gain by telling lies about him.

"Possibly so."

"Tell us whether or not one of these men said a statement to you in a threatening way about this subject."

"Yes—Mr. Bozeman."

"What did Mr. Bozeman say to you?"

"He said, 'Well, I'd like to see you in the penitentiary, also.'"

Before he surrendered his client to cross-examination by the state, Seale asked Judge Bacon for a motion *in limine* to prevent Hannah from asking Ladner about any previous acts of misconduct without first approaching the judge and getting a hearing in the judge's chambers. The damage to his client, Seale argued, would be irreparable if, for example, Hannah blurted out a question such as "Have you ever hit anybody before?"

The prosecutor objected strenuously. "Mr. Seale raised the issue of self-defense yesterday," Hannah argued. "As a matter of fact, his client said he was acting in self-defense. That opens the door for any and all extraneous offenses whereby Mr. Ladner might have been the aggressor. It does not require a conviction. . . . That is not the law in the state of Texas," Hannah said, "and it's the state's intention to begin immediately to show extraneous offenses. We want to question him about other prior beatings he's been involved in."

Judge Bacon granted Seale's motion. He added, however: "Don't misunderstand the court. The court is not ruling that the matters are not admissible at this point. They will be taken on an individual basis without the presence of the jury."

John Hannah had long had a theory that bad cops brutalized prisoners with impunity not only because their victims were captive, which made them vulnerable to even more abuse if they complained, but also because prisoners had no credibility and wouldn't be believed even if they did have the courage to complain. In Texas terminology, it would be an old-fashioned "pissing match," the word of a criminal against a man wearing a badge, hardly a level playing field. And, Hannah knew, Ladner had brutalized suspects for years. The prosecutor figured he'd just try out his theory on the imposing-looking defendant.

"There was a soliloquy [*sic*] between you and Mr. Seale regarding that the very worst possible place for you to commit a crime would be in jail," Hannah started off. "And it was because, as you and Mr. Seale developed that, why, there would be people in there who would want to testify against you, is that correct?"

"I believe I said 'possibly,' sir," Ladner replied, clearly sensing a setup.

"Possibly? Well, let me ask you a few questions about that, because the way I had been thinking about that last night," Hannah said, drawing it out, "it seems to me, Mr. Ladner, that that would be the very best possible place for you to beat somebody up, because of these reasons. See if you agree and let me ask you some questions. . . .

"For one thing, you have heard the previous testimony in this trial where people who witnessed or heard what you were doing, sir, were reluctant to give statements over there and refused to give statements to law officers and Texas Rangers, didn't they?"

"I have heard that testimony, yes. . . ."

"And you also heard testimony that they refused to talk until they saw either the grand jury or the Federal Bureau of Investigation, haven't you?"

"Yes sir."

"Okay, can we conclude from that, Mr. Ladner, that indeed it would be a *good* place to beat somebody up because people are afraid to testify against you? Couldn't we conclude that from the testimony?"

"Possibly, yes," Ladner conceded.

"Couldn't we also conclude . . . if it ever got to trial," Hannah continued, "and they came over to testify against you, that every one of you could say to that jury, 'He's just a little ol' burglar,' or 'He's just a little ol' thief, been in jail several times, and look at me, I wear a badge. . . .'

"Every person in the jail testifying against you, sir, would be somebody that you could call a criminal, and you would hope the jury would not believe them because of that, would you agree with that?"

"Yes."

Hannah was building toward a crescendo, and Floyd Addington sensed the prosecutor was about to drop Ladner into the grease. Addington objected but was overruled.

"So instead of the worst place to commit a crime," Hannah continued, his voice rising, "it would be the best place in the world for a psychotic bully to beat somebody up, wouldn't it, Mr. Ladner?"

Paul Buchanan objected that Hannah was being argumentative. The judge agreed, forcing the prosecutor in a new direction.

Hannah began poking holes in Ladner's arrest of Garner and his testimony. "And the evidence you gathered up, Mr. Ladner, was a six-pack full and two whiskey bottles, is that correct?"

"Yes sir."

"And you didn't bring the empties in?"

"No, I didn't."

"That was not a very proper gathering of the evidence, was it?"

"Probably not, sir."

Hannah turned to his notes and found an underlined passage. "As I recall your testimony and as I look over the grand jury testimony," the prosecutor said, "you always either said 'sir,' or you said '*Mr. Garner*,' or one time, when you were feeling really warm and fatherly toward him right after he had assaulted you at the jail, you referred to him as '*son*?' "

"Yes sir, I—yes sir."

"And you think that you want the jury to believe that you never addressed Mr. Garner except 'sir,' 'son,' and '*Mr. Garner*,' is that correct?"

"As far as I know, sir."

"And especially when you . . . were feeling warm and cuddly toward him and call him 'son,' was right after he jumped up, hit you on the face with one fist, hit you on the neck with the other fist, and that's when you lapsed, then, to this warm, snuggly feeling where you said, '*Son*, do you want to make a phone call?' " Using a different inflection, Ladner tried to demonstrate how the same words wouldn't sound as affectionate as Hannah had made them.

The gloves were off, and Hannah was trying to demean the witness. "Were you puffing any after all of that struggle?" Hannah asked.

"No sir."

"Then you are in better shape than the defense counsel led on?"

"I'm pretty fat," Ladner said. "I'm not slim and trim like you, but I can do a little work."

"Are you a pretty agile man?"

"Well, I can't say that I am."

It was time for a little theater. The prosecutor, no small man himself, asked the hulking lawman to step down from the witness stand. They would re-enact the scuffle in the jail cell; Hannah would play Loyal Garner, Jr. Emotions were running high, and with both men standing eye to eye, Glenda Shelton worried something awful was about to happen.

Hannah maneuvered Ladner around until the chief agreed the distances were approximately what they had been in the detox cell.

"And you had on numerous occasions said that he was—you were one foot from him?" Hannah asked.

"Yes sir, just about this distance, just about this far beside him. . . ."

"And he jumped up and lunged at you?"

"No sir, I didn't say that."

"No, you didn't," Hannah said. "What you said is 'He ran at me.' "

From the audience, the two men appeared to be almost touching.

"I want you to explain to the jury how a man as close to you as I am now, how a person can run at him?"

"He got—he jumped up and he said—"

"He jumped up and said what?"

Ladner was flustered. "What did I just tell you?" the former chief asked.

"Tell the jury again. They want to hear it and your lawyer wants to hear it."

" 'I am, white motherfucker,' " Ladner said, quoting Garner.

"And he run at you and you agilely stepped out of the way?"

Ladner changed his stance and said, "I stepped forward like this. Mr. Hyden grabbed him from behind."

The prosecutor looked at the witness skeptically and asked him to return to the witness stand.

As he had in his grand jury appearance, Ladner testified Garner had struck him only twice, once in the ear and once in the neck, both times in the detox cell. But Hannah produced the earlier statement Ladner had written for Ranger Roscoe Davis. According to Ladner's statement, Garner also struck him in the book-in room. Hannah read aloud from the statement: " 'He hit me, Thomas Ladner, again with his fist.' . . . True or untrue?" the prosecutor asked.

"That's true there, sir."

"Well, but the statement . . . pardon?"

"I meant to say that he hit *at* me again."

Later, Hannah asked about the intensity of the "glancing" blow Ladner had delivered with the blackjack to Garner's head.

"I don't know how hard it was, sir."

"And he didn't hit your arm enough to throw it off balance, to keep you from hitting him flat?" Hannah asked. "Because if you had, that probably would have cut him, wouldn't it?"

"I've never seen one cutting anybody, sir."

Hannah couldn't believe his good fortune. Ladner was setting himself up as an expert on blackjacks, someone with experience.

"You've never seen one cut anybody, have you, Mr. Ladner?"

"No, I haven't."

"As a matter of fact, you can usually hit people with them and it doesn't cut anyone and you can get away with it, isn't that true, Mr. Ladner?"

"That's not necessarily true."

"Tell me how many times you've seen people hit with those that it didn't cut them, Mr. Ladner."

"Several times."

"Tell us who they were."

"I can't tell you exactly who they were. . . . I just can't remember right now."

Poking and probing, the prosecutor carried Ladner through a series of points Seale had established with Ladner's testimony. Hannah got Ladner to admit that Garner hadn't staggered "to any appreciable degree" during the arrest and that he didn't appear "an almost comatose, dope-crazed .33 [intoxicated] black man."

"As a matter of fact," Hannah asked, "Mr. Loyal Garner, Jr., was acting so unintoxicated and so un-dope-crazed and so unhallucinogenic that he was left in the processing room without any officers in there with him, wasn't he?"

"He was left in the processing room, yes sir, him and Mr. Maxie."

Going back to Ladner's account that he struck Garner only one glancing blow with the blackjack, Hannah asked, "Then can you offer the jury any explanation of how Mr. Garner got these blows to his head that killed him?"

"No sir, I can't."

"It's a mystery, isn't it?" Hannah asked facetiously.

"Yes sir, it is, because I did not hit Mr. Garner but one time and that's all that I hit Mr. Garner."

Of the battered, unraveled blackjack that Ladner had surrendered to Ranger Davis, the prosecutor asked, "And it's been used to such an extent that it is raveled?"

"Is split around the edges, yes sir. . . . Roscoe Davis, somebody, had cut it or something."

Hannah was convinced the only reason Ladner and Hyden took Garner to the book-in room was to beat him outside the presence of witnesses. Their claims that they were merely taking him to make a phone call were too ludicrous to believe.

"So we have a person that has been offered a phone call and refused?"

"That's right," Ladner replied.

"And he asks for a phone call, attacks the person who is going to let him make a phone call?"

"Yes sir."

"And *then* he says that he wants a phone call?"

"Yes sir."

"And then he gets up to where the phone is and refuses?"

"That's correct."

"Now, that doesn't fit into our human experience either, does it?"

"Well, it's according to what he was thinking," Ladner responded. "He might not have wanted me in there with him when he made the phone call."

Satisfied he had picked the bones of Ladner's testimony, Hannah turned to Judge Bacon and said, "Your Honor, at this time I would like to ask Mr. Ladner the questions that the court has previously ruled that I could not ask him."

Hannah's comment propelled John Seale from his chair, objecting as he rose. Judge Bacon ordered the jury out of the courtroom and the lawyers into his chambers, so that the audience—and reporters—wouldn't hear the conversation.

"Mr. Hannah well knows . . . that when a motion *in limine* has been granted that there is to be no mention in the presence of the jury," Seale argued. He referred to the judge's earlier ruling that before Hannah could ask any questions about Ladner's alleged previous wrongdoings, he would have to obtain the court's permission—out of earshot of the jury. The prosecutor's comment in front of the jurors told them there was something, at least, about Ladner that the judge hadn't allowed Hannah to ask.

"We're talking about the statements made in the presence of the jury," the judge said.

"I understand that I'm so instructed," Hannah replied. "Thank you."

"It shouldn't occur again," Judge Bacon said sternly. "It *better not* occur again."

Hannah renewed his request to probe previous instances in which the chief had used his blackjack. "What I would like to do at this time— *with the court's blessing*," he was careful to add, "so that the court can judge for himself—is to put witnesses on the stand to show, in fact, that this man has beaten other people and not in self-defense."

Paul Buchanan, the defense team's board-certified defense specialist, led the argument against admitting prior allegations of beatings at the hands of Ladner. "In this particular case," Buchanan argued, "there is no way in the world that you're not going to have a peace officer that's been working on the job for as many years as this man has, that you're not going to be able to find some reprobate that's going to say, 'Yeah, I was beaten up and I was treated unfairly.' "

"What particularly bothers me," Hannah interjected, "is the argument that there should be a special exception for law officers. The argument that's gone through all this case is they're [jail witnesses are] just people that's not worth worrying about anyway, is especially prevalent to me, and I ask that the court reject that argument out of hand."

Judge Bacon finally agreed to review the potential witnesses' testimony to see if it was admissible in the trial, but only in the privacy of his chambers. "We're not going to try this to the press," he said. "We'll bring those witnesses in here. We've got a lot of press here. I'm instructing the counsel that this is not a gag order, but I'm instructing counsel in fairness to everyone concerned, that you not go out and tell the news media what you're intending to prove."

The judge had been careful in his warning to direct it to "counsel," but Hannah knew the judge's comments clearly were directed at him. It didn't matter. Half a loaf was better than none. He'd be glad, even in the privacy of the judge's chambers, to show him snapshots of testimony from people Ladner had beaten through the years.

No lawyer defending a police officer on brutality charges would want Leonard Green on the stand. The visual image of the forty-eight-year-old wheelchair-bound amputee would be, in legal jargon, inflammatory. And Lloyd Armstrong, claiming his missing teeth were knocked out with Ladner's blackjack, would be little better.

After hearing both men's recollections in the privacy of his chambers, Judge Bacon made his ruling: Armstrong would testify; the jury, however, would not be allowed to hear Green's testimony.

The judge apparently ruled against Green's testimony because the incident was nine years old—precisely the reason Hannah wanted to introduce it. It showed, the prosecutor contended, a pattern and trend, that Ladner had been abusing suspects for at least nine years. Green, with his handicap and virtually no arrest record, clearly was the stronger witness. Armstrong's multiple arrests for intoxication, the prosecutor suspected, would be easily discredited, just as the defense had done with his witnesses from the county jail.

When his cross-examination of Thomas Ladner resumed in the courtroom before the jury, Hannah used his last few questions to inquire about the circumstances of Lloyd Armstrong's arrest. "Did you hit him?"

"No sir. . . ."

"Had no injuries?"

"He had some injuries."

"Did he hit himself?"

"No, he fell. . . ."

"And what happened when he fell?"

"He hit a car door," the former chief said. "It was open and he hit the running board of the car with his chin."

Paul Buchanan's questioning of his client, Bo Hyden, took less than five minutes. The lawyer read both charges from the indictment, that Hyden had subjected Garner to bodily injury by hitting him with a slapjack and causing him to fall against a wall, and that he had denied Garner reasonable medical attention. After each charge, Buchanan asked, "Did you do that, Bo?"

"No sir," Hyden answered both times.

Buchanan apparently was content to allow Ladner's recollection of the confrontations in the Sabine County Jail stand. He passed the witness to Hannah.

The young former deputy appeared ill at ease but amiable under the prosecutor's scrutiny. At times Hyden was detached and impassive, as if he had been a third-party observer and not a participant in the events that led to Garner's death.

Under cross-examination, Hyden's recollections of the arrests, the book-in, the confrontation in the detox cell and the trip to the book-in room generally tracked those in Ladner's testimony. Surprisingly, though, there were two critical junctures at which Hyden's testimony failed to support Ladner's.

"Did you ever see Loyal Garner, Jr., hit Mr. Ladner?" Hannah asked.

"No sir."

"Did you ever see Mr. Ladner hit Loyal Garner, Jr.?"

"No sir."

The catalyst for the battle in the detox, according to Ladner, had been

Garner hitting him, first in the ear, then in the neck. Hyden said he didn't see the prisoner throw the punches. Nor, the former deputy said, did he see Ladner deliver the glancing blow with the blackjack.

"You saw nothing except a scuffling, is that right?" Hannah asked.

"Right."

"I had just gotten slammed into a steel door," Hyden explained.

Hannah pursued his attempt to prove that the three officers conspired the morning after Garner's injury to cover up a beating. Establishing that all three officers were at the sheriff's office the morning of December 26, Hannah asked Hyden: "Did you discuss anything about what happened the night before?"

"We just couldn't believe that he was in the hospital or anything was bad wrong with him, no sir."

The prosecutor's last questions of Bo Hyden were well crafted, and elicited a curious response from the suspended lawman. "Did you see anything that Loyal Garner did that deserved a beating that would put three subdural hematomas in his head?" Hannah asked.

"I didn't see him do anything but run from Mr. Ladner, is all I saw."

"And, of course, Officer, you know that that's not justification for beating anyone, don't you?"

"That in itself, no sir."

John Seale was too skilled to leave hanging in the air the implication that Ladner hadn't been justified in his use of force. Having gotten Hyden to recount being thrown against the cell door and to acknowledge that while he didn't see Garner hit Ladner, Garner's arms nonetheless were "in a position to swing," Seale asked: "In your opinion, did Mr. Ladner have any choice to do other than what he did?"

"No sir."

Sitting in the witness stand in the cavernous and formal courtroom, Billy Ray Horton was cowboy boots at a black-tie dinner. He had been indicted on civil rights charges just five days before his fifty-eighth birthday, and he wore his years hard. His deep-creased face was more accustomed to khakis than to the western-cut coat and tie he wore, and he looked more like someone's grandfather than an accused cop facing ninety-nine years to life in prison.

Horton was from the country, so far removed from Hemphill that the trip entailed a succession of narrower roads until finally the pavement petered out into three miles of low-water dirt road. Since his wife, Mary, had died a year earlier, Horton had lived on the ranch with one of his two children, a twenty-six-year-old daughter.

The former chief deputy's answers and demeanor were deceptively tough, endorsing Bill Martin's assessment that Horton was "raised tough, brought up tough." The three black prisoners were loud and belligerent, he testified, when he walked into the jail Christmas night. "So I walked back there and asked them what their problem was," he testified. "They said they wanted to 'make a phone call, motherfucker.' "

Horton said he later was in the dispatcher's room, talking with Mary Russell, when he heard a loud conversation across the hall in the book-in room. "I thought, 'There's going to be problems,' " Horton recounted under questioning by his lawyer, Floyd Addington. "I got up and went out across the hall. I pulled the door behind me shut, and I don't believe the door was all the way shut in the book-in room . . . and I pulled it to when I went in so that Mary wouldn't hear all of that language.

"When I walked in there, Bo had said . . . 'Mr. Garner, if you're not going to make a phone call, you've got to go back to your cell.' And I believe he caught him by his left arm . . . and he reached and grabbed Bo's flashlight off the table.

"Well, I walked [over] there and I grabbed the flashlight. I set it over on the table, the long table. He slung Hyden aloose, and, like I say, there was that chair, he run into it back and forth, it was all over the floor. And they grabbed at him again and he either got tangled up in that chair or he got tripped or something, and fell into the wall."

Horton said he later helped Garner to his feet. "He shook us and said, 'Turn me loose, I'll go, I'll walk,' and I turned him loose."

"And did he walk back to the detox?"

"Yes sir."

Horton said he "saw a little blood on the left side of his hair, but there was nothing to cause alarm."

Later that night, while waiting with Johnnie Maxie for Constable Bubba Johnson to return Maxie's call, Horton testified, Maxie told him "that they're supposed to pick up a load of drugs and haul them back, load some in Weirgate, some in Hemphill, and the rest in Many."

Even before trial, Hannah had worried about the jury's perception of Bill Horton. The lawman's family had been a fixture in Sabine County since the county's formation. Horton, whatever his role, hadn't been seen doing anything to Loyal Garner, Jr., by any of the jail witnesses. Whatever Horton had done in the book-in room had been known only to Garner, who obviously couldn't testify against him, and to Horton's two colleagues. The prosecution's questioning of Horton would be critical.

Hannah moved quickly on cross-examination to Johnnie Maxie's purported confession to Horton. Noting that Horton went home after the phone conversation between Maxie and Constable Johnson, Hannah asked him: "You've got a man giving you a statement, and my question to you is, why didn't you get him to write it out that night?"

"He wouldn't give me a statement . . ." Horton replied.

"Then explain to the jury how a man he saw instantaneously the next morning, by the name of Clyde 'Preacher' Kirk, who he never had seen before, [how Maxie] immediately gave him a statement? Can you explain that?"

"No, I can't."

On Christmas night after the phone call to the Newton County constable, Horton testified, he had escorted Johnnie Maxie back to the detox cell.

The prosecutor was groping for a way to show the jury that Horton knew the extent of Garner's injuries but offered no medical help, as charged in one count in the indictment.

"Wouldn't it have been the appropriate thing, sir, after having seen blood on this man's head before that," Hannah wanted to know, "when you go in his cell again to at least—just being a decent human being, much less a jailer—to look and see if he's injured?"

"But I didn't."

"But you didn't," Hannah repeated incredulously.

"No sir."

"And he died?"

Buchanan objected and the objection was sustained before Horton had to answer the question.

The prosecutor moved to a line of questioning that, if it didn't elicit a confirmation from Horton, might nonetheless demonstrate a hidden side to the docile-appearing defendant.

"Are you a man who curses, Mr. Horton?" Hannah asked.

"Sometimes, yes sir."

Hannah recalled the testimony from jail inmates that they heard someone, presumably Horton, outside the detox cell warn, "If you don't be quiet back there, we're going to come in and kick some ass." "Is that something," Hannah asked, "that you would ever say?"

"I would say it," Horton replied, "but I didn't say it that night."

"Have you ever said it before?"

"I might have—I don't remember."

"Well, perhaps you don't remember saying it that night?"

"I'm sure I'm not above saying it."

The prosecutor returned to the issue of failing to provide medical attention. Dr. Gonzalez had testified that at least one of the blows Garner suffered would have incapacitated him immediately. Recalling Hyden's testimony that as he and Horton escorted Garner back to the cell after the trip to the book-in room, Hyden saw blood on Garner's shirt, Hannah asked, "Did you see that?"

"No sir, I sure didn't."

"How is your eyesight?"

"Not as good as it ought to be," Horton said. "I think he probably seen something that I didn't see. I'm not saying he's wrong. . . ."

"And y'all let Mr. Garner just walk on through the door then?"

"James Hyden walked up and pulled the door open and Mr. Garner went around and went in," Horton testified. "He could have fell face down on his head or whatever when he went in. I didn't see nothing."

It was late in the day, after Hannah called Lloyd Armstrong as a rebuttal witness, that both sides rested in *State of Texas v. Ladner, Horton, and Hyden.*

27

GOD, FLAG, AND SABINE COUNTY

As he had so many times before in civil rights trials, and never without success, John Henry Hannah, Jr., rose from the prosecutor's table and approached the jury with righteous indignation. "Whatever verdict you arrive at," he said, staring jurors in the eyes, "will be the one that this county has to live with in its history."

His wasn't so much a closing argument as it was a challenge. The jurors' decision, he told them straightforwardly, wasn't merely about three law officers accused of abusing their authority and killing a man. It was way more important than that. Their decision was a referendum about *them*, about Hemphill and Sabine County. "The verdict that you arrive at determines what type of people are in this county," he said, "and what type of people have served on the jury."

Thomas Ladner, Bill Horton, and Bo Hyden all were charged with the same counts, but Hannah acknowledged the differences in their involvement. "I think the evidence in this case shows that they're all guilty of both counts," he said. "But the degree of culpability, I think, varies considerably.

"Thomas Ladner, who I believe the evidence has shown is a psychological and physical brute, down to Mr. Horton and Mr. Hyden, who had moral failure on the night of December twenty-fifth, when they knew what they should have been doing, but yet didn't do it. . . .

"In fact, I don't believe they did intend to kill anybody. I believe that this blackjack had been used many times without killing anybody, and I believe it was intended to be used on that night, not to kill anybody, but to teach some loudmouths a lesson. But it did kill. . . . They intended to violate someone's civil rights, and they did. And after they did, they violated the civil rights again by not taking him to a doctor."

The prosecutor's voice softened noticeably when his thoughts turned to the victim. "Loyal Garner, Jr., never spent a night in jail in the thirty-five years of his life except when he ended up over there," he said, pointing toward the jail. "That was the kind of person he was. From a poor, black family, for a man to exist thirty-five years without spending one night in jail says something about the caliber of that man, and that's the type of man he was. . . .

"But assuming, just assuming, if you want to, that Loyal Garner, Jr., was a dope-smuggling, heavy-drinking fellow—and that's a big assumption, because there is nothing in his prior life that could lead you to conclude that at all—does that give him any less rights to be not subjected to a beating in that jail?

"It has nothing to do with this case. It was offered to you by the defendants so that you will begin to think, 'Gosh, he was a dope dealer, maybe he needed to be killed anyway.' That's what they hope you will think."

How, Hannah wanted to know, could Garner, "a man with a record better than mine and I daresay better than maybe some of you," suddenly become "a dope-crazed drug dealer?"

Periodically, the prosecutor interspersed his own characterizations of the three lawmen. Horton's "aiding and his assistance in this involved . . . a cover-up," he said. "I think Mr. Horton probably knows Thomas Ladner is a brute," Hannah said. "I think Mr. Horton is probably a little afraid of Thomas Ladner himself."

Bo Hyden, Hannah surmised, "looks up to Thomas Ladner—bigger, stronger, meaner. . . . Mr. Hyden had a moral failure that night in the presence of Thomas Ladner. . . . I don't think he's an evil man, but he didn't do what he should have done that night."

Hannah wasn't nearly so charitable to the huge former lawman who sat stone-faced across the room. Hannah attacked not only Ladner but Sabine County's entire system of justice. In the end, he implied, they actually were one and the same. It was dangerous ground for an out-of-town lawyer dependent on a small-town jury. "Now, Thomas Ladner—you can see the way this county is run," the prosecutor said. "It's continuing right up to this moment. It's continuing during this trial.

"Let me give you a little slice of life and explain it to you of Sabine County, Texas, in the law-enforcement system as controlled up to that time by Mr. Thomas Ladner.

"I put a witness on the stand yesterday by the name of Lloyd Armstrong. Lloyd is the man with no teeth." Hannah picked up a blackjack. "This is what removed the teeth.

"Thomas Ladner also told us on the stand—and you could see when it came out that it was one of those statements that you want to draw it back in. I said, 'Thomas,' something about 'won't this cut people?' You remember what Thomas said, sitting over here? 'Never cut anybody before.'"

Holding the blackjack up, Hannah said, "This thing has been used, used, and *used* in that county jail. . . . Indeed, it probably had never cut before, and indeed, I'm sure, it never killed before. But it killed on that night."

Hannah returned to Lloyd Armstrong, who, he said, suffered a crushed mouth at the hands of the city's chief of police. Hannah's anger was apparent in his voice, and he clearly was pushing the envelope not only with the jury but with all of Sabine County. "Of course, none of these things are going to happen to you people. . . . They're not, because you're not poor, you don't get into trouble, and you don't have to worry about that. Dr. Winslow is not going to be arrested and brutalized. A schoolteacher is not going to be arrested and brutalized. But you don't have any power and you possess no friends if you drink a little and throw flower pots or you're accidentally black and have a Louisiana license plate. Then you're in serious trouble in this jail over here, and you have a serious problem in this county about that.

"You can say 'It will never happen to me,' and I guarantee it won't, because you're who you are—but it's *you* people that are going to have to make a decision whether it continues."

Referring to Ladner as "Big Tom," Hannah painted a frightening picture of the town's former police chief and of life in Sabine County. "'Big Tom' had beat his teeth out the night before," Hannah said of Armstrong, "and he's getting him to plead guilty the next morning with his mouth sewed shut. Now, that's the way things happen in this county. . . ."

Texas law allows the state to split its closing arguments, taking half before the defense summation and half later. It was what Hannah had chosen to do, but before he sat down, the prosecutor gave jurors his version of the events that led to Loyal Garner, Jr.'s death.

The catalyst that triggered the lethal chain of events, Hannah speculated, was the dispatcher, Mary Russell. "They had probably made this lady mad and she went back, and then Horton went down . . . and he said, 'If you don't be quiet, I'm going to come in there and kick your ass. . . .' And I think as he was leaving, somebody with a smart mouth in detox—I suspect maybe Alton, might have been Johnnie, I doubt Loyal Garner, Jr.—after they left, [said] 'You'll have to bring four or five with you.' And they could hear it down here. Thomas could hear it and Bo could hear it. And Thomas is the type of person that there ain't gonna be no smart niggers in his jail."

As he dropped into his chair, Hannah knew his initial summation had been emotional and bare-knuckled. He had been brutally honest, at least as far as he was concerned. Ladner, Horton, and Hyden, as contemptuous as their beating of Garner had been, were symptoms of a far greater problem. The prosecutor was even more convinced after watching justice as it was meted out in Hemphill's seat of justice. His remarks, particularly his "slice of life" analogy about life in Sabine County, he suspected, had been dangerous.

The defense lawyers had snapped upright, in fact, when they heard Hannah mention his "slice of life in Sabine" commentary, and they jotted notes to themselves. For the next two hours, the jurors would hear Seale, Buchanan, and Addington defend not only their accused clients, but the jurors themselves and life in general in Sabine County. The enemies clearly were the outsiders who meddled in the affairs of good people. In the end, the defense for Ladner's, Horton's, and Hyden's actions, as espoused by their lawyers, was more than self-defense; it also was small-town virtue, patriotism, God, and law and order. Indeed, self-defense became but a footnote in the rhetoric.

Even before John Seale opened his mouth, his fair-complexioned face was flushed. Always eloquent and earnest, the lawyer galvanized the defense with his first sentence. "Before going any further," he said, "let me open by saying to you that, in spite of what some people and some civil rights groups and some members of the media have wanted so bad, and in spite of what John Hannah wants so bad, race has never been an issue in this trial. Think back. Who in this courtroom, in this trial, have you heard use the word 'nigger'? Only one. Race has never been an issue in this trial."

Deftly, he took jurors back over the witnesses they had heard, methodically singling out pieces of testimony and evidence here and there that supported the officers' actions. He paused after capsuling the testimony of the jail inmates. "Now you tell me that that's the kind of people the state wants you to use in convicting three people in this county who, on the other hand, have been good citizens of the county."

For contrast, the courtly lawyer moved swiftly to the outsiders, ostensibly applauding Hannah for "doing his job" but skillfully reminding jurors that the special prosecutor's fees were paid by the Southern Poverty Law Center.

"On the other hand," Seale said, "witnesses like doctors are not supposed to be advocates. And Dr. Gonzalez, who said, 'Aw, folks, I'm not just a pathologist, I don't just check a body to see what it is, I got into it as a *forensics* pathologist,' trying to make a case. And how did he get into the case? He got into the case by the JP up in Tyler, Judge Beaird, the same one who called him . . . and said he wanted to have an inquest hearing and let Morris Dees, the lawyer with the same outfit that's paying Mr. Hannah, go in there and impersonate a district attorney and get into Roscoe Davis's file. . . .

"Slice of life," Seale said, spitting out the phrase.

"So what has this case become?" he asked. "It's become an *indictment* not against these three men but against Sabine County and everything that has to do with Sabine County. Everything is a conspiracy. . . .

"At the same time," Seale said, pointing at the three former officers, "why do these men—one of them as old as I am, fifty-six or fifty-seven years old, over there, another one forty-one, and another one in his thirties—why have those three leopards changed their spots and become dishonest, dirty, crooked, conniving men? Where is there anything that's been presented to you in this case that would suggest or support any such thing? . . . No, these men didn't get together and make up anything."

Feisty by nature and personally angered by Hannah's initial closing, Paul Buchanan resurrected a seemingly routine objection Hannah had made a day earlier in which the prosecutor characterized Horton's Army service as "irrelevant" and not material to his credibility. "Well, I'll tell you what [relevance] it has, Mr. Hannah, in the 'slice of life' in Sabine County. We admire our veterans," Buchanan said, turning toward Thomas Ladner. "And if I have not, Mr. Ladner, I'll thank you for your service that you gave us in Vietnam, because for every one of us that are here, someone died over there so that we might be free. And I think that has to do with credibility."

Hannah had to have wondered if it would have made a difference to the jury if they knew that Buchanan was neither a veteran nor a resident of Sabine County.

The bearded and pudgy Buchanan, wearing a western-cut suit and cowboy boots, had moved to the prosecution side of the table and was attacking Johnnie Maxie's credibility when Hannah interrupted him in mid-sentence. "Excuse me, Counsel," the prosecutor said, "don't wave your hand in my face."

Buchanan ignored him and picked up where he left off. "If they decide to start—"

"Counsel," Hannah broke in again, making no attempt to cloak his anger. "Your Honor," Hannah said tersely, "would you instruct him not to wave his hand in my face?"

"Don't wave your hand in his face, Counselor," Judge Bacon said. "This is not to say you may not gesture. Proceed."

Buchanan moved on, aiming his remarks at the special prosecutor.

"We've got a special prosecutor from the Southern Poverty Law Center here," Buchanan said loudly. "Personally, I think this is the kind of case where P. T. Barnum would have been excellent as special prosecutor because P. T. says, 'There's a fool born every minute,' and if he believed that, then this is the kind of case he could have chomped right into. . . . I think Walt Disney might have worked real well . . . [He] is great at taking reality and turning it into fantasy. . . .

"This case reminds me of a little kid's game called Gossip," Buchanan said derisively. "You start off on one end saying, 'So-and-So got hit,' and by the time you get to the last little kid, 'He bludgeoned him to death.' "

The lawyer was flamboyant in his recollection of Alton and Johnnie Maxie's testimony, opining to the jury that he had "heard enough perjury here to kill a horse."

Approaching the end of the time allotted him by the court, Buchanan shifted his tone from berating skepticism to sincerity.

"I do believe that one day God's justice will be established on the face of the earth," he said quietly. "But until it is, we've got these silly systems that we have to live with that are wrought with human errors, and the only thing we can do as humans is bind together occasionally and scream, 'Enough is enough!'

"I ask you to take the first step in a way to rebuild a reputation and return a verdict of not guilty, and send a message, send a true and *honest* message, about the real life in Sabine County."

The defense of Sabine County, already having evoked speeches of God and country, was not yet complete. Horton's attorney, Floyd Addington, was particularly upset with Hannah's characterization of Ladner and Horton, so much so that it reminded him of a line from a country music song. "The only thing that makes me angry about it is when you use this type of testimony for prosecution and then ask twelve persons of this county . . . to convict my client, and to call Thomas Ladner a 'psychotic bully,' and convict Bo Hyden, and further call Billy Ray Horton a liar from his testimony," Addington said.

"I believe it's Merle Haggard—and I may be with the wrong country-and-western singer—but folks, when you get to that point, 'You're walkin' on the fightin' side of me.' Because Billy Ray Horton is a citizen of this county, a veteran of the armed services, honorably discharged, married and raised a family here, and has been a very good contributing citizen for a long time, as the previous evidence shows."

Like Buchanan before him, Addington singled out Hannah personally, implying that the prosecutors' remarks had been so off-target that he had been embarrassed for him, what with his having been "U.S. attorney and all of these other things." But Horton, he said, "looks out there, and there is the Smith County district attorney sitting there, and there is the Smith County assistant district attorney sitting there from Tyler. And we've got lawsuits being filed for three hundred thousand dollars by the same people that are paying Mr. Hannah.

"Now can you imagine what kind of celebration there would be in Alabama tonight with a conviction . . . insofar as that civil case is concerned?

"I think you can reasonably conclude that the Southern Poverty Law Center dug those people up [the Maxie brothers], and what do they have to gain? Three hundred thousand dollars for each of these guys plus Mrs. Garner."

Having tied Hannah and the Southern Poverty Law Center together in the same noose for their "unusual prosecution," Addington told jurors their verdict was "the declaration of your independence from anything that taints your decision.

"It's not a declaration of independence of Sabine County, because that's not an issue here," he said. "We can try that later on, I guess, sometime, someplace, maybe in the newspaper, the press, on TV, whatever, but you twelve folks, you citizens of Sabine County, can declare your independence of any of this other outside interference and base your verdict on this evidence and this evidence alone."

John Hannah had lobbed a rock at the defense with his "slice of life in Sabine County" commentary, and he had gotten a boulder in return. He was painfully aware, as he prepared for his last few minutes with the jury, that he had to do damage control—but not before he cleared up one last major piece of evidence, one that had nagged at him since Dr. Grover Winslow's testimony, and a point the defense, in his opinion, repeatedly had tried to blur.

"There has been a lot of argument about how drunk Loyal Garner, Jr., was," he began immediately. "They have tried to make him falling-down, staggering drunk, somewhere between a .27 and a .33, which, as their doctor says, is comatose. . . .

"Here is the medical report, the lab test, the lab test that was done at eight A.M. The lab test says, 'Alcohol, 0.075; *unit of measurement, milligrams per deciliter.*'" Milligrams per deciliter, he wanted to scream, is not a percentage. He wrote the measurement on the chalkboard.

"They have made Loyal Garner a drunken fiend by trying to manipulate the records," Hannah contended. "Speaking of perjury . . . ? Speaking of perjury . . . ?"

Lest members of the jury see themselves portrayed in his critical comments about Sabine County, Hannah tried to explain: "I think the people over here are no better and no worse than people all over this world. Some of them are better, some of them are worse, but you have, and have had, a problem down at the jail. And if you return a verdict of not guilty," he warned, "those men tomorrow will be eligible to put those badges back on. . . . They can go to work back in the jail arresting people and treating them basically the way they want to."

He had scrawled notes of points he wanted to rebut from his opponents' closing arguments. The clock was running; he'd have to be quick.

He was not the one, he pointed out, who interjected race into the trial, but rather a witness from the jail who overheard Ladner's conversation in detox.

"And he said . . . he either heard them say 'you black bastard' or 'you black son of a bitch.'"

All three defense attorneys had managed in their final remarks to underscore Hannah's relationship with Morris Dees and his organization. It had to be addressed.

"A lot has been said about my association with the Southern Poverty Law Center," Hannah said. "I am not ashamed of that. Perhaps the word 'poverty,' perhaps it embarrasses those people. . . . It doesn't embarrass me at all to work with an organization that tries to do something about poverty and brutality and injustice whenever they can."

He glanced at his watch, jolted by how little time he had left.

"Ladies and gentlemen of the jury," he said, speaking as quickly as he could, "you have had a vicious crime committed in that jail, a vicious, brutal crime that they attempted to cover up, including lying to you about the medical records and attempting to cover it up till this jury rested. The cover-up continued, and they have attempted to do it right up to while they were putting on evidence."

Returning a guilty verdict, Hannah knew, would require unusual courage among the jurors. He wanted them to know he understood the consequences they faced. "To go back into the community and live with your verdict may be a tough proposition," he said. "But you're always going to have to live with yourself and say, 'Did I do what was right in regard to that case? Did I take the easy way out and dismiss it?'—and go away and perhaps be applauded by a few and congratulated on how you stood up to those ol' agitators? . . . or will you do what you really can live with and say, 'I participated in 1988 in protecting and defending the Constitution of the United States?' "

Hannah glanced fleetingly toward Corrine Garner, who was seated beside her late husband's parents, then faced the jury.

"Let me leave you with this. Let me leave you with the last words that we know that Loyal Garner, Jr., ever said." Hannah's voice broke. "Corrine, at least you have this knowledge.

"He said, 'All I wanted to do was call my wife. All I wanted to do was call my wife.' "

28

ALL OR NOTHING

DEPENDING ON HOW WELL they read the jury, always a dangerous proposition for a lawyer, John Seale and Paul Buchanan set themselves up to be heroes or goats. By their strategy, their clients would either be convicted on the civil rights charges—and face potential ninety-nine-year sentences—or walk out scot-free.

The defense lawyers knew that, despite strict orders to the contrary, jurors sometimes compromised on verdicts. Holdouts voting not guilty, for example, could be lured into the guilty camp by the majority with promises of reducing the charge to a lesser crime. The defense lawyers, already fairly confident of an acquittal, didn't want jurors tempted into such a compromise by considering lesser charges.

Hannah objected strenuously to what Buchanan called the defense's "all or nothing" charge to the jury. The defense strategy was obvious to Hannah, particularly so with a jury he, too, suspected was in the defense camp. "We ask," Hannah told the judge, "that lesser-included offenses . . . specifically, the lesser-included offense of bodily injury and serious bodily injury, be applied to all counts and all defendants. . . . The statute does not require that death occurred *therefrom*—that is, the beating— but just that death occurred." In order to win a guilty verdict, Hannah argued, he didn't have to prove that Ladner killed Garner with a blackjack, just that the former chief inflicted "bodily injury" on the prisoner—a proposition he believed was obvious from the evidence. (In fact, a previous Texas jury had found an officer guilty of civil rights violations for having pulled a prisoner's hair.)

Seale and Buchanan, however, fought for a more restrictive instruction, one that required jurors to determine whether Ladner's blackjack actually *killed* Garner. The distinction, Hannah knew, was more than semantics. The defense was forcing jurors to unanimously agree to an additional conclusion, in effect determining cause and effect.

It was yet another major victory for the defense when Judge Bacon ruled that the jury, in order to find the officers guilty on the first count, would have to agree that Ladner's blow, or blows, did, in fact, kill Loyal Garner, Jr.

Any hope John Hannah had in the jury's only black member he abandoned early in the trial. Being the only black juror in a controversial killing with racial overtones would be tough for anyone, but Dorie Mae Handy, the forty-year-old domestic worker, was hardly the kind who would dig her heels in against overwhelming pressure. She appeared disoriented, sometimes arriving late and requiring help to find her appointed seat. Seldom did she look toward the counsel table and almost never toward the audience. If any evidence particularly interested her, the reaction wasn't reflected on her face. Most of the time, the housekeeper simply sat in the jury box with her head bowed, too shy or ill at ease to even look up. The judge, all six lawyers, and, indeed, her eleven colleagues on the jury were white. She was conspicuous by her color.

Nor was Handy any more assertive in the privacy of the jury room. Juror Mary Pritchard, whose pregnant daughter had been the catalyst for Willis Garner's arrest in the courtroom, said later that Handy had been "intimidated" from the beginning. "She sat there with her head down," Pritchard recalled. "She ran out of cigarettes, and she wouldn't ask anyone for a cigarette. I said, 'Here, take one.' She'd take it and apologize. . . . We'd invite her to come in and eat with us. I think she did one day, but most of the time she'd walk over to the drugstore and have a sandwich with her husband. She just didn't talk much.

"She had worked for Wilma Hinson [another juror] cleaning house. About a year earlier, Mrs. Hinson's daughter had lost her diamond ring. Mrs. Handy found it cleaning her house, and she put it up on the bar. Honesty was not the question, just the ability to think."

The jury had deliberated only a few minutes, Pritchard recalled, when Billy Ray Horton's name came up. "Mrs. Handy said, 'Oh, no. I don't want anything to happen to Mr. Bill.' I think Bill had taken she and her husband to jail numerous times, but they just thought the world of him. We told her, 'Oh, no, no, don't do it that way, do it from your heart. You have a say just like we all do.' "

After only thirty minutes behind closed doors, the jury sent out a message to Judge Bacon. Customarily, judges send bailiffs to round up all the lawyers in the case so they can be notified of correspondence from the jury. Hannah had been out on the courthouse lawn under the pecan tree, smoking a Marlboro. He just happened into the judge's chambers after the judge already had taken action on the note.

The jury wanted to know if it could find Ladner guilty and still acquit Horton and Hyden. "Well, what'd you tell 'em, judge?" Hannah asked.

The judge hadn't given them an answer, he said, but merely referred them back to the jury's written charge. And based on the instruction, jurors, in order to find the two deputies guilty, had to hold the deputies responsible for not stopping Ladner from hitting Garner.

Inside the deliberation room about an hour later, Pritchard recalled, the jury dispensed with Horton and Hyden. They would be acquitted.

The initial votes on Ladner were "seven–five, something like that, maybe seven–three with two not voting. But it was never the majority saying guilty," Pritchard recalled.

Handy, she remembered, voted guilty. Another member of the minority voting group for a guilty verdict, Pritchard recalled, was a housewife who "thought just because a lawyer made a statement, it was true. She said a lawyer would not get up and lie," Pritchard said. "But we told her they were not under oath, they were not in the stand.

"She said, 'But I have heard that Thomas has been mean to prisoners for a number of years. And if y'all can guarantee me that he'll never be a law officer again. . . .' I said, 'We can't do that. And you can't go by what happened a long time ago or what happened the day before court. You have to go totally by what the people under oath said, and when there's conflict, you just have to sort out black from white.'

"She was sincere," Pritchard said of her fellow juror. "She goes to church every Wednesday night, every Sunday, and every Sunday night. Probably the top button unbuttoned on a shirt would be low-necked to her. . . . But if a neighbor had the flu, she'd be the first one there with a pot of dumplings."

Universally, Pritchard said, jurors doubted the testimony of the two black eyewitnesses, Johnnie and Alton Maxie, particularly when weighed against those of people they knew.

"Mrs. Ray, she was the emergency room attendant. . . . The Maxie brothers testified they [the officers] had washed his shirt and thrown it on the floor of the cell wet. Mrs. Ray said he had his shirt on and it was completely dry. . . .

"And Mary Russell, she checked the cells once an hour. . . . If there had been a puddle of blood there, she would have seen it. She would not have protected the deputies. I just don't believe she would."

Even the strongest admonishments from judges fail to insulate the purity of justice against the fallibility of human nature. And the intrusions into court-ordered objectivity were fierce in a tiny town of thirteen hundred embroiled in controversy.

"As jurors, we really weren't supposed to talk about the trial," Pritchard recalled, "but you'd go to the grocery story and everybody would want to talk." She recalled specifically some unsolicited advice she received during the trial about her seventeen-year-old daughter, Stacey. "People would be saying, 'Don't let Stacey be going into Hemphill at night. Don't let Stacey be alone in the house. Those people from Louisiana, you don't know what they'll do. They could burn your house.' I said, 'Don't tell me this. I've got to get up in the morning and go over there and do what I think is right, not what I think is best for me.' "

The eerie advice had come on the heels of the ominous visit by Sheriff Blan Greer to Pritchard's coffee shop after Willis Garner had been evicted from the trial for breathing on Pritchard's daughter. The unnerving implications about her daughters' well-being couldn't have gone unnoticed, but they didn't stop the juror, she said, from "doing what I had to do."

As if there already weren't enough intrigue, Pritchard recalled Sheriff Greer's abrupt and authoritative appearance in the jury room about six-thirty P.M., after they had deliberated for a half-day with no verdict.

"Mr. Blan just came and said, 'Get your purses and anything else you need, and leave everything else.' We just looked. He said, 'Get in a straight line, when you get to the bottom of the court, form two lines and don't speak, don't look. . . .' We didn't know what was going on. We didn't know if there was a bomb threat or what. . . . The law from Woodville, from everywhere, was there with cars to transport us.

"Human nature," she admitted, "has us to expect the worst."

When the puzzled jurors were loaded into the police cars, they were taken to the Sabine County Hospital. There were no death threats or bomb scares; since they had begun their deliberations, Judge Bacon wanted the jurors sequestered overnight. The hospital was the only place in town large enough to accommodate both the jury and the bailiffs who would ensure they were undisturbed.

Judge Bacon had issued the standard warnings to jurors: "It is only from the witness stand that the jury is permitted to receive evidence" and "You should not consider or mention any personal knowledge or information you may have." If anyone remembered his warnings the next day, he or she disregarded them, turning instead to the kind of facts perhaps known only to small-town jurors.

"So many of those boys [jail inmates] would testify to what they saw and heard," Pritchard recalled. "And Danny Bragg, of the auto parts store in Hemphill, he had been in that new jail as a guest. He said from there in the holding tank, you can't see down the hall. And so far as to what they could hear, well, Glen Harper works for the telephone company. He was in charge of the layout and doing the telephone systems [for the jail]. He said it was soundproof as much as it could be, and so far as hearing plainly what was said, you couldn't.

"They wouldn't let the jury go into the cells," she explained, "but the telephone man was a juror and he had no reason to lie. And the people that know him would probably come closer to believing him than their preacher."

Still, according to Mrs. Pritchard, there were "a couple of people who, for personal reasons we knew, just weren't voting [for acquittal]. We said, 'Well, tell us why you feel this way and maybe I'll want to change my vote. You tell me what has you so thoroughly convinced, and I might see the light.' . . . They'd say, 'No, I'd just rather not say.' "

It was then, according to Pritchard, that Danny Bragg, the parts store owner, jarred the jury into a unanimous verdict. Ironically, neither the dead victim nor the three lawmen accused of killing him were even mentioned in the final, critical minutes of decision making in *State of Texas v. Ladner, Horton, and Hyden*. The final argument was an emotional appeal for the future of Sabine County.

According to Pritchard, Bragg stood and said: "Y'all, Sabine County is a good place to live. It's a good place to raise children. What we do today is going to make history. It's our whole county, the growth of our whole county is going to depend on what we do today. So give it a lot of thought."

Tears started flowing down his cheeks, Pritchard recalled, and he continued. "If we get a bad name out of this, no one will ever want to move to Sabine County, and everyone will want to move away. Your children and your grandchildren are going to be affected by the decision we make today."

At 1:38 P.M. on July 15, after ten and a half hours of deliberation, the jury announced to Judge Bacon it had reached a verdict. Twice, as the clerk read the verdicts, the judge had to silence the audience, which overwhelmingly voiced its approval. All three defendants were acquitted on both counts.

Twelve minutes later, Thomas Ladner, Billy Ray Horton, and Bo Hyden emerged among cheers from the Sabine County Courthouse as free men.

"I'm proud of the people of Sabine County," Bo Hyden said in his only comment to the press. "I'm proud to live in this county."

Six years earlier, in June 1982, John Hannah, Jr., had tasted his only political defeat, narrowly losing a bitter Democratic runoff to Jim Mattox for Texas attorney general. Mattox, a Dallas lawyer and former United States congressman whose strength was in the urban areas, had dodged Hannah's reputation as a tough-fisted crusader during his tenure as United States attorney for the Eastern District of Texas. Instead, he attempted to portray his tattooed opponent with the East Texas drawl as a rough-edged country boy too unsophisticated to be the state's top lawyer. Indeed, Mattox had made an issue of Hannah's bootstrapped law license, implying it made him less of a lawyer. Hannah had taken the unaccustomed loss philosophically, telling friends it wasn't "the end of the world," and that it was "just a job."

The loss in Hemphill, however, was complete. It left him feeling hollow and lower than he'd ever felt. Battling adversaries was a part of hanging out the shingle. As a top federal prosecutor, Hannah had tried more civil rights cases than anyone else in Texas, never losing one. But from the day he had gone to the appeals court to get a continuance to ensure Johnnie Maxie's appearance as a witness, everything had told him the odds were against him. He'd anticipated the loss, but the verdict nonetheless was strikingly personal.

Pushed by reporters for a comment only minutes after the verdict, Hannah tried to cloak his dejection. "I do not believe that the totality of the surrounding circumstances in regard to this trial produced a fair result," he said, choosing his words cautiously. "This could sound like sour grapes from the losing side, but I do have a right to seek justice elsewhere. The results were unfair."

Then he announced he would take transcripts of the trial and witnesses to the United States Justice Department and ask for federal indictments on charges of conspiracy to violate civil rights. It wasn't an off-the-cuff comment to the media; it was a vow.

On the same day he suffered his most agonizing defeat, a man whose integrity and experience placed him among the handful of men Hannah most admired wrote the special prosecutor a letter. It was a letter Hannah cherished and would later hang on his wall:

Dear John:

You've been privileged during the course of your career to participate in some of the great issues of your time. You have enjoyed the sweet taste of victory and drunk from the bitter cup of defeat. It can never be said that John Hannah is counted among those cold and timid souls who know neither victory nor defeat.

I have watched your struggles from both afar and from ringside. I have agreed and disagreed with positions espoused. Such is the nature of this rather peculiar system we have. Through it all, I have always observed that you chose the high road in the best traditions of this old and honored profession.

However, this week you reached that plateau reserved for the truly great. In that courtroom in Hemphill, Texas, you were not fighting alone for truth and justice. You were walking with Darrow, Lincoln, Marshall, Fortas and Brandeis.

I am proud to call you friend.

The letter was signed by United States District Judge Robert M. Parker, chief judge of the Eastern District of Texas.

29

DOUBLE JEOPARDY

*If there's justice for all in a free society, then it seems like there's
justice for whites only in this society. The message to me is that, as
black folks, we better be careful.*

—The Reverend Will Smith, black Church of
Christ minister, July 15, 1988, after the Hemphill trial

———————

WITH NO TIME TO CELEBRATE his victory, a weary John Seale was one
hundred miles northwest of Hemphill by the next morning, arguing in
yet another courtroom. Thomas Ladner, Bill Horton, and Bo Hyden still
stood indicted on murder charges in Judge Joe Tunnell's 241st District
Court in Tyler; and now, just seventy-two hours before they were to face
their second trial, Seale was pleading for a writ of habeas corpus to have
the charges thrown out.

A day earlier, the defense lawyer argued, a jury in Hemphill had found
the three former lawmen innocent of violating Loyal Garner, Jr.'s civil
rights. To try them now in Tyler for murdering Garner, Seale maintained,
District Attorney Jack Skeen would have to rely on the same witnesses
to prove virtually the same facts. Such a proceeding would violate the
former officers' Fifth Amendment rights. The impending murder trial,
Seale told Judge Tunnell, would constitute double jeopardy and violate
the doctrine of collateral estoppel, which means that once an issue of
fact has been determined by a final judgment, that issue can't be litigated
again between the same parties.

Jack Skeen, the Tyler prosecutor, had anticipated the habeas corpus
attempt, and produced case law that he said showed no double jeopardy.
Skeen also produced as a witness John Hannah, who told Judge Tunnell
that the Hemphill trial had not been a fair and unbiased proceeding.

Judge Tunnell, known among Smith County lawyers as a tough, sometimes brash, but evenhanded judge, was unmoved by Seale's interpretation of the law. Thomas Ladner, the judge announced, would stand trial for murder on August 8, three weeks away. The other two former lawmen would be tried later.

Tunnell's decision stunned John Seale. "I was so convinced that we were right on the issue of double jeopardy," Seale said later, "that I knew Judge Tunnell was going to say, 'Yes, this is double jeopardy,' and wasn't going to let these men be tried a second time for the same thing. And when he ruled against us that day, all of my elation and happiness over the verdict the preceding day went down the tubes. I was devastated. . . ."

Dashed hopes aside, Seale had a reputation among his peers as a judicial street fighter of sorts, accomplishing whatever it took to win. "He's a guy who'd fight just as hard over a $500 case as a $500,000 case," one adversary would recall. "And if he lost the $500 case, he'd appeal just as quickly. Cases are not just 'cases' to John. It's more personal than that. He hates to lose worse than any lawyer I ever saw. He's a lot like a bulldog. He just won't let go."

As he drove south on U.S. 69 from Tyler toward home, Seale knew he'd be traveling the same highway again in less than seventy-two hours. He was taking his argument to the Texas 12th Court of Appeals in Tyler.

"I told every customer in my beauty shop, 'Y'all walk those cops, I've had it,' " Nora Helms said.

When Nora and Andy Helms had transplanted their family from Houston to Sabine County, they couldn't have imagined a more tranquil and serene setting to raise a family. Their expectations went downhill almost immediately, particularly after Andy Helms's brief and embattled tour as Hemphill's city marshal. The ensuing harassment of their daughter Kathy by police, particularly Ladner and Horton, had left the beautician and the professional fishing guide embittered and vocal in their criticism of local law enforcement.

When the acquittal came on July 15, Nora Helms wasted no time in following up on her promise. "I told Andy, 'If those people are stupid enough to let them off on this killing, then I damn sure don't want to live here anymore,' " Mrs. Helms said later. "I don't want to live in a town with people like this."

She was preaching to the choir. Andy Helms, who never opted for tact when eye-to-eye confrontation would send the same message, had alienated many of Hemphill's more prominent citizens with his remarks about "ignorant, lying rednecks."

The couple packed the family's belongings and moved to Carthage, a small town two counties north of Sabine.

The acquittal of the three lawmen in Hemphill stung Vollie Grace almost as badly as Garner's death. Grace was well into organizing a second protest rally when he read in the newspaper that the state circuit appeals court in Tyler had agreed to hear the officers' appeal on double jeopardy. Clearly, the appeal meant postponement, if not the demise, of the murder charges. The newspaper, Grace noted, painted a bitter battle. Defense attorneys accused Tyler officials of pursuing the murder charges for "publicity and politics." Tyler District Attorney Jack Skeen was quoted as saying, "The indictments are based on the facts, and that is my only comment."

The latest legal machination, Grace believed, was even more reason for his rally, which he planned for the steps of the same courthouse where Ladner, Horton, and Hyden had been acquitted. Already he had elicited guarantees from as far away as Louisiana and Arkansas, ensuring at least 350 marchers, many from NAACP chapters. One hundred of those were coming from the predominantly black Christians Against Capital Punishment in Shreveport. "We plan to join them because we have the same problem around here in Shreveport—racism and prejudice," said Lorenzo Wilson, the group's leader. "When black people are killed here by police, it's only 'coincidental' or 'in the line of duty.' I know it will make a difference. We have white support as well as black support. It's a way of letting people know that they are not alone."

And alone was precisely how Grace felt. Rumors had been fast and furious in Sabine County after he circulated word of the August 6 rally. "They scared a lot of black people," Grace recalled, "saying that the Klan was coming in."

Fear and loathing, in fact, was rampant throughout Sabine County, not just among blacks. Mary Pritchard was invited by a couple who operated a dry goods business on the town square to watch the rally from their store. "They wanted me to come over and let's get upstairs where you couldn't get hurt and watch the marchers," Pritchard recalled. "I said, 'No, I'm staying in Pineland.' I didn't think there'd be any trouble

—maybe a little scuffling, a little fighting. But in other places, you hear about them burning buildings, and I didn't want to be upstairs if the building's on fire. And so far, me and my children were doing just fine. I said I didn't want to put myself in a position where I could receive bodily injury. I didn't want to make anybody mad." Rumors of potential violence, including threats that the Ku Klux Klan would appear to protest the rally, were so rampant that the United States Justice Department sent Efrian Martinez, a community relations mediator from Houston, to help defuse the tension.

Grace, as was his custom, decided to deal with the tension head-on. He paid another visit to Sheriff Blan Greer. "If I see any Klan," Grace told him, "I'll know what kind of message you're trying to send to me and to this county."

Grace and other blacks in the community were certain, even if they couldn't prove it, that there were Klan members in the county. If nothing else, simple geography made it a distinct possibility. The state Klan headquarters for years had been located in Vidor, a tough, blue-collar refinery-and-shipbuilding town on the outskirts of Beaumont, about one hundred miles south of Hemphill. Less than a year before Garner's death, the Klan had held a statewide rally in an isolated rural area near Talco, less than one hundred miles north of Hemphill.

Grace's meeting with Greer confirmed what he suspected about the sheriff's perception of minorities. "The sheriff said, 'Vollie, there's a boy around here wanting to see you.' I went around the jail looking for a *boy*—you know, a *child*. . . . The sheriff pointed to Martinez and said, 'There he is now.' He was talking about a Mexican-American *man*," Grace recalled. "But he was a *boy* to Greer. . . . And that's one of the reasons we've never had a black in law enforcement."

Under the surveillance of reinforced law enforcement officers from throughout East and Southeast Texas, nearly four hundred marchers, most of them black, met at the Macedonia Baptist Church on the outskirts of Hemphill. Among them were Corrine Garner and the mother of Kenneth "Hambone" Simpson. Peacefully, they marched two miles to the town square, arriving at the steps of the county courthouse just as the noon whistle sounded. A surprisingly large number of whites lined the square to watch the unprecedented event, during which speaker after speaker deplored the acquittal of Ladner, Horton, and Hyden. Why, they asked, had justice died in Sabine County?

As he stood on the steps, Grace also spotted a few blacks not among the marchers but standing with the whites on the sidewalks. "On the day of the rally," Grace recalled, "there were black men who got up and left their homes, left their wives at home, and went to town to stand among the white people . . . so that they wouldn't be considered being with the demonstrators. Some were so scared, they left town that day. It was tough."

A reporter for National Public Radio interviewed a retired white man among the spectators who said he lived on Toledo Bend Reservoir. "Looks like some blacks aren't gonna have jobs after this," the retiree said.

John Hannah, Jr., was not among the marchers in Hemphill. He was, however, on the phone and writing letters to Washington, trying to make good his vow to get federal intervention in Garner's death. With the scheduled murder trial in Tyler in limbo before the state circuit appeals court, the former special prosecutor doubted privately that the Hemphill cops ever would be tried again in Texas courts. As a former U.S. attorney, however, Hannah knew there were no prohibitions, or double jeopardy issues, in the federal government trying the officers for federal civil rights violations, regardless of what had occurred in state courts.

Following up on his phone call to lawyer Barry Kowalski in the civil rights division of the Department of Justice in Washington, Hannah wrote a four-page letter on August 9. He detailed seven rulings by Judge O'Neal Bacon that, he maintained, "were calculated to bring about an acquittal. . . . I beg you to investigate and seek an indictment in this case," Hannah wrote. "A terrible wrong has been done both to Loyal Garner Jr., the victim, and the judicial system. The Justice Department is going to be the only one that may correct it."

A month later, an obviously frustrated and impatient Hannah wrote yet another letter, this one to Kowalski's boss, Assistant Attorney General William Bradford Reynolds, head of the Civil Rights Division in Washington. Claiming that "justice was not done in this case," Hannah wrote: "The defendants in this case have not truly yet had to stand trial. I encourage your action. . . . I believe that the great majority of the citizens of this area (of whatever color) are shocked and outraged by the notion that these former law officers might escape being tried in a fair courtroom with a fair judge presiding."

He enclosed a copy of an editorial in the *Lufkin Daily News,* an uncommonly spunky small-town paper that had won the Pulitzer Prize for revealing the U.S. Marines' negligence in the death of a young Lufkin recruit. Noting that the federal government had the authority to enforce civil rights, managing editor Phil Latham, who had condemned police brutality in Hemphill, had written: "Are you listening, Washington? Do it. Just do it."

At the Southern Poverty Law Center in Montgomery, Morris Dees and Richard Cohen were readying Corrine Garner's civil lawsuit for trial. They had not, however, abandoned hope of criminal charges against Ladner, Horton, and Hyden. Dees, too, wrote Kowalski, claiming the Sabine County trial had been a "farce." "Barry, this case is history repeating itself," he wrote. "During the 1950s and 1960s, law enforcement officers routinely murdered blacks and were acquitted." Dees referred to the 1958 case of Woodrow Wilson Daniels, the black killed in Water Valley, Mississippi, by a white sheriff, which he had discovered in his research. "The evidence is strikingly similar to the Garner case," Dees said. "In the face of clear physical and medical evidence that the sheriff beat the prisoner to death with a blackjack, the white Mississippi jury acquitted.

"Please . . . begin the grand jury investigation immediately, while the evidence is still fresh. This will prove to be one of the most meritorious police brutality cases undertaken by the Justice Department."

As early as January, the FBI had compiled an investigative report that contained not only statements from the inmates at Sabine County Jail and the three officers but also indications that previous civil rights violations could have occurred in Hemphill. As soon as he had reviewed the report, United States Attorney Bob Wortham in Beaumont had approved the Garner case for federal prosecution. Indeed, FBI agents from Beaumont had monitored much of the ensuing state proceedings. But following its policy of interceding only when state officials fail to take action, federal prosecutors had been awaiting the results of the Texas civil rights and murder trials. With the state circuit appeals court considering the legal merits of the scheduled murder trial, Hannah suspected, the federal prosecutors undoubtedly would await the court's ruling. Then the decision to file federal charges would have to come from Washington, not from the United States attorney in Beaumont.

Paranoia gripped tiny Hemphill in the aftermath of the acquittal and the NAACP-sponsored rally. Not that there ever had been an appreciable amount of racial interaction anyway, but now the chasm was complete —whites and blacks, distrustful of each other, found sanctuary only among their own race. Even some whites were cautious about being seen talking to other whites, particularly with those few who had publicly criticized law enforcement. Continued rumors of violence spread like beaded water on a windshield, but few could be authenticated, and most townspeople merely attributed the rumors to agitators among both whites and blacks.

Thomas Ladner, for the most part, did, too. Then his phone started ringing, he said, with death threats. "They'd say, 'You're a nigger killer. You got twelve hours to live, then you'll be a dead sonofabitch.' I got calls from California, Chicago, wherever," Ladner recalled. "It didn't bother me, but I was concerned for my kids and my wife. Somebody already broke into the [house] trailer a month before and stole a microwave and a bunch of stuff. I think it was just a thief." Better safe than sorry, Ladner moved his family from the mobile home to his mother's farm near Fairmont.

Shortly before midnight on a Sunday in late August, someone entered the back door of Ladner's mobile home on the isolated two-acre clearing south of Hemphill. According to Bill Barcheers, the emergency medical technician who doubles as Hemphill's fire marshal, the mobile home was doused with kerosene, apparently, and set afire. "Somebody torched the place, no question about that," Barcheers said. "We took some prints off the back door, a good set, but we didn't have nothing to match them with."

The arson ignited fears anew. Whites inferred that blacks had set the fire in retaliation for the acquittals. Blacks claimed whites, maybe even Ladner himself, set the fire to implicate blacks and to collect the insurance to pay legal fees.

"At the time," Barcheers said, "we weren't getting any cooperation from anybody. We were black sheep, and nobody wanted to get involved in our mess." On his own, Barcheers followed some leads. "We had some suspects in Louisiana," he said, "but we didn't have enough probable cause to get them fingerprinted." Someone in town, Barcheers said, had seen a black man speed up to a pay phone shortly after the fire would have been set. Then he sped out of town to the Y intersection, taking the road toward Louisiana, the fire marshal said.

Barcheers asked the state fire marshal to investigate, but the case, he said, died of neglect.

Two months after Thomas Ladner, Bill Horton, and Bo Hyden were found innocent by their peers in Hemphill, the specter of murder charges vanished. The Twelfth Texas Court of Appeals in Tyler ruled that in order for the state to prosecute the lawmen on murder charges, prosecutors "must necessarily relitigate all of these issues" already determined by the jury in Hemphill. "The doctrine of collateral estoppel prohibits the State from so doing, and that ingredient of double jeopardy protection prohibits prosecution of the Smith County indictments. . . ." The indictments in Tyler were thrown out.

The thirteen-page ruling that granted freedom to the officers, ironically, was issued in the same city that had tried so desperately to send them to the penitentiary. Dismissal of murder charges, to many people's way of thinking, exonerated not only the lawmen but the entire white population of Hemphill. A half-page advertisement appeared the next day, September 14, 1988, in the *Sabine County Reporter*. The ad listed the names of twenty-four citizens and businesses, including Barcheers EMS and Big 4 Construction, whose owner, Billy Joe McGee, had given Ladner a job after he was indicted and suspended in Garner's death. "The citizens and businesses listed below," the advertisement read, "are proud of the law enforcement officers and agencies in Sabine County. We all hope that our community can pull together to overcome the ordeal that we all hope is over now."

But in Jack Skeen's mind, the battle was far from over. "I just knew we had to appeal," the Tyler district attorney recalled. "I felt like if we could get to the Texas Court of Criminal Appeals in Austin, we could reverse the Tyler appeals court. That's all I thought about, was how soon we could get to Austin."

The normally docile Skeen had made up his mind to try the former cops for murder long before the civil rights trial in Hemphill. But driving to Hemphill to monitor Hannah's prosecution in Judge O'Neal Bacon's court had renewed Skeen's commitment. "I was even angrier at what they had done," he said. "These men needed to be tried for murder."

Some of the most respected lawyers in Texas wouldn't have bet a plug nickel that Skeen would ever see the former lawmen in court for murder; nor did many expect him to even try. The case had become a legal roller coaster. Politically, the out-of-county case had been a gamble anyway. He had done his best, lost it to a circuit appeals court, and now, they reasoned, the Tyler DA would walk away from it without any political damage.

Instead, Skeen committed his entire appellate staff to drafting the appeal to the Texas Court of Criminal Appeals, the state's highest criminal court. And to just about everyone's surprise except his own, he won. On October 25, the Texas Court of Criminal Appeals wrote: "Contrasting the allegations in the murder indictments with the indictments and jury charge in the civil rights prosecution, it is apparent that the issues are far from identical." The court reinstated the murder indictments against the Hemphill officers and remanded the cases to Judge Tunnell's court for trial.

The reinstated charges set off a bitterly personal reaction among Ladner, Horton, Hyden, and their lawyers, who long had blamed Morris Dees and Richard Cohen and their Southern Poverty Law Center for their continuing legal problems. Three days after the ruling, in one of the most bizarre chapters yet in the convoluted legal saga, Horton and Hyden sued Dees, Cohen, and the Southern Poverty Law Center in Hemphill. John Seale dissuaded Ladner from joining in the civil suit, saying he "didn't see a lot of merit in it." Horton and Hyden claimed they had enjoyed an "impeccable reputation" before the Poverty Law Center tried to subvert and manipulate Sabine County's judicial system. The lawsuit was breathless in its litany of wrongdoing purportedly orchestrated by the Poverty Law Center: civil conspiracy, malicious prosecution, libel, slander, intentional interference with employment, invasion of privacy, and intentional and negligent infliction of mental anguish.

The reason for their persecution, Horton and Hyden claimed, was greed. "The Southern Poverty Law Center is an operation which is supported by solicitations to the public, and its own acts have resulted in a personal fortune of millions of dollars by its principal," the deputies alleged. "The defendants, Southern Poverty Law Center, Dees and Cohen, sitting in Montgomery, Ala. . . . saw an opportunity to gather a larger fortune by destroying the lives and reputations [of Horton and Hyden]. . . ."

The lawsuit referred to a direct mail letter, like the one Paul Buchanan received shortly before the civil rights trial, in which Dees asked for donations to litigate the Loyal Garner, Jr. case. "In only slightly veiled language, the mailing compared [Horton and Hyden] to the Ku Klux Klan and implied that all southern white people were racist and, based on this hate mail, they requested the recipient to send in money to the Southern Poverty Law Center."

If Dees and Cohen were genuinely concerned about the lawsuit filed against them, they didn't acknowledge it publicly. When they referred to the lawsuit at all, they described it as merely a "nuisance suit," filed to create a smoke screen and to vent the former deputies' anger. "It's a frivolous suit," Dees said. He paused, then added, "It's also the craziest suit I've ever seen."

Cohen filed a perfunctory motion three weeks later, asking for a change of venue. "[We] object to venue being in Sabine County . . ." he said, "because there exists in Sabine County, Texas . . . so great a prejudice . . . that [we] cannot obtain a fair and impartial trial." Without naming anyone, the motion also alleged a conspiracy in Hemphill against the Poverty Law Center "instigated by influential persons."

When he died December 27, 1987, in a town he never before had visited, Loyal Garner, Jr., left a wife who worked part-time as a cook at a cafe in Florien, six children ranging in age from thirteen to three, and a $10,000 mortgage. Exclusive of the eleven dollars in bills and $1.67 in change he was carrying at the time of his arrest, Garner left an estate worth $664.97. His legacy to his children amounted to $110.83 each, except for Corey, the youngest, who got $110.82.

Corrine Garner could expect little financial help from her in-laws. Sarah Garner received $262 a month from Social Security; Loyal Sr., listed on income tax forms as a self-employed woodcutter, grossed $4,242 in 1987.

Overshadowed in the media by the twists and turns of the criminal prosecutions, Richard Cohen and Poverty Law Center investigator Joe Roy quietly pursued the Garner family's civil lawsuit.

Using Cohen's court-ordered discovery, Roy, the white former Montgomery police officer, scoured the Sabine County Sheriff's Department phone records and arrest reports even as Hannah was prosecuting the officers. He confirmed the phone calls, which he and Cohen dubbed the "body-snatching calls," to Tyler Justice of the Peace Bill Beaird in which Sabine County officials tried to force the release of Garner's body. And they documented it was almost seven hours before sheriff's officers finally called Texas Ranger Roscoe Davis to investigate Garner's death—hardly the "immediate" action the sheriff had testified to in his grand jury appearance in Hemphill.

To prove that, as Cohen had alleged in his lawsuit, excessive force and brutality in Sabine County were "so common . . . as to constitute a custom that represents expected, accepted municipal policy," Roy had used the jail logs to locate Lloyd Armstrong and Leonard Green, among others.

The fruits of Roy's investigation were reaping big dividends in the depositions, which, while they weren't taken in a courtroom in front of a judge or jury, nonetheless were sworn and admissible should the case go to trial.

Cohen, using Roy's information as ammunition, shot holes in previously announced "official" versions. He was a relentless and skilled questioner, wearing down and flustering his witnesses in depositions. At one point in his questioning of Sabine County Judge Royce C. Smith, for example, Cohen pushed the judge about his phone calls to Judge Beaird in Tyler: "You wanted the body released to Sabine County, correct, Judge?"

"The interest was getting an autopsy," Smith said, after conferring with his lawyer.

"You wanted the autopsy done in Sabine County, didn't you, Judge?"

"No sir. There's no facility to do one in Sabine County, no sir."

"Isn't it the case, Judge Smith, that you told the justice of the peace that Sabine County had ruled the death an *accident*?"

"I don't recall that, no sir."

Before the young lawyer finished with Sabine County's highest elected official, Judge Smith had said "I don't recall" or "Not that I remember" thirty-eight times.

On November 23, four months before the civil case was to go to trial, attorneys representing the city of Hemphill agreed to an out-of-court settlement in the case filed by the Southern Poverty Law Center in behalf of Corrine Garner, her children, and her in-laws. United States District Judge Robert M. Parker sealed the settlement, saying it was "deemed confidential and prohibited from public disclosure." He agreed, however, to allow attorneys to make the following public statement: "The city of Hemphill and the Garners have compromised and settled their differences on a basis that is fair to all parties. The precise terms of the agreement are confidential and may not be disclosed." Beyond the approved public statement, Cohen would say only that "the Garners and the children have been provided for." But a court document inadvertently left unsealed and later withdrawn from public view showed the settlement to be $300,000, with provisions for a trust fund for each of Garner's six children.

The court's docket, a record of the settlement hearing, bore the notation "Richard Cohen announces he waives any claim to attorney fees."

30

CONVICTION

THAT BLACKS WOULD LOOK hopefully toward the Smith County Courthouse for justice in the death of a black man was an ironic footnote in the history of the nondescript beige building.

Thirty-three years earlier, when the courthouse was newly opened, Texas was swept up in the bitterness of school desegregation. The future of integration in Texas, some said, not to mention the future of the NAACP, would be determined in the Tyler courthouse. The Texas NAACP, in the aftermath of the landmark *Brown v. Board of Education* ruling, had filed a wave of lawsuits to force the integration of public schools in the state. Texas Attorney General John Ben Shepperd, an outspoken segregationist whose home was fifty miles north, had chosen Tyler as the place to stop the black organization in its tracks.

In September 1956, before a major hearing in the case was scheduled, a crowd of whites carrying Confederate flags confronted an equally large group of blacks on the sidewalk in front of the courthouse. Emerging from a car in the midst of the chaos was Thurgood Marshall, a lawyer who had come to defend the NAACP and who later would become the first black associate justice of the United States Supreme Court.

The segregationists, according to historian Michael Lowery Gillette in *The NAACP in Texas, 1937–1957,* "could hardly have had a more sympathetic ally" than Shepperd. "A native of Gladewater, he was deeply conservative and reflected the prevailing racial attitudes of the state's most prejudiced region." Shepperd had accused NAACP lawyers of recruiting black students as plaintiffs in the desegregation lawsuits, a violation of state barratry laws, which prohibit lawyers from soliciting clients. Among the records Shepperd sought in his investigation were the NAACP's membership rolls. Making public its members' names would subject them to intimidation by the segregationists in power. The lawsuit, if successful, threatened to push the black rights organization to the brink of extinction in Texas.

Thurgood Marshall, who regarded the Texas case as critical to the school integration movement throughout the nation, had agreed to provide certain records to the attorney general. But when state investigators arrived to collect them, according to Gillette, they found Marshall "sitting at his desk excising the members' names from each document." Inside the Smith County Courthouse, Marshall "emerged as the dominant figure," Gillette wrote, impressing his adversaries with his quick knowledge of the law and a keen sense of humor.

Only a change in attorneys general and Marshall's ability to compromise saved the NAACP in Texas. The new attorney general, Will Wilson, agreed not to revoke the group's charter in Texas as a nonprofit organization; in return, Marshall agreed, the NAACP would not violate the barratry statutes. The Texas NAACP had been crippled in the Smith County Courthouse, but not killed.

In the best of circumstances, the wheels of justice grind slowly. Given all the paperwork the Garner case fed into the machinery, the system all but ground to a stop. On October 25, 1989, nearly two years after Garner died, the Texas Court of Criminal Appeals finally ruled out double jeopardy, paving the way for the reinstatement of the murder charges against Ladner, Horton, and Hyden. The new trial date was set for April 16, 1990, allowing for District Judge Joe Tunnell's docket and the participating lawyers' schedules.

Two weeks before the trial was to begin, and even as Smith County District Attorney Jack Skeen was readying for the on-again, off-again murder case, John Seale relentlessly was groping for yet another way to throw out the murder charges. His appeals in state courts exhausted, Seale had moved his battle to federal court, filing a writ of habeas corpus in an attempt to nullify the upcoming trial. In the eleventh hour, Skeen had had to dispatch assistants Michael Sandlin and Frank Henderson, both critical to the preparation of his murder case, to federal court in Beaumont to argue against Seale's latest motion.

U.S. District Judge Howell Cobb denied Seale's writ, which again claimed doubled jeopardy.

Thomas Ladner, whose retainer to Seale had been exhausted even before the verdict was returned in the Hemphill trial, was getting more than his money's worth. Undaunted and unpaid, Seale moved on to the United States Fifth Circuit Court of Appeals in New Orleans, reurging his double-jeopardy argument and asking for emergency relief to stop the impending trial in Tyler.

"We were scheduled to pick a jury on Monday, and on Friday we still didn't know if we were going to trial," Skeen recalled. "We had two fronts going at the same time. I was up here with assistants preparing for trial while my other assistants were down arguing the federal court order. It was in the evening hours on Friday that we finally learned the Fifth Circuit was going to overrule the writs and allow us to proceed to trial."

And even after Skeen had put out legal fires in two states, the murder trial still wasn't a certainty for April 16. On April 11, after a "fainting episode," Judge Tunnell, who was to be the presiding judge, was rushed to Medical Center Hospital, the same hospital where Garner had died. Doctors diagnosed the judge's illness as "sick sinus syndrome," a condition that made his heart rate precariously slow.

If Judge Tunnell had a reputation for being tough—a fact to which most lawyers in his court would sign affidavits—he now only added to the image. Doctors implanted a permanent pacemaker and discharged him forty-eight hours later. At nine A.M. Monday, April 16, precisely on schedule, Judge Tunnell gaveled the trial, which now consolidated all three defendants, to order. He introduced a letter from his doctor attesting to his health and said, simply, "I would not be here if the doctor had any apprehensions or concerns about my being able to preside."

Jeff Haas, a young Tyler lawyer and a recent addition to the defense team, quickly replied, "I don't have any concern, Your Honor." Haas, representing Billy Ray Horton, had practiced in Judge Tunnell's court before. He replaced Jasper attorney Floyd Addington, who had been indicted shortly after the Hemphill trial on charges of theft and misapplication of $100,000 in proceeds from an estate he represented.

Quickly, the lanky, gray-haired jurist launched through a pile of pretrial motions. Some of Judge Tunnell's decisions were so markedly different from those of his colleague in Hemphill that a lay person would wonder if the judges read from the same law. In Tyler, for example, the defense would not be allowed to tell the jury Johnnie Maxie was an informant unless "other testimony makes it relevant." After having to ask what the Southern Poverty Law Center was, the judge determined that the defense would not mention any participation of the Southern Poverty Law Center in the case. "To the extent of my ability to do so," Judge Tunnell said, "I'm going to eliminate or minimize any racial overtones in this case. The Poverty Law Center clearly injects race into it."

The judge agreed the defense could discuss Johnnie Maxie's prior arrests for drunk driving because it could have relevance to his arrest in Hemphill for public intoxication. He refused, however, to let the defense allege "they were dealing drugs unless it has some relevance to some issue in the trial of this case."

"Are you going to permit me to tell about Johnnie Maxie making a phone call to the constable?" Seale asked.

"I may or may not," Judge Tunnell said. "If it is relevant, I'm going to permit it, but if it is not, I will exclude it."

Skeen would be able to show the jury the autopsy pictures Hannah had been denied in Hemphill, but only for "limited purposes" of explaining Garner's injuries. The judge did not, however, want Skeen "waving" them in front of the jurors for effect.

During recess, a visiting lawyer, remarking on the judge's occasional and pointed jabs at lawyers, asked a local attorney if the judge was always that irascible. "Actually," the local lawyer replied, "his heart problem has made him a kinder, gentler judge."

As they had in the 1956 NAACP trial, blacks drove to Tyler from throughout East Texas to witness the most important civil rights trial in recent Texas history. Their hopes for justice for Loyal Garner, Jr., were not buoyed when a nine-woman, three-man, all-white jury was seated.

Pearlie Henderson, the head of the local NAACP chapter and the man who had reported Garner's death to FBI officials, sat emotionless in the courtroom as he had so many other times. The Garner family, enduring the ordeal of their second trial, sat near the front, with the patriarch, Loyal Sr., a black baseball cap covering his gray hair, seated stoically at the end of the aisle.

Only three days into the trial, and despite Judge Tunnell's best efforts, as he put it, to "eliminate or minimize any racial overtones" in the Garner case, the defense asked for a mistrial based on comments and implied threats, according to Seale, made by the NAACP in a television report. The report, aired three times by KLTV in Tyler, was an interview with an NAACP spokesman, who proclaimed the Garner case "one of the most important cases ever tried." The trial was a barometer, he said, for determining whether civil rights for blacks had advanced or declined. A guilty verdict, he said, would show progress; an acquittal "would be taking us fifty years back." Should the Hemphill officers be acquitted, the NAACP spokesman said, the organization would "take some sort of action."

The comments, Seale argued to Judge Tunnell, "put into this case an absolute sense of community pressure on the jury to return a verdict of guilty . . . with the further connotation or statement that a not-guilty verdict would amount to going back fifty years in time, but the most important thing being the threat of action by the NAACP.

"In this connection, Your Honor," Seale said, "we also intend to offer evidence of the fact that following a previous not guilty verdict involving these same people, that one of their homes was burned and it was found to be arson, and the arsonist has not yet been apprehended or located."

Judge Tunnell polled the jurors, none of whom said they had seen the TV report. The judge denied Seale's motion for mistrial.

Four days later, the issue of race reappeared, this time directly in the Smith County Courthouse, and Judge Tunnell sequestered the jury to shield it from bigotry. A reporter using the first-floor men's room, one used occasionally by members of the jury, discovered a warning scrawled on a stall. Someone had written: "Hemphill niggers go home or die." Above the warning were two Ku Klux Klan hoods, and beneath it, the phrase "Klan Jam '90," an apparent reference to an earlier Ku Klux Klan rally in northeastern Texas. When the defense attorneys again asked Judge Tunnell to declare a mistrial, he once more polled the jurors, asking them if they had seen any "writings or signs" in the restrooms. None had, and the motion for a mistrial was summarily denied.

Buchanan, fearful that sequestering the jury could send an ominous message to the jurors about Ladner, Horton, and Hyden, argued unsuccessfully against "locking up the jury." "I just think that if something like this were to happen in the future," he said, "these jurors would be sharp enough to understand that there are idiots out there on both sides of this issue that would like to, for whatever sick reason, deny one or more sides in this case a fair trial. . . ."

One of the witnesses investigator Joe Roy dredged up for Richard Cohen's ongoing grilling in the civil depositions had been Ronnie Felts, the Hemphill sawmill owner who also was the town's mayor for six years, and as such, had been Thomas Ladner's boss. When Cohen questioned the mayor, he discovered that Felts had had a conversation with Ladner the morning after the alleged beating. And Cohen, though he had not developed the information in time to help Hannah's case in Hemphill, had elicited a strange twist to the conventional account of the events of Garner's death. The Poverty Law Center lawyer knew that Felts, an affable, forty-nine-year-old college graduate, would make a damning and ironic witness for Jack Skeen's prosecution.

Felts's testimony on the witness stand in Tyler spawned a low roar in the courtroom and stone silence at the defense table. Early in the morning of December 26, he testified, Ladner had appeared at his doorstep. Declining an invitation to come inside, the chief appeared worried and asked the mayor, who was still in his slippers, to step outside. At the time, the mayor recalled, Ladner mistakenly believed Garner already had died in the Sabine County Hospital. Their conversation, as Felts recounted it under oath, not only contradicted the three officers' version of the arrests and the confrontations in the Sabine County Jail but also implicated for the first time Chief Deputy Billy Ray Horton in delivering some of the blows Loyal Garner, Jr., suffered.

Ladner and Hyden were backed into the road beneath Drag Strip Hill on Texas 87 when a "pickup came wobbling up the road," the mayor recalled from his conversation with the chief.

"They were not on the road on patrol at that time, is that right?" asked Assistant District Attorney Frank Henderson.

"That was my understanding."

Felts testified that Ladner told him he and Hyden had gone to the detox cell to get Garner so he could make a phone call. When he opened the door, Ladner told the mayor, Garner lunged at him. "He just sort of sidestepped him and he hit the wall," the mayor said.

"Who hit the wall?"

"Garner. . . . He didn't go into detail. I assumed he ran into it head-on."

The audience reacted with loud whispers.

"Just a minute," Judge Tunnell interjected. "Let's have no audience reaction."

"He just said he hit the wall," Felts continued. "Then he got hold of him and—and was carrying him up to the book-in room and—and on the way up there, he had to catch him from behind and on the way up there, he kicked him in the shins all the way up there or something."

"Who kicked who in the shins?"

"Garner kicked Ladner."

In the book-in room, the mayor recalled Ladner told him, Garner "just decided he was going to leave." Garner "went for a flashlight that was on the desk.

"He didn't get the light," Felts continued. "Bill beat him to the light, and Thomas started trying to grab him again, and then he got his slapstick out of his back pocket. . . .

"I asked him, did he hit him? He said, 'Yes sir, I did.' He said, 'But I hit him just a glancing blow with my left hand with my slapjack.' He said, 'I can't do nothing with my left hand. . . .' He said, 'If I had got it in my right hand and got a good lick at him, I would have hit him pretty hard.' But he said after that, the slapjack got away from him and they all went into a scramble on the floor. . . ."

"Did the chief tell you about any blows being struck by any other officer?" Henderson asked.

"He said that only one other one—he just said that Bill got in a couple licks with a flashlight and he didn't know who all else hit who or what all happened in that scramble."

Felts's testimony was devastating to the defense, and on cross-examination, all three defense lawyers walked around it as if it were a coiled snake. Messing with it, they knew all too well, could be fatal, if it weren't already. After asking only a few perfunctory questions, they quickly passed the witness and retreated.

Hannah, who had assisted Skeen's prosecution team however he could, was trying a case in another court the day Felts testified. He had had no indication that Ladner had confided in the mayor the day after the jailhouse battle. When he heard that Felts had submarined the officers, Hannah was rocked by the irony. With defendants, lawyers, judges, and anybody else it could muster, Hannah believed, Hemphill had embraced its own and had walked lockstep against the outside world. Now, it was the town's mayor, of all people, who had devastated its case.

Felts's recollection of his conversation with Ladner, particularly the portion about Horton hitting Garner "a couple licks with a flashlight," also helped Hannah solve a mystery that had been nagging at him since the trial. Hannah couldn't understand why Horton had refused his offer of immunity in return for testifying against Ladner and Hyden. It had been a trade-off, Hannah now surmised: Horton wouldn't testify against his two colleagues for fear they would implicate him in the beating in the book-in room.

If Ronnie Felts was aware of his damning impact on the officers' case, he didn't show it. The judge declared a recess after his testimony, and by chance, Felts and Ladner walked out of the courtroom at the same time.

"Well," Felts told Ladner, "I hope I helped you."

On advice of counsel, Thomas Ladner, Bill Horton, and Bo Hyden declined to testify in their own behalf. Instead, the court reporter who had recorded their testimony before the Smith County Grand Jury two years earlier merely read those accounts into the record and before the jury.

Paul Buchanan had scoffed before the trial when John Seale confided he had an ominous feeling about trying the case in Tyler. "He was depressed from day one about trying that case in Tyler," Buchanan recalled later. "He said he had bad vibrations about being in that county. He would joke about having the beer iced down and not touching it until he reached Angelina County, and then he'd pop the top. He wasn't about to do it in Smith County. He was just real concerned. He felt an overwhelming prejudice against the defendants up there."

But damned if Buchanan wasn't beginning to believe Seale was clairvoyant.

The defense faced all the familiar faces again—the Maxies, Corrine Garner, the jail inmates, Texas Ranger Roscoe Davis, and Dr. Virgil Gonzalez, whom Buchanan had dubbed "the pathologist from hell." And Felts wasn't the only new face. Skeen, a strong believer in expert witnesses, was taking no chances. Now there was yet another medical expert, Dr. Ron Donaldson, the neurosurgeon who performed the emergency surgery on Garner and who hadn't been called for the Hemphill trial for fear of duplicating Dr. Gonzalez's medical testimony.

Like the Maxie brothers, Dr. Donaldson, too, claimed to have found *bruises* on Garner's head. And, the doctor testified, the bruises couldn't have resulted from any emergency medical procedure to save Garner's life.

Assistant District Attorney Wayne Dickey led Dr. Donaldson through CAT scans and X rays, the doctor pointing out damage to Garner's brain.

"Can you put that into layman's terms, so they can understand . . . how much force, in your opinion, would it cause, or take, to cause that type of injury?" Dickey asked. "Can you relate it to something the jury can understand?"

"Most of the people we see with that kind of injury," Dr. Donaldson said, "have had a high-speed automobile accident. I would think you would have to be going fifty or sixty miles an hour and have a sudden stop and hit something.

"It would also take an enormous amount of force if you were hit with something. . . . I would describe that as if you hit somebody with, say, a baseball bat. Then it would not be a bunt, but trying to hit a center-field flier to somebody."

Dickey asked if a person suffering such a blow "would be conscious and able to walk around and talk and perform functions."

"Not in my opinion."

Wayne Dickey was in charge of presenting most of the medical evidence and he was pleased with the jurors' reaction to Dr. Donaldson's appearance. His testimony hadn't been full of arcane references to medical terms no one understood; it was, instead, filled with analogies of car wrecks and baseball grand slams that evoked strong mental images. The contemplation of that kind of violence even made a couple of the jurors wince visibly.

More foreboding, Skeen's able young assistant knew, was Dr. Winslow's "drunk and belligerent" premise. The theory, the prosecution was certain, had been a "rabbit trail" to provide a rationale for the officers *having* to use violence on Garner Christmas night. Dr. Winslow's extrapolated conclusion that Garner had been drunk—at least three times the legal limit—had been told convincingly to the Sabine County grand jury, the inquest jury in Tyler, and the civil rights jury in Hemphill. On cross-examination, Dickey was waiting.

The prosecutor elicited Dr. Winslow's confirmation that a blood test performed in his own hospital on December 26 showed Garner's blood contained .075 percent alcohol. Dickey then handed the doctor an analysis from SmithKline Bio-Science Laboratories in Beaumont, the lab that had tested blood drawn from Garner at the same time. The SmithKline report specified that Garner's blood had been tested for, among other drugs, ethanol alcohol; the report did not note that any alcohol had been detected.

"They did not report any level of ethanol, did they?" Dickey asked.

"They did not," Dr. Winslow admitted. The physician claimed, however, that despite ethanol being listed among the tests performed, the lab might not actually have tested for it. "We only asked for the drugs and not for the alcohol."

Dickey was mildly incredulous at Dr. Winslow's interpretation of the absence of alcohol in the independent lab report. But he knew he had planted a significant seed of doubt with the jury; now he had to make it bear fruit. How, Dickey asked, did Dr. Winslow arrive at the formula for extrapolating the purported .075 alcohol content of Garner's blood on December 26 to arrive at the .337 content it would have been a night earlier during Garner's arrest?

Dr. Winslow had consulted a Beaumont pathologist, Dr. Gary Werntz, he said. The pathologist had told him that the body metabolizes, or breaks down, alcohol at the rate of .016 to .023 per hour.

Did Dr. Winslow also tell the expert that Loyal Garner, Jr., the subject of his inquiry, was in a *coma?*

"Oh, yes," Dr. Winslow said, "he knew that."

Dickey moved closer to the witness, grasping a letter from Dr. Werntz. The prosecutor read from Dr. Werntz's letter: "Since ethanol is metabolized in the liver, no such extrapolation can be made in an individual with an impaired [liver] condition."

Only about 10 percent of the alcohol in the body is oxidized through the lungs and is disposed of through the skin; the liver handles the remaining 90 percent. In a coma, the liver would have been shut down, Dickey contended, making it virtually impossible for the organ to metabolize any alcohol.

"All I know is my original question in talking and corresponding with Dr. Werntz was that he was familiar with everything," Dr. Winslow replied. "As far as what he says now, I could not answer."

A wave of confidence swept Dickey. In his mind—and he hoped in the minds of the jurors—he had proved that Garner could not have been drunk when he was arrested. Savoring the feeling, the prosecutor elected to ride the crest. He had scrawled a tidbit on his legal pad from an interview with Corrine Garner and now was the time to test it. He called the doctor's attention to Corrine's arrival at Sabine County Hospital on December 26.

"Do you remember her first question to you was, 'What was wrong?,' and your initial response was, 'This was not the result of police brutality'?"

The question appeared to catch Dr. Winslow off guard. "I certainly don't remember making that statement," he said. "I would not say I did or did not."

Jack Skeen had achieved enviable success in his six years as Smith County's chief prosecutor. And while no one ever would accuse the sturdy, sandy-haired prosecutor of being flamboyant or dramatic, everyone who knew the forty-four-year-old bachelor gave him high marks for diligence, perseverance, and integrity.

Skeen wasn't an eagle in the courtroom; he wasn't a soaring orator with dramatic phrases and gestures. He was an intensely focused groundhog with an eye toward the hole. Always, Skeen knew where he was headed. He made a checklist of elements to be proven and another of the witnesses and evidence that could deliver that proof. Methodically, he would set out, amassing voluminous and impenetrable detail by the time he finally chose to rest. His trip frequently was so quiet and earnest that his adversaries had been lulled into complacency.

And as he proved in the Garner case, the most controversial and publicized in his career, Skeen was not afraid to make the trip.

Methodically in his closing arguments, Skeen summarized and underscored the key elements of his murder case against Ladner, Horton, and Hyden. He elected to split his arguments, taking half his time first and the other half after Seale, Buchanan, and Haas had made their final pleas to the jury.

Loyal Garner, Jr., he emphasized, was not drunk. Even more basic was the fact that Ladner and Horton had no justification for even going to the detox cell.

"I'll tell you right now, ladies and gentlemen," Skeen said, "the evidence shows at that point the defendant Ladner was on a mission. He had these three men in his custody. They hadn't given him a lick of trouble. He didn't even have to handcuff them. He had them off the road, in his custody, in the detox cell of the Sabine County Jail, a secure cell built for the purpose of leaving individuals in there to allow them to sober up, if they are intoxicated in the first place. . . . Nothing in it they can hurt themselves with, nothing in it they can hurt anybody else with. . . ."

Simply, Garner was killed, Skeen said, "for hollering."

"The evidence shows when he went out of detox and he went up to processing, he was alive. The evidence shows without any doubt what-

soever that when he came out of the processing room . . . where he had
been with defendant Ladner, this defendant Horton, and this defendant
Hyden, that for all practical purposes, Loyal Garner, Jr., was a dead man."
Skeen emphasized Mayor Ronnie Felts's testimony, saying Ladner had
told "the best story he can to his boss because he knows at that point he
is in trouble because he knows where Loyal Garner, Jr., is—up at Sabine
County Hospital." The prosecutor recounted Ladner's version to Felts of
Horton grabbing the flashlight off the desk. "Of course, we know what
Ronnie Felts testified that Ladner told him . . . [what] defendant Bill
Horton did with the flashlight."
Skeen expressed horror at the unconscious Garner being dragged back
to the cell and left overnight without medical treatment. "If that is not
the grossest indifference to human life in a murder I have ever seen, I
don't know what is," he said.
John Seale had noticed Garner's children seated in the front row in
the final hours of the trial, and he strongly resented what he believed
was the prosecution's ploy to play on the jury's sympathy. "It was a
tragedy, of course, for the Garner family," Seale opened, "and I certainly
do sympathize with them. It was not only a tragedy for the Garner family,
but it was a tragedy for three other families, too. The election could be
made to have taken children out of school and brought them up here
and sit them up here to try to get your sympathy . . . because these men
all have children, too. But I don't want to appeal to sympathy."
Seale shifted gears, singling out Alton and Johnnie Maxie as the weak-
est links in Skeen's case. "You cannot convict these men unless you
believe Johnnie and Alton Maxie completely," he said, trying to reduce
his defense to the simplest elements. Seale had sketched a score card,
he said, of the times the Maxies' testimony conflicted with that of other
witnesses. "If Johnnie is right," Seale said, "sixteen [witnesses] lied. . . .
Alton scores a little bit better. Alton cuts it down to thirteen. . . .
"Has it become, to use the expression, a 'swearing match,' between
Johnnie Maxie and Alton Maxie on the one hand and the three defendants
on the other? No, not at all. It has become those two men's testimony
against everyone else."
The defense lawyer was arguing all he had, and it forced him into
potentially treacherous ground. He attacked Skeen's portrayal of Garner
as a family man. Garner and the Maxies, he said, planned "to have a
Christmas afternoon get-drunk party, and that is exactly what they did."

He returned to Garner's children in the audience. "And this wonderful family man, and I apologize to even have to argue this, but it was *their* election to bring these folks in here and sit them up on the front row."

Buchanan's anger made Seale's a misdemeanor. The bearded lawyer with cowboy boots announced he planned to do "some screaming and hollering" for "the holy hell" Bo Hyden had endured. The prosecution, he said, glaring at Skeen, was "founded totally in dishonesty"—a remark that prompted the first of many objections from the prosecutor.

From the exhibit table, Buchanan grabbed an autopsy photo that showed a series of marks on Garner's forehead. "You see those marks, how uniform they are?" Buchanan asked, shoving the picture toward the jurors. "The prosecution knew when they asked Dr. Donaldson, 'Isn't it consistent with being whipped upside the head . . . getting the bruises from this slapjack?' [and] Dr. Donaldson beautifully answered, 'Yeah'— okay, all right, that's your testimony, you live with it, you die with it— now, he knew, he knew when he asked that question they were placed there by the EEG. He *knew* it, but he didn't want to go the honest route. He wanted to go the dishonest route. . . ."

Buchanan's attack continued over Skeen's objections. Judge Tunnell consistently overruled the prosecutor's pleas, reminding him he would have "the last reply."

"You know what else is dishonest?" Buchanan asked. "For them to have the audacity . . . to attack these fine people coming up here from Sabine County and say they all must be in cahoots, they all must be lying."

Throughout the trial, defense attorneys had objected to Skeen's penchant for repeating key, and generally damning, testimony in front of the jury. Finally, Buchanan had the opportunity to vent his anger. "I didn't go to the Adolf Hitler School of Truth and have to repeat things. Our case was short, clean, and concise. It didn't have any lies in it. It didn't have any dishonesty in it, and it didn't need to be repeated twenty times to make it the truth. That is what we learned in World War II. The Nazis decided if you told something twenty times or one hundred times or one thousand times, soon it would become the truth."

Buchanan was bold in his final comments, not only asking for a not-guilty verdict but wishing "there was a place in there you could write an apology for the things these men have had to go through."

Young Jeff Haas moved quickly to distance his client, Bill Horton, from the flashlight and any blows Garner had suffered. The state's own witnesses, Roscoe Davis and Dr. Gonzalez, the lawyer said, agreed that "the cause of death was not a flashlight, that there was no cuts, there was no external indication. . . .

"V. V. Gonzalez . . . finally admitted, no, in his opinion, it wasn't a flashlight because it wasn't a smooth or soft, flat object, which is what he felt would have been needed to cause the blow that, in his opinion, caused the death of Loyal Garner, Jr.," Haas said. "Let's get that flashlight issue out of the way." Having tried to extract his client from the actual blows, Haas added: "Thomas Ladner and James Hyden, surely in retrospect, used bad judgment and slapped Loyal Garner upside the head."

Jack Skeen wasn't his normal sedate self when he got his last shot at the defense.

"I've seen lawyers like Paul Buchanan do that before," Skeen told the jury almost apologetically, "and I'll tell you they have one common thread . . . and the common thread is, they always represent somebody who, the evidence shows, is one hundred percent guilty."

Before he sat down, the prosecutor tried to take the legal complexities out of the case. "It [the law] simply provides that you can convict each one of these defendants as a principal actor, or you can convict each one of these defendants as a party acting with one of the other defendants."

In Texas, juries first determine guilt or innocence. In the event of a guilty verdict, and if the defendants have asked that a jury instead of a judge assess punishment, jurors resume deliberations to determine the sentence.

On Thursday, May 3, 1990, the nine women and three men sent Judge Tunnell a note saying they had reached a verdict in *State of Texas v. Thomas Ladner, Billy Ray Horton, and James "Bo" Hyden.* By judicial practice, the three former Hemphill police officers and their attorneys stood as the verdict was read.

All three were guilty of murdering Loyal Garner, Jr. None revealed any emotion or said a word.

At the bar of a Bennigan's restaurant near their hotel, a distinguished, gray-haired lawyer and his younger colleague, a bearded man in a suit and cowboy boots, bemoaned their fate and that of their clients. Eventually, their conversation turned from legal issues to gallows humor, the kind lawyers, cops, and reporters use to salve experiences most people seldom see.

"I was drunk as a skunk," Buchanan recalled later. "Somebody said something funny, and I blacked out and fell off the stool." He got up rubbing his head. "I got a hell of a bump on my head," he deadpanned. "I'll probably be dead in two days."

Late the next day, after Skeen had implored them to remember Garner's children with a life sentence and the defense attorneys had pled with them for probation, the jurors returned to court with the punishment.

The sentences were read in alphabetical order.

Horton: Ten years.

Hyden: Fourteen years.

Ladner: Twenty-eight years.

John Seale, Paul Buchanan, and Jeff Haas announced they would appeal the convictions to the Texas Court of Criminal Appeals. Horton and Hyden were released on bonds of $25,000 each, pending the outcome of their appeals. Because Texas law requires defendants sentenced to fifteen years or more to be imprisoned during their appeals, Ladner was not eligible for bond.

"Mr. Ladner will be taken into custody by the sheriff," Judge Tunnell said, "and confined to jail."

EPILOGUE

EXCEPT FOR HIS TESTIMONY in Hemphill, Thomas Ladner had not spoken publicly since Loyal Garner, Jr., died on December 27, 1987. In February 1991, with the approval of his attorney, Ladner agreed to talk with me.

He was incarcerated in Jester II, a sprawling, one-story minimum-security prison stuck in the middle of monotonous rolling farm land thirty miles south of Houston. It was a unit for first-time, generally younger offenders.

The state of Texas had issued him a number, 548099, as it had so many others Ladner himself had sent to prison.

The visit was less than ideal. He sat on the other side of a clear Plexiglas wall, and we were forced to speak loudly through a metal opening resembling that in a bank teller's booth. A guard stood within earshot a few feet from him.

Prison regimen had diminished neither Ladner's girth nor his attitude. The relaxed atmosphere in the minimum-security unit, he explained, was night-and-day different from his first days in the Texas Department of Criminal Justice at Huntsville, a notoriously tough place for an ex-cop.

"I was in a single cell and had gangsters on both sides of me," he said. "I had two guards with me when they moved me anywhere, and they'd make all the inmates get back against the wall in their cells. They were yelling, 'We know who you are!' I was scared, I don't mind telling you. I almost had a mental breakdown."

Three days later, two guards shackled Ladner in a van and drove him from the main prison complex to Jester. "The prison people apologized. They said, 'We don't have a place for you.' They said, 'We're sending you to Jester II. They'll take good care of you down there. If you open your mouth one time, you'll spend the rest of your time in TDC locked down by yourself.' "

For eight months, Ladner was confined in a single cell for his own safety. When I spoke with him, he recently had been moved into a dorm with thirty-eight inmates. Sixty percent of them, he said, were black, and all were aware that he was a former cop convicted of beating a black man to death. "There hasn't been one problem," Ladner said. "They said they had been expecting me, figuring I'd be here. But they think the other two ought to be here, too."

Ladner straightened himself in his chair at the recollection of Bill Horton and Bo Hyden, and he glanced down at his arms crossed on the counter. He appeared ready to say something, but apparently thought better of it and checked himself.

It had been nine months since bailiffs led him from the courtroom in Tyler, he said, and he had neither seen nor talked to Horton or Hyden.

Soon he was slumped on his arms again and affable, recounting how he'd received more than four thousand letters of support. "The town thought we got shafted," Ladner said. "After the Garner thing, I only went to Hemphill a dozen times. I just stayed out and worked. I told my mother and wife when we got to Tyler, 'Get ready. I'm going to prison.' I said all along I'd get thirty-five to forty years. It was no surprise to me. But I felt like I didn't deserve any more time than they did." The bitterness at his former colleagues was open but fleeting; it was gone almost as soon as it appeared. Bitterness, he said, was something he tried not to dwell on. Still, talking about the Garner case produced emotional responses.

"The media was really bad," Ladner said. "The TV people knocked my oldest sister down. They were always rude. I just made it a rule not to talk to them. Looking back, maybe we didn't do it right.

"The stories were all the same—Garner was black, we were white. *They* made it a race issue. I've never been prejudiced with black people. I was raised with them, rode the school bus with them, lived with them. The black people in Hemphill will tell you I've treated them fairly. I've only had problems with one black—Vollie Grace.

"Every time I turned on the TV, I saw John Hannah. I wasn't mad at him. He was doing what lawyers get paid to do. But Jack Skeen isn't a truthful man. Even John Hannah said in closing arguments that we didn't mean to kill Garner. Jack Skeen said we did."

Toward the end of our allotted time, Ladner turned uncharacteristically philosophical. "I've always had God on my mind," he said. "There's a joke that you always find God here in prison. But before I ever got here, I'd always tried to live a pretty decent life. I've turned all this over to God and let Him deal with it."

The guard was edging closer, and Ladner knew our time was gone. For the first time, the hulking ex-cop appeared ill at ease. He already had pulled back his chair to get up when he awkwardly leaned back toward the hole through which we spoke.

"There's nobody in the world sorrier than I am about what happened," he said. "I wished I could have been in a position to talk to Mrs. Garner and her family, but I just couldn't. I doubt they'd believe me about anything I said anyway.

"But I know the truth about what happened. And nobody meant to kill anybody. I can tell you that."

Bill Horton and Bo Hyden have continued their silence. Both remain free on appeal bonds, pending a ruling from the Texas Court of Criminal Appeals on the murder charges against them and Ladner. John Seale and Paul Buchanan, aware their clients couldn't afford their legal fees, told the court they would pay the appeals out of their own pockets.

On September 21, 1991, while the state appeals were still pending, a three-judge panel of the United States Fifth Circuit Court of Appeals in New Orleans voted two to one against Ladner's appeal in federal courts. Seale, steadfastly contending that Ladner's second trial violated the double-jeopardy provision of the Fifth Amendment, took his battle to the United States Supreme Court, which refused to hear the case.

In the aftermath of two trials in Texas courts, there still remains the specter of additional civil rights charges against Ladner, Horton, and Hyden in federal court. United States Attorney Bob Wortham and federal civil rights lawyers from Washington continued their grand jury investigation even after the murder convictions in Tyler. Lawyers on both sides acknowledge, however, that federal charges are merely "an ace in the hole" and probably never will be filed unless the Texas Court of Criminal Appeals overturns the murder convictions against the three former officers.

Corrine Garner and her six children still live in the modest little home on the outskirts of Florien next door to Garner's parents. She hasn't remarried, and if the money from the settlement of her lawsuit has changed her family's life-style, it's not obvious.

Time, Corrine said, has eased some of the bitterness, and the boys no longer talk about avenging their father's death. "They're beginning to realize that no matter what a person does, it's not because of their race," she said. "You can't spend your life living in colors."

Bill Beaird, the justice of the peace in Tyler who forced an inquest into Garner's death and ultimately ruled it a homicide, was defeated for re-election to a third term.

"You're looking at another victim of the Garner case," he said. "Some people around here didn't appreciate me getting involved in an out-of-county killing, especially a black's."

John Henry Hannah, Jr., was appointed Texas secretary of state in December 1990. In appointing him, Governor Ann Richards said: "I wanted someone who was ethical, who was tough, who was wise, who's brilliant and who's real good-looking. The name of John Hannah immediately came to mind."

Hannah's first assignment, Governor Richards said, would be to push sweeping ethics reform in Texas government.

Vollie Grace's new chapter of the NAACP has 150 members, who, he believes, will never again tolerate the kind of civil rights abuse that killed Loyal Garner, Jr. He's relieved justice was done in Garner's case, but he's resentful and embarrassed justice had to be administered one hundred miles away.

"Yeah, the right thing got done," Grace said, "but it didn't happen here, not where we live. We can't continue to look to the future and expect other people to do what we can't do for ourselves. That's not the way it ought to be."

Ten months after the Tyler trial, I talked with Bill Barcheers, one of Ladner's high school classmates and the emergency medical technician who took the unconscious Garner to the hospital in Hemphill and, later, to Tyler.

The aftermath of the murder convictions, he said, splintered Hemphill, maybe permanently. "It's made the town more racial," Barcheers said.

"Blacks are demanding more, which has drawn together the white community. There wasn't a lot of prejudice before this. The whites and blacks stayed separate, and everybody liked it that way."

Shortly before he spoke with me, Barcheers said, two federal civil rights lawyers from Washington, "a Jewish-looking guy and a weird-looking woman," interviewed him, leading him to believe federal charges still might be filed one day.

The federal government and the media, Barcheers said, created Hemphill's problems and the racial bitterness that still exists. "There wasn't a race problem here until you people told everyone there was," he said.

"Why kill Loyal Garner, anyhow?" he asked. "If they wanted to kill someone, why not kill someone here they didn't like? If they just wanted to kill a nigger, we got some right here that need killing."

His comment made me look up from my notebook, and he stared defiantly for several seconds. Then he added an afterthought: "And some whites, too."

Barcheers said he holds himself partly responsible for the murder convictions against his friends in Tyler. "Garner was dead, per se, when I picked him up at the jail," Barcheers said. "We just caused a whole bunch of trouble by keeping him alive. I wish I had let him die before we got to Tyler. I've always felt a little guilty about that. He was dead anyway. It won't happen again."

Had it not been for happenstance in Los Angeles—that George Holliday, a plumber, had gotten a new video camera—Rodney King, a twenty-five-year-old black man, undoubtedly would have faced a lengthy jail sentence. He would have been charged with failure to stop for police. And to explain away King's broken leg, fractured cheekbone, concussion, injuries to both his knees, and nerve damage that partially paralyzed his face, officers almost certainly would have claimed King attacked them, and charged him with resisting arrest.

Were it not for Holliday's video, shot from his balcony on March 3, 1991, the incident would have been merely another night in the city, a controversy that would have hinged on the word of a single black man against that of police. Though twenty-three LAPD officers and four California highway troopers were present when King was kicked seven times, clubbed more than fifty times, and shocked with an electric stun gun, none of the officers stopped the beating or broke the "Cop's Code" to

report it. One of the four officers charged in King's beating had been
suspended previously for kicking and hitting a handcuffed man; another
was under investigation for making racial slurs and physically abusing
two black college students.

The beating of Rodney King occurred while this book was being written, and it reminded me of a comment by Ronnie Felts, then the mayor
of Hemphill.

"People are trying to make Hemphill something evil," Felts had said,
"but I don't think race relations are bad here at all. It's no different here
than in Georgia, or in New York City, for that matter."

Or Los Angeles.

Statements and testimony in the Garner case documented that Thomas
Ladner and Bill Horton had beaten and brutalized unarmed citizens for
years with impunity—even after they were reported to the FBI. The
record shows their victims were white and black, their only common
bond that they were socially, economically, and politically disenfran-
chised. They would have been the kind easy for Ladner, Horton, and
Hyden to spot beside the road: decrepit car, modest clothes, maybe too
drunk to remember, but generally the kind unlikely to hire a lawyer and
sue—or to be believed by the FBI.

Hemphill is a microcosm of Deep East Texas, where disenfranchise-
ment is a legacy that encompasses the overwhelming majority of blacks.
White inmates in the Sabine County Jail swore Ladner and Hyden underscored their threats to Garner with "nigger" and "boy." The Southern
Poverty Law Center called Garner's death a "racially motivated killing."

Beatings by police, the law center claimed, were so common in Sabine
County they represented "expected, accepted municipal policy." There
were no videotapes, but there was a well-known legacy of abuse that
extended far beyond the county.

But in every public statement he made, Sheriff Blan Greer denied
knowing that officers had beaten prisoners in his jail.

Dr. Grover Winslow, one of the town's most prominent residents,
treated an amputee who claimed to have been brutalized in the jail,
stitched the mouth of a man who claimed Ladner had beaten him with
a slapjack, and fought—valiantly, by all accounts—to save the life of an
unconscious man who had been brought to the hospital directly from the
jail. Nonetheless, Dr. Winslow noted publicly that he'd never witnessed
injuries he attributed to police abuse.

Mayor Felts knew that Ladner had hit a teenager in the head with a club, and had cautioned him on previous occasions about being verbally abusive. Yet, when Garner died, the mayor likened the death to an "industrial accident."

If police abuse in Sabine County wasn't apparent to the county's chief law-enforcement officer, the doctor who ran the emergency room, or the mayor, it apparently was obvious to others in the community. A housewife on the Hemphill jury, a holdout for convicting Ladner on civil rights charges, reluctantly had agreed to change her vote if she could be guaranteed the chief would never carry a badge again. She'd heard "bad stories about Thomas," she said.

To a degree, the sensational Rodney King beating in Los Angeles and untold others like it throughout the nation add credence to Felts's claim that Hemphill is no different than thousands of other towns and cities. Indeed, a California jury, as its counterpart in Hemphill had two years earlier, acquitted its officers on brutality charges. But in the riotous aftermath of its most notorious civil rights case, Los Angeles also appointed a blue-ribbon commission to investigate its law enforcement. A survey of 650 LAPD officers showed that one-quarter agreed that "racial bias on the part of officers toward minority citizens currently exists." That prejudice, they acknowledged, "may lead to the use of excessive force."

Jesse Brewer, a retired, thirty-eight-year veteran of the Los Angeles Police Department, testified before the blue-ribbon citizens investigative commission after the King beating. Said Brewer: "We know who the bad guys are. Reputations become well known. . . . We know the ones who are getting into trouble more than anyone else. But I don't see anyone bringing these people up and saying, 'Look, you're not conforming, you're not measuring up.' "

"The problem of excessive force in the LAPD," the select Christopher Commission concluded in its 288-page report, "is fundamentally a problem of supervision, management, and leadership."

Except for the meeting Vollie Grace convened in Hemphill at the Macedonia Baptist Church to discuss police brutality, there has been no official inquiry into Sabine County law enforcement.

Eleven months after Loyal Garner, Jr.'s death, Sheriff Blan Greer ran for re-election, winning by an 82 percent margin—the largest in his twenty-three-year career.

CAST OF CHARACTERS

THE VICTIM

LOYAL GARNER, JR.: A father of six and never before arrested, Garner was a truck driver who lived with his family in Florien, Louisiana. He was arrested for drunk driving on Christmas evening in 1987 in Hemphill, Texas. Two days later, he was dead of massive head injuries.

THE FAMILY

CORRINE HOLDEN GARNER: Loyal Garner, Jr.'s widow.
SARAH AND LOYAL GARNER, SR.: Garner's parents.

THE LAWMEN

THOMAS LADNER: The chief of police in Hemphill, Ladner was one of two officers who arrested Garner and, after two trials, was convicted of Garner's murder.
JAMES "BO" HYDEN: A deputy sheriff for the Sabine County Sheriff's Department who, with Ladner, arrested Garner. He was convicted in Garner's murder.
BILLY RAY HORTON: The chief deputy for the Sabine County Sheriff's Department, Horton was convicted of murdering Garner.
BLAN GREER: Sabine County's chief law-enforcement officer, Greer was considered to be the most powerful politician and among the wealthiest

residents of the county. He had been sheriff more than twenty years when Garner was arrested.

HOLTON "BUBBA" JOHNSON: A law-enforcement officer in Newton County, Texas, Constable Johnson testified that Garner and two friends were on a drug trafficking mission when they were arrested in Hemphill.

THE WITNESSES

JOHNNIE MAXIE: An oil-field laborer and a lifelong friend of Garner's, Johnnie Maxie had asked Garner to drive him to Newton, Texas, on Christmas afternoon to pick up a car. He was arrested with Garner and witnessed Ladner's attack on him.

ALTON MAXIE: Accompanying his brother, Johnnie Maxie, and Garner on the trip to Newton, Alton Maxie was arrested with the pair and witnessed Ladner's attack on Garner.

ANGUS BOZEMAN, WELTON GENE SANGWIN, AND KEITH ALLEN MILLER: Inmates in the Sabine County Jail on Christmas night, 1987, they heard racial slurs and a beating in the detox cell.

TRENT TAYLOR: An inmate-trusty in the Sabine County Jail, he was ordered by Ladner to mop up blood in the jail after Garner was dragged down the hall from his cell to the book-in room.

JIMMY EARL MOORE: An inmate in the Sabine County Jail, Moore saw officers dragging the bloody and unconscious Garner back to his cell.

THE LAWYERS

JOHN SEALE: A veteran attorney from Jasper, Texas, Seale represented Ladner, winning an acquittal in Hemphill on civil rights charges. After losing the later murder trial in Tyler, Seale took Ladner's case to the U.S. Supreme Court, where he ultimately lost.

PAUL BUCHANAN: A criminal defense specialist from Beaumont, Texas, Buchanan represented Hyden. He won an acquittal on civil rights charges in Hemphill, but lost Hyden's murder trial in Tyler.

FLOYD W. ADDINGTON: A defense attorney from Jasper, Addington won an acquittal for Horton in Hemphill on civil rights charges. He withdrew from Horton's case after his law license was revoked on a felony conviction unrelated to the Garner case.

JEFF L. HAAS: A criminal defense lawyer from Tyler, Haas represented Horton in Tyler on murder charges.

JOHN HENRY HANNAH, JR.: A former state representative, federal and state prosecutor, and defense attorney, Hannah was retained as a special prosecutor to try Ladner, Horton, and Hyden on civil rights charges in Hemphill.

BILL A. MARTIN: The longtime district attorney for the Hemphill area, Martin, who already had announced he would not seek re-election, stepped aside to allow Hannah to prosecute the civil rights case in Hemphill.

CHARLES MITCHELL: Martin's assistant, Mitchell was co-counsel in the civil rights prosecution in Hemphill. He later became district attorney.

JACK SKEEN: As district attorney for Smith County, Texas, in Tyler, Skeen had criminal jurisdiction because Garner died in a Tyler hospital. He fought in appeals court for the right to try Ladner, Horton, and Hyden on murder charges. He won convictions against all three.

MORRIS DEES: Co-founder of the Southern Poverty Law Center in Montgomery, Alabama, Dees litigated some of the landmark civil rights cases in the South. He represented Garner's survivors in a civil suit against Ladner, Horton, Hyden and the city of Hemphill.

J. RICHARD COHEN: As legal director of the Southern Poverty Law Center, Cohen spearheaded the civil suit in behalf of Garner's survivors, producing key evidence, some of which was used in the criminal prosecution of Ladner, Horton, and Hyden.

THE JUDGES

JUDGE W. B. "BILL" BEAIRD: A Tyler justice of the peace, Beaird refused to release Garner's body to Hemphill authorities until an autopsy was performed. He later conducted an inquest jury that determined Garner's death was a homicide.

JUDGE O'NEAL BACON: With jurisdiction in the Hemphill area, District Judge Bacon presided over the civil rights trial of Ladner, Horton, and Hyden.

JUDGE JOE TUNNELL: Based in Tyler, Judge Tunnell presided over the murder trial in which Ladner, Horton, and Hyden were convicted.

THE ACTIVISTS

PEARLIE HENDERSON: As head of the Tyler chapter of the NAACP, Henderson notified the FBI shortly after Garner died and encouraged agents to launch a civil rights investigation into his death.

VOLLIE GRACE: A self-employed contractor and lifelong resident of Sabine County, Grace formed the Concerned Citizens for Sabine County and the first local chapter of the NAACP in Hemphill in the aftermath of Garner's death. He later planned a protest demonstration when the officers were acquitted on charges in Hemphill.